Praise for
The Secret Life of Things

"Mark Blackwell has assembled a group of lively, provocative, and readable essays. We are lucky to have them. . . . *The Secret Life of Things* is an erudite and enjoyable guide, well-written and wide-ranging."

—Henry Power, *Review of English Studies*

"Blackwell's collection marks the arrival of a substantial new body of work. Admirably inclusive . . . *The Secret Life of Things* will be useful for anyone who is working on objects in eighteenth-century narrative."

—Sophie Gee, *Times Literary Supplement*

"Blackwell's collection brings together some of the best previously published essays on eighteenth-century thinginess, such as Aileen Douglas's essay on it-narratives and empire (1993) and important new work by Barbara Benedict, Jonathan Lamb, Deidre Lynch, Markman Ellis, Lynn Festa, and Blackwell himself, among others. . . . [This] is a valuable collection for eighteenth-century studies and for 'thing theory' more generally."

—Cynthia Wall, *Modern Philology*

"I think [this volume] represents essentially the best-case scenario for the edited collection of literary criticism that is organized not for a series or as primarily a teaching tool but as the best way of compiling a field's state of knowledge on an emerging topic. . . . [It] remains an indispensable resource for scholars working on a host of topics related to the it-narrative and the animated objects of eighteenth-century literature."

—Jenny Davidson, *Studies in English Literature*

"Complex and sophisticated . . . Blackwell's volume both carefully scrutinizes it-narratives and provides interesting perspectives on them."

—Melora G. Vandersluis, *Style*

"The collection . . . adroitly consolidates, assesses, and extends the best work available in this fruitful intersection of theory and culture. The book boasts some of the most distinguished scholarly critics of the eighteenth century operating in the field today, and one finds herein numerous instances of scintillating and luminous critical prose. . . . Recommended."

—A. W. Lee, *CHOICE*

"*The Secret Life of Things* fully realizes the ambitions that Mark Blackwell established for the volume—both to leaven the history of prose fiction and to contribute to our understanding of eighteenth-century attitudes towards the new object world—ambitions that square with those of the Bucknell series in which it appears, devoted to eighteenth-century literature and culture."

—Bill Brown, *Eighteenth-Century Fiction*

"By bringing our attention to a genre that realizes the apparently impossible condition of material objects behaving as narrative protagonists, Blackwell's collection destabilizes our received impressions of eighteenth-century narrative as an evolving institution of realism. . . . [I]ntriguing analyses and claims fill *The Secret Life of Things*."

—Julie Park, *Eighteenth-Century Life*

The Secret Life of Things

The Bucknell Studies in Eighteenth-Century Literature and Culture

The Bucknell Studies in Eighteenth-Century Literature and Culture aims to publish challenging, new eighteenth-century scholarship. Of particular interest is critical, historical, and interdisciplinary work that is interestingly and intelligently theorized, and that broadens and refines the conception of the field. At the same time, the series remains open to all theoretical perspectives and different kinds of scholarship. While the focus of the series is the literature, history, arts, and culture (including art, architecture, music, travel, and history of science, medicine, and law) of the long eighteenth century in Britain and Europe, the series is also interested in scholarship that establishes relationships with other geographies, literature, and cultures for the period 1660–1830.

Titles in This Series

Dan Doll and Jessica Munns, ed., *Recording and Reordering: Essays on the Seventeenth- and Eighteenth-Century Diary and Journal*
Ziad Elmarsafy, *Freedom, Slavery, and Absolutism: Corneille, Pascale, Racine*
Regina Hewitt and Pat Rogers, eds., *Orthodoxy and Heresy in Eighteenth-Century Society*
Susan Paterson Glover, *Engendering Legitimacy: Law, Property, and Early Eighteenth-Century Fiction*
Catherine Jones, *Literary Memory: Scott's Waverley Novels and the Psychology of Narrative*
Sarah Jordan, *The Anxieties of Idleness: Idleness in Eighteenth-Century British Literature and Culture*
Deborah Kennedy, *Helen Maria Williams and the Age of Revolution*
Chris Mounsey, *Christopher Smart: Clown of God*
Chris Mounsey, ed., *Presenting Gender: Changing Sex in Early Modern Culture*
Frédéric Ogée, ed., *"Better in France?": The Circulation of Ideas across the Channel in the Eighteenth Century*
Roland Racevskis, *Time and Ways of Knowing Under Louis XIV: Molière, Sévigné, Lafayette*
Laura Rosenthal and Mita Choudhury, eds., *Monstrous Dreams of Reason*
Katherine West Scheil, *The Taste of the Town: Shakespearian Comedy and the Early Eighteenth-Century Theater*
Philip Smallwood, ed., *Johnson Re-Visioned: Looking Before and After*
Peter Walmsley, *Locke's* Essay *and the Rhetoric of Science*
Lisa Wood, *Modes of Discipline: Women, Conservatism, and the Novel after the French Revolution*
Mark Blackwell, ed., *The Secret Life of Things: Animals, Objects, and It-Narratives in Eighteenth-Century England*
Evan Gottlieb, *Feeling British: Sympathy and National Identity in Scottish and English Writing, 1707–1832*

www.bucknell.edu/universitypress

The Secret Life of Things

Animals, Objects, and It-Narratives in Eighteenth-Century England

Edited by
Mark Blackwell

BUCKNELL UNIVERSITY PRESS
Lewisburg, Pennsylvania

First paperback edition 2023
ISBN 978-1-68448-470-6

Library of Congress Cataloging-in-Publication Data

The secret life of things : animals, objects, and it-narratives in eighteenth-century England / edited by Mark Blackwell.
p. cm.
Includes bibliographical references and index.
ISBN-13: 978-0-8387-5666-9 (alk. paper)
ISBN-10: 0-8387-5666-2 (alk. paper)
1. English fiction—18th century—History and criticism. 2. Material culture in literature. 3. Material culture—England—History—18th century. 4. Consumption (Economics) in literature. 5. Property in literature. 6. Animals in literature. 7. Human-animal relationships in literature. I. Blackwell, Mark, 1966– II. Title.
PR858.M38S43 2007 823.509355—dc22 2006019363

A British Cataloging-in-Publication record for this book is available from the British Library.

bucknelluniversitypress.org

Distributed worldwide by Rutgers University Press

MANUFACTURED IN THE UNITED STATES OF AMERICA

Contents

Acknowledgments

ACKNOWLEDGMENTS, I TAKE IT, CATALOGUE DEBTS SO GREAT THAT they can only be recognized, not repaid. I have much to acknowledge. Thanks are due first to the contributors to this volume, scholars with whom I am honored to be associated, collaborators who have manifested exemplary goodwill and patience with their deliberate editor. Greg Clingham and the anonymous reader at Bucknell University Press provided invaluable advice about *how* to make this a better book, while Julien Yoseloff and his confrères at Associated University Presses *did* the making, a thing wonderful to behold. Grants from the Steven Moseley Fund and the Richard Cardin Fund of the University of Hartford's College of Arts and Sciences helped me to pay for color images and to secure freelance professional assistance with the proofing and indexing of the volume. Indeed, I owe an incalculable debt to the provider of that assistance, Lynne Lipkind, whose eye for a misplaced en dash is matched by her ear for the poetry of the everyday. (Reader, I married her.) Finally, Josiah and Xavier—our "best piece of poetry"—deserve thanks for suffering their dad's visits with his it-child, this curious talking thing you hold in your hands.

Introduction: The It-Narrative and Eighteenth-Century Thing Theory

Mark Blackwell

In "Thing Theory," an essay that serves as the introduction to a collection entitled *Things* (2004), Bill Brown considers the cyclical modishness of "things" as an academic and artistic subject before declaring that every "decade of the [twentieth] century" had "its own thing about things."[1] No one can dispute the geographical, temporal, and disciplinary range of the essays collected in Brown's volume, yet his introductory emphasis on the twentieth century continues in subsequent pages, the largest number of which are devoted—perhaps disproportionately, perhaps appropriately—to things of the last century. Nonetheless, three of the volume's essays—Jonathan Lamb's "Modern Metamorphoses and Disgraceful Tales," W. J. T. Mitchell's "Romanticism and the Life of Things: Fossils, Totems, and Images," and Jessica Riskin's "The Defecating Duck, or, the Ambiguous Origins of Artificial Life"—demonstrate that even the eighteenth century had a thing about things.

Was there "thing theory" in the English eighteenth century? One recalls, of course, James Boswell's famous account of his conversation with Samuel Johnson about George Berkeley's "ingenious sophistry to prove the non-existence of matter." "I observed," Boswell writes, "that though we are satisfied his doctrine is not true, it is impossible to refute it. I never shall forget the alacrity with which Johnson answered, striking his foot with mighty force against a large stone, till he rebounded from it, 'I refute it *thus*.'"[2] Yet Boswell's anecdote does not convey us beyond the stark opposition between an idealism that denies the objective status of things, on the one hand, and the crudest empirical account of the mute resistance of matter to subjective manipulation, on the other. Like the foot and the stone, Johnson's and Berkeley's very different senses of things make brief contact only to rebound from one another, without leaving much trace of having touched. Johnson's refutation of Berkeley, then, does not offer promising evidence of a period interest in "the way objects and subjects animate one another," as Bill Brown puts it.[3]

Johnson's refusal to engage theoretically with Berkeleyan idealism—like Boswell's tantalizing assertion that Edmund Burke had intended to answer Berkeley but instead decided to pursue a political career, leaving thing theory in the lurch—suggests that it may not be in the work of philosophers and men of letters that one should look for such a theory. More satisfactory, perhaps, is the second book of William Blackstone's *Commentaries on the Laws of England* (1765–69), entitled "Of the Rights of Things." Blackstone examines "those rights which a man may acquire in and to such external things as are unconnected with his person."[4] First, Blackstone traces a speculative genealogy of property from temporary appropriation for use to exclusive ownership of "the very *substance* of the thing to be used"; then he differentiates things, defined as "objects of dominion or property," from persons; and finally, he distinguishes "things real"—permanent and immoveable property, such as lands and houses—from "things personal"—"all sorts of things *moveable,* which may attend a man's person wherever he goes."[5] Myriad possible property arrangements lead Blackstone to enumerate multiple and complex categories of thing—hereditaments, for instance, form a class that mingles moveable and immoveable species of property and includes both "corporeal" and "incorporeal" things.[6] Blackstone's interest in property law ensures his attention to the intricate relations between persons and things, and though the emphasis falls squarely on the ways in which human claims tease things into a new life as property, Blackstone seems equally cognizant of the ways in which people have been shaped by their changing relationships with the things they own.

It is the gambit of this collection that one of the richest records of things' growing importance as emblems of "a particular subject-object relation" in eighteenth-century Britain comes in an odd subgenre of the novel, a type of prose fiction in which inanimate objects (coins, waistcoats, pins, corkscrews, coaches) or animals (dogs, fleas, cats, ponies) serve as the central characters.[7] Sometimes these characters enjoy a consciousness—and thus a perspective—of their own; sometimes they are merely narrative hubs around which other people's stories accumulate, like the stick around which cotton candy winds. Variously called "it-narratives," "novels of circulation," "object tales," and "spy novels," the subgenre boasted such phenomenally successful works as Francis Coventry's *The History of Pompey the Little; or, The Life and Adventures of a Lap-Dog* (1751) and Charles Johnstone's *Chrysal; or, The Adventures of a Guinea* (1760–65). *Chrysal* was even included in the *Ballantyne's Novelists' Library* (1822), one of the early nineteenth-century anthologies that began to establish a canon of great novels.

Despite the evident popularity of it-fictions in the second half of the eighteenth century and their continuing importance in the nineteenth century, the form has languished in critical purgatory. *Chrysal* has dropped from even the most eccentric list of the period's canonical works, as have its literary counterparts. Indeed, most twentieth-century considerations of novels like *Chrysal* have been confined to editorial introductions and to the sweeping and encyclopedic critical surveys more commonly written before 1950. In *The Restoration and Eighteenth Century (1660–1789)* (1948), the third volume of *A Literary History of England,* George Sherburn connected it-narratives with other satirical novels "hark[ing] back to the picaresque pattern," though "instead of a human adventurer," he noted, "they . . . frequently substitute some unhuman piece of 'currency.'"[8] Some years earlier, Ernest Baker had traced a similar genealogy in *The Novel of Sentiment and the Gothic Romance* (1934), volume 5 of *The History of the English Novel,* but dismissed works like *Chrysal* by proclaiming their literary interest "insignificant."[9]

Nonetheless, a growing body of work published during the last decade or so is reviving interest in the it-narrative and reassessing its significance by approaching the form through broader literary, cultural, and social questions about eighteenth-century England. This critical momentum can be measured by the appearance of substantial articles in major journals—*PMLA, Critical Inquiry*—and by the attention devoted to such fiction in important recent books, including Markman Ellis's *The Politics of Sensibility: Race, Gender, and Commerce in the Sentimental Novel* (1996), Deidre Lynch's *The Economy of Character: Novels, Market Culture, and the Business of Inner Meaning* (1998), Liz Bellamy's *Commerce, Morality, and the Eighteenth-Century Novel* (1998), and Laura Brown's *Fables of Modernity: Literature and Culture in the English Eighteenth Century* (2001). The momentum can also be gauged by the dedication of two sessions at the 2002 MLA Convention in New York to objects and animals in the eighteenth century—"The Agency of Objects without Subjects" and "Sympathy and the Lives of Animals"—and by the two panels entitled "The People Things Make" at the 2004 ASECS meeting in Boston. The waxing interest in the relationship between literature and material culture outside of eighteenth-century studies—Bill Brown's *A Sense of Things: The Object Matter of American Literature* (2003) serving as perhaps the most vivid example—further suggests that scholars may at last be ready to reconsider the place of it-narratives in both literary and cultural history. Lorraine Daston's *Things That Talk: Object Lessons from Art and Science* (2004), like Brown's *Things* and various works growing from material culture studies, testifies to an exploding interest in "thing theory" which transcends the limits of discipline and historical period. Indeed, Rebecca Zorach's "Theory of Everything" recently surveyed this academic trend for the *Boston Globe,* asking, "So, are 'thing studies' the next big . . . thing?"[10] If Zorach and the editors of the *Boston Globe* are to be trusted, "thing studies" are a phenomenon of sufficient cultural and intellectual force to command the attention of a broad reading public.

Discussing how to write "the biography of a thing," Igor Kopytoff proposes a number of crucial questions:

> What, sociologically, are the biographical possibilities inherent in its "status" and in the period and culture, and how are these possibilities realized? Where does the thing come from and who made it? What has been its career so far, and what do people consider to be an ideal career for such things? What are the recognized "ages" or "periods" in the thing's "life," and what are the cultural markers for them? How does the thing's use change with its age, and what happens to it when it reaches the end of its usefulness?[11]

Kopytoff's category of thing-biography is doubly significant to this collection. First, it provides one way of describing it-narratives themselves. Kopytoff notes that "biographies of things can make salient what might otherwise remain obscure," and indubitably some it-fictions provide a perspective on eighteenth-century British culture unavailable by other literary means.[12] The it-narratives discussed in this volume are curious records of British society's relationship with its material environment, chronicles of its attitudes toward the things it valued and the things it took for granted. But it-fictions are also things themselves, print objects that formed part of both the literary and the material culture of eighteenth-century Britain.

The essays assembled here approach it-narratives—or novels of circulation—from various theoretical and historical vantage points, but together they begin to sketch the cultural biography of a neglected literary form. The first part, "The Stories Things Tell," establishes a set of broad critical contexts that open varied perspectives on the phenomenon of it-narratives. Barbara Benedict explores the relationship between commodity culture and the waning belief in occult powers as it is expressed in period fiction, particularly poltergeist narratives. Jonathan Lamb discusses *The Rape of the Lock*'s exploration of the ontological indistinction between persons and things through the lens of still-life painting. Deidre Lynch's essay, previously published in *Eighteenth-Century Fiction,* traces the importance of things in sentimental fiction in order to outline an alternative history of characterization capacious enough to account for it-narratives. Finally, Markman Ellis identifies a discourse of counter-sensibility that emerges as anxieties about the affection lavished on lapdogs begin to put pressure on ideas about things and theories of sympathy.

A second, longer part, "Approaching It-Narratives," collects essays focused more narrowly on the it-narrative. Liz Bellamy offers an encyclopedic survey of the genre, discussing problems of generic definition and nomenclature and including both a checklist of eighteenth- and nineteenth-century examples and a distribution analysis of different types of circulation narrative. Aileen Douglas's seminal essay, first published in *Eighteenth-Century Fiction,* treats the it-narrative as a complex register of both burgeoning commercialism and a growing imperial culture. The next three essays deal in different ways with the genre's immersion in print culture. Christopher Flint, whose essay first appeared in *PMLA,* argues that "the appearance of speaking objects in eighteenth-century fiction projects authorial concerns about circulating books in the public sphere." My own contribution discusses the relationship between generic identity and hack-writing in it-fiction, while Hilary Englert situates it-narratives in the context of period copyright debates.

The subsequent three essays explore the ways in which it-narratives reflect and comment upon larger social phenomena and thus provide fresh accounts of the genre's oft-remarked topicality. Ann Louise Kibbie reads one of the best-known it-narratives, Charles Johnstone's *Chrysal,* against the background of the virulent anti-Semitism stirred up in the wake of the Jewish Naturalization Act. Bonnie Blackwell interprets it-tales as allegories of the circulation of women as sexual objects whose market value declines over time, while Nicholas Hudson discusses the ways in which some of the formal innovations of it-narratives serve an emergent middle-class ideology.

A short final part entitled "It-Narratives in Transition" rounds out the collection by gesturing toward transformations in the genre that come in the nineteenth century. Lynn Festa traces the it-narrative's progressive reinscription as a form of didactic children's literature at the turn of the nineteenth century, examining "the different ways eighteenth- and nineteenth-century examples of the genre endeavor to align the moral and economic ends to which things—and narratives—may be put." John Plotz's essay concludes the volume and carries us tentatively into the twentieth century by situating nineteenth-century diamond narratives by Christina Rossetti, Anthony Trollope, and Wilkie Collins in the context of twentieth-century thing theory, on the one hand, and eighteenth-century it-narratives, on the other. His contribution, like this introduction, encourages us to ponder the different ways in which eighteenth-, nineteenth-, and twentieth-century writers have thought things through by thinking through things.

The Secret Life of Things brings new texts, and new ways of thinking about familiar ones, to our notice. By attending to exactly the sorts of prose fictions overlooked by studies that emphasize richly characterized, psychologically complex novels as the terminus ad quem of eighteenth-century narrative evolution, and by focusing on works especially popular during the last half of the eighteenth century, this volume adds to recent work done by the likes of Deidre Lynch, in *The Economy of Character* (1998), Clifford Siskin, in *The Work of Writing* (1998), Leah Price, in *The Anthology and the Rise of the Novel* (2000), and Thomas Keymer, in *Sterne, the Moderns, and the Novel* (2002), to enrich and complicate the history of prose fiction. Moreover, by exploring a genre that offers a unique perspective on humans' relations with objects, the essays assembled here advance important work on eighteenth-century consumer culture and attitudes toward things—work begun, for example, by Neil McKendrick, John Brewer, and J. H. Plumb's *The Birth of a Consumer Society: The Commercialization of Eighteenth-Century England* (1982), John Brewer and Roy Porter's *Consumption and the World of Goods* (1993), and Ann Bermingham and John Brewer's *The Consumption of Culture, 1600–1800: Image, Object, Text* (1995).

Notes

A very different version of this introduction, entitled "The It-Narrative in Eighteenth-Century England: Animals and Objects in Circulation," first appeared in the online journal *Literature Compass* 1 (2004).

1. Bill Brown, "Thing Theory," in *Things*, ed. Bill Brown (Chicago: University of Chicago Press, 2004), 13. This volume derives from *Critical Inquiry* 28.1 (2001).
2. George Birkbeck Hill, ed., *Boswell's Life of Johnson*, rev. ed., 6 vols. (1934; rpt. Oxford: Clarendon Press, 1971), 1:471.
3. Bill Brown, *A Sense of Things: The Object Matter of American Literature* (Chicago: University of Chicago Press, 2003), 16.
4. William Blackstone, *Commentaries on the Laws of England*, 4 vols. (1765–69; Chicago: University of Chicago Press, 1979), 2:1.
5. Ibid., 2:4, 16, 384.
6. Ibid., 2:17–18.
7. Brown, "Thing Theory," 4.
8. George Sherburn, *The Restoration and Eighteenth Century (1660–1789)*, vol. 3 of *A Literary History of England*, ed. Albert C. Baugh, 4 vols. (New York: Appleton-Century-Crofts, 1948), 1031.
9. Ernest A. Baker, *The Novel of Sentiment and the Gothic Romance*, vol. 5 of *The History of the English Novel*, 10 vols. (1929; rpt. New York: Barnes & Noble, 1957), 52.
10. *Boston Sunday Globe*, January 9, 2005, sec. F5. For a critical discussion of recent "commodity histories," see Bruce Robbins, "Commodity Histories," *PMLA* 120.2 (2005): 454–63.
11. Igor Kopytoff, "The Cultural Biography of Things: Commoditization as Process," in *The Social Life of Things: Commodities in Cultural Perspective*, ed. Arjun Appadurai (Cambridge: Cambridge University Press, 1986), 66–67.
12. Ibid., 67.

The Secret Life of Things

I

The Stories Things Tell

The Spirit of Things

Barbara M. Benedict

> There are more things in heaven and earth, Horatio,
> Than are dreamt of in your philosophy.
>
> —William Shakespeare, *Hamlet*

SCHOLARS HAVE LONG CLAIMED THAT THE EIGHTEENTH CENTURY banished the mysteriousness of the world and the magical animation of nature in a cold shower of empiricism, secularism, and consumption. Keith Thomas has argued that the scientific advances and religious and governmental policies of the period resulted in the loss of belief in witchcraft, and studies of the rise of science further document a concomitant distrust of the inexplicable as merely the unexplained.[1] Such publications as Henry Oldenburg's *Philosophical Transactions* analyzed the effects of unseen forces as the result of nature, while journalism throughout the period responded to readers' inquiries about strange events with secularist logic, exposing apparently unnatural events as the result of fraud, or perceptions tainted by ignorance and superstition.[2] Critics have linked this attitude not only to the surge in consumer products, but to a consumerist attitude that enveloped belief itself.[3] However, the passion for consumption did not drive out contemporary fascination with the occult. Rather, writers represented spiritual meaning in the new idiom of the consumerist century: things.

Things and ghosts seem opposites: the first all material form, the second all immaterial spirit. Both things and ghosts, however, lie on the margins of form and formlessness, materiality and meaning: things metaphorically connote the soulless body, ghosts the bodiless soul, and both express the problem of finding selfhood in the nexus of spirit and form. As Mary Douglas explains in her analysis of pollution and ritual, "all margins are dangerous" because they delimit social, state, and personal control.[4] For eighteenth-century writers, both ghosts and things embody a self at the margins of will and form, a self beyond physical confines that can appear and vanish with ominous consequences to the individual's fate. Most vitally, both enact and yet conceal power relations that shape the self.[5] The representation of things thus allows eighteenth-century writers to explore the relations between materiality and morality, form and formlessness, body and soul, and to express anxiety about unseen powers that control human beings. In the literature of the long eighteenth century, occult objects become a literary motif that dramatizes the struggle between humans having power over things, and things having power over humans.

A familiar moral discourse already enveloped things in literature.[6] Since the medieval period, sacred objects and relics in the Catholic tradition were believed to hold God's spirit, most cogently in the Host, and eighteenth-century collecting practices mimicked this reverence for things, albeit desacralized.[7] Conventional Protestant doctrine, however, held that objects embody the irreligious pursuit of wealth and worldly power over the pious worship of God. In the seventeenth century, satirists such as Aphra Behn and Samuel Butler portrayed apparently skeptical scientists as deluded by the mysterious power of collectible objects and scientific instruments.[8] Both religious and satirical writers thus depict objects as sapping spiritual strength and diverting social and intellectual energies; indeed, as in many cultures, early modern objects often appear to possess evil power or to house devils.

Things in literature hence become a site of cultural struggle between a religious and a secular approach to meaning. Narratives of occult things with lives of their own document the power of commodities to determine human identity as personal possessions in the bourgeois culture increasingly embodied intangibles like social status, power, and sexuality, and as emerging capitalism dissevered product from perceptible labor. As the material of consumption, objects also incarnate the satanic power of secular desire over spirituality. Moreover, such objects refuse relationship, existing entirely in and of themselves, in a sphere whose detachment from quotidian concerns parallels but never intersects with the religious. Contemporary culture reinforced this uneasiness about the status and power of things. As several critics have observed, the "spiritualisation of commerce" that, especially in the credit craze of the 1720s and the South Sea Bubble disaster, made wealth and property impalpable, clearly subjected humans to unseen forces.[9] In addition, eighteenth-century thinkers remained uneasy about the limits of identity and physicality, a keen concern dramatized in the fad for automata, public frauds, and instances of professional credulity: the cases of Mary Toft, mother of seventeen rabbits and fragments of cat, for example, or the fraudulent Bottle Conjuror, who promised to shrink into a beer bottle.[10] Through the conjunction of the advent of empirical science, unmonitored consumption, and the flight of the supernatural from mainstream culture, things come to embody the ambiguity of the material and the uncertainty of significance in a world of lost meanings.

Ghost tales also belong in a literary tradition dating from classical writings and the Bible that was revisited in the late seventeenth and eighteenth centuries.[11] Many religious accounts employ vengeful ghosts and prophetic visions as traditional arguments for reform and the restoration of justice after the courts and the Church have failed. Throughout the century, too, broadsides and pamphlets rehearsing episodes from Joseph Glanvill's *Saducimus Triumphatus* (1681) report the return of the dead to lay the doubt of their skeptical friends, or retell the hugely popular Drummer of Tedworth haunting.[12] In the eighteenth century, these generally appear as rustic documents designed for antiquarian pleasure and/or as class-inflected refutations of empirical philosophy. *The Yorkshire Wonder* (1698), for example, which chronicles the resurrection of a man two days after his death, proved so popular that it reappeared as *The Surrey Wonder* in the following century. In all such works, ghosts enact people's outrage at the severance of their relationships with government, God, or history. Such stories use a traditional idiom to urge traditional ends: they reestablish the importance of the very relationships in which things intervene, and urge the role of moral conviction and social responsibility in personal identity.

Because of this traditionalism, ghost stories were threatening to writers wedded to enlightenment principles of self-advancement and rationalism. Mannered fictions and topical satire thus coopt the literary conventions of the supernatural either to reify the occult into a literary commodity or to deride superstition.[13] Journalists, including Daniel Defoe, and late-century novelists like Ann Radcliffe, Horace Walpole, and Matthew Gregory Lewis also used ghosts to titillate lurking readerly superstition; Margaret L. Carter explains that such stories use mediating narrative structures to allow speculation about the immaterial realm and to "invite the reader to identify with the protagonist's uncertainty."[14] However, they do so within the confines of literary practices that also invite disbelief or pragmatism by framing the occult within secularist or empirical assumptions. Poems such as Charles Churchill's *The Ghost* (1761), a progress of superstition culminating in a parody of the Cock Lane Ghost incident, and ballads such as that describing the haunting of Admiral Byng after his execution in March 1757 hitch the absurdity of a belief in the occult to outrageous abuses of public trust: both dramatize public credulity.[15] Another example, Susanna Centlivre's 1709 comic farce *The Man's bewitch'd; or, The Devil to do about Her,* was revived in 1767 in an abbreviated form as *The Ghost,* with the ghost scene foregrounded to exemplify trickery. Here, the truewit Captain Constant attempts to reclaim his inheritance by pretending that the ghost of his father has appeared to redress his wrongs in a passage burlesquing Glanvill's Drummer of Tedworth tale (1662). The Captain's confederate, Clinch, reports that "he haunted us six days like the Devil; sometimes like a shag dog—sometimes like a white pidgeon—At last he came in the shape, Sir, of his own shape; and with a hollow voice, he says—Clinch says he do you know me. Yes Sir says I, I do. Then addressing himself to my master, don't be afraid, said he."[16] In eighteenth-century literary culture, the occult, commodified in genre and trope, often signals consumer deception.

Ghost stories directed to a broader audience evoked as pious, however, more ambiguously negotiate the complex relationship between beliefs and things both in form and subject. In these works, the deception embodied by the occult concerns the status of physical reality and empirical language. Several religious pamphlets and chapbook tales pit empiricism against faith by portraying clichés as real. *The Wonder of Wonders, or Strange News from Newton in Yorkshire* ([London?], 1675), for example, recounts the story of a woman whose house was pelted by stones until, opening the door, she saw the handsome gentleman of whom she dreamed, turned to stone in her courtyard. Albeit readers may construe him as her adulterous lover, the pamphlet functions as a marvel, an empirical objectification of a hidden—an "occult"—event. This clash of denotative against connotative language complicates the use of empiricism as interpretative strategy by making words slide between registers of meaning. Collections of apparitions frequently contrast reports of visionary armies and monsters that require allegorical interpretation with individuals' visions expressed in a journalistic idiom. Whereas metaphorical visions concern the polis and demand a public decoding, visions concerning the self speak literally.[17] *God's Awful Warnings to a Giddy, Careless, Sinful World* (1795), for example, contains famous tales of prophetic visions that ride on the margins of words and objects. While the vision of a cloud-beast at the head of an army in a sky-continent receives an allegorical gloss from Richard Brothers, the tale of a man who disregards a personal, divine warning stands without comment. In this story, ignoring the advice "*not to go to work,*" the victim suffers the collapse of a vertebra in his neck "so that his head fell, and he has never since been able to hold it up."[18] This linguistic instability expresses the opposition of secular and spiritual impulses—to work or to worship—by eliding literal and metaphorical description. Such ghost stories literalize language; in making metaphor material, they explore the materialization of ideas and the ghostly meanings behind physical phenomena.

The relationship between material forces and moral power also preoccupied religious thinkers, particularly when physicality seemed divorced from meaning, as in madness, delusions, and dreams, instances that threatened the supremacy of reason and self-preservation, both concepts that grounded enlightenment principles of humanism and sociability.[19] Accordingly, popular theorists were concerned to rationalize the behavior of physical phenomena as the result of a controlling, intelligent force. Some explain the occult as God's power working with humanity's own rational impulses to circumvent wayward will by acting directly on the body. William Freke's *The Divine Grammar; or, Select Rules Leading to the more nice Syntax and Articulate Construction of Dreams, Visions and Apparitions* (1703), for example, categorically defines "THE FOUNTAIN OF MONITION" as bodily movements motivated by a consonance of the animal being and the deity:

> When the Creature acts not of his own Volition, 'tis the Spirit operates in him to his proper Designs.
> When the Creature ceases from Action by Sleep or otherwise, he makes a new Theatre for the Spirit to act.
> Creatures unreasonable have Monitions to be regarded by the Creatures reasonable that approach them.
> The Dog dreams to shew the Master himself his Fate, and as he is unworthy of a kinder Notice.
> The Madmen light-headed and sick, have Extasy Dream and Vision, to instruct their Nurses and Intenders what the Divine Will and Pleasure concerning them is.
> Creatures reasonable have Dream, Vision and Apparition for their own Sakes and Goods; and if so be they would not [s]light them, have Eyes and see not, Ears and hear not, etc.
> God hath, doth, and for ever will thus shew to all, that he is, and continues Really and in Act the universal Lord of all, and that nothing is, or can be befallen us, but what is by his Decree and Pleasure.[20]

This pamphlet portrays the self as an objectified body pulled into action by a great will: we are things moved by God. Characteristically, this explanation identifies the unseen as strictly divine and dispels the mystery of unaccountable movements, dreams, and sights by blaming humanity's blindness to God and God's own preference for mysterious ways. It argues that, since the spirit moves the material, and that material, rightly seen, reveals the spirit, the material becomes a lens for the divine purpose.[21] At the same time, using a traditional Christian idiom, the writer represents identity as a division between the body-thing and the soul within.

The benignity of a materialized occult provided many Protestant writers with a way to acknowledge occult and material forces without giving in to superstitious fears of the devil. The idea that occult phenomena worked through things to profit and protect humans cleansed the occult and humans alike of devilry, as long as that devilry was kept separate from material things. In "*An Essay on the History and Reality of Apparitions.* Being an Account of what they are, and what they are not; whence they come, and whence they come not" (1727), Daniel Defoe defines supernatural events as a means for advancement. Refuting earlier claims that devilish spirits abound, he argues that spirits act as guardians of property and save both goods and souls—indeed, souls implicitly through goods.[22] These, however, are not human souls but a divine species designed to warn humans against external and moral dangers; in his open-minded exploration of kinds of apparitions, Defoe declares, "I exclude no Species of Spirits, but the departed unembodied Souls of Men."[23] Moreover, these spirits act on human intuition; they never act directly on property. By reinscribing the distinctions between divinity and materiality, Defoe consequently circumvents the marginality of both the human ghost and the occult object.

Defoe's antagonism to the intrusion of the ghostly into the real permeates *A Journal of the Plague Year* (1722), where apparitions exist as fearful delusions destructive to the social and material world. In one instance, crowds perceive an apparition predicting by gestures the deaths of hundreds, but the enlightened narrator, H.F., wedded to the empirical world, sees nothing:

> In this narrow Passage [from Petty-France into Bishopsgate Church Yard] stands a Man looking thro' between the Palisadoe's into the Burying Place; and as many People as the Narrowness of the Passage would admit to stop, without hindring the Passage of others; and he was talking mighty eagerly to them, and pointing now to one Place, then to another, and affirming, that he saw a Ghost walking upon such a Grace Stone there; he describ'd the Shape, the Posture, and the Movement of it so exactly, that it was the greatest Matter of Amazement to him in the World, that every Body did not see it as well as he. On a sudden he would cry, *There it is: Now it comes this Way.* Then, *'Tis turn'd back;* till at length he persuaded the People into so firm a Belief of it, that one fancied he saw it, and another fancied he saw it; and thus he came every Day making a strange Hubbub, considering it was in so narrow a Passage, till *Bishopsgate* Clock struck eleven; and then the Ghost would seem to start; and as if he were call'd away, disappear'd on a sudden.[24]

H.F.'s description of the ghost's behavior echoes Shakespeare's description of Old Hamlet's ghost, a popular source of occult literary tropes itself shaped by Shakespeare's reading of Lewes Lavater's 1570 *Of Ghostes.* Such literary language underscores not only the fictionality of the ghost, but also its sphere of significance. Form without substance, a mockery of materiality, ghosts speak of a metaphorical world beyond the physical. As such, they have no place in Defoe's material universe. Furthermore, since people grow terrified of walking through the passage, these forms impinge on social space and take up property.[25] Indeed, the apparition projects further usurpation of space:

> This Ghost, as the poor Man affirm'd, made Signs to the Houses, and to the Ground, and to the People, plainly intimating, or else they so understanding it, that Abundance of the People, should come to be buried in that Church-Yard; as indeed happen'd: But that he saw such Aspects I must acknowledg [*sic*], I never believ'd; nor could I see any thing of it my self, tho' I look'd most earnestly to see it, if possible.

As in the incident of the angel in the sky, H.F. cannot verify this sighting, but he reports it as a premonition that the space would, indeed, be occupied by nonhuman bodies, "as indeed happen'd." Yet these are the opposite of ghosts: they are all body without spirit, the dead.[26]

While *A Journal of the Plague Year* polices the margins of body and spirit, many of Defoe's fictions explore the relationship between the supernatural and property, itself maddeningly fugitive, as devilish agency. Many critics have noted the conflict in Defoe's work between self-determination and submission to Providence, a conflict that complicates his moral message by implying that salvation lies in accumulating goods.[27] Even *Robinson Crusoe* (1719), most evidently a tale of spiritual salvation, entangles identity in possession by chronicling Robinson's recovery of property. Most notoriously, while intently raiding his wrecked ship for useful items, Crusoe discovers a stash of money and exclaims "O Drug! . . . what art thou good for? Thou art not worth to me, no not the taking off of the Ground; one of those Knives is worth all this Heap; I have no Manner of use for thee. E'en remain where thou art, and go to the Bottom as a Creature whose Life is not worth saving. However, upon Second Thoughts, I took it all away."[28] When he gives possession of himself to God, he comes to possess wealth and land: his identity is accumulated along with his things. *Roxana; or the Fortunate Mistress* (1724), as the title ironically indicates, documents the slippery descent of the heroine as she exchanges her identity for that of an owned object of admiration.[29] Whereas these and other novels depict the general lure of wealth, the addictive power of specific things to subsume human identity most vitally informs Defoe's great novel of acquisitiveness, *Moll Flanders* (1722).

In *Moll Flanders* things possess a devilish power. They overtake Moll's agency and pull her will-lessly into action.

> Wandring thus about I knew not wh[i]ther, I pass'd by an Apothecary's Shop in *Leadenhall-Street*, where I saw lye on a Stool just before the Counter a little

> Bundle wrapt in a white Cloth . . . This was the Bait; and the Devil, who I said laid the Snare, as readily prompted me, as if he had spoke, for I remember, and shall never forget it, 'twas like a Voice spoken to me over my Shoulder, take the Bundle; be quick; do it this Moment; it was no sooner said but I step'd into the Shop, and with my Back to the Wench, as if I had stood up for a Cart that was going by, I put my Hand behind me and took the Bundle, and went off with it, the Maid or the Fellow not perceiving me, or any one else.
>
> It is impossible to express the Horror of my Soul all the while I did it . . . I could never tell which way it was [that I was going], nor where I went, for I felt not the Ground, I stept on . . . my Blood was all in a Fire, my Heart beat as if I was in a sudden Fright.[30]

The voice of things that "lye" summons Moll so strongly that she responds as a witch to the call of the devil: she floats or flies through the air, inflamed with passions that supersede reason. Penetrating her very body, the things she steals infuse her with their own occult powers, yet their power is Satan's lie: they will betray her.

The sexual innuendo of Moll's response to the bundle also underscores its function as a material body. It contains: "a Suit of Child-bed Linnen . . . very good and almost new, the Lace very fine; there was a Silver Porringer of a Pint, a small Silver Mug and Six Spoons, some other Linnen, a good Smock, and Three Silk Handkerchiefs, and in the Mug, wrap'd up in a Paper, Eighteen Shillings and Six-pence in Money" (234–35). Since these domestic items are the accoutrements of a family with a newborn child, the bundle symbolically embodies both the family triad of father, mother, and child, and an infant in swaddling clothes. Carrying it in her arms, Moll serves to parody motherhood by bearing not a child, but things. Moreover, by purloining the bundle, Moll intervenes in all the familial relationships it represents. She reenacts the sexual transgression of adultery by sliding between the bundle's original owner and the owned object in an act of instinctive passion, while her symbolic bearing of an illegitimate child mirrors her literal bearing of a bastard son pages earlier (141). In place of the sanctioned relationships of ownership and family, Moll substitutes the passionate duality of illegal possession between object and thief. As in adultery, however, the object as a body itself is complicitous: it asks to be taken. The lying bundle thus betrays its own function as a representative of familial love, and, as a speaking body, it draws Moll into sin. The object becomes the body without a soul.

This very physicality enacts objects' dangerous power to replace moral with material values. The silver, silk, lace, and money within the bundle signal the collection as rich: they incarnate the temptation of wealth, which is to substitute things for relationships, accumulation for charity. This is enabled by the objects' fungibility. Although Moll yearns to hear "News of the Loss," there is none: despite the penumbra of family history hanging over the bundle, the objects it contains bear no physical marks of ownership (236). Whereas Desdemona's handkerchief is irreplaceable, unmistakable, and uniquely valuable as a gift, not as a handkerchief, these objects do not carry their meaning beyond Moll's consciousness. They are items circulating in a free economy, and because they are exactly the same as dozens of other items, they can be fenced without questions. The bundle thus allows Moll to replace social meanings with the solipsistic relationship between the self and accumulated riches. Consequently, as the objects enrich Moll, so they possess her mind, and this possession fills her with the anguish of ownership: "All the while I was opening these things I was under such dreadful Impressions of Fear, and in such Terror of Mind, tho' I was perfectly safe, that I cannot express the manner of it" (235). Furthermore, they define her public identity: "I sat me down and cried most vehemently; Lord, *said I,* what am I now? A Thief! why, I shall be taken next time and be carry'd to *Newgate*" (235–36). Not only has the bundle made her into a thief, but it has made her a thing in its place, liable to be "taken next time" and "carry'd" off, just as she has taken it. The object has made an object of her self.

Objects not only make the self a thing, however; they also make other people into things. As Moll rapidly becomes addicted to stealing things, not merely out of need but out of desire, she fails to differentiate material from human objects of use and possession. From the "Bundle" of infant-clothes, she next "stoops" to a child when satanically "tempted" by "the same wicked Impulse that had said, *take that Bundle*" (237). Her subsequent description characterizes the child as "it":

> I talk'd to it, and it prattl'd to me again, and I took it by the Hand and led it along till I came to a pav'd Alley that goes into *Bartholomew Close,* and I led it in there; the Child said that was not its way home; I said, yes, my Dear, it is; I'll show you the way home; the Child had a little Necklace on of Gold Beads, and I had my Eye upon that, and in the dark of the Alley I stoop'd, pretending to mend the Child's Clog that was loose, and took off her Necklace and the Child never felt it. (206)

The gleam of the golden beads almost drives Moll to murder, and although fear prevents her, she moralizes to herself that "I had given the Parents a just Reproof for their Negligence in leaving the poor little Lamb to come home by it self" (238). By contrasting the Biblical language of "poor little Lamb" with the hungrily mercenary "my Eye upon that," Defoe emphasizes how things obscure religious and humane meanings: the sinister metaphor in "I'll show you the way home" intensifies the conflict of literal and spiritual meanings. Things' seductive fungibility is contagious, spreading from the objects to Moll's relationships with people, themselves made objects for her use.

Once she develops into an accomplished thief entirely focused on accumulating money, Moll regards all relationships as material that she can cash in. While recognizing that the child's string of golden beads represents its mother's "Vanity" and her own moral descent, Moll nevertheless sees it as "worth about Twelve or Fourteen pounds," and even as she criticizes the common practice of exchanging goods attained with life-risking thievery for "a Trifle," she describes other thefts in terms of the money they net (238, 241). Shortly after the above incident, Moll pretends to help a woman whose house is afire in order to steal another bundle. This theft symbolizes her detachment from the world of relationships:

> It is with Horror that I tell what a Treasure I found there, 'tis enough to say, that besides most of the Family Plate, which was considerable, I found a Gold Chain, an old fashion'd thing, the Locket of which was broken, so that I suppose it had not been us'd some Years, but the Gold was not the worse for that; also a little Box of burying Rings, the Lady's Wedding-Ring, and some broken bits of old Lockets of Gold, a Gold Watch, and a Purse with about 24 *l.* value in old pieces of Gold Coin, and several other things of Value.
>
> This was the greatest and worse Prize that ever I was concerned in, for indeed, tho', as I have said above, I was harden'd now beyond the Power of all Reflection in other Cases, yet it really touch'd me to the very Soul, when I look'd into this Treasure, to think of the poor disconsolate Gentlewoman who had lost so much . . . I confess the inhumanity of this Action mov'd me very much. (253)

Rings and lockets, both "old fashion'd" symbols of loving bonds, become loot in Moll's possession. The warning messages of the "burying Rings," the watch, and the broken lockets mean nothing to her: chronicled in a litany, they are all golden material, her own "gold chain" of worldly wealth shackling her to materiality and blinding her to time. The impersonal "gold" survives the fracturing of life and relationships told by the rings, lockets, and chain, as earlier Moll's mentor, her "governess," melts stolen plate into amorphous silver, guaranteeing its anonymity for sale (246). As Moll betrays the victim of this theft, so she severs the objects she purloins from their social meanings. Objects become formless wealth, their very materiality swallowed by their demonic power to possess her soul.

Moll's initial descent dates from the objectification of her own body as material exchangeable for money. This pattern facilitates her objectification of people as she progresses from raiding the infant-bundle, to the child, to the male body. As Stuart Sim explains, when Moll accepts £500 to marry her lover's younger brother, she becomes a "commercial object," and reified herself, discovers "that the only way to escape from reification is to reify others."[31] When Moll recounts her dealings as a prostitute, she passes over "the bed, etc. . . . I need say no more," but she details what she takes from her clients. Often, these objects symbolize gentlemanly status: "I Took this opportunity to search him to a Nicety; I took a gold Watch, with a silk Purse of Gold, his fine full bottom Perrewig, and silver fring'd Gloves, his Sword, and fine Snuff-box" (277). Head, hands, purse, prowess, and social identity, the body and the soul of her lover, have been translated into commodities for the taking. Accumulating fungible lovers as collected things, Moll's dealings in sex again symbolize her transgressive substitution of materiality for spiritual values, and the triumph of a materialistic definition of relationship over a moral one that is the foundation of pornography.[32] As she uses her own body as a thing exchangeable for money, her identity spirals into the appetite for acquisition.

Moll Flanders ends with a repentance and, presumably, redemption of its heroine, now rich and married, that readers often find implausible. Much of the problem lies in Defoe's technique, whereby catalogues of objects hold the meaning of the narrative so powerfully that readers vicariously share Moll's acquisitive triumph, with the result that the symbolic power of providential fortune dims beneath denotative literalism. Moreover, Moll's tumbling series of adventures itself turns the story into a litany of sketchily connected incidents. This episodic narrative echoes formally the thematic motif of accumulating separate things. Thus, the conventional moral, reliant on a mental process of reflection and a formal sequence of causal connections, works against both the narrative and the thematic modes. Appearing hastily at the end, it functions as another episode and another way of accumulating gold—this time, in heaven. The notorious ineffectuality of this ending shows that things remain the embodiment of cultural power and meaning in a novel about accumulation.

As objects' fascinating powers empty Defoe's moralistic narrative of the immaterial values he ostensibly recommends and overtake his protagonist's personality, their evasive power to determine the meaning of humans also shapes satirical genres. Famously, in Alexander Pope's *The Rape of the Lock* (1714), spiritualized things in the form of sylphs govern women's passions and determine their actions. Moreover, material items in the poem possess a transformative power.[33] The commodities on Belinda's dressing table gild her into a divinity, whereas Moll's made her a devil. Tea-table consumables convert the internecine plotting of the cards into a spiritual celebration, and the cards play the people in Canto III. While human lives evaporate into metaphor and cliché in Canto V's battle, in the Cave of Spleen objects come alive: "living Tea-pots," a walking pipkin, sighing "Jar," and talking "Goose-pye."[34] Crowned with capital letters, objects have souls, spirits, and material bodies that transform people into commodities. Pope, indeed, describes the central act of rape and division by a symbolic action in which the object commits the human crime: the "glitt'ring *Forfex,*" that closes to "divide" (3.147–48). At the end of the poem, Belinda herself has been transformed into "*This Lock*" (3.149), a poetic object that fastens her, made from Pope's linguistic commodification of the adornment of her maiden's head. Again, in *Epistle to Burlington* (1731), things can overwhelm people by their social power, sheer size, and number. Timon, hypnotized by the conviction that things will make him great, stands surrounded by his swollen estate and is dwarfed by his possessions:

> Who but must laugh, the Master when he sees
> A puny insect, shiv'ring at a breeze!
> Lo, what huge heaps of littleness around
> The whole, a labour'd Quarry above ground.
>
> (lines 107–10)

Timon's possessions, rivaling his greatness, transform him into an "insect." Pope's objects upstage people as the vessels of social meanings.

Gothic fictions often dramatize this competition for control between possessor and possession in order to explore the marginality of identity in a postempirical world where physical meanings fail to correspond to spiritual significance. In Horace Walpole's *The Castle of Otranto* (1764), the ghostly and gigantic helmet and sword testify to Manfred's usurpation, as do the ancestral portrait that sighs and climbs down from the wall and the waving black plumes of the huge casque that has descended abruptly into the castle. Uncontrollable, supernatural, and simultaneously material and immaterial, these phenomena embody the swollen power of emblems of ownership to determine owners. Indeed, Manfred's very character as the tyrant of the tale is both identified and usurped by huge, occult things. The objects in Ann Radcliffe's novels, set on the Catholic continent, also play out the tension between self-possession and objects' power of possessing. The fine paintings, tapestries, and richly wrought furniture that she describes bear witness to the tyrannies of a proud, feudal, and superstitious past. In *The Mysteries of Udolpho* (1794) especially, these things lure Emily away from reason into the world of fluctuating impressions. The waxen figure of death, for example, seems so lifelike to Emily that she believes it real evidence of murder. Similarly, music and scenes of natural beauty have a hypnotic effect on sensitive characters. In Radcliffe's novels, the power of art to dislodge life parallels the power of superstition to infect. Like the sensations of love, beauty, and fear, art objects can suspend thought by dangerously possessing the imagination.

Whereas these portrayals of objects' power to erode personal and social control focus on elite objects that mesmerize the imagination and emotions, poltergeist ghost narratives traditionally locate this power in quotidian things. Such things attack both the body and the household possessions that constitute people's most intimate objects.[35] Self-propelled objects, a common feature of witch stories, had traditionally been evidence of devilish possession, but in the eighteenth century, empirically minded observers regarded them as more ambiguous evidence of unidentified forces, either natural or supernatural. Typically, stones and man-made objects hurl themselves at people or move slowly through the air; victims hear things knocking, rapping, and scratching; property burns itself out in fires; objects grow unnaturally hot, cold, or slimy.[36] Clothes often move on their own, or even reject their wearers; *Pandaemonium, or the Devil's Cloyster* (1684), for example, reports that a young man's perriwig bounced from its box and tore itself to shreds, and a shoestring "was observed (without the assistance of any hand) to come of its own accord out of his Shoe, and fling itself to the other side of the Room; the other was crawling after it."[37] Most poltergeists prefer domestic items, characteristically the plates, glasses, candlesticks, and kitchen objects overturned by the Stockwell Ghost in 1772.[38] Noisy, stinky, and violent, such objects infringe on humans' control over their own bodily sensations and households. The dislocation of sensual evidence from perceptible agent characterizes even conventional ghost events. In the famous Cock Lane Ghost affair, for example, the supernatural phenomena of occult scratching and tapping drew wide audiences, even including skeptics. Such hauntings dramatized for eighteenth-century observers the tenuousness of the relationship between sensation and cause, the invisible will and the material world, invisible agency and visible matter.[39]

Whereas the Cock Lane Ghost affair replays the conventional trope of ghost narratives by centering, Hamlet-like, on a spirit demanding punishment for her undetected murderer, a parallel incident focuses instead on the phenomenon of malicious material that acts without a detectable origin. *A Narrative of Some Extraordinary Things that Happened to Mr. Richard Giles's Children, at the Lamb, Without Lawford's-Gate, Bristol; Supposed to be the Effect of Witchcraft* eschews blaming a human for the disruptions, instead identifying maddened objects as the source of evil.

Moreover, whereas the Cock Lane Ghost was motivated to redress a public crime, the bad things in Durbin's account aim to upset the domestic home. Although first published in 1800, long after any possibility of the kind of official investigation that laid the Cock Lane Ghost, Durbin's *Narrative* had purportedly been circulated in manuscript from 1761. This dating suggests that the piece was written in response to the notoriety of the Cock Lane Ghost incident, and that the publisher hoped to capitalize on the Cock Lane Ghost's fame with a narrative that spoke more widely and generally to the audience's experience.

The centrality of objects in the story results largely from the pragmatic, empirical style and familiar setting of the narrative. Fashioned to appeal to the audience's domestic experience by recording incidents that might happen in any middle-class household, the tale concerns the ten-month torment of two children, beginning on Friday, November 13, 1761 and lasting until a cunning-woman exorcizes the demonic forces. In the convention of verification dating from Glanvill's *Saducimus Triumphatus* and perfected in Defoe's 1706 *True Relation of the Apparition of one Mrs. Veal,* the frame of the pamphlet guarantees its empirical authenticity. Along with a title specifying the location and date of events, the editorial preface defends the probity, piety, and disinterestedness of the witness Durbin, who, like Glanvill and Robert Boyle, was a scientist, a "Chymist," and who verifies his narrative by asserting himself "an Eye and Ear Witness of the principal Facts herein related."[40] While the editor grants that "every man should abound in his own opinion," he "thinks the following is a *clear case,* and that from it every impartial reader will draw the following conclusion": that the story is authentic (7–8). Thus, the narrative functions conventionally as a journalistic record of a practical, skeptical, meticulous observer's mental and visual impressions as he tests the possibility of the occult. Durbin presents himself as an everyman whose obscure status intensifies the domestic immediacy of the story: this kind of haunting could happen to anyone.

The ubiquitous danger of mad things receives more verification than this proof of Durbin's reliability. Like Defoe's *True Relation,* it appears bound with authenticating testimonials, in this case "A LETTER From the Rev. Mr. Bedford, late Vicar of *Temple,* to the Bishop of Glocester . . . Who had Dealings with Familiar Spirits" that functions to reassure readers of the text's piety by invoking the spiritual authority of the Church (6). The most powerful "proof," however, is material:

> Till within a few years of his death, he preserved the *glass* and *pins* mentioned on page 31. &c. which he often shewed to his particular friends. Such forms as the pins were crooked into, the Editor believes [n]ever met the human eye. There was scarcely a known form in nature that corresponded

> to any of them. It would have tortured the ingenuity of man to have even imitated them, much more, to have invented the vast variety of fantastic figures which several scores of these pins exhibited. To *describe* them is impossible, and to *paint* them equally so. The glass, which was an old-fashioned one, has been shewn to several, and it was nipped round at the foot in the manner described on page 14.

These bewitched pins defeat description. By asserting that material objects that exist *beyond* the text and *outside* language prove the narrative, the preface thus reinforces the predication of the poltergeist genre: that objects have power beyond human structures of meaning. Pins traditionally were used to test witchcraft, and thus already exist for readers as household objects with a subversive cultural significance. Interestingly, Adam Smith also cites pins as the quintessential example of his theory of added labor in *An Inquiry into the Nature and Causes of the Wealth of Nations* (1776). Here, they serve as examples of doubly added value; embodying both the labor of the maker and the labor of the unmaker, they have moved outside the sphere of use into the sphere of symbolic meaning. This technique of citing an object's materiality as proof of a reality both literal and metaphorical, physical and occult, appears everywhere in ghost fiction. In *True Relation,* for example, Defoe repeatedly points to the color, texture, and freshness of Mrs. Veal's dress as evidence of her spiritual reality.[41] In Durbin's account, however, the material evidence is still more powerful because it constitutes the means that caused pain: the pins work as both agent and evidence.

As phenomena on the margin of the natural and supernatural, inspirited objects thus are paradoxically both material and immaterial, like the sylphs in *The Rape of the Lock.* The *Narrative of Some Extraordinary Things* emphasizes this ambiguity by cataloguing the transformations of the invisible power from essence to object. It opens by identifying the evil spirit occupying the house as a concatenation of immaterial impressions that make a bodiless body. The editor recounts that Durbin met the spirit by appointment and heard

> a loud knocking on the opposite side of the wainscot . . . Lifting his eyes toward the place where the noise seemed to be, he discovered a coloured luminous appearance, of a circular form, about the size of a common plate: the colours resembled those of the rainbow: the brighter ones were extremely vivid, and deeply shaded with the *red, blue,* and *indigo.* The Writer believes that Mr. *D*[urbin] said, he then asked some questions, but what they were, he cannot now recollect. (7)

Shaped like a plate, armless, legless, headless, the apparition is all center; it escapes the substance and form of earthly bodies. Both this manifestation itself and the supernatural power to change form have precedents in ghost-tale publications: in the 1680s tale, *A most Strange and Dreadful APPARITION of several Spirits & Visions*, for example, supernatural agents appear as rats, as pigeons, and as "a round circumference like to Foot-balls" before revealing themselves to be human spirits.[42] A darkly glowing essence of forceful will, the poltergeist is pure agency whose terrifying power lies in its ability to become any thing. It manipulates the borders of form and formlessness.

This manipulation of the physical world inspires independent objects with specific agency. While Durbin includes reports of ghostly apparitions, he himself witnesses only objects rebelling against their roles. Such objects include the victims' bodies. His account thus records the torment of a Mr. Giles's two young children by meticulously describing the trajectories and behavior of things and human parts which, albeit presumably driven by this spherical spirit, seem to act on their own. The tale recounts that the household ignored scratching sounds, believing them made by pigeons, although on Sunday, December 6, "several persons said they saw the finger of a hand near the children" (9). However, after Giles's daughter Molly reports that her clothes seem to move on their own, her father investigates, suspecting thieving servants, and, when she attempts to clear under the bed, observes that "it" pulls the hanger out of her hand and sees her clothes box move. Hearing of these events, the skeptical Durbin determines to test the poltergeist. The first proof is the impression on the girl's flesh of the live spirit-thing:

> December 18, 1761, hearing that Mr. Giles's children, Miss Molly and Dobby, were afflicted in an extraordinary manner, for a fortnight past, I went there this day, and saw Molly sewing, and found she had marks on her arms given on a sudden, like the marks of a thumb-nail; which I am satisfied she could not do herself. As I watched her, I saw the flesh pressed down, whitish, and rise again, leaving the print of a fingernail, the edges of which grew red afterwards. (9)

In this empirical description, Molly's own flesh acts as an occult object, sinking and rising, whitening, creasing, and reddening of its own accord. Although she complains that she feels painfully bruised, Molly seems to exercise no power over her own body. In another instance, "I saw the flesh at the side of her throat pushed in, whitish, as if done with fingers though I saw none. Her face grew red and blackish presently, as if she was strangled," but when Durbin touches her, she recovers (12). Whereas Moll Flanders uses her body as a thing in an exchange economy, Molly's body abuses her, yet both enact the severance of body from human spirit.

The rebellion of things, including the body, against their owners and appointed functions turns the orderly, manufactured household world into a site of revolution. The objects in the Lamb's Inn enact the anxiety eighteenth-century people felt about formless powers infiltrating, indeed possessing, domestic forms, and turning form inside out. In the ensuing episodes, animated domestic objects overturn themselves while familiar things attack the domestic space and its inhabitants:

> The curtains [in the children's bedchamber] moved up and down, as if drawn by pullies. Things were thrown over the bed, and the chamber-pot whirled around the room several times, and several other things done contrary to nature . . . We were told how the great table was, by an invisible power, turned quite upside down, with the four legs upwards, twice in an hour, in presence of three or four persons. The carpet that was on it being laid smooth on the floor in an instant, as if placed so by two men. I think by the size of the table, two men could scarcely turn it over. Mr.— — —, saw a chair move from the wall and fall down. Mr.— — — was sitting in the room with Mr. Giles and others, and they saw the poker and shovel rise from the chimney, and seemed to be thrown to the other end of the room. A key that was hanging up came five yards and struck Mr. Giles on the head. (11–12)

The violation of "nature" Durbin observes lies in the human agency of inhuman objects and the reversal of power between the maker of things and the thing made. In other instances, objects direct their animus at the family's nursemaid, fighting back against her efforts to keep them in order. Durbin reports that, when he went upstairs to investigate knocking, he spied on a case of drawers "a wine-glass, which I saw glitter in the sun, and was astonished to see it rise from the drawers without hands. It rose gradually about a foot, perpendicularly from the drawers; then the glass seemed to stand, and thereupon inclined backwards, as if a hand had held it; it was then flung with violence about five feet, and struck the nurse on the hip with a hard blow," leaving a bruise (14–15). In contrast to the obedient nursemaid, the wineglass rejects its purpose and creates disorder. This behavior illuminates the real danger these rebellious objects present: by acting on their own, without a central purpose or identifiable motive, they represent the chaos of matter divorced from divine will, of things alienated from human meanings, of anarchy. Both by their meaningless violence and by their rejection of the purposes for which they were made, these objects reprise satanic ingratitude. They battle their creators and disrupt the hierarchy of man and thing. The narrative locates in the immediate domestic sphere the Christian struggle between material and spiritual, body and soul.

Correspondingly, it becomes syntactically impossible for the narrator to evade agency. Like other narrators of poltergeist experiences, this narrator gradually shifts from describing the behavior of these separate things to attributing their actions to "it." "It" first appears when the uppity objects themselves have a new kind of significance. Durbin reports that on January 3, "they told me a silver dobbin had been flung at them, nobody being near the place where it came from. *It,* (I mean the invisible agent) had now a new trick. Whenever Molly drank tea, or any liquor, it threw it about. She could carry the dish steady to her mouth, but when she went to sip, it pushed her elbow, and threw it about" (13). By such brutal treatment of money, food, and commodities, "it" subversively violates conventional categories of significance, making what humans deem valuable into rubble. In addition, "it" can endow amorphous liquids with form and motive power and invade the body: "it" repeatedly bites and pinches flesh, leaving rank spittle, as well as nail and bite marks; smacks cheeks; pulls on knitting needles; flings glasses and cups about the room; and rolls the children's chamber pot. Variegated, malicious forms have collapsed into a central, evil agency: demonic power has turned the household and the body against themselves.

Nonetheless, the specific manifestations that this demonic power prefers further dramatize the threat anarchic objects present. Both the behavior of the bad things and the substances that "it" attacks, evokes, or emits transgress the borders between form and amorphousness, inside and outside. The Lamb's Inn objects unleash formless matter: they release the contents of wineglasses and chamber pots, blood from the body, sputum, and tears. By spilling, hitting, hurling, and pushing, they violate their assigned functions of containing mass and space. Similarly, the substances they smear about dramatize the body's inability to shore itself up against leakages. Douglas notes that "spittle, blood, milk, urine, faeces or tears by simply issuing forth have traversed the boundaries of the body. So also have bodily parings, skin, nails, hair clippings and sweat."[43] By both transgressing their own forms and releasing excremental materials that themselves transgress the borders between controlled form and fluid formlessness, these objects enact the breakdown of the borders of human control and prove the dangerous independence of property from ownership. Douglas explains, "ritual pollution . . . arises from the interplay of form and surrounding formlessness. Pollution dangers strike when form has been attacked."[44] Self-acting objects enact the violation of form and order.

To reassert control, the narrative compresses the amorphous energies into a form that carries with it a comprehensible motive, and then expels it. Thus, even as the relationship between "it" and the self-propelled objects remains ambiguous, episodes increasingly resemble familiar witch narratives. Durbin reports that the children are, more than once, magically transported to bed. At other times, "it" behaves like the Tedworth Drummer, beating a tattoo, panting "like a bull-dog under the bed," and filling the room with "an insufferable smell, like putrified blood, &c. from a shambles" (45). These variations in occult agency mark the transformation of the narrative from an empirical account of the malicious agency of domestic things to a conventional haunting. Indeed, a third of the way through the narrative, "it" suddenly becomes "she." This female power squeaks "like a large rat caught by a cat," bites, leaves tooth marks and saliva, and soon acts and sounds like a person, swearing "damme" at the nurse, upsetting the pan on the fire, tearing clothes, and crookedly driving a pin so hard into the nurse's leg that they could scarcely remove it. At last, "it" admits to being a woman, a widow, in fact a witch, employed for ten guineas by a malevolent neighbor to cause diverse mischiefs: the creature actually appears as "usual," dressed in "a dirty chip hat, and a brown ragged gown.—She was of a middle size, and had a sharp nose" (34). Formless hostility has turned out to be domestic malice. The narrative ends by reporting that, on the advice of a cunning-woman, the children's urine was boiled, whereupon "beautiful colours came out of it, like the rainbow," signifying the expulsion of "*Malchi,*" the disembodied devil that first flooded the house (54). Even as the story devolves into a conventional witch tale, Durbin dryly concludes, "how far the *cunning* woman may have contrived this [rainbow], I will not pretend to say" (55). Thus, while the narrative reinscribes the margin of form and formlessness by banishing the amorphous power through a transgressive and liquid substance that dissolves into air, it also retains the ominous possibility of uncontrollable things acting on their own. The border between static form—well-behaved objects—and dangerous spirit may have been formally restored, yet not everything has been adequately explained.

A Narrative of Some Extraordinary Things is pulled between the descriptive modes of an empirical, scientific report and a witch story. This strain shows how the occult in the eighteenth century is subsumed into the genre of logical causality and control, the novel, through a process of objectification provided by describing things.[45] The rational explanations that begin to structure the novel in the later eighteenth century, here manifested by the witch, gradually stifle the empirical observation of inexplicable phenomena. Thus, the anarchy represented by separately existing, individually significant, and independently acting material is organized by a structure of repetitive cataloguing, and the observation of separate things is swallowed into the contemplation of a central meaning. Like *Moll Flanders,* Durbin's *Narrative of Some Extraor-*

dinary Things employs an episodic form that both focuses on the material object at the center of each supernatural event and reinforces the accumulation of segregated incidents. Like the things that fly, shatter, and fall, each incident occurs separately, yet together they form a pattern that becomes the moral. The "*Things*" in the book's title further tightens the link between narrative episode and physical object: since each minitale recounts the behavior of a particular object, both are "*Things*." Narrative thus orders chaotic material. Such material includes the body. The depiction of Molly's body as a thing battled by other things echoes the objectification of Moll Flanders's body: Molly's, too, appears defined by its physicality until the pamphlet's witch-explanation inserts a social and moral context that repositions it as a vehicle for a soul. As in Defoe's novel, the tacked-on, conventional ending supplies causality and morality.

The narrative of the Lamb's Inn affair articulates the cultural anxiety in the eighteenth century about the incompatibility of elastic meanings and material objects through a literary mode that seeks to reconcile form and formlessness, thing and spirit. Beginning as a scientific report that depicts objects as agents in themselves, it develops into a chronicle of the family's relationships with their neighbors, servants, and each other. Things' malicious powers are revealed to derive from traditional witchcraft as the occult power shifts from a "plate"-shaped manifestation of formless energy, to a series of malicious material items, then to a central, indefinable "it," and finally to a conventional witch, complete with cat, hat, and robe. Like *Moll Flanders* and such Gothic novels as *The Mysteries of Udolpho,* Durbin's chronicle both expresses the terrifying power of objects and enacts their control. As in *The Rape of the Lock,* the agency in manufactured objects appears finally as human passion, but whereas Pope's satire shows things triumphing, in novelistic structures, the occult is safely drained out of commodity culture and returned to the devil when things relinquish their occult power to become part of the family. At the same time, as in Pope's epic, the ominous power of shapeless forces to take over things, including the body, remains a threat to self-possession, social control, and religion. The amorphous rainbow force still hovers somewhere in the air, seeking other things to possess.

The spiritualization of commodities in eighteenth-century literature betrays contemporary anxiety about the location of power. Material and yet beyond definition, things stand poised between a world of puritanical doctrine and religious adjurations against the lure of lucre, and a world of materialism, progress, and empiricism. As agents of the power of new public culture over the individual, objects can pervert the will, define the owner, rend relationships, and enact theft, violence, loss of identity, and mystery. Especially in their mutability and fungibility, they possess supernatural power over individual meanings and identities; they can make and unmake selves; they even take over conscience and consciousness. Because of their replicability and fundamental indifference to human possession or loss, things embody the terrible hazards of living in a world of soulless material powers. They are absolute material: bodies without souls. For eighteenth-century writers, things are the devils of the empirical age.

Notes

1. Keith Thomas, *Religion and the Decline of Magic* (Harmondsworth, UK: Penguin Books, 1971); Michael Hunter, *Science and the Shape of Orthodoxy* (Woodbridge, UK: Boydell, 1995), esp. 167–79.

2. Both periodicals and travelogues specialized in uncovering deceit and dissolving superstition. See, for example, *The Athenian Mercury* (1691–97), *The British Apollo: Curious Amusements for the Ingenious* (1708–11), *The Spectator* by Joseph Addison and Sir Richard Steele (1711–12, 1714), and the imitations of these journals throughout the century; also William King's *A Journey to London* (1698), Ned Ward's *The London Spy* (1698–1700), John Gay's *Trivia, or the Art of Walking the Streets of London* (1716), and subsequent picaresque journeys into London.

3. For example, Neil McKendrick, John Brewer, and J. H. Plumb, *The Commercialization of Eighteenth-Century England* (London: Hutchinson, 1983); *The Consumption of Culture, 1600–1800: Image, Object, Text*, ed. Ann Bermingham and John Brewer (London: Routledge, 1995); Emma Clery, *The Rise of Supernatural Fiction, 1762–1800* (Cambridge: Cambridge University Press, 1995).

4. Mary Douglas, *Purity and Danger: An Analysis of Concept[s] of Pollution and Taboo* (1966; rpt. London: Routledge, 2002), 150. All quotations refer to this edition.

5. Fredric V. Bogel explores the theme of immateriality and the "pervasive awareness of . . . the insubstantiality" of human experience in *Literature and Insubstantiality in Later Eighteenth-Century England* (Princeton, NJ: Princeton University Press, 1984), 24, passim. In a different context, in *The Devil and Commodity Fetishism in South America*, Michael T. Taussig points out that confrontation with the devil—or the occult—enacts the confrontation with unjust exchanges and relationships in a capitalist culture (Chapel Hill: University of North Carolina Press, 1980), 221–22. This ethnographical insight suggests usefully that things also represent relationships, typically obscure ones.

6. See Susan Stewart, *On Longing: Narratives of the Miniature, the Gigantic, the Souvenir, the Collection* (Baltimore: Johns Hopkins University Press, 1984); Susan M. Pearce discusses the religious value of things in *Museums, Objects and Collections: A Cultural Study* (Leicester, UK: Leicester University Press, 1992), esp. 92.

7. See *The Origins of Museums: The Cabinet of Curiosities in Sixteenth- and Seventeenth-Century Europe*, ed. Oliver Impey and Arthur Macgregor (Oxford: Clarendon Press, 1985); Barbara M. Benedict, "The 'Curious Attitude' in Eighteenth-Century Britain: Observing and Owning," *Eighteenth-Century Life*, n.s., 14.3 (1990): 59–98, esp. 67–77; Kenneth Hudson, *Museums of Influence* (Cambridge: Cambridge University Press, 1987), 18–38; Clive Wainwright, *The Romantic Interior* (London: Victoria and Albert Museum, 1990), 9–10; Marjorie Swann, *Curiosities and Texts: The Culture of Collecting in Early Modern England* (Philadelphia: University of Pennsylvania Press, 2001).

8. See, for example, Samuel Butler's *The Elephant in the Moon* (1676), Thomas Shadwell's *The Virtuoso* (1676), Aphra Behn's *Emperor of the Moon* (1687), and Gay, Pope, and Arbuthnot's *Three Hours After Marriage* (1717).

9. Clery, *The Rise of Supernatural Fiction,* 7; Catherine Ingrassia, *Authorship, Commerce, and Gender in Early Modern England: A Culture of Paper Credit* (Cambridge: Cambridge University Press, 1998), 17–39; also Sandra Sherman, *Finance and Fictionality in the Early Eighteenth Century: Accounting for Defoe* (Cambridge: Cambridge University Press, 1996), esp. 26–27.

10. Dennis Todd, *Imagining Monsters: Miscreations of the Self in Eighteenth-Century England* (Chicago: University of Chicago Press, 1995); *At the Borders of the Human: Beasts, Bodies, and Natural Philosophy in the Early Modern Period,* ed. Erica Fudge, Ruth Gilbert, and Susan Wiseman (Houndmills, UK: Macmillan, 1999); Barbara M. Benedict, *Curiosity: A Cultural History of Early Modern Inquiry* (Chicago: University of Chicago Press, 2001), 71–92.

11. See, for example, John Beaumont's *An Historical, Physiological and Theological Treatise of Spirits, Apparitions, Witchcrafts, and Other Magical Practices* (London: D. Browne et al., 1705), which retells stories from Glanvill, among other texts; also *A Critical and Philosophical Enquiry into the Causes of Prodigies and Miracles, as related by Historians* (London: Thomas Corbett, 1727). Much of this repeats material from R.H.'s translation of Lewes Lavater's book, *Of Ghostes and Spirits Walking by Nyght* (London: Henry Benneyman for Richard Watkyns, 1572), which collects ancient and religious sources.

12. Harry Price, *Poltergeist Over England: Three Centuries of Mischievous Ghosts* (London: Country Life, 1945), 44.

13. Clery, *The Rise of Supernatural Fiction,* 95–105.

14. Margaret L. Carter, *Spectre or Delusion?: The Supernatural in Gothic Fiction* (Ann Arbor, MI, and London: UMI Research, 1987), 3, passim.

15. C. Churchill, *The Ghost* (London: W. Flexney, 1763). See, for example, [E. Smith], *A Dialogue between the Ghost of A— — —l B— — —, and the Substance of a G— — —l: Shewing the Difference between a Chop and a Pop* ([London]: A. Smith); also, from the opposite point of view, *A Full and Particular Account of A Most Dreadful Apparition which appeared to a certain Great Man* [London, 1757?], and the broadside "Admiral B–G in Horrors at the Appearance of the Unhappy Souls, who was Kill'd in the Engagement crying for Revenge" [1756?].

16. Susanna Centlivre, *The Ghost. A Comedy of Two Acts* (London: J. Williams, 1767), 1.11. In *The Man's bewitch'd; or, The Devil to do about Her,* the identical passage with different punctuation appears in act 2 (Dublin: J. Jones, for George Ewing, 1737), 32. See also *Susanna Centlivre,* ed. Jacqueline Pearson, vol. 3 of *Eighteenth-Century Women Playwrights,* gen. ed. Derek Hughes (London: Pickering and Chatto, 2001).

17. For example, "*A True and Perfect Account of a Strange and Dreadful Apparition* which lately infested and sunk a Ship . . . And of the Strange Deliverance of John Pye, Master, and Nine Men more" (London: Robert Clavel, 1672) characteristically reports a sailor's vision of a dead man as evidence of God's special Providence in sparing him.

18. *God's Awful Warnings* (London: G. Ribow, 1795), 2.

19. See Michel Foucault, *Madness and Civilization: A History of Insanity in the Age of Reason* (New York: Vintage Press, 1973).

20. William Freke, *The Divine Grammar; or, Select Rules Leading to the more nice Syntax and Articulate Construction of Dreams, Visions and Apparitions* (London, 1703), 1.

21. In "*A True Narrative of the Sufferings and Relief of a Young Girle;* Strangely Molested By Evil Spirits and the Intsruments [*sic*], in the West," Francis Grant, Lord Cullen similarly argues that, "though what [Satan] does . . . may, by . . . artful disposal of *Matter* and *Form;* appear surprising: Yet he cannot work *against Nature,*" for the devil does all his work with God's permission (Edinburgh: James Watson, 1698), v.

22. See Richard Baxter's claim that "Corporeal Crassitude is an abasement, and therefore fittest for the more Ignoble sort of Spirits" in *The Certainty of the World of Spirits* (London: T. Parkhurst . . . and J. Salisbury, 1691), 221; also the claim that "the *Devils* are so many, that some Thousand, can sometimes at once apply themselves to vex one Child of Man" in *The Wonders of the Invisible World* (Boston; rpt. London: John Dunton, 1693), 5. Richard Bovet's "*Pandaemonium, or the Devil's Cloyster. Being a further Blow to Modern Sadducism,* Proving the Existence of Witches and Spirits" (London: J. Althoe, 1684) warns against "Mischievous Spirits (who like Beasts of prey) watching all Occasions to entrap" superstitious people (90–91).

23. [Daniel Defoe], *An Essay on the History and Reality of Apparitions* (London: J. Roberts, 1727), 55; see chapter 4, entitled, "Of the Apparition of Spirits Unembodied and which never were Embodied; not such as are vulgarly called Ghosts" (25). This tome was republished under the pseudonym Andrew Moreton as *The Invisible World Disclos'd* in 1729.

24. Daniel Defoe, *A Journal of the Plague Year,* ed. Paula R. Backscheider (New York: Norton, 1992), 24. All citations refer to this edition.

25. Cynthia Wall points out that Defoe considers space a commercial product in *The Literary and Cultural Spaces of Restoration London* (Cambridge: Cambridge University Press, 1998), esp. 96.

26. Carol Houlihan Flynn analyzes Defoe's struggle with the materiality of self in *The Body in Swift and Defoe* (Cambridge: Cambridge University Press, 1990).

27. See, for example, George A. Starr, *Defoe and Casuistry* (Princeton, NJ: Princeton University Press, 1971); also Stuart Sim, *Negotiations with Paradox: Narrative Practice and Narrative Form in Bunyan and Defoe* (New York and London: Harvester, Wheatsheaf, 1990), esp. 142, 150.

28. Daniel Defoe, *Robinson Crusoe,* ed. Michael Shinagel (New York: Norton, 1994), 43.

29. Many critics have commented on Defoe's depiction of the fungibility of body and money. See, especially, Bram Dijkstra, *Defoe and Economics: The Fortunes of* Roxana *in the History of Interpretation* (Houndmills, UK: Macmillan Press, 1987). David Trotter observes that both Roxana and Moll, "because they are women, must discipline themselves to circulate, body and soul. An economy of trade enters their lives at every point to convert meaning into event, signifier into signified, asset into cash . . . they are already caught up in the spiral of limit and transgression" (*Circulation: Defoe, Dickens, and the Economies of the Novel* [Houndmills, UK: Macmillan Press, 1988], 41).

30. Daniel Defoe, *The Fortunes and Misfortunes Of the Famous Moll Flanders* (London: W. Chetwood et al., 1722), 234–35. All citations refer to this edition.

31. Sim, *Negotiations with Paradox,* 152.

32. Lynn Hunt, Introduction to *The Invention of Pornography: Obscenity and the Origins of Modernity,* ed. Lynn Hunt (New York: Zone Books, 1993), 36–39.

33. See Jonathan Lamb's essay in this volume.

34. Alexander Pope, *The Rape of the Lock,* ed. John Butt (New Haven, CT: Yale University Press, 1963), 4.49–52; all citations to Pope's poems refer to this edition. Jonathan Lamb richly describes the way Pope's objects "act on passive human beings" in his essay in this volume. David Fairer comments on the vitality of Pope's objects as part of Pope's exploration of the imagination: "On entering Belinda's world the physical data become part of an internal drama, and alongside the critique is a sense of wonder at how they impinge on thought and feeling" (*English Poetry of the Eighteenth Century, 1700–1789* [London: Longman, 2003], 52).

35. Mihaly Csikszentmihalyi and Eugene Rochberg-Halton, *The Meaning of Things: Domestic Symbols and the Self* (Cambridge: Cambridge University Press, 1981), 58.

36. Sacheverell Sitwell, *Poltergeists: An Introduction and Examination followed by Chosen Instances* (London: Faber and Faber, 1890), 32–33; Hereward Carrington, *Historic Poltergeists*, Bulletin 1 (London: International Institute for Psychical Research, 1935), 45.

37. Bovet, *Pandaemonium, or the Devil's Cloyster*, 182.

38. See "*An Authentic, Candid, and Circumstantial Narrative, of the Astounding Transactions at Stockwell*, in the County of Surry, On Monday and Tuesday, the 6th and 7th Days of January, 1772" (London: J. Marks, 1772); the twenty-year-old servant Ann Robinson later confessed.

39. Andrew Lang, *Cock Lane and Common Sense* (London: Longman's, Green, 1894), 31.

40. *A Narrative of Some Extraordinary Things that Happened to Mr. Richard Giles's Children, at the Lamb, Without Lawford's-Gate, Bristol; Supposed to be the Effect of Witchcraft . . . By the Late Mr. Henry Durbin, Chymist* (Bristol, UK: R. Edwards; London: T. Hurst and W. Baynes; Bath, UK: Hazard and Browne, [1800]); all citations refer to this edition.

41. See also "*A Strange, True, and Dreadful Relation of the Devils appearing to Thomas Cox, a Hackney Coach-Man;* who lives in *Cradle-Alley* in *Baldwins-Gardens* (London: E. Mallet, 1684), which similarly verifies time, place, and the devil's accoutrements, a parchment scroll and a hat (5). Robert Crookall observes that apparitions either wear replicas of the clothes of the living or "white robes" that conform to scriptural descriptions of angelic costumes in *The Next World—and the Next: Ghostly Garments* (London: Theosophical Publishing House, 1966), xx, 18.

42. *A most Strange and Dreadful APPARITION of several Spirits & Visions* (London: J. Clarke, 1680), 2.

43. Douglas, *Purity and Danger*, 150.

44. Ibid., 130.

45. See John Bender, *Imagining the Penitentiary: Fiction and the Architecture of Mind in Eighteenth-Century England* (Chicago: University of Chicago Press, 1987).

The Rape of the Lock as Still Life

Jonathan Lamb

During the seventeenth century still life changes direction. From its close alliance with emblems and Christian symbols, it shifts towards a less schematic and less iconographical representation of things. One of the earliest Northern European still lifes was Rogier van der Weyden's Braque triptych (1450) exhibiting various symbols of spiritual qualities, such as bottles, boxes, fruit, and bread, each expressive of purity, piety, and self-abnegation and placed alongside their saintly exemplars. Sometimes these symbolic objects were painted on the backs of pictures. A painting of the virgin and child of 1470 attributed to van der Weyden carries on the reverse a trompe l'oeil of a towel, basin, and books, symbols of purity, virginity, and piety. It was possible to compile a whole language of ordinary things. In still lifes of the later sixteenth and early seventeenth centuries, cherries and pears stood for paradise, strawberries for salvation, red currants for the incarnation of Christ, gooseberries for his sufferings, and so on.[1] Van der Weyden and Bartholomew Bruyn the Elder started painting skulls on the back of portraits, making way for the still-life *vanitas,* whose centerpiece is usually a death's-head often accompanied by a legend teaching the shortness of life and the transience of earthly pleasure. In later vanitas still lifes the traces of emblematic images are clearly visible: a knocked-out pipe, legal settlements and testaments, an hourglass, a broken wineglass, a stopped watch, not to mention the skull that sits so often at the center of the composition.

But the eschatological emphasis on a narrative of death, judgment, heaven, and hell is displaced by the luscious impressions of the surfaces of things. A vanitas by Heda or Freck shows how brilliantly and digressively ordinary items appear when they are not being interpreted—the glow of the tobacco, the tiny dimples on a stoneware jug, the mottlings on the surface of a skull. Attention was shifting from Christian symbolism to the things themselves, objects isolated from action or narrative, insolent in their insignificance.[2] The motive for such a change is variously ascribed to the rise of natural science and the growing demand for accurate illustrations of species, especially the novelties arriving from the New World; to the rise of a world market in commodities, on whose axis the Dutch were very firmly perched; to the recovery of the Roman *xenion,* the bowl of fruit offered to strangers often illusionistically painted on the walls of houses, and its association with the ekphrases of Philostratus; to the taste for curiosities and marvels, expressed in heterogenous collections of strange and unique things among which still lifes were often included, both as registers and instances; to the iconoclasm that swept Northern Europe after the Reformation; and so on. But most historians of still life are agreed that the change begins in the studio, with experiments made by artists in the use of pigments and glazes, the casting of light and the deepening of shade, and the arrangement of the objects represented. There is a growing concentration on the surface of the thing and the surface of the work, as if nothing of any importance lay behind it. Cornelis Gysbrecht's paintings of picture-backs are destitute of emblems or skulls; they are just the backs of pictures with nothing on them at all.

The loss of an ethical or eschatological dimension in vanitas still lifes encourages a kind of superficiality which is typical of much still life in the later seventeenth century. The best examples are neither interpretable nor narratable. It is pointless to ask who left the table with the food half-eaten, why they are no longer there, or to whom these bits and pieces belong. The only point is to admire the sheen of the knife-cuts on a cheese or a ham, or the exquisite rendition of something as ordinary as a broken breadcrust. Still lifes are as remarkable for their accuracy as they are for the absence of any action. They are pitched at a level where, as Norman Bryson says, "there are no events, none of the dreams of history."[3] The irrelevance of human interests to these scenes is evident in the reflecting surfaces of metal and glass objects, where as often as not no trace of the human is to be seen. The things emerge into the light from an intense darkness, and they look in their isolation as if they belonged only to themselves.

This emptiness is mentioned frequently as a disquieting element in still-life composition, but one quite different from the skull of the standard vanitas, because it has no human point. "Is vitality or mortality the sovereign principle here?" asks Simon Schama of the *pronkstilleven* (swank still lifes), without offering an answer.[4] Hal Foster characterizes trompe l'oeil still lifes as "not alive, not dead, not useful, not useless . . . the pictorial effect is often one of deathly suspension or . . . eerie animation."[5] Norman Bryson says still life reveals to the human eye "the look of the world before our entry into it or after our departure from it."[6] A fascinating hollow then rather than a door to the last judgment and eternity is what the later vanitas still lifes exhibit. Bryson tries to explain how this effect is obtained even in pronkstilleven, which more than other still lifes seem to celebrate the sensual pleasures made available by artifacts in a secular commercial world. Of Kalf's technique Bryson says that it outdoes the appeal and even the price of the original thing—the Chinese porcelain, the nautilus shell goblet, the Venice glass—by evacuating the space once filled by the reality of the thing with "a virtuosity that circles endlessly round a kind of void."[7] That is to say, the pleasure caused by these exquisite things is not at all the pleasure of possession. As for the artist, all that labor expended for what?

Reformation in the Netherlands was delayed by Spanish rule, but when it arrived the churches were cleansed of images. Altars were washed with lye to leave "an unadorned nowhere," naves stripped to reveal "an enabling void."[8] Pieter Saenredam painted the huge uncluttered interiors of Dutch churches, delivering mass and volume in the tones of butterscotch, according to Roland Barthes, who says of these pictures, "Never has nothingness been so confident."[9] Saenredam was a conscious iconoclast. He publicly derided the discovery of alleged images of Catholic priests in cross sections of a rotten apple tree in Haarlam in 1628.[10] In his pictures of churches Saenredam doesn't entirely evacuate icons, but they possess no more significance than the images of writing in still lifes and trompe l'oeils, where script is not for reading but for viewing. His church interiors are not opened by the eye of an imagined spectator, but by the experience of looking and the desire to make that experience visible. As Svetlana Alpers puts it, his are the views of architecture viewed, pictures of the sensation of space rather than of the space itself. To this extent they are aligned with what she calls the benchmark genre of still life and its studio experiments with light, shade, and color. Similarly, Caravaggio makes still lifes out of history painting, and Cézanne makes still lifes out of landscape, reducing time and space to the measure of an art where the coloring of a surface is literally all that counts. Of Velazquez's transformation of portraiture into still life—for instance, his picture of Luis de Gongora—Svetlana Alpers has said, "The sharpness of these depictions involves a kind of denial, an avoidance, a lack of interest in what lies beneath the surface of the paint."[11]

None of these examples of still life and its variants provides a specimen of the sublime, where iconoclasm loosens artistic intensity from the tyranny of the image. On the contrary, the iconoclasm of still life heightens interest in the appearance of things. This heightening is caused by the emptying of meaning from signs or tokens of spiritual value, returning to the thing itself its proper qualities which were formerly read and interpreted, and awarding to the sensation of those qualities an importance independent of other concerns. This may be fetishism of a distinct kind, where the fashioning of a thing neither represents nor symbolizes a deity, yet generates a glamour beyond the ordinary, as if what had been made or painted had a life of its own. Often this glamour was noted and deplored. The still-life artist Johannes Torrentius, collected by Charles II, was imprisoned for sorcery in the Netherlands because he left no trace of a brush on his canvasses.[12] Desymbolized or fetishized still life could acquire a power distinct from the artist's—so distinct that the painter Marinus van Reymerswael, a specialist in representing velvet and brocade, eventually took revenge upon images for their independence by destroying them.[13]

There is a drawing by Paul Klee of 1920 called *Die Büchse der Pandora als Stilleben* (fig. C-1) reproduced in Dora and Erwin Panofsky, *Pandora's Box.*[14] It shows a vase (the original "box") filled with flowers. On the side of the vase a genital ornament or crack seems to emit a black vapor that curls into a rebus of pubic hair. Vase and hair, boxes and vanities, ornamental outsides and potentially shocking insides, all keyed to a notion of the feminine as trouble on a grand scale, is summed up by Klee as still life, a genre not notorious for its misogyny although certainly hospitable to certain kinds of fetish, as Laura Mulvey points out when talking of this very drawing.[15] What is happening in Klee's still life? Is something secret or uncanny being disclosed? Is the box being opened, or opening itself? In fact part of the contents of the vase-box is already on display as an arrangement of flowers. The vapor or hair blots out the central flower by extending the genital design from which it originates. It adds extra details to the image or flaw upon its surface, where perfunctory traces of hair already frame the vaginal divide, as if to demonstrate that the container and what it holds occupy the same plane.

This dark stain is equivocal then. It seems both to emerge from a crack in the vase as a smoky token of what is hidden inside, and at the same time to consolidate the outside by adding another membrane to the surface of the vase. If this is an image of a fetish, it is an instance of Freud's female hair, so obsessively handled by artists such as Fuseli and Beardsley, where the phallus that is allegedly missing from the female genitals is embodied in some analogous or contiguous token of them: hair of the head or pubic hair. Freud's fetish, like Hobbes's idol, is the image of nothing, circling a void similar to Kalf's when his virtuosity substitutes for the value or significance of a thing the brilliant arrangement of pigments laid on a surface. In Klee's picture the fetish-hair supplements what can only ever be a surface, no matter how much the view of the hidden phallus is desired. Any move in the direction of depth creates only the trace of more hair, not hair's referent, as one surface (the vase) gives way to another (the paper on which it is represented). It strikes me that it is the oscillation between these two possibilities, of a surface conveyed to the eye as both image and reality, that leads Klee to assign the name of still life to his picture.

Given the Pandoric scope of Pope's *The Rape of the Lock,* where a woman's hair, confounded with her pubic hair, is lost in a world of vanities symbolized by the charming fragility of China vases, there is room to ask whether the poem has anything in common with still life. Can literature align itself with the benchmark genre along with history painting, landscape, and portraiture? Helen Deutsch has shrewdly noted how closely its sheer superficiality reproduces the trompe l'oeil effect of some still lifes.[16] Along the same lines, I want to suggest that the oscillation of the eye between the view of a thing and the view of that view, so typical of generic still life and its optical counterpart, the camera obscura, plays an important part in the layering of surfaces and the hollowing out of centers in *The Rape of the Lock*—so much so that no basis remains for a satiric or commonsense narrative of such a state of affairs. When a probed surface yields only more surface, there is no ulterior duty that superficial characters neglect, and no hidden deficiency or sin that their flaws betray. The only mistake in this kind of world is idolatrously to suppose that there is something desirable, disgusting, or significant underneath the paint, when really there is only nothing.

There is a semi–still life by Jan Weenix, called *Port de Mer* (fig. C-2), which rehearses the temptations leading to this mistake. It shows a lady standing between two men near a dockside. One of the men is a huckster offering her trinkets for sale. She has turned away from him towards a gentleman-lover who holds up a mirror in which her reflection can be seen, and from that too the lady seems inclined to turn away. Caught between two temptations to vanity, the woman has nowhere to turn but the foreground, where a still life of fruits and game is laid out. Weenix's picture is a compendium of the issues raised by Pope in *The Rape of the Lock,* where the contents of a woman's dressing table, filled with toys and cosmetics and topped by a mirror, become of concern to the men as well as the women of the poem. The men would like to see an easy transition from one sort of female vanity to another. First comes the consumption of the alluring commodities of worldwide trade ("all that Land and Sea afford") which deck out a female for the marriage market.[17] Then come the lover's compliments, a ritual indulgence that precedes the removal of the woman from the protection of her father to that of her husband. Thus she enters the market to purchase one sort of commodity so that she might be purchased in turn as another.

Like Weenix's lady, however, Belinda has no inclination to regard her dressing table as this sort of trade route to marriage. But in turning aside from the proffered flatteries of trade and courtship, her options are limited to the things that contingently fall within her purview. In *Port de Mer* these are to be found in the clutter of the still life. Similarly, on the dressing table Belinda sees heterogeneous items, "Puffs, Powders, Patches, Bibles, Billets-doux," and in the world at large she spots a disorderly congeries of species: "Men, Monkies, Lap-dogs, Parrots" (1.138, 4.120). The diverse things that largely make up the scenes of *The Rape of the Lock* offer themselves to the female eye in the same way as the still life in *Port de Mer*. They present themselves as largely fortuitous, variously pleasing, and totally uninterpretable. Nothing in the cluster is differentiated by moral, economic, or practical value, and no meaning is attached to the relation between indifferent objects. Bibles are flanked by patches and billets-doux without archness. Like the rarities that are collected, as Shaftesbury observed, for rarity's sake, these various objects are gathered together for the sake of variety.

Weenix and Pope raise the possibility of value-free encounters in a world where the prevailing assumptions are all on the side of trade, calculation, and *marriage à la mode*. They show how things and women might manage to subsist without the government of prices, morals, husbands, and other instruments of intelligibility and social control, and how they might thrive simply among shapes, textures, colors, and surfaces. That this more eligible, insignificant world is not significant at some higher level is evident in the failure of the vanitas, unsuccessfully introduced first by Clarissa and then the poet when they remind Belinda of the passage of time and her own mortality. She ignores them both. Frail china jars are not icons of mutability, commodities for exchange, or storage containers. Their painted surface, emphasized by their hollowness, is their charm, and the pleasure of the eye is their only purpose.

In his *Remarks on Mr Pope's Rape of the Lock* (1728) John Dennis points astutely if impatiently to those aspects of the poem that most strongly resemble the distinctive qualities of still life. Although Pope claims to have a literary model for his piece in heroic poetry, Dennis argues that in fact it has none, for the heroine lacks any leading traits ("a Chimera, not a Character"), and there are no incidents of note save the cutting of the lock, which is then lost.[18] The poem is filled with descriptions instead of episodes and ends with nothing resolved, so any resemblance it may have to epic is arbitrary and unconvincing (9–10). Although the poet promises to treat general themes appropriate to heroic poetry (such as love and conflict) he deals in nothing but frivolous particulars (31). The machinery introduced so ceremoniously in the expanded five-canto version of the poem fails to organize a dramatic conflict or to promote an outcome, for these little gods are denied foreknowledge and, to make things worse, they desert their protégée at her moment of greatest danger (24–25). Dennis goes on to complain that occult lore is deployed as a kind of microscope ("the false Opticks of a Rosicrucian Understanding") to exalt trifles to a specious importance (28). He points out that the extension of the machinery into the personifications of the allegory of the Cave of Spleen makes no sense and confounds the sequence of cause and effect (45). Since the little world of the poem lacks solid antecedents and a definite closure, he declares it to be deficient in the two articles of neoclassical verisimilitude, namely the narrative (or "fable") and the moral. "It is a very *empty Trifle,* without any Solidity or *sensible Meaning*" (6). Dennis returns again and again to the theme of its emptiness. Pope, he says, "seems to take pains to bring *something* into a Conjunction Copulative with *nothing,* in order to beget *nothing*" (53).

Dennis contrasts *The Rape of the Lock* with Boileau's *Le Lutrin,* a mock-epic of the travails of a pulpit to which Swift's *Tale of a Tub* and *The Battle of the Books* are both indebted. Boileau's satire has a narrative filled with incidents. Dennis cites the midnight sortie to the vestry made by Lamour, Brontin, and Boirude, armed with tools to repair the wrecked pulpit. An owl that has roosted there makes them think that the pulpit has learned to speak, but when the bird flies off they resume their task and carry off the pulpit to the body of the church. While they are engaged in this work, their enemy the prelate has a dream in which the pulpit has come alive and is rampant in his choir stall. The point about the dream and the mistake about the owl is that they are shown indisputably to be delusions. Pulpits are made by human labor and their placement affects passions and politics—human nature, in short—ensuring that the narrative has a human origin and a human end. The thing itself can never act or speak on its own behalf. In the ensuing battle in the bookshop volumes turn into missiles because human feelings have become engaged, not because of any impetus found in calfskin and paper. If we were searching for a painterly parallel with *Le Lutrin* we would find it in Rembrandt's *The Flayed Ox,* where the subordination of the thing to human needs and human perceptions is expressed by the signs of the labor expended on it, both in the resemblance between the carcass and the frame in which it is suspended, and in the broad and undisguised brushstrokes with which the resemblance is achieved. This raises a question about things and their relations to humans in Pope's poem, where there is literally nothing to differentiate the automatism of an artifact from the actions of a man or woman. In the Cave of Spleen this is made grotesquely obvious.

Dennis is troubled by the replacement of this human point of reference with artifice in *The Rape of the Lock.* Belinda's beauty, he notices, is owing almost entirely to her toilette; as for her lock of hair, it is totally artificial, the result of the application of bodkin, comb, essence, paper, curling tongs, and lead fillets. A natural beauty, Dennis affirms, "wants neither *Flounce,* nor *Furbelow,* nor *torturing Irons,* nor *Paper Durance*" (14). He cannot understand why Belinda, young and beautiful, is presented by Pope as if she were a kind of Lady Wishfort ("a decay'd superannuated Beauty" [13]) who (we remember) derives such complete advantages from her toilette that the slightest symptom of emotion threatens to shatter her appearance. With nothing more substantial to Belinda than the supplements that color her face and mold her form, he calls her *"an artificial daubing Jilt"* (18).

I think it is hard to disagree with Dennis on any score, for if one were to base the standard of good poetry on its attention to the deeply incised and ineradicable marks of character and human nature, one would find little to approve of here. Of the three leading duties of poets and artists—a proper regard to moral, character, and coloring, in that order—Pope has concentrated exclusively on the last. Consequently in Belinda's world there is nothing to choose between people and things: husbands and lapdogs, women and china vases, belles and barges compete on the same level. Even lost chastity is classed as a superficial impediment to the social whirl, equivalent to a coffee stain. Whether in the region of earth, hell, or heaven of this miniature cosmogony, the distinction between human agents and things is blurred. On earth things invariably move like automata, without the need of human intervention: caskets unlock themselves, patchboxes fall without being touched, pins extend themselves in rows, fans clap, boxes breathe, gowns plait themselves, and sleeves are self-folding. In the preparation of coffee, berries crackle and mills turn round on their own to produce a liquid which, when drunk, acts on passive human beings by putting ideas into their heads. In the underworld this process is completed when people are so far affected by things they actually turn into things themselves. In the Cave of Spleen we are shown men and women metamorphosed into teapots, goose pies, bottles, and jars: still lifes that can move and speak. In the upper sphere of the moon, human passions and intentions are preserved as useless remnants, trompe l'oeils of performative words that never worked:

> There broken Vows, and Death-bed Alms are found,
> And Lovers' Hearts with Ends of Riband bound;
> The Courtier's Promises, and Sick Man's Pray'rs,
> The Smiles of Harlots, and the Tears of Heirs.
>
> (5.117–20)

At all three levels humanity is shown to be impotent if it relies only on its own faculties of will and speech. Unless it acquire the attributes of things it cannot act on its own behalf.

Between the earth and the moon is the sphere dominated by the sylphs, the "machinery" that in epic poetry embraces the power of gods and fate. Here they preside over the machine-like movements of things and people in the world below. The sylphs take the credit for every happy chance that looks like design: the powder that doesn't blow away, the perfume that keeps its scent, the sleeve that doesn't lose its crease. They supervise the replacement of human nature with supplements: clothes, gestures, and speech that assume the public form of human personality. Real passions and purposes are displaced by bustling artifice. The descriptions that usurp what ought (in Dennis's opinion) to have been a moralized narrative are all of things doing things.

This is why machines are so important. The sylphs and the gnomes personify the energy and glamour acquired by things when they free themselves from time, value, and meaning. If hair looks just right, or a sleeve is folded with becoming negligence, then the sylphs have done it. They are the name of good luck, grace, and the je ne sais quoi—whatever it is that gives artifice an appeal independent of nature. They are busy in preserving the activity of brocades, watches, locks, necklaces, and fans, all of which must hang, flash, and gleam with maximum éclat. It is of no importance what these things looked like before, or what they might become, as long as in the present moment their effect is sudden and ravishing. Contrariwise, if a pimple rises on a nose or a headdress falls inexplicably awry, the gnomes are responsible. As the sylphs promote the happiness of accidents, so the gnomes personify the hostility that can break out between people and things. The sylphs are like Willem Kalf in making the best of beautiful artifacts, while the gnomes are like Maerten de Stomme or Jan Steen, who show things broken, upset, and scattered.[19] Between them the upper and lower echelons of machines comprise the two contradictory impulses of still life: the voluptuous iconoclasm of Pieter Saenredam and destructive iconoclasm of Marinus van Reymerswael. The pleasurable investment of energy in an idol that represents nothing defines the upper level of light, while the obscurity and darkness of the lower regions consorts with the pain of knowing the indifference of gods and fetishes to human wishes. In this respect the poem sustains a direct link with its Homeric original, insofar as fate is driven by the impetuosity of its human victims ("too soon dejected, and too soon elate") whose ebullience or melancholy carries them beyond the range of moral intelligence and into the domain of things.[20]

In the tradition of the best of the still-life artists, the sylphs leave no trace of their work, so it is necessary to discriminate nicely between the fortuitous motion of things and the compositional genius of the machines, who are both the effect and the cause of that motion. Under the right circumstances things form into a mobile cluster or vortex that is particularly arresting in its beauty or absurdity. The most beautiful of these is found in the barge trip down the Thames, but it is preceded by another: Ariel's own example of "the moving toyshop of the heart," "Where Wigs with Wigs, with Sword-knots Sword-knots strive, / Beaus banish Beaus, and Coaches Coaches drive" (1.100–102). Unlike the heroic synechoches from which this couplet is derived ("Now Shield with Shield, with Helmet Helmet clos'd"), the vortex it describes annihilates the difference between accoutrements and the human beings who wear or use them.[21] The effect is of ekphrasis rather than a narrative. Beaus and wigs compete on the same ground for the sole advantage of being seen. Importance is measured by lines of sight, and the whole point of a display of fashions is the capture of the spectator's eye by the happiness of the arrangement. When Belinda imagines an existence antithetic to this one of things in motion before a public gaze, it is a state of invisibility, out of sight, where no one is looked at and nothing is seen. As there is no other purpose to looking than to be pleased by the sight, and none to being seen than to arrest the gaze, so the only standard to be observed is that of taste—the taste of the sylphs who have contrived the whole show, the taste of Belinda, who will award its successive moments a glance or a smile, and the taste of the spectator who overlooks this looking. As far as she is concerned, the show works like a camera obscura, printing a train of unmediated images on her eye that exactly corresponds to the motions and outlines of the artificial things parading in front of her. Thus Belinda's mind, or heart, is moved in the same rhythm as the images passing across her eye, and proportionately to their salience. Her thoughts and feelings exactly correspond to the visibility of a ride in the park, a trip on the Thames, or a game of cards, untroubled by reflection or anticipation. What the sylphs contrive is apparently no different from what Belinda herself perceives, and what she perceives is what is taking place in front of her. So what is the difference?

At this point it is worth comparing Pope's poem with Gay's *The Fan,* another Scriblerian piece inspired by Boileau. It concerns the invention of the fan by Venus, which is followed by a discussion among the gods about the narratives most appropriate to be painted on its expanded surface. The fan originates in a Cytherean toyshop, where all the trifling objects of female vanity are put together, among which the toilette stands supreme. The fan is conceived by Venus as a machine, "this fantastick Engine," whose purpose is not to multiply the artifice of patches, pulville, pins, and paint, but to focus it.[22] Otherwise the burgeoning particularities of fashion would be too dazzling:

What Force of Thought, what Numbers can express,
Th'inconstant Equipage of Female Dress?
. . . .
Should you the rich Brocaded Suit unfold,
Where rising Flow'rs grow stiff with frosted Gold,
The dazled Muse would from her Subject stray,
And in a Maze of Fashions lose her Way.

(1.229–44)

So the story the fan will "unfold" is intended to limit or control this disorienting extravagance. Momus suggests satires of female inconstancy. Diana says the stories of Dido and Aeneas, Oenone and Paris, and Ariadne and Theseus will teach woman to avoid shame, and to do without the disguise even of a fan. But Minerva compares the fan-machine to another engine, the camera obscura, whose virtue is to show the world exactly as it is:

Thus have I seen, Woods, Hills, and Dales appear,
Flocks graze the Plains, Birds wing the silent Air
In darken'd Rooms, where Light can only pass
Through the small Circle of a convex Glass.

(3.15–19)

The fan as camera obscura will show the authentic and tragic outcomes of vanity, pride, and self-love.

Let vain *Narcissus* warn each Female Breast,
That Beauty's but a transient Good at best.
Like Flow'rs it withers with th'advancing Year,
And Age like Winter robs the blooming Fair.

(3.127–30)

Strephon gives Corinna this Minervan fan, a camera obscura functioning as a vanitas, whereupon she corrects the errors of her heart and they get married. The truth of the fable has to be a moral one—for Gay as well as for Dennis—and the art of composition and synthesis that provides the vehicle of the moral brings the indiscipline of social art into symmetry with natural order ("Woods, Hills, and Dales"). The particulars of modern life must yield to this sort of synthesis, or the picture will scatter into unrelated fragments, like a fallen china vase.

It is clear that Pope's notion of the realism of the camera obscura is far more extensive and less convenient than Gay's. Twice in the course of his poem he introduces a moral similar to Minerva's, first with Clarissa's commentary on the rape, then in the Ovidian compliment to Belinda at the end. Like Minerva's they are variations on the vanitas and warn the heroine of her own mortality. Clarissa recites what Dennis would have expected to be the moral of the poem:

> But since, alas! frail Beauty must decay,
> Curl'd or uncurl'd, since Locks will turn to grey.
> Since painted, or not painted, all shall fade,
> And she who scorns a Man, must die a Maid;
> What then remains, but well our Pow'r to use,
> And keep good Humour still whate'er we lose?
>
> (5.25–30)

The poet too tells Belinda she will die in the flesh ("When those fair Suns shall sett, as sett they must, / And all those Tresses shall be laid in Dust") though her name will live in his poem (5.147–48). Neither warning is followed by any sign of reformation of manners. Clarissa's wins no votes at all among the women, while the poet's promise of immortality seems suspiciously like those worn-out performatives preserved in the sphere of the moon. The furthest Pope is prepared to go in limiting the multifarious images of his camera obscura is to assume, via the machinery, that it is a contrivance (Dennis's "false Opticks") that makes the whirligig of fashion worth looking at. So the machinery of Pope's poem accomplishes the very opposite of Gay's: it multiplies the details of fashion instead of summarizing them; it dazzles, quite deliberately and beautifully, especially when describing the effects of machinery at work:

> Loose to the Wind their airy Garments flew,
> Thin glitt'ring Textures of the filmy Dew;
> Dipt in the richest Tincture of the Skies,
> Where Light disports in ever-mingling Dies,
> While ev'ry Beam new transient Colours flings,
> Colours that change whene'er they wave their Wings.
>
> (2.63–68)

Descriptions like these force the reader to note that Pope's camera obscura works equally as a kaleidoscope or a magic lantern to the extent it reflects nothing that is not artificial, and that what it composes is already the stuff of composition. Indeed, Pope goes further than Addison, who located the camera obscura in his aesthetic system of the double principle on the grounds that it confounds the works of nature with those of art: "For in this case our Pleasure arises from a double Principle; from the Agreeableness of the Objects to the Eye, and from their Similitude to other Objects: We are pleased as well with the comparing their Beauties, as with surveying them, and can represent them to our Minds, either as Copies or Originals."[23] In Pope's hands the image, whether viewed or viewed as viewed, is always a copy, and the movement of its parts is neither the trace of nature nor of time, but of the self-activity of made things. Except for the failed attempts at a vanitas by Clarissa and the poet, he makes no space in his camera obscura for the implied observer of the image, capable of critically distinguishing art from nature and the observer from the world.[24] The metaphor of the *Epistle to Burlington* that has nature painting as the landscape artist plants is literalized in *The Rape of the Lock* in respect of colors that are laid on in layers, starting in the dressing room. All nature then becomes a toilette. The sky is a rotating prism or a paintbox; nature is a palette. The iridescence of vapor, like the spontaneity of a blush, has already been appropriated by art, and improved by it. A blush made of Spanish red is superior to the real thing, "purer" (1.143), like eyes made keener by belladonna; while the spectrum of colors seen in a splash of water is much more remarkable when observed through "the false Opticks" of the machines. If Saenredam gives us not views of architecture, but views of architecture viewed, so Pope gives us paintings of pictures being painted.

By means of such improvements in art everything is brought to the surface and all things are rendered completely superficial. The process begins at the dressing table where Belinda paints herself better cheeks and eyes, and sculpts her hair. Then come the sylphs who add paint to paint, drawing "fresh Colours from the vernal Flow'rs" and borrowing tints from "Rainbows ere they drop in Show'rs" (2.95–96). Finally there is the poet's painting of the painters of paint, the amazing description of airy things whose fluid bodies are "half-dissolv'd in Light" (2.62). At every stage in these successive applications of paint, the result is beautiful: Belinda's face, her clothes, the light that illuminates her ornaments and her skin. The effect may be compared with Kalf's pronkstilleven inasmuch as the brilliance of the image entirely supplants nature and makes a hollow where the original Belinda might once have stood. This provokes Dennis to feel (as Bryson and Barthes put it) that the artist is circling a void, playing triumphantly with nothingness. Hazlitt felt this too, but with more delight, describing *The Rape of the Lock* as "the most exquisite specimen of *filagree* work ever invented. It is admirable in proportion as it is made of nothing."[25]

To be sure, Pope doesn't skirt the issue of glorious outsides and empty insides: "But now secure the painted Vessel glides" (2.47). But there is little or no figurative play on "painted Vessel." The world of the poem allows no coign of vantage from which it may be called a "painted" vessel or a painted "vessel," or, for that matter, a "painted vessel." The same is true of Belinda's complaint after the rape when she wishes the baron had taken from her hairs less in sight. Like the pubic hair spreading over the surface of Klee's vase, these less visible hairs still belong to the surface, although they may (like the metamorphoses of the Cave of Spleen) be cast in the shade. There is nothing behind or beneath that surface to give the hairs an oblique or figurative point. Pope means literally what Gay offers only ironically when he writes of a china jar and a woman, "How white, how polish'd is their skin, / And valu'd most when only seen!"[26] When Garth makes this sort of parallel between a female and a thing in *The Dispensary,* comparing a grieving woman with an animate jewel, for example—"How lately did this celebrated Thing, / Blaze in the Box, and sparkle in the Ring"—her superficiality is reproached with a thingness edging in a humiliating way towards the genital.[27] This is more explicit when Etherege disparages the ornaments of an Austrian countess: "The Thing that wears this glitt'ring Pomp / Is but a tawdry ill-bred Ramp."[28] There is a large vein of misogynist satire in the 1690s which tackles female artifice in the harshest terms, a whited sepulcher or a Pandora's box, as in this paraphrase of Virgil's fourth eclogue published in Dryden's *Sylvae:*

> Pomatums, Washes, Paints, Perfumes they use,
> And never think they can be too profuse.
> False Shapes, false colour'd Locks they wear,
> False Smiles, and Looks more false than is their Hair.
> Thus they, like Actors 'till the Play is done,
> Have nothing on that they can call their own.[29]

This is even more disastrously true of Swift's Corinna, who divests herself of so many prostheses in *A Beautiful Young Nymph going to Bed* that there is scarcely anything of her left. The moralization of female fashion ends up with a disgusting or sexual reading of the thing-as-nothing disguised by artifice. Shaftesbury directly equates women's devotion to the falseness of fashion with the effeminacy of men who delight in still lifes, "so that whilst we look on paintings with the same eyes as we view commonly the rich stuffs and coloured silks worn by our Ladys . . . we must of necessity be effeminate in our Taste and utterly set wrong as to all Judgment and Knowledge in the kind."[30]

In Pope's poem empty things with painted surfaces are constantly juxtaposed with the heroine of Pope's poem, and not in any satirical way, for the beauty of the surface makes satire irrelevant. Look on her face and you'll forget her faults, he promises. So enveloping are the superficies of things it becomes pointless to distinguish between things, humans, and spirits except in the degree to which these surfaces are more or less pleasurable to look at. Pope calls Belinda his muse, painting her as part of the machinery, just as the machinery painted her as an exquisite empty vessel, or as she painted herself purer blushes out of breathing boxes and self-opening caskets. Such overpainting doesn't thicken the pigment; it sets up a potentially infinite series of reflections of paint and the act of painting in which very little difference is to be detected. From these reflections the natural and the human elements—at least those that would be recognized as such by Dennis, Shaftesbury, and Etherege—have been expelled, as they are from the reflections sent from the shining surfaces of pewter and silver in the paintings of Jan Lievens and Jan van der Welde. If Belinda's mind is like the whirligig of fashion or a camera obscura, where moving images are cast upon a blank surface unmediated by a reflective or critical presence, then Pope supplies the ekphrasis suitable for such machinery. His absorbed descriptions of things beautifully made speak solely of their remarkable effects, as Homer does in his ekphrasis of Achilles' shield, or Philostratus in the descriptions of still lifes he gives in his *Imagines*.

Dennis is right to observe then that there is nothing to interpret in this kind of painting, and nothing to learn from it. Like a still life it refuses the frame of narrative, and it introduces the temporality of the vanitas only to emphasize its irrelevance. If it shows a bible and a billet-doux together, it is not to dignify one kind of writing at the expense of another but just to picture it, like the writing in a still life or a trompe l'oeil. It is one more thing among the clutter of other artificial things that constitute the subject, medium, and end of the work. The sparkling cross worn by Belinda, for example, is neither a symbol of faith nor an icon of providential care. It means nothing at all, which is why Jews might kiss it and infidels adore it without danger of apostasy.

The conflict in the poem, specifically the battle over the lock of hair, emerges from the refusal of characters such as the baron and Clarissa to regard a painted surface simply as a treat for the eye. They want to find out what lies beneath it, what it represents, and what it means. It is evident from the baron's hecatomb of gloves and garters that he regards the lock as a trophy of sexual triumph even before he cuts it off. Regardless of whether the triumph has actually taken place, or whether he likes looking at the lock, or whether he likes Belinda, to wear it on his finger would be to have the world understand it as an authentic sign of his prowess, the trace of the genital "thing." Even Thalestris believes this to be the case. All the destructive impulses in the poem arise from this desire to symbolize and to interpret things—locks, motions, looks, and eyes. Such idolatry stands in contrast to the iconoclasm of Belinda and the sylphs, who set up no images on the whirligig of fashion that signify any ulterior or higher intention, or which cannot easily be replaced with others. Pope travestied the tendency to read these images as signs when, as Esdras Barnivelt, he published *A Key to the Lock*. The sparkling cross on a white breast alludes, Barnivelt says, "to the Ancient Name of Albion, from her white Cliffs, and to the Cross, which is the Ensign of England."[31] Later he contradicts himself, arguing that Belinda represents the Whore of Babylon, and the cross on her breast, "the Ensign of Popery" (30). But her dressing table is worst of all, as it figures a Catholic altar and "plainly denotes Image Worship" (29).

The history of still life shows how likely it is that an iconoclastic art will attract the charge of idolatry, partly because its exponents are so alert to it, like Pieter Saenredam and van Reymerswael, and partly because it delivers things so minutely and exactly that the spectators cannot believe it innocent of a hidden or general meaning. As a Roman Catholic writing a poem about members of the Catholic aristocracy, Pope knew the risks he took of having cynosures interpreted as symbols. Dennis's discovery of the emptiness of the poem was really Pope's vindication. The closest the iconoclasm of still life approaches idolatry is in the form of the fetish, the idol that stands for nothing and that nothing can represent, though it exerts nonetheless a strange magnetism over its spectators. I have said the lock of hair is a fine example of a Freudian fetish, an impossible female phallic substitute, and no doubt Lord Petre's original motive for taking it was linked dimly to an urge to restore what was missing from his memory of his mother. However, the fetish in its original African form of a god fortuitously constructed out of fragments provides a better idea of the machinery of the poem, and its perpetual construction of deities out of the appearances, toys, and trivia of the world. More specifically, Dennis's characterization of machinery as the copulation of nothing with something, whose offspring will be more nothings, relates the fetishism of *The Rape of the Lock* to the dazzled muse of *The Fan,* where fashionable nothings uncontrolled by a synthesizing moral threaten a crisis of taste. The reaction of Belinda to the loss of the lock at the beginning of the fourth canto resembles the introduction of Eden in *Paradise Lost* in its elaboration of the nothing which the lock represents. In an extended litotes, or an exploded je ne sais quoi, six things are numbered as instances of loss with which Belinda's might *not* be compared.

As a thing of nothing, the hair belongs to some other standard of value than the sign systems of trophy hunters and ambitious critics. In still life the occupation of space by things representing no system of order proclaims the independence of each from a narrative framework and its promise of intelligibility. Each of these things gleams with self-subsistence, taking its place in the scene with utter literalism, like the man in Pantagruel's mouth found planting cabbages, who denied any allegorical dimension to his work which was, he said, simply planting cabbages. Everything in a still life declares this independence, and the result is a series of present moments so fully and intensely described that their relation to other moments is set aside in favor of the momentary visual triumph of the image of the thing. So changes may occur, such as the change of tresses into dust or beautiful faces into skulls, but they are neither remembered nor foreseen in the way a narrative would demand.

There is a case perhaps for treating the dressing table, like the still life, as a utopic space of a specifically feminine kind. Halfway between an artist's studio and a compendium of the world, this is a zone of feminine labor where paintings are produced for the world's enjoyment, as they were in the studios of the still-life artists Maria van Oosterwyck, Clara Peeters, and Rachel Ruysch. Velazquez was fascinated by this zone. His pictures *Christ in the House of Mary and Martha* and *The Black Servant* show women in the foreground at work in kitchens, while in the background the main narrative of a history painting proceeds. In this repositioning of the quotidian, Velazquez develops the techniques of early still-life artists, such as Beuckelaer and Aertsen, who miniaturized historical scenes within large frameworks of market stalls overflowing with food. Velazquez's most intriguing contribution to this painterly mock-epic is his painting of the contest between Arachne and Minerva, *Las Hilanderas,* where female art runs up against the moralizing strain of the goddess and is forced to capitulate, as it is again—with the same goddess—in *The Fan.*[32]

Svetlana Alpers has offered an extended and extraordinary reading of this picture which is centered, like Pope's poem, upon a rape, and which again, like the poem, places the heroic dimension in the background so that women's work can come to the front. She shows how Valazquez has ordered it as four artificially lit interiors or boxes, each inside the other, anticipating some of the innovations of Philippe de Loutherbourg's *eidophysikon* (a camera obscura in which pictures moved instead of the landscape). First comes the tapestry of the Rape of Europa, woven by Arachne. A copy of Titian's painting, the scene includes, as the second box, Minerva's punishment of Arachne, who in her picture has slandered one god and dared to compete successfully with another. So Minerva's spear is raised, ready to turn the woman into a spider. Then, as in a theater, three women partly observe this outcome, and partly gaze out towards the frame that contains them. This final frame includes five women, two (*las hilanderas* [the spinners]) actively engaged in spinning the threads destined for tapestry work, with three others busy at ancillary tasks. Simplified, the arrangement is like a mirror, with five working women set against five heroic, courtly, or divine women. Whether parallels can be drawn between the woman in the foreground at the spinning wheel and Minerva, and between her companion reeling the thread and Arachne, Alpers leaves open. She is more fascinated by the loosening of Velazquez's style as his attention moves from the center box to the last frame, where his brushwork is free, original, and voluptuous, and the unconstrained gestures of the women (particularly she who holds the thread) respond to the *sprezzata desinvoltura* of the artist. Altogether the effect, says Alpers, is one of peculiarly vivid over-painting, "and instead of making art out of life, [Velazquez] draws life out of art."[33]

Belinda's dressing table, situated between the *Iliad* in one direction and iridescent machinery in the other, accomplishes the same transformation. Pope's position relative to this space, and to the broader world on which it draws for its colors and textures, might be compared with Velazquez's. There is in fact no "real" world to depict, no moral to draw from worked surfaces that open only on to more surfaces, only art breeding art. When Samuel Pepys saw a flower-piece by Simon Verelst, he was so taken with it that he confessed, "I was forced again and again to put my finger to it to feel whether my eyes were deceived or no"; he further admitted, "I was never so pleased and surprised with any picture."[34] Pepys's sensuous encounter with nothing but the experience of colors laid on canvas might be compared to the pleasures of laboratory experiments ("What raptures can the most voluptuous men fancy to which they are not equal?") or to the delight of those looking through a microscope ("They complain at first that they see nothing, but soon they cry out that they perceive marvelous objects with their eyes").[35] The utopias to which these experiences give rise, such as Bacon's *New Atlantis* and Swift's *Gulliver's Travels*, lay a similar emphasis on the pleasures of the eye, pleasures to which all subaltern delights give way in More's *Utopia*.

A utopia of pleasing visual sensations is based likewise on nothing. Having links neither to the past nor the future, and none to the natural or customary world, utopias are filled with things resembling nothing that is known or familiar. They are necessarily comparable with nothing, which is why even the most positive declarations in a utopia are framed in double negatives. Whatever might bid to have value, like gold, is transformed by art into an exquisite toy or ornament. Whatever might offer itself as the bulwark of civil society, such as marriage and the family, submits to the strange utilitarianism of the immortal commonwealth. When customary values invade the unfamiliar structures of *The Rape of the Lock*, things lose their autonomous, bright, and unexchangeable qualities and assume the dull tints of property. The enemy defined by the sylphs is "Man" (1.114), in the sense of both a masculine agent and a representative of the species. The antithesis of the rape inflicted on women by Man is painting, and the antithesis of Man is a lock of woman's hair, a thing that cannot be symbolized or possessed without entirely disappearing. The lock is an idol that breaks itself as soon as ever it is supposed to mean more than nothing.

Notes

1. Sybille Ebert-Schifferer, *Still Life: A History,* trans. Russell Stockman (New York: Abrams, 1999), 87.

2. Jean Baudrillard, "The Trompe-l'Oeil," in *Calligram: Essays in New Art History from France,* ed. Norman Bryson (Cambridge: Cambridge University Press, 1988), 54.

3. Norman Bryson, *Looking at the Overlooked: Four Essays on Still Life Painting* (Cambridge, MA: Harvard University Press, 1990), 80.

4. Simon Schama, "Perishable Commodities: Dutch Still-Life Painting and the 'Empire of Things,'" in *Consumption and the World of Goods,* ed. John Brewer and Roy Porter (New York: Routledge, 1993), 483.

5. Hal Foster, "The Art of Fetishism: Notes on Dutch Still Life," in *Fetishism as Cultural Discourse,* ed. Emily Apter and William Pietz (Ithaca, NY: Cornell University Press, 1993), 257.

6. Bryson, *Looking,* 143.

7. Ibid., 126.

8. Joseph Leo Koerner, *The Reformation of the Image* (Chicago: University of Chicago Press, 2004), 88, 84.

9. Roland Barthes, "The World as Object," in Bryson, *Calligram,* 106.

10. Svetlana Alpers, *The Art of Describing: Dutch Art in the Seventeenth Century* (Chicago: University of Chicago Press, 1983), 80–81.

11. Svetlana Alpers, *The Vexations of Art: Velázquez and Others* (New Haven, CT: Yale University Press, 2005), 241.

12. Alan Chong, Wouter Th. Kloek, and Celeste Brusati, *Still-Life Paintings from the Netherlands, 1550–1720* (Zwolle: Waanders, 1999), 132.

13. Schama, "Perishable Commodities," 485.

14. *Pandora's Box: The Changing Aspects of a Mythical Symbol,* Bollingen Series 52 (New York: Pantheon, 1956), plate 59, facing p. 113.

15. Laura Mulvey, *Fetishism and Curiosity* (London: British Film Institute; Bloomington: Indiana University Press, 1996), 54–59.

16. Helen Deutsch, *Resemblance & Disgrace: Alexander Pope and the Deformation of Culture* (Cambridge, MA: Harvard University Press, 1996), 118.

17. Geoffrey Tillotson, ed., The Rape of the Lock *and Other Poems,* 3rd ed., vol. 2 of *The Twickenham Edition of the Poems of Alexander Pope* (London: Methuen: New Haven, CT: Yale University Press, 1962), 200 (5.11). Further quotations refer to this text and will be cited parenthetically by canto and line number.

18. John Dennis, *Remarks on Mr Pope's Rape of the Lock* (London, 1728), 11. Further references will be cited parenthetically.

19. Bryson, *Looking,* 122.

20. Simone Weil, *The Iliad, or, The Poem of Force: A Critical Edition,* ed. and trans. James P. Holoka (New York: Peter Lang, 2003), 59.

21. See Tillotson, The Rape of the Lock, 153 n.

22. Vinton Dearing, ed., *John Gay: Poetry and Prose,* 2 vols. (Oxford: Clarendon Press,

1974), 1:68 (2.80). Further quotations refer to this text and will be cited parenthetically by canto and line number.

23. Joseph Addison, *Spectator* 414 (June 25, 1712), in Donald F. Bond, ed., *The Spectator,* 5 vols. (Oxford: Clarendon Press, 1965), 3:550.

24. Jonathan Crary, *Techniques of the Observer: On Vision and Modernity in the Nineteenth Century* (Cambridge, MA: MIT Press, 1991), 38–39.

25. Quoted in Deutsch, *Resemblance,* 67.

26. "To a Lady: On Her Passion for *Old China,*" in Dearing, *John Gay: Poetry and Prose,* 1:293 (lines 37–38).

27. Samuel Garth, *The Dispensary,* 2nd ed. (London, 1699), 88.

28. George Etherege, quoted in John Dryden, *Sylvae: or, the second part of poetical miscellanies* (London, 1702), 225.

29. Dryden, *Sylvae,* 221.

30. Cited in Bryson, *Looking,* 177.

31. [Alexander Pope], *A Key to the Lock,* 4th ed. (London, 1723), 13.

32. See Bryson, *Looking,* 150–55.

33. Alpers, *Vexations,* 158, 177.

34. Quoted in Chong et al., *Still-Life Paintings,* 262, 66.

35. Thomas Sprat, quoted in Alpers, *The Art of Describing,* 108; quoted in ibid., 6.

Personal Effects and Sentimental Fictions

Deidre Lynch

SENTIMENTAL NOVELS ARE CLUTTERED WITH THINGS. THE EMOTIONAL attachments that people form with possessions in these mid-eighteenth-century fictions can seem as freighted with consequence as the emotional attachments that people form with one another. Indeed, modern readers of Henry Brooke's *The Fool of Quality* or Laurence Sterne's *A Sentimental Journey* might be pardoned for finding it hard to distinguish the one sort of relationship from the other—even if, convinced of the folly of fetishism, we tend to believe that the difference between, say, ownership and friendship is a difference worth preserving. The keepsakes that clutter sentimental fiction (the lockets that protagonists wear next to their hearts; the sleeve buttons or snuffboxes that pairs of characters exchange to memorialize their first meeting or last, teary-eyed parting) work instead to collapse that difference. While they instructed their readers in emotional responsiveness, sentimentalist novelists were more than ready to make props of objects of this kind, objects particularly valued because they are the surrogates for particular persons. This practice marks the novelists' fashion-consciousness. On the testimony of the *Oxford English Dictionary,* which dates the word *keepsake* to 1790, it was only in the eighteenth century that keepsakes came to be identified as a distinct kind of material good.[1] That by 1790 members of the propertied classes had learned to *want* to give and to receive keepsakes from one another bespeaks the reciprocal influence between eighteenth-century people's love affair with feelings and their fascination with the new opportunities for acquisitiveness that they discovered in shops. And that new readiness to countenance superfluous expenditure that historians of this century's "consumer revolution" have recognized—people's new willingness to disregard luxury's traditional association with vice and instead value the luxury good as a vehicle for the finer feelings—also lies behind the marketability throughout the era of a literature designed to procure for its readers the "luxury of tears."[2]

Writers such as Brooke, Sterne, Henry Mackenzie, and Sarah Scott vindicated the psychology of refinement suitable to the new consumer culture not only by finding increasingly nuanced ways of discriminating human emotions, but also by exemplifying the diversity of the portable properties that humans might feel emotional with or about. Hence the clutter. Sensibility is both the capacity to feel when, and as, others do and also, as one eighteenth-century definition maintains, that "peculiar . . . habitude of mind, which disposes a man to be easily moved, and powerfully affected by surrounding objects."[3] The (only semi-) satiric imitator of Sterne who takes a "Sentimental Journey from Islington to Waterloo Bridge" knows he should let nothing (no thing) "escape" him: "The traveller . . . should extract reflections out of a cabbage stump." While providing a "recipe" for sentimental writing, another imitator of Sterne models what it means to extend sentiment to "inanimate objects" by "exclaim[ing], with the lady to the amputated wheel-barrow,—'Unhappy vehicle! little didst thou think at morning-dawn . . . that ere six hours elapsed—for one leg lost—thy master should desert thee—peace be with thee.'"[4] Satirists who worked this vein emphasized the irony of a situation in which sentimentalists encouraged their public to be (in the standard phrase) "tremblingly alive" to dead matter.

The satires of sentimental animism had a point. A carriage for hire that sits alone and "unpitied" in an inn yard in Calais is able to arouse in Sterne's Parson Yorick the sense of obligation that he had been incapable of mustering in his earlier encounter with the Franciscan friar. "Much indeed was not to be said for it—but something might—and when a few words will rescue misery out of her distress, I hate the man who can be a churl of them."[5] It seems apt that Yorick's piteous words acknowledge his obligation to a *desobligeant*—that they personify (bestow personhood on) a carriage that seats one person only. It is as if the communicative and emotive powers that sentimentalism projects onto objects work not just as well but even better when they are exerted in the absence of persons with whom we might connect them. Sterne acknowledges this, as the parodists note when they register the materialism in his sentimentalism. He reveals objects and subjects as competitors. Of course, it is also the usual business of the sentimental novel to subordinate the former to the latter. These fictions often measure well-being by, in good liberal fashion, assessing people's ability to hold on to their prized possessions. Yorick thus opens his narrative by protesting the insecurity of property in France. We are meant to share his dismay at the prospect that should he die in France the *droits d'aubaine* would consign his "shirts and black pair of silk breeches" and even the picture of Eliza he wears round his neck to King Louis (27), even if Yorick's heir should happen to be on the spot.[6] Sarah Scott's eponymous hero Sir George Ellison begins his career as a social reformer in a characteristic manner when, having freed the slaves on his wife's plantation, he assigns to each "a small share of peculiar property." Later, Sir George takes pains to ensure that his kinsman Sir William will, despite the lunacy that has robbed him of his legal status as a free agent, retain his right to enjoy his own fortune. In Sir George's humanitarian worldview, even the mad should preserve a relation to the possessive pronoun, and so Sir William is made a pet owner, someone who, supplied with guinea pigs, birds, rabbits, and squirrels, is in a position to refer to "*his* creatures."[7]

This essay tells its own story about characters' personal effects—a story about the changing idioms that eighteenth-century fiction developed to represent persons and things. Complicating this story is the ideological flexibility that enabled these idioms to retain their utility at a time when, impacted by new concepts of intellectual property, for instance, or by the policies of dehumanization that underwrote colonial slavery, the interrelations between human identity and property were drastically and multiply reconfigured. The precise manner in which ownership remakes a thing as a belonging, remakes a person as a proprietor, and binds moveable property, despite its moveability, to its proprietor is culturally and historically conditioned: a particular individual's title to a particular thing becomes meaningful only in the context of the diverse styles of possessing that together, at a given moment, define the social domain. This means, as anthropologist Nicholas Thomas comments, and as eighteenth-century fictions demonstrate at length, that "objects change in defiance of their material stability."[8]

My principal strategy here for doing justice to what is historically specific about the ways in which "objects changed" as they organized and reorganized eighteenth-century persons' affections is to attend (as I will most closely in the penultimate section of this essay) to the give-and-take relations linking the period's sentimental novels to the so-called novels of circulation that, in the middle decades of the century especially, moved as nimbly from the shelves of circulating libraries as did those now better known "crying volumes."[9] When the men and women of feeling who populate sentimental fiction avow the "feelings of a friend" for chairs and tables or talk to wheelbarrows or carriages, the animism at stake in these episodes pales in comparison with the more robust variety of animism that distinguishes the novels of circulation, in which ordinarily inanimate, silent objects—tokens of exchange such as a banknote or a guinea, or bits of erstwhile personal property such as a coat or a slipper—commence talking in their turn.[10] By thinking about what the sentimentalists' characters and the objects they endow with sentimental value might owe to others' representations of characters who *are* objects and who (as we shall see) use their animation and gift of gab to narrate their own lives, adventures, and opinions, I hope to show how eighteenth-century fictions schooled their readers in how belongings (a category in which works of fiction themselves were increasingly coming to be comprehended) may best be preserved as people's "own."

I initiated this project in *The Economy of Character.* In that book I began to outline the shifting role that the possessive adjective plays (and along with it the exchange relations that at once underpin and problematize the category of personal property) within the history of the literary character: the history, that is, of that insubstantial, inanimate being that novelists should, or so we believe, animate and endow with a "life of its own." I set out there to challenge the idea that the work of the British novel was by definition, and from the start, that of representing individual interiority. I suggested that, rather than understand character in these representational terms, we might do better to elaborate a pragmatics of character and investigate how readers in the eighteenth century *used* their encounters with the beings peopling their books to accommodate themselves to a new world of commercialized social relations—and, within that world, to apprehend and explain a marketplace being filled up with novelties, cope with the embarrassment of riches, and make their possessions truly private. In formulating that suggestion, I had recourse to the material culture of sentimentalism: the sorts of personal effects crowded into the sentimentalists' inventories. I found sleeve buttons, lockets, and snuffboxes unexpectedly important. The present essay scrutinizes more closely the forms of affection and styles of possession provoked by these trinkets and by the pieces of money for which they were exchanged. It thus scrutinizes more closely the paradoxes that attend on sentimental proprietorship. My hunch is that to track the fate of personal effects in sentimental fictions and to recover the "it-narratives" within texts that we have read as transcripts of human feelings might prompt us to rethink how, over the course of the eighteenth century, characterization—indeed, notions of what might count as a character—changed.

Of course, linked as it is with familiar narratives both about the "rise of the novel" and the rise of that individualism that "the novel" is ostensibly tailor-made to reflect, the success story that frames most examinations of the history of characterization also pivots on the discovery of personal effects, albeit in a different sense of the term than the one I've invoked. Ian Watt recalled the special effects in the arsenal of the Hollywood filmmaker when he made Samuel Richardson's use of the letter-form the equivalent in its importance for the developing novel of "D. W. Griffith's technique of the close-up . . . for the film." Watt's scheme grants precedence, that is, to "personal effects" such as Richardson's technique of writing to the moment: technologies for getting up close and personal with characters that permitted the novel to realize its potential as a "full and authentic report" of "human experience."[11] For Watt, personal effects in this sense of the term represented the motor force of the history of the novel.

William Warner points out that the priority that *The Rise of the Novel* accorded to the representation of private subjectivity distinguished Watt's narrative of the novel's progress from earlier accounts of novels' mimetic capacities, accounts more appreciative of the social panoramas readers can also find in fiction. This concentration on personal effects (and on Richardson at the expense of Fielding) also, Warner notes, allowed Watt to tap the prestige that reliably accrues to explanations of "the birth of the modern subject." By associating eighteenth-century fiction with the "new psychological genres" that, in the wake of James-inflected accounts of "point of view," were at the forefront of critical discussion in the 1950s, Watt managed to retroactively psychologize eighteenth-century writing. This move helped secure for *The Rise of the Novel* the remarkable currency it has enjoyed since 1957.[12] (By 1965, W. J. Harvey was able to take for granted the premise that it is the individuality of the individual characters that makes a novel a novel. In his view, novelists *must* accept their characters as "asserting their human individuality and uniqueness in the face of all ideology.")[13] Yet, at the same time, this choice of priorities also aligned Watt's account with certain romantic-period discussions in which the figure of the character had likewise served to relate the history of novels to the history of individualism. Perhaps it would be possible to explain the persuasiveness of Watt's account by pointing to how it managed to appear new *and* familiar at once. For instance, when, in chapter 6 of his *Lectures on the English Comic Writers* (1819), William Hazlitt outlines *Don Quixote*'s claim to the title of "first novel" it can seem as if he has somehow read Watt already. Hazlitt emphasizes the irreducible singularity of each of Cervantes' characters, who, he writes, "are never lost in the crowd." In his view of novels, the claims of character should override those of plot, and he is therefore happy to note that the actions portrayed in *Don Quixote* arise "not out of the situation of life in which [the characters] are placed, but out of the peculiar dispositions of the persons themselves." And when Hazlitt turns in earnest to compiling a romantic-period "rise of the novel" narrative, when he moves from Spain to England (a short distance as it happens, since he regards Cervantes as a "naturalised" British subject, practically "of native English growth"), he continues to discover these seemingly autonomous, self-expressive characters. He sees them now as artifacts of England's regard for the individuality of real individuals. In the reign of George II, he explains, accounting for why the novel rose when it did, "a security of person and property . . . had been established, which made every man feel of some consequence to himself . . . Each individual had a certain ground-plot of his own to cultivate his humors in."[14]

The terms Hazlitt uses to delineate the stage on which literary history unfolds ally the novelistic character's ideal scene of action with sentimentalism's paradise of small proprietors. They no doubt pleased W. J. Harvey, who using literary criticism to fight the Cold War, warned in *Character and the Novel* that there could be no novels under communism. But if the broad outlines of this liberal story of character's progress were and are familiar, there is some oddity in the way Hazlitt alludes to the history that John Locke's *Second Treatise* (1690) offers when it explicates the invention of property. As cultivator, Hazlitt's individual "mixes" his labor with his "humors" and, in approved Lockean fashion, makes them his property: makes them personal effects in a doubled sense of the term. By virtue of this labor, they have something "annexed" to them that "excludes the common right of other men." Hazlitt is exploiting the pun on the possessive adjective that Locke also relied on, with momentous results, as he moved from the premise that "his body" was "his" body to the conclusion that his "property" was also "his"—was private property—and in the same way. (What obliges us to term the Locke of the *Second Treatise* a punster is that in English the possessive adjective *only sometimes* implies the legal status of possession. Other languages, by making different kinds of possessive adjectives available, make it simpler to distinguish between the alienable and inalienable and discriminate the sort of relation that is implied when, for instance, one writes of Locke's *Treatise* from that implied when one writes of Locke's intelligence or cultivation of his humors or Locke's mother.)[15]

Hazlitt's extended metaphor for the rise of the novel has been set up so as to make the "peculiar dispositions" that render a person or a character who he is seem as substantial, as indisputably and objectively *real,* as articles of personal property. It is not clear, however, that such an analogy makes it easier to conceive of literary characters, along the lines Hazlitt means to adumbrate, as possessed of "lives of their own"—as expressing nothing, and being like nothing, but their own, original selves. After all, the effort of ascribing quiddity to the "self" is as much undermined as it is supported by Locke's account of our property in our persons. There the claims Locke makes for *self-possession* suppose both inalienability and alienability, both ideals of integrity and autonomy *and* a "fragmented relationship in which 'a person as transactor' owns" the self as commodity.

In this respect, Hazlitt's allusion to Locke seems perfectly, if unwittingly, apt: for, as eighteenth-century Britons were well aware, at no time more so than when they thought about what characters in their books represented and what could be done with them, the metaphor of "the property body" that grounds liberal thought is, in potentially perplexing ways, "always and everywhere public and private."[16] Indeed this very conjunction of public and private is built into the eighteenth century's understanding of the character. This is why readers and writers living under King George II, during the character's salad days, would have been perplexed at how that later narrative of the character's progress invokes and depends on a narrative about humanity's growing tolerance of the variations that individuate private persons. (Of course, scholars of the fictions that follow the "novels of the 1740s" are likewise put at a disadvantage by this narrative, which requires us to supply proofs that the novel's "rise" did continue, that the novels of the later rather than early eighteenth century contributed properly and in a timely manner to a movement toward "more complex psychological fiction." We are all too aware that, measured by Watt's criteria, the novels that we study represent, mortifyingly, the "sagging" of the erstwhile rising form.)

As I have indicated, the familiar account opposes characterization categorically to public institutions and social conventions. Yet for individuals living in the first half of the eighteenth century "characters" was first and foremost a designation for the legible, graphic elements of writing.[17] From the Greek for a stamp or an impress, the term "characters" denoted those distinguishing marks that visibly separate persons and things from other persons and things, and that also, in their guise as the material, replicable elements from which language is composed, refer to a *public agreement* about how their culture makes sense. The puns many early-eighteenth-century novelists elaborate—and, enthralled with letter-writing and physiognomy, they frequently arrange for one character to read another precisely as we read her, which is, quite literally, like a book—suggest their determination to think of characters accordingly: think of them not just as what or whom they represent but also as their means of representation. In Eliza Haywood's fiction, for example, lovers' reunions are mediated by "characters": they arise, that is, at the moments when a lover recognizes, in an epistle or in the verses penciled on the base of a garden statue, his beloved's "dear obliging characters." Daniel Defoe's *An Essay upon Literature* (1726) engages with characters in ways that thwart the expectations aroused by that value term "literature" (it presents literature as an object of study better suited to twentieth-century departments of communications than our departments of English). Defoe's history of characters concerns "types impressing their Forms on Paper by Punction or the Work of an Engine."[18] He engages various alphabet systems, typefaces, the inscriptions that, stamped on coins, transform previously unembossed disks of metal into current money. He extols characters of these sorts as the means that enable communication to take place over a distance. Defoe would not be disconcerted to learn that as I compose this paper I am able to command my computer to execute a "character count": for him, as for our more wired contemporaries, character designated a typographic object, a unit of information. And, for all his centrality to Watt's account of how fiction took an inward turn, Samuel Richardson likewise brought a technocratic interest (shaped in his printing shop) to his notions of how characterization could advance the project of redesigning the social order. Touting the moral efficacy of fictional (rather than "dry") narrative, promising his readers that they too might expect to be reissued in improved editions, Richardson contends in the Hints toward a Preface to *Clarissa* that the "Characters sink deeper into the Mind of the Reader, and stamp there a perfect Idea of the very Turn of Thought, by which the Originals were actuated, and diversified from each other."[19]

Character belongs, in statements like Richardson's, to the field of discourse: this is in conformity to the local intellectual conditions of early-eighteenth-century England, a culture exhilarated by what it could do with moveable type. Modern readers, by contrast, think of the literary character as existing apart from and prior to the words that represent it. We think of the literary character as what the writing is written about. Eighteenth-century commentators are able to think of the character *as* the writing.[20] Predicting a long line of nineteenth-century humanist commentators on novels, Hazlitt teaches readers to raise questions about characters' autonomy and authenticity, to adjudicate whether, rather than being the playthings of circumstance or plot ("manners or situation"), the characters of a novel are possessed of dispositions and humors "peculiar" to themselves. But such questions about a character's intrinsic nature—about whether a character is indeed like nothing but himself, "unfellowable"—are in a sense beside the point when, as with Richardson, Defoe, and Haywood, we engage writers who value characters, in the first instance, as cultural instruments for generalizing meaning, for revealing the general principles that hold a conversable society together, and for socializing and redeeming particularity.[21] The early novelists' punning on "character" as well as on a series of related terms, their habit, for instance, of pointedly directing readers' attention to the "characters" that betray the authorship of an epistle or to the "lines" that make a hero's face recognizable as his own, constitute their self-reflexive admission that their own practices of characterization must comply with recognized public conventions for sense-making.

In this context, characters do not matter primarily because, as W. J. Harvey would later assert, each "asserts its uniqueness." Characters matter instead in some measure *because* they are matter: because the materiality of written language, the thing-like qualities that ensure language's participation in the phenomenal world, ensure as well that agreements and arguments that are inscribed in characters will be accessible to public scrutiny. Language embodied in written or printed characters "resists mystification from being treated as a purely private or hidden property."[22] The anti-oral biases of a print culture, geared up for the exchange, copying, and commercial circulation of information conveyed in graphic form, help motivate the character-writers' embrace of the corporeality of language. Of course, in this period of physiognomic enthusiasms, this idea of language also intersects with an ideal of a legible, telltale body, one marked with characters that externalize character. It intersects as well with a homiletic tradition, originating in the middle ages, that compared the "character," in the sense of the word that concerns personality, to the coin. Sermons in this tradition proposed that the self might be considered the issue of God's Mint or saw in the coin imprinted with the inscription that turned it into legal tender an image of the individual separated from its originary state of innocence by the lineaments—corresponding in turn to the lines and marks to be discovered on the face—of the virtues and vices. This character-coin analogy, we should note, implies a narrative. As befitted a Protestant culture nervous about cloistered virtues, and a commercial culture anxious to see the "dead stock" of bullion enlivened by financial investment, the coin was described as existing in order to circulate within the marketplace of the world. It was thought of as having been sent out from the Mint to be marked up by experience.

This narrative that recounts the so-called purchase of experience organizes numerous mid-eighteenth-century novels—Tobias Smollett's *Roderick Random*, Sarah Fielding's *David Simple*, or her brother Henry's *Tom Jones*, to name a few. In works such as these, the universal conversation enjoyed by the protagonist, which brings him into contact with "every kind of character from the minister at his levee, to the bailiff in his spunging house; from the dutchess at her drum, to the landlady behind her bar," represents another means by which the character and the piece of current money come to associated.[23] These fictions can seem bent on treating their principal characters as investment capital: the vehicle empowering them to get more characters still. Each text looks to be intent, too, on charting the social order to its farthest reaches, doing so by means of a peripatetic, conversable protagonist who, like current money (as described in 1757) "cherishes and invigorates the whole community."[24] Modern readers may be justified in viewing the social context that novels elaborate as being there to explain the characters. But taking seriously the linkages among numismatic, physiognomic, and "characteristic" signs that so interested early and mid-eighteenth-century writers means that we should also try to think of the characters as there to produce the sense of a social context.

The flagrant unworldliness of many sentimental protagonists of the 1760s and 1770s—Brooke's Fool of Quality, say, or Mackenzie's Harley, who, deviating from the standard peripatetic model for mid-century protagonists, leaves home too late and returns too soon—might seem to disqualify them from this work. At the least, this unworldliness seems to suggest that by the last third of the eighteenth century the typographical emphases that had oriented the "character" toward publication, publicity, and the public had become easier to discount. In this respect, sentimental fictions do seem to know their allotted place within the familiar rise-of-the-novel narratives recounting how fiction got personal and people got individual. In seeming to exemplify an intermediate stage in the development of the individuated novelistic character—in seeming to provide precursors to the style of character Hazlitt talks about, whose humors are his and his alone, or to the style of character that Watt finds in the psychologically discriminating work of Jane Austen, sentimental fictions appear to affirm the narrative of progress in characterization that these figures and others outline. I want not so much to challenge as to complicate this view. (It has, after all, the disadvantages, also evident in accounts that ascribe "preromanticism" to the literary productions of this period, of casting sentimental fictions as lesser versions of what they merely foreshadow.)

To do so, I want to return to personal effects in the first sense in which I used that term. I want to think about how often in sentimental novels we see the fungibility that is demanded of characters who participate in the exchange relations of "sentimental commerce" (Yorick's phrase) pitted against an ideal of integrity that is modeled when characters keep their keepsakes and so keep themselves to themselves. I want to think about how often sentimentalists arrange for intimate, absolute proprietorship—the style of ownership that Locke's account of the property body was supposed to model—to take shape against a backdrop of other, imperfect and compromised sorts of possession. What suggests that the status of the (self-possessed and self-possessing) character in sentimental fiction is more enigmatic than our critical narratives have allowed us to suppose is this paradox: that in this venue thinking about what is *personal* very often becomes intertwined with thinking about *money*. And when sentimental novels do that thinking, they turn to citing the books they jostled with on mid-century circulating library shelves, the narratives of circulation.

In what remains of my essay I mean to outline how these works intertwine the personal with the fiduciary, and by doing so propose a conjectural account of how the British novel negotiated the shift between the two notions of character and the two ways of estimating their use and value that I have already outlined. Let me begin by considering the narratives that people, starting in the eighteenth century, learned to spin out of their keepsakes and souvenirs—for, as Susan Stewart has demonstrated, stories invariably accompany this species of object. The keepsake's narrative is a story of dispossession. (It is our nostalgia that makes us value it as a metonymic object, one memorializing the special experience of which it was a part. But nostalgia's demands are insatiable, and this keepsake, accordingly, records loss as much as preservation. It records, that is, its status as a mere substitution.) At the same time, paradoxically, it is also a story of possession of the most absolute, intimate kind. (Thus this nostalgic story in itself is the property of the possessor and not the object, for, inalienable and ungeneralizable, that story can encompass the experience of one particular person only. In this way, when a souvenir is purchased or a keepsake is bestowed upon a "significant other," the possessor is in a position to "inscrib[e] the handwriting of the personal beneath the more uniform caption of the social.")[25] The second of the two quotations from the 1790s that the *Oxford English Dictionary* provides when it exemplifies the earliest usage of "keepsake" is from *The Mysteries of Udolpho* of Ann Radcliffe, preeminent poet of the memorializing impulses we bring to our personal effects. The heroine Emily's maidservant, Annette, refers to "'a beautiful new sequin, which Ludovico [another servant] gave me as a keep sake,'" and which she "'would not [part] with . . . for all St. Marco's Place.'" Ludovico's choice of a memento to bestow upon his beloved underlines and exacerbates the paradox that I have already associated with property in general: the paradox that to call something property is to apprehend it as both, simultaneously, a private and a public concern. This is so because Annette's prize possession the "sequin" is (again, as the *Oxford English Dictionary* indicates) an Italian *coin,* and because money is so very odd a form of personal possession.[26]

Adam Smith evoked that oddity when he remarked, in *The Wealth of Nations,* on how "the same guinea . . . [that] pays the weekly pension of one man today, may pay that of another tomorrow, and that of a third the day after."[27] Spinning out Smith's sentence so that it describes a sequence of adventures extended over several volumes of print, authors throughout the eighteenth century adopted the guinea's—or shilling's, banknote's, halfpenny's, or rupee's—point of view as they delineated at length the serviceability that secures current money, which can substitute itself for any sort of good or service, a welcome wherever it goes. The banknote narrator and hero of Thomas Bridges's 1770 narrative begins its story, for instance, in the possession of a poet, with whom, as we might expect, knowing poets, it does not remain long. When the poet uses the note to pay for his lodgings, the note makes its way (taking its readership along with it) to a grocer, who pays it out to a doctor, who in his turn pays it out to an old woman, as hush money and as restitution that he owes her after impregnating her daughter. This daughter acquires the banknote next, but it quickly slips out of her hands to pass to her silk-mercer's. This sequence unfolds in the first sixty pages of Bridges's first volume. "Who would not be a banknote to have such a quick succession of adventures and acquaintances?" (2:25).

The popularity enjoyed by these autobiographies of money—or by, for that matter, the autobiographies of, variously, a hackney coach, an old black coat, and so on, that sprang up in the middle decades of the century to emulate the money-narrators' success—might be a function of the programmatic way in which their cataloguing of "acquaintance" in both high society and low, town and country, made the otherwise ungraspable, anonymous totality, "society," appear something that a solitary reader might *know,* and made it appear, too, something that cohered as a system of mutual interdependence. If money indeed "cherishes" the community, a banknote's report on how it has kept on moving from hand to hand should count as a significant labor of love. This is so because when, through this panoramic project of characterization, the banknote narrator attests to its prolonged circulation, it attests to the ongoing power of the social agreements that make pieces of metal and paper into the populace's means of measuring and representing value. It also makes this circulation appear tidily, reassuringly circular, as if the economy really did rotate round a single axis in the reassuring ways that the metaphor of "circulation" implies. What goes round *can* come round, when you share things' point of view. Eighteenth-century authors often arrange for some persons among the circulating objects' multitudinous acquaintance to perform their walk-on roles twice. Ending his second volume, the banknote eagerly points out that he is back in "the clyster-pipe of the little apothecary that in my first volume got so tumbled about by the blind man and his dog" (2:204). In similar fashion, Pompey the Little, the eponymous canine protagonist of Francis Coventry's 1751 book, does, however circuitous his route, find his way back to Lady Tempest, the owner succeeding the gentleman newly returned from the Grand Tour but preceding the hackney coachman.

But leaving aside such consolations, audiences might well have been perturbed by these works' demonstration that smart-aleck objects know more about the interrelations that compose a society than do human beings (who might wish to think that society is their creation): their epistemological advantage is the more troubling because these objects also make no bones about the fact that they are saved or disbursed, immobilized or put in motion, only according to human whims, and that their purchase of experience depends on our consumption patterns. The world they portray is, furthermore, a parlously slippery place, so that, even though a lapdog or banknote can end up on a highly intimate footing with its possessor (the banknote momentarily finds itself tucked into a "milliner's stomacher" [1:158]), the story line reiterated throughout these narratives is always one of loving and leaving. The leaving may be par for the course when it comes to, for instance, the account that a hackney coach gives of its passengers, but almost all the object-heroes of eighteenth-century literature are blithely ready to dispense with personal attachments, sharing—if not in law, then in fact—the disconcerting propensities described by the lawyer hired by the lady who feels her title to Pompey is superior to Lady Tempest's: dogs, say the lawyer, "follow any body . . . [and] have a strange undistinguishing Proneness to run after People's heels."[28] The banknote even refers to itself as "walk[ing]" (1:158), endowing itself with a pair of legs the better to make the point crucial to its genre—that money is never at home except in the state of circulation and, in seeking to be everybody's, ends up being nobody's.

Frequently, however, it *is* a piece of money that is at center stage at those moments when objects occasion the artless expression of affection which is the hallmark of sentimental fiction. I am thinking here of how Sterne and Mackenzie (following Henry Fielding's lead) each arrange to convert the social instrument of money into a personal effect. A vignette common to *A Sentimental Journey* and *The Man of Feeling* demonstrates how a coin may be converted into property so personal—and property which is, quite precisely, of sentimental value—that to be parted from it would be like losing a body part, or as Sterne's sentimental traveler says, referring in this case to what it would mean to lose the snuffbox bestowed on him by the Franciscan friar, like losing "the instrumental parts of my religion" (44).[29] (The complication, of course, to which I'll attend shortly, is that these scenes of possession are necessarily haunted by the picaresque stories that peripatetic money has been recounting in other persons' books.)

After Parson Yorick gives a French *fille de chambre* a crown along with a piece of his advice (the payment working to make his exhortations more endearing), she promises to set the coin aside—"En vérité,

1. This hand-colored engraving (after Thomas Rowlandson) of *A Sentimental Journey through France and Italy* (London: T. Tegg, 1809) memorializes Yorick and Father Lorenzo's sentimental exchange of keepsake snuffboxes. Courtesy of the Yale Center for British Art, Paul Mellon Collection.

Monsieur, je mettrai cet argent apart" (90)—and later reenters his story to show her benefactor the purse that she has fashioned for that express purpose. She has made the little purse of green taffeta, she says, handing it to him, to "hold your crown" (117). As the other books' garrulous money-narrators insist at such length, money exists to be spent, and so Yorick's words about why she instead might keep the money in fact bring into view just what it could be exchanged for—"ribbons" (90). But this coin escapes the general fate. In Mackenzie's *The Man of Feeling* we witness through Harley's eyes a comparable refusal to treat cash as cash. Wending his way through the London streets, Harley encounters "a fresh-looking elderly gentleman" whose physiognomy impresses him, as do his expressions of benevolence: so much so that when his new acquaintance lacks even a "farthing" of spare change and is thereby prevented from donating alms to the beggar who accosts him, Harley steps into the philanthropic breach.[30] Harley, the stranger, and a friend of Harley's new friend then make their way to a public house, where they begin a game of piquet, and where, oddly enough, the same would-be philanthropist produces ten shilling pieces to serve as markers of his score. Harley, however, is characteristically quick to put a brave face on the matter and to explain away the incongruity between the actual state of the gentleman's pocketbook and what had transpired earlier in the gentleman's encounter with the beggar. Musing to himself, our hero observes that "inanimate things" will create affection "by a long acquaintance." He continues, "if I may judge by my own feelings, the old man would not part with one of these counters for ten times its intrinsic value; it even got the better of his benevolence! I, myself, have a pair of old brass sleeve buttons" (31–32).

When Yorick and Harley advocate or justify others' earmarking of their moneys (or, in the case of the not-so-benevolent old gentleman, apparent earmarking), what Sterne and Mackenzie are staging is, of course, a scene of fetishism. Harley's association of the coin and the sleeve button, the latter an object that is also converted into a keepsake in Brooke's *The Fool of Quality,* makes this point for me.[31] Thinking about what a button and a coin might share, we highlight their tactility and tininess: each object asks us not only to touch it but to cup it in our palm and secrete it away. (It is noteworthy, furthermore, that buttons have historically been fashioned of the same precious metals used for circulating specie. If we sometimes do end up wearing our cash, for example, sporting waistcoats adorned with "buffalo nickels" for buttons, there is reason to think, too, that in a nation chronically short of specie, especially in small denominations, and not ready to commit wholly to a paper currency, eighteenth-century Britons might sometimes have ended up spending their buttons. Matthew Boulton, the commercial magnate whose lucrative button trade inaugurated Birmingham's era of industrial prosperity, for brief periods supplemented that manufactory with a contract from the Crown to mint copper twopences and pennies and, later, three-shilling pieces.)[32]

The attachments to money put on view here might also be said to be fetishists' in that they overthrow "normal" criteria for value. As a designation for the illusions of those moved in the wrong (irrational, outlandish) ways by the wrong species of objects, *fetishism* entered Western Europe's conceptual repertory when colonial trade first brought far-flung cultures, and with them incommensurable economies of the object, into a new, unstable proximity. In the aftermath of that reconfiguring of the atlas, objects themselves came to move in new ways, as they traversed the heterogeneous spaces of uneven economic development demarcated by the globe's new trade routes.[33] Within this novel theater of cross-cultural to-and-fro, valuables from one zone could metamorphose into trifles in another, and vice versa: "objects [would thereby] change in defiance of their material stability." The fetish (pidgin, from the Portuguese, *feitiço*) begins its historical life as a creation of this metamorphosis-working border zone: as a thing demanding to be comprehended exclusively in terms of its irreducibly sensuous "thingliness," impeding the capitalist marketplace's drive to understand everything via the abstraction of exchange value, and standing outside the ambit of trade.[34] The peripatetic rupee-narrator of Helenus Scott's 1782 *Adventures of a Rupee* is fated to become a fetish in just this creolized mode when, as a consequence of its dislocation from India, it ceases to be "a current coin" and loses its ability to refer beyond itself, to the abstract system of exchange value underwriting the Mughal state. In fact, the English sailor who takes the rupee with him on his return from the Maratha War had therefore "resolved to keep me, for a present of true love, as he called it, to Molly Black."[35] (Sailor Jack's sentimental impulse works momentarily to link up the *Adventures* to the "crying books" but is quickly short-circuited by the demands of Scott's genre. If "adventures" are to continue, a keepsake cannot be kept.)

Diverted from exchange, but not receiving the sort of treatment they would get from the miser who simply suspends rather than annuls exchange relations, the talismanic shillings and crown and rupee demand a special sort of consideration. Though money, they are not being considered *either* as "a measure of value"—valued for how they might determine and represent the worth of the commodities on offer in the marketplace—*or* "as treasure—value itself."[36] In fact, according to the jurist William Blackstone, *curiosities*—the category of thing that the rupee by its own confession has entered in exchanging India for England (103)—are property that it is no felony to destroy or to detain, "because their value is not intrinsic, but depending solely on the caprice of the owner."[37] (The distinction Blackstone asserts appears, however, to elude the pawnbroker who agrees to receive the rupee as a pledge and who thereby grants it the opportunity to make additional, copy-worthy acquaintance among his customers). At the same time, the scene that presses money into service as the most personal sort of personal effect operates to join what, according to recent scholarship, fiction of the mid-eighteenth century supposedly sunders—public and private spheres, "the indirect relations of the commercial state" and "the direct relations of the affective community." The keepsake coin marks the point of intersection, even as it sets objective and subjective determinations of value at variance.[38]

Credit for first devising this sentimental scenario should perhaps go to Henry Fielding, who arranges for Joseph Andrews, following an incident in which that hero is attacked by thieves, to stubbornly refuse to cash in the little piece of broken gold that he wears fastened with a ribbon to his arm. That gold piece is the token of Joseph's love for Fanny: Fielding may intend his readers to infer that when these two pledged their troth, they broke a coin in halves between them to commemorate the compact. For this reason, despite being unable to pay the reckoning at the Dragon Inn, Joseph is resolved to keep his gold out of circulation. He has earlier refused to let it be produced in evidence against his assailants, and now, too, though it represents the sum total of Joseph's wealth, and though Mrs. Tow-wouse avers, incontrovertibly, that she "'never knew any Piece of Gold of more Value than as many Shillings as it would change for,'" this "coin" will not be spent. When so challenged, Joseph instead "hug[s]" his property "to his bosom." His gesture invites us to identify his gold piece with the strawberry mark that is imprinted over his heart and that will, at the end of his story, effect the recognition of his true identity.[39] And for this reason Joseph's gesture also invites us to remember the tradition of comparing coins to characters, of comparing the legends that are inscribed on coins' surfaces and make metal disks into legal tender to the so-called characteristic marks that make bodies into telltale, self-evident transcripts of identities and enable foundlings to be identified and "owned." Hence one Mrs. Fielding who contributes her story to the many tales of bereavement that get told in Brooke's *The Fool of Quality:* "If heaven should ever bless me with more children, said Mrs. Fielding, I have determined to fix some indelible mark upon them, such as that of the Jerusalem letters, that . . . I may be able to discern and ascertain my own offspring from all others."[40]

I am not the first to remark the high profile money enjoys in sentimental novels, which for eighteenth-century readers must in many respects have represented guidebooks to money's uses: object lessons demonstrating the power that those disbursing it have to assign an objective value to all sorts of actions and things. In delicate situations, money clarifies roles and sets limits on people's entitlements. Sentimental fiction taught readers to have faith in money.[41] But those vignettes in *Joseph Andrews, The Man of Feeling,* and *A Sentimental Journey* that render money a keepsake go out of their way to belie such instruction. In these scenes money's value depends on its not circulating. It depends on money's being divested of its money-like qualities. By this means the scenes reveal current money's oddity as a category of *private* property. For example, cash, once lost, cannot necessarily be recovered with the sanction of the law: a 1758 ruling of Lord Mansfield's maintained that the "true owner" of stolen money could not claim it after it had been paid away honestly in a bona fide transaction, not simply because money "leaves no Ear-Mark" (a rationale that Mansfield mentions only to reject), but instead because of "the Currency of it."[42] (At the time of her second encounter with Yorick the fille de chambre, tellingly, still refers to the contents of her little purse as his crown, not her own. Her slip suggests that in reality the coin belongs to neither.) By its very nature money suspends us between possession and exchange. If we spend "our" money, it really is no longer our property. But if we refuse that spending power and keep our keepsake coins out of circulation, this money ceases to *be* money.

As they traffic in an idea of "sentimental" value, the three scenes I have just considered emphasize money's dual nature. They underline this duality as they adjudicate between the quiddity of the coin—the set of special associations that supposedly make each one of the benevolent elderly gentleman's ten shillings irreplaceable, however much it resembles anybody else's shillings—and the abstract, impersonal qualities that allow a coin to function as (in Marx's terms) a general equivalent, a stand-in for anything that is up for sale, anytime and anywhere. In the peculiar way in which they annex a memory to a piece of money and make it into the prop for character's story "of his own," these scenes suspend the powers of representativeness that were supposed to make money a medium of civility. The narrative of the keepsake momentarily displaces the narrative of circulation.

If we recall how eighteenth-century culture associated the mechanical production processes that create money and printed texts with the ethical production processes that create *character* (that imprint the self with traits and characteristics), these scenes have a further effect. One might postulate that the dual status that money has in these scenes correlates with the two ways in which character might be conceptualized, with the two alternatives that the first half of my essay outlined. My earlier discussion turned backward from the sui generis particularity of the authentic literary character (the wholly individuated character whom a novel-lover like Hazlitt can celebrate without apology) to the social conventions for which written characters stand, the same social conventions that make a character a readable artifact. As money is personalized in the sentimental scenes we have been considering—recast along asocial lines so that it no longer tells its tale of social agreement, fetishized so that it absorbs into itself the history of the processes of mechanical reproduction (and the history of the people) that made it—so, in our narratives about the novel's rise, character will be personalized too, and made singular and self-referential in an analogous way. In this way, sentimental fiction accommodates, albeit with the irony that attends on all our attempts to make property an intimate article, the designs of those who like Hazlitt wish to recount the narrative of character as a success story of personal effects.

This value given currency within the text of sentiment suggests another reason to ascribe significance to the scenes that show us a coin withheld from exchange. In their capacity as men of feeling, George Ellison, Harry Clinton, Harley, and Yorick plunge into the transactional universe of a market culture. Reputed to be charitable to the needy, they spend freely. These sentimental protagonists thus move, as their shillings and crowns do, from one scene of exchange to another. For in sentimental fiction even the needy bring something to market: the stories of their suffering. All those madwomen, beggars, and slaves enable these protagonists to spend their cash and purchase the vicarious pleasures of sympathy. If, with this plot convention in mind, we align the social mobility of current money with the universal conversation and sympathy that are required of these protagonists, then what we see in those vignettes centered on the keepsake coin is a suspension of narrative: a hovering between plot and plotlessness. Explaining why Harley will not leave home and enable his narrative to begin, why he defers his Grand Tour, the narrator of *The Man of Feeling* speaks to the appeal such an impasse might exert: "It will often happen in the velocity of a modern tour, and amidst the materials through which it is commonly made, the friction is so violent, that not only the rust, but the metal too, will be lost in the progress" (4). In this quotation the character *himself* (conceived of as independent of social circumstances and preexisting any plot) appears as the cosseted coin at center stage in our vignette. Furthermore, the cosseting is the condition of the character's survival, of his remaining *himself*.

Yorick suggests something similar in the episode in *A Sentimental Journey* where, in conversation with the French aristocrat who has assisted him in his quest for identity papers, he responds candidly to the Count's request for his impressions of the French. This is the passage, from the chapter titled "Character," in which our hero gets homesick and waxes nostalgic for the alternative to the hyperurbanity that distinguishes his Frenchified life.

> Should it ever be the case of the English, in the progress of their refinements, to arrive at the same polish which distinguishes the French . . . we should . . . lose that distinct variety and originality of character, which distinguishes them, not only from each other, but from all the world besides.
>
> I had a few king William's shillings as smooth as glass in my pocket; and forseeing they would be of use in illustration of my hypothesis, I had got them into my hand, when I had proceeded so far—
>
> See Monsieur le Count, said I, rising up, and laying them before him upon the table—by jingling and rubbing one against another for seventy years together in one body's pocket or another's, they are become so much alike you can scarce distinguish one shilling from another.
>
> The English, like ancient medals kept more apart, and passing but few peoples hands, preserve the first sharpnesses which the fine hand of nature has given them—they are not so pleasant to feel—but in return, the legend is so visible, that at the first look you see whose image and superscription they bear. (114)

Prior to this scene, we have watched as, using Shakespeare as the character reference who will secure his introduction to the Count, Yorick has ended up defining himself as a copy who stands in derivative relation to an "original" Yorick: "I took up *Hamlet* . . . I laid my finger upon YORICK, and advancing the book to the Count, with my finger all the way over the name—Me, *Voici!* said I" (109).[43] His owing his character to a character (or, as the typography emphasizes, to the six characters Y, O, R, I, C, K) means, of course, that our hero has refuted in advance his claims about English originality, but that irony merely compounds those ironies which are (as we have seen) already at stake in this reimagining of money along asocial lines—this dramatization of the dual nature of money and of character.

Yorick's "antient medals" may be classed with Joseph's gold, the benevolent gentleman's shillings, and the crown in the fille de chambre's purse, but what about his shillings "rubbed smooth as glass" by their participation in a long series of fiscal transactions? Yorick has upped the ante with this image. I suggested above that money converted into a keepsake, made the object of a more absolute, immaculate mode of ownership, ceased to be money. In Yorick's scenario, however, when money does what money is *supposed* to do, which is to jingle and rub in one body's pocket or another, it *likewise* ceases to be money, losing the inscriptions with which it was endowed. (And indeed around 1774, when many decades had lapsed since the last sizeable coinage, the inscriptions on silver were in general so effaced that it was apparently difficult to discern whether a coin was "English" or "foreign.")[44] Diminished in their material substance, those King William's shillings leave the bearer with less to call his own. At the same time, dwindling into illegibility, they have ceased to perform their *public* function of giving material shape to the immaterial fiction of civil society. And, presumably, if the jingling and rubbing Yorick dramatizes continue, this money ceases to *be* altogether—instead worn away to nothingness.

With Yorick's assistance, I have spelled out what is wishful about the manner in which the sentimental text polarizes circulation and the sentimental possession of property, something it does each time it tells the story of the keepsake. The novels underline that wishfulness, insofar as they often arrange for personal effects and the impersonal medium of money to trade places. Cash is "held apart" in a sentimental novel. The same cannot be said of the articles of personal property: those things we customarily endow with sentimental value and distinguish with a "characteristic mark" (a cipher or motto) that denotes ownership start behaving within sentimental novels as if they were the peripatetic protagonists of narratives of circulation. The latter, as one might expect, return obsessively to sites where personal effects can regress to the state of impersonal commodity: object-narrators frequently introduce readers to what a talkative Black Coat calls "new vamper[s] of old commodities" and have us visit pawnshops and auction rooms.[45] Sentimental fiction's knickknacks—its snuffboxes, hankies, and portrait miniatures—do something similar. They too tend to be whisked out of persons' pockets and, once they are set wandering, made subject to handling by all and sundry. Personal property's fate in sentimental novels inverts impersonal money's.

This is the lesson of that miniaturized narrative of circulation folded into *A Sentimental Journey* that recounts how La Fleur's *gage d'amour* is given by his inamorata to a footman, who gives it to a seamstress, who gives it to a fiddler (130). A comparable fate is suffered by Tristram Shandy's handkerchief (marked with an S in the corner), which finds its way into Maria's possession (139), as it is by Yorick's starling. The bird, Yorick insists, "was my" bird, and he bears it as the crest to his coat of arms, a choice of crest that suggests that Sterne himself, behind the scenes, is seizing an opportunity both to pun on his name (via the homophony linking "Sterne" with "starn," the North-of-England dialect word for starling) and to assert *his* title as owner. (All those printed asterisks that speckle Sterne's book, concealing names and euphemizing naughty bits, work to similar ends: as *little stars, star-lings,* they function as the characteristic marks memorializing, even as the book circulates, the author's rights in his literary property.) And yet that bird that is so definitely Yorick's has, at the time of his writing, been set adrift on the seas of civic finance, and passed to Lord A, who traded it away to Lord B, and "so on—half round the alphabet" (99).[46]

❧

What does the wishful thinking manifested in *A Sentimental Journey*'s disquisition on "character"—this attempt to put the brakes on the story of money's and character's mobility—mean for that other story to which sentimental fiction ostensibly contributes, that romantic-period success story about individuals, characters, and novels? I would like to answer that question in two ways.

First, if sentimentalism marks a transition in the history of characterization, perhaps that transition does not need to be understood as a passage between a less and a more perfect mimesis of a less and a more perfect individualism. In *The Economy of Character* I propose that an alternative account of how characterization changed might take for its point of departure the modeling of sentimental possession that engrosses the sentimental novel. I suggest that rather than looking for improvements in novels' mimetic powers, we might instead contemplate how a new way of using characters might have been engendered by

[38]

I have borne this poor ſtarling as the creſt to my arms.—Thus:

—And let the heralds officers twiſt his neck about if they dare.

2. The "Poor starling" is all too soon whisked out of Yorick's possession, and it afterward passes through the hands of a long series of Peers and then Members of Parliament. Nonetheless Yorick has arranged to give "this self-same bird" pride of place on the coat of arms that blazons forth his identity, as this page from the second volume of *A Sentimental Journey* (1768) attests. Courtesy of The Lilly Library, Indiana University, Bloomington, Indiana.

an era of consumer revolution—an era that, to a limited degree, saw a democratization of consumption, and in which, more importantly, the boundaries of wealth and class appeared increasingly permeable, as luxuries that were once confined to an elite few came to seem as if they might potentially be every person's property. The result of such transformations? Imagine the novelty of a situation in which exact replicas of my favorite Wedgwood snuffbox were likely to be wending their way by pack boat or wagon from Newcastle to Bangor, while another such shipment of "my" snuffboxes headed for York. As this outline for a fiction to be entitled *The Adventures of the Mass-Produced Snuffboxes* suggests, eighteenth-century Britons had increasing reason to bear in mind what was uncertain and complicated in possessive individuals' relation to possessions. In their era of nascent consumerism, personal effects must have seemed less personal than they had hitherto.

The idea that a character has a life (better still, an inner life) of its own—that a character's identity is a matter of hidden depths and meanings that are nowhere stated in print—may itself have been serviceable for readers anxious to personalize their reading experience. At a time when books, as well as snuffboxes, were at once being cherished as keepsakes and looking more and more like mass-produced commodities, to reconceptualize the meanings of literary characters in this way may have represented a way of alleviating such pressures.[47] To cast the character's significance as an inside story aligns the character with the coin that is held apart. It separates characters from exchange relations; it decommodifies them as it detaches them from the social text. Under these arrangements, one may value one's knowledge of a character as an immaculately personal, personal effect.

The keepsake's story memorializes this desire for property that would be truly self-expressive and private. At the same time, of course, it also underlines its wishful quality. When our keepsake is our money we have not abrogated that connection with the marketplace that compromises our pleasure in having. Instead, the market continues to figure in our story, as a defining line of self-expression. This suggests a second way in which the story of sentimental money can help us reassess the history of how characterization ostensibly improved and the novel took its so-called inward turn: the story highlights what is wishful in that reinvention of "character" that allowed us to forget the older meanings of that term. As I have noted, in the early eighteenth century "character" directed people toward the system of linguistic and fiscal exchanges that composed the public sphere. It prompted them to think about the social infrastructure and the mechanisms of social consent that, ironically enough, ascribed meaning and value to the most personal of communications or personal effects. Our postromantic understandings of what novels and characters do are bound up with that irony: and what indicates that this is the case is that so often in literary history, when we reflect on how characters have been redemptively set apart from the market, we acknowledge that such a luxury is "rarely allowed by history": having sentimentalized them, the best we can hope for is to have postponed characters' demise.[48] Those King William's shillings that Yorick brandishes haunt the history of the history of novels, doing so precisely as ghosts of themselves.

Thus when Hippolyte Taine recounted his own version of the narrative of novelistic progress and charted how in the eighteenth century "novels of adventure" came to be superseded by "novels of character," he returned in telling ways to those coins. In his *History of English Literature* Taine wrote: "All these novels are character novels. Englishmen, more reflective than others, more inclined to the melancholy pleasure of concentrated attention and inner examination, find around them human medals more vigorously struck, less worn by friction with the world, whose uninjured face is more visible than that of others." An elegiac undertone imbues Taine's definition of what the English novel is and renders it a description of what the English novel may imminently cease to be: it is a mere matter of time before the wear and tear of the world will take a toll on these human medals too. At its inception, the "character novel" is already in its twilight years. In *English Comic Writers* Hazlitt, while intending as Taine does to write a story of character's triumph, writes, instead, another story about character's imminent demise. In his narrative the very processes of circulation and publicity by which literature is sustained undermine the possibility of literary character: "It is . . . the evident tendency of all literature to generalise and *dissipate* character, by giving men the same . . . point of view, and through the same reflected medium." To further suggest how literature makes itself impossible, Hazlitt too has recourse to the story of money's fate: "In proportion as we are brought . . . together, and our prejudices clash one against the other, our sharp angular points wear off."[49]

In *A Contribution to the Critique of Political Economy* Marx contemplated a coin worn down by its wanderings in the world and noted that "while other beings lose their idealism in contact with the outer world, the coin is idealized by practice, becoming gradually transformed into a mere phantom of its golden or silver body." Perhaps such ghostliness is de rigeur for the novelistic character too: perhaps only a ghost could bring about the reconciliation between ideality and materiality that novel readers wishfully expect of their reading matter. Sentimental fictions' morbid moments might owe something to the novelists' recognition that death—the last debt to nature—conveniently resolves the difficulties characters have in calling property their own. (Richardson's Clarissa, who can only prove her entitlement to her grandfather's estate by willing it away upon her death, provides a celebrated example. Sarah Scott's George Ellison argues, analogously, that the best sort of benevolist is the dead property owner: the death of the man who wills away his property to another means that this property is the sole species of charitable gift that does not abridge the liberty of its recipient.)[50] One cannot help but note, too, how often sentimental protagonists elide the boundaries between life and death—as if by positioning them liminally between presence and absence their authors are acknowledging that the characters who come alive in the pages of our novels can do so only fleetingly. That the first thing that Sterne's readers knew about Yorick was, thanks to Tristram Shandy's earlier narration, the manner of his death in 1748 makes the 1768 novel centered on him a ghost story, and it is fitting that our sentimental traveler's Shakespearean namesake entered literary history posthumously, as one dead long since. Object rather than subject ("thingsake" from the grave), Yorick is dead matter, his role in Shakespeare's drama determined by the props department rather than casting.[51] In this sense, Yorick the sentimental traveler is another it-narrator.

After he compares his bashful, homebody hero to a coin whose rust has not yet been rubbed off through travel, the narrator of *The Man of Feeling* observes that the typical Briton—the typical member of that nation of singular originals and real characters—does not even dare to "pen a *hic jacet* to speak out for him after his death" (3). At the same time that it sets the communicative functions of written characters at variance with the self-possession that permits the character to be himself, Mackenzie's metaphor destines the real character to an unmarked grave. In this situation of pathos we may locate the point of intersection between the history of characterization and the history of sentimentality: the character with a life of its own lives, by definition, on borrowed time.

Notes

A shorter version of this essay originally appeared in *Eighteenth-Century Fiction* 12.2–3 (2000): 345–68. The editors' permission to reprint is gratefully acknowledged.

1. *OED2*, s.v. "sentiment."

2. On sensibility and consumer culture, see G. J. Barker-Benfield, *The Culture of Sensibility: Sex and Society in Eighteenth-Century Britain* (Chicago: University of Chicago Press, 1992).

3. "Question: Ought Sensibility to be Cherished or Repressed?," *The Monthly Magazine* 2 (October 1796), quoted in Markman Ellis, *The Politics of Sensibility: Race, Gender and Commerce in the Sentimental Novel* (Cambridge: Cambridge University Press, 1996), 5.

4. Thomas Hood, "A Sentimental Journey from Islington to Waterloo Bridge,"

first published in the *London Magazine* in 1821, rpt. in Alan B. Howes, ed., *Sterne: The Critical Heritage* (London: Routledge & Kegan Paul, 1974), 367; G. M. Woodward, "Modern Sensibility," in *The Comic Works in Prose and Poetry of G. M. Woodward* (London: Thomas Tegg, 1808), 27.

5. Laurence Sterne, *A Sentimental Journey through France and Italy*, ed. Graham Petrie (Harmondsworth, UK: Penguin, 1986), 37. Subsequent references to *A Sentimental Journey* are to this edition and appear parenthetically in the text of my essay.

6. Compare the concerns expressed by the eccentric country gentleman Mr. Fenton in Henry Brooke's *The Fool of Quality:* "It is affirmed that the civil constitution of England is the best calculated for the security of liberty and property of any that ever was framed by the policy of man; and originally perhaps, it might have been so" (*The Fool of Quality* [1766–70; London: Macmillan, 1872], 149).

7. Sarah Scott, *The History of Sir George Ellison*, ed. Betty Rizzo (Lexington: University Press of Kentucky, 1996), 14, 142–47; my emphasis). Sir William's title to his chattels is, in a sense, presented as more secure than that of the sane: Sir George "considered Sir William as possessed of a *double* right to the enjoyment of his own fortune, first, as it solely belonged to him, a legal and material right; for if it was not his, it was no body's; no other person could justly lay claim to it: his other title was founded in humanity, no one being so true an object of compassion; for, in his opinion, no poverty was so much to be pitied as the poverty of the understanding" (146; my emphasis).

8. Nicholas Thomas, *Entangled Objects: Exchange, Material Culture, and Colonialism in the Pacific* (Cambridge, MA: Harvard University Press, 1991), 125. Wolfram Schmidgen has recently published an insightful book on the mutable manner in which property defines identity within eighteenth-century Britain's possessive cultures: *Eighteenth-Century Fiction and the Law of Property* (Cambridge: Cambridge University Press, 2002).

9. "Crying volumes" is the term for sentimental novels that Thomas Bridges's garrulous banknote uses when, in Sternean fashion, he interrupts his narrative of his adventures to address "Mr. Circulator of greasy volumes" (i.e., the proprietor of a circulating library) and to survey, with this interlocutor, the marketplace in which Bridges's book must compete for a readership: see *The Adventures of a Bank-Note*, 4 vols. (London: Thomas Davies, 1770–71), 3:5. Subsequent references to this work appear parenthetically in my text.

10. Henry Mackenzie, "Account of some Peculiarities in Mr. Umphraville—of Attachment to inanimate objects and to Home," *The Mirror* 61 (December 7, 1779), and *The British Essayists* (London: C. J. Rivington et al., 1823), 29:20.

11. Ian Watt, *The Rise of the Novel: Studies in Defoe, Richardson, and Fielding* (Berkeley and Los Angeles: University of California Press, 1957), 25, 32.

12. William B. Warner, *Licensing Entertainment: The Elevation of Novel Reading in Britain, 1684–1750* (Berkeley and Los Angeles: University of California Press, 1998), 38, xiv, n. 3.

13. W. J. Harvey, *Character and the Novel* (Ithaca, NY: Cornell University Press, 1965), 25.

14. William Hazlitt, *Lectures on the English Comic Writers* (London: Taylor & Hessey, 1819), 217, 242–43.

15. John Locke, "The Second Treatise of Civil Government," in *Two Treatises of Government*, ed. Thomas I. Cook (New York: Hafner, 1969), 134. I draw here on Alan Hyde's discussion of the body as property in *Bodies of Law* (Princeton, NJ: Princeton University Press, 1998), 55, 38.

16. See Hyde, *Bodies of Law*, 55, 28. In the first citation, Hyde is quoting Patricia J. Williams's *The Rooster's Egg* (Cambridge, MA: Harvard University Press, 1995).

17. For a more detailed account of eighteenth-century characterization's affinities

with the discourses of physiognomy, numismatics, and typography, see Deidre Shauna Lynch, *The Economy of Character: Novels, Market Culture, and the Business of Inner Meaning* (Chicago: University of Chicago Press, 1998), 29–47.

18. Eliza Haywood, *Love in Excess, or, The Fatal Enquiry,* ed. David Oakleaf (Peterborough, ON: Broadview Press, 1994), 75; Daniel Defoe, *An Essay upon Literature: Or, An Enquiry into the Antiquity and Original of Letters* (London, 1726), 2. On novelists' punning on "character," see also David Oakleaf, "Marks, Stamps, and Representations: Character in Eighteenth-Century Fiction," *Studies in the Novel* 23.3 (1991): 295–311, and Patrick Coleman, "Character in an Eighteenth-Century Context," *The Eighteenth Century: Theory and Interpretation* 24.1 (1983): 51–63.

19. "Hints of Prefaces for Clarissa," in *Clarissa: Preface, Hints of Prefaces, and Postscript,* introd. R. F. Brissenden (Los Angeles: William Andrews Clark Library and the Augustan Reprint Society, 1973), 12.

20. A comparable distinction separates a modern conception of sentiment from that of a culture able to treat the term as a designation not just for the feeling but also for feeling's vehicle, the "epigrammatical expression . . . often of the nature of a proverb" that makes it communicable and available for public consumption. See the *OED2,* s.v. "sentiment."

21. Jonathan Lamb takes the reply that Henry Fielding's Tom Thumb makes when asked about what the giants he has captured are like ("Like nothing but themselves") and makes this remark the starting point for a fascinating discussion of the status of singularity for Sterne: see his *Sterne's Fiction and the Double Principle* (Cambridge: Cambridge University Press, 1989), chap. 2, "Originality and the Hobbyhorse."

22. Richard W. F. Kroll, *The Material World: Literate Culture in the Restoration and Early Eighteenth Century* (Baltimore: Johns Hopkins University Press, 1991), 20.

23. *Tom Jones,* ed. Sheridan Baker (New York: Norton, 1973), 526. Compare John Barrell, *English Literature in History, 1730–80: An Equal, Wide Survey* (New York: St. Martin's Press, 1983), chap. 3.

24. Anon., *An Essay upon Money and Coins,* Part 1 (London: G. Hawkins, 1757), in John R. McCulloch, ed., *A Select Collection of Scarce and Valuable Tracts on Money* (London, 1856; rpt. New York: Augustus M. Kelley, 1966), 402. Locke had noted earlier how money memorializes a social contract of sorts, namely, that gold and silver are by "general consent the common pledge" for all the exchanges that can take place in civil society (*Some Considerations of the Consequences of the Lowering of Interest and Raising the Value of Money* [1692], quoted in James Thompson, *Models of Value: Eighteenth-Century Political Economy and the Novel* [Durham, NC: Duke University Press, 1996], 57).

25. Susan Stewart, *On Longing: Narratives of the Miniature, the Gigantic, the Souvenir, the Collection* (Baltimore: Johns Hopkins University Press, 1984), 135–38; I quote 138.

26. Ann Radcliffe, *The Mysteries of Udolpho,* ed. Bonamy Dobrée (Oxford: Oxford University Press, 1980), 342.

27. *An Inquiry into the Nature and Causes of the Wealth of Nations: A Selected Edition,* ed. Kathryn Sutherland (Oxford: Oxford University Press, 1993), 177.

28. [Francis Coventry], *The History of Pompey the Little; or, The Life and Adventures of a Lap-Dog* (London: M. Cooper, 1751), 262.

29. I discuss these episodes in somewhat different terms in *The Economy of Character,* 112–19.

30. Henry Mackenzie, *The Man of Feeling,* introd. Kenneth C. Slagle (New York: Norton, 1958), 29–30. Subsequent references are to this edition and appear parenthetically in the text.

31. The eponymous fool of quality, Harry Fenton, asks a poor man what he wishes in payment for the "priceless" lesson he has given him in the benefits of moderating

one's anger: "plucking a button from the upper part of my coat—I will accept of this token, my darling, says he" (*The Fool of Quality,* 256). When Thackeray gives the eighteenth-century novel a Victorian overhaul in *The History of Henry Esmond* (1852) he remembers such eighteenth-century love affairs through and with buttons: at the end of the novel we discover that during the visit she paid Henry in prison Rachel purloined a gold sleeve button from the arm of his coat and has ever since secretly worn it next to her heart.

32. For information on Boulton and buttons, see Neil McKendrick, "The Commercialization of Fashion," in Neil McKendrick, John Brewer, and J. H. Plumb, *The Birth of a Consumer Society: The Commercialization of Eighteenth-Century England* (Bloomington: Indiana University Press, 1985), 69–76. On Boulton and coins, see A. E. Feaveryear, *The Pound Sterling: A History of English Money* (Oxford: Clarendon Press, 1931), 175.

33. Patricia Spyer, "Introduction," in Spyer, ed., *Border Fetishisms: Material Objects in Unstable Spaces* (New York: Routledge, 1998), 1–3; Schmidgen, *Eighteenth-Century Fiction,* 116–21.

34. Jonathan Lamb, *Preserving the Self in the South Seas* (Chicago: University of Chicago Press, 2001), 147. Lamb draws, as do Schmidgen and the contributors to *Border Fetishisms,* on the germinal work of William Pietz, whose article "The Problem of the Fetish" appeared in three parts in *RES* 9 (1985): 5–14; *RES* 13 (1987): 23–44; and *RES* 16 (1988): 105–21.

35. Helenus Scott, *The Adventures of a Rupee, Wherein are interspersed various anecdotes Asiatic and European* (London: J. Murray, 1782), 103. Subsequent references are to this edition and appear in the text.

36. Thompson, *Models of Value,* 34.

37. William Blackstone, *Commentaries on the Laws of England* (1770), quoted in Lamb, *Preserving the Self,* 110.

38. Liz Bellamy, *Commerce, Morality, and the Eighteenth-Century Novel* (Cambridge: Cambridge University Press, 1998), 126.

39. I quote here from Henry Fielding, *Joseph Andrews and Shamela,* ed. Douglas Brooks-Davies (Oxford: Oxford University Press, 1980), 83, 57.

40. *The Fool of Quality,* 155. A "Jerusalem letter" is the tattoo that pilgrim-visitors to Jerusalem sometimes wore in testimony of their visit (*OED*). Fielding's and Brooke's readers would know that coins, sometimes sliced in half or clipped into easily identifiable shapes, often numbered among the "tokens" that were left with the anonymous infants who were deposited at London's Foundling Hospital (opened 1745); those tokens would enable parents returning at a later date to claim their children to identify them.

41. Compare Robert Markley, "Sentimentality as Performance: Shaftesbury, Sterne, and the Theatrics of Virtue," in *The New 18th Century,* ed. Felicity Nussbaum and Laura Brown (New York: Methuen, 1987), 210–30, and Ellis, *The Politics of Sensibility,* 129–35.

42. Thompson, *Models of Value,* 138.

43. See Lamb, "Originality and the Hobbyhorse."

44. Feaveryear, *The Pound Sterling,* 156.

45. Anon., *The Adventures of a Black Coat, Containing a Series of Remarkable Occurrence and Entertaining Incidents* (London: J. Williams, 1760), 42.

46. Given that Sterne alludes here to the narratives of circulation his contemporaries were writing, it seems fitting that the snuffbox that Yorick received from the friar and that he preserves as he "would the instrumental part of his religion" is appropriated by the anonymous author of *The Adventures of a Hackney Coach* (London: G. Kearsley, 1781), who mentions how great a price that box would obtain—"if Yorick's heirs would

dispose of it" (73)—and who also begins his narrative with the pretense that "an old worn-out pen of Yorick's" has found its way into his hand ("Dedication," n.p.). Yorick failed, or so it would appear, to keep his keepsakes.

47. The literature of sensibility, we know, seemed in especially vexing ways to be too easily replicated, and by the end of the eighteenth century, it had become all the fashion to claim that sentimental expression had become devalued and insipid through being too much in circulation. One reader lamented the mechanical reproducibility and marketability of these personal effects in a 1793 poem: "Yorick! indignant I behold / Such spendthrifts of thy genuine gold!" (Anon., "To Sensibility," *The Looker-On* 60 [June 23, 1793], quoted in Ellis, *The Politics of Sensibility*, 195).

48. The phrase is W. J. Harvey's in *Character and the Novel:* after he insists that novels cannot be written in an illiberal society, he adds that liberalism "is a luxury rarely allowed by history" (26). His book ascribed to the character the glamour of the soon-to-be-doomed.

49. Hippolyte Taine, *The History of English Literature,* trans. H. Van Laun, new ed., 4 vols. (London: Chatto and Windus, 1877), 3:268; Hazlitt, *Lectures on the English Comic Writers,* 305–06.

50. I owe the quotation from Marx to Susan Eilenberg's *Strange Power of Speech: Wordsworth, Coleridge, and Literary Possession* (New York: Oxford University Press, 1992), 261, n. 62. For George Ellison's reasoning about the right to make a will and his related argument that the best charitable gifts come, very precisely, from nobody, see *The History of Sir George Ellison,* 112–13 and 125. Participants in the mid-eighteenth-century debates about whether there was such a thing as literary property defined objects of property in ways that made the relations of the dead to the living crucial to their definitions, which are for this reason alone worth consulting. See, for instance, Mr. Baron Eyre, who in 1774 argued that if "Ideas" were "convertible into Objects of Property," they "should bear some feint [*sic*] Similitude to other [such] objects": but, in fact, "They cannot pass by Descent to Heirs; they were not liable to Bequest; no Characteristic Marks remain whereby to ascertain them" (*The Cases of the Appellants and Respondents in the Cause of Literary Property in The Literary Property Debate: Six Tracts, 1764–1774* [New York: Garland, 1975], 32).

51. Michael Seidel, "Narrative Crossings: Sterne's *A Sentimental Journey,*" *Genre* 18.1 (1985): 7; Robert Chibka, "The Hobby-Horse's Epitaph: *Tristram Shandy, Hamlet,* and the Vehicles of Memory," *Eighteenth-Century Fiction* 3.2 (1991), 130.

Suffering Things: Lapdogs, Slaves, and Counter-Sensibility

Markman Ellis

IN HIS *GENERAL HISTORY OF QUADRUPEDS* (1790), RALPH BEILBY ARGUED that writing a history of the dog—a "truly valuable creature . . . so eminently useful to the domestic interests of men"—would be a task equivalent to a history of mankind. It would begin with man and dog equal in "their original state of simplicity and freedom," but following the gradual "progress of civilisation," the history would conclude with man alone at the "head of the animal world" in "manifest superiority over every part of the brute creation." The key to the story, Beilby added, was that mankind's rise to preeminence and domination over the animals had only been possible through the assistance of "one so bold, so tractable, and so obedient as the Dog," without whose aid man could not have "conquered, tamed, and reduced other animals into slavery." Mankind was master, but only because of the faithful role of his gangmaster and enslaver, the dog.

The popular success of Beilby's natural history was to no small extent guaranteed by the book's generous provision of wood engravings of each of the animals by Thomas Bewick. For each of Beilby's kinds of dog, Bewick supplied a descriptive plate, together with ten ornamental tailpieces illustrating social interactions between dogs and mankind. Alongside depictions of the utility and faithfulness of working dogs to mankind were others giving evidence of mankind's failure to reciprocate. One of the vignettes showed two boys in the act of hanging a dog from the branch of a tree, throttling the animal with a noose around its neck. The boys appear to view the dog's death with equanimity—one sits in an easy posture on the ground, the other watches with arms folded—and they seem to have killed it for sport.[1] Dog-baiting was just one of the forms of cruelty to animals examined in the first plate of William Hogarth's series *The Four Stages of Cruelty* (1751). The accompanying verses describe the

> various Scenes of Sportive Woe
> The Infant Race Employ

3. Thomas Bewick, "[Vignette of Dog-Baiting]," in Ralph Beilby and Thomas Bewick, *A General History of Quadrupeds. The figures engraved on wood by T. Bewick* (Newcastle upon Tyne, UK: S. Hodgson, R. Beilby, and T. Bewick, 1790), 174. © The British Library Board (672.G.20).

And tortur'd Victims bleeding shew
The Tyrant in the Boy.[2]

Thomas Gainsborough's large-scale fancy picture, *Two Shepherd Boys with Dogs Fighting* (fig. C-3), well received when exhibited at the Royal Academy in 1783, depicts a tussle between two dogs and two boys in a rural setting. While the two hounds battle it out in the foreground, the boys react in different ways to the struggle. One looks on with sentimental concern, raising a stick as if to separate the dogs before they kill each other. The other, however, restrains his companion's arm, more interested in seeing the cruel spectacle of their fight.[3] These three images celebrating the atavistic relish for cruel sports argue that Beilby's teleology underplays the darker side of mankind's rise to domination over the animal kingdom, a barbarism noticed by his reference to animal slavery. As if to underline this, a tiny detail in the background of Bewick's woodblock depicts a gallows from which hangs a human corpse. Reading this plate as a narrative, Bewick would seem to imply that cruelty to animals leads to a life of crime terminated by the death penalty. But this plate could also be read as an analogy, in which Bewick argues that both dog-baiting and the death penalty are actuated by the same cruel and inhuman motives.

What conclusions can be drawn about these images depicting the pleasure derived from cruelty to animals? They seem to undermine the oft-made argument that the eighteenth century saw the emergence of a new moral understanding of animals among philosophers and writers alike. In this period, the problem of human and animal relations could not be extracted from the wider discussions of inequality, distress, and feeling. Dix Harwood argued in 1928 that eighteenth-century literature evinces a "flourishing tenderness toward animals."[4] According to Keith Thomas in *Man and the Natural World* (1983), "new sensibilities" in British culture developed a conception of the animal as an appropriate object of human sympathy by observing its capacity to suffer. Thomas argues that writers and philosophers working in the Shaftesburian tradition drew from the observation of animals' capacity for suffering the conclusion that they should be included within moral debate and treated with kindness.

There is no shortage of contemporary opinion that might be marshaled in support of this view. As the nonconformist divine Philip Doddridge explained in his *Lectures on Pneumatology* in 1763, "virtue obliges us to avoid whatever would be grievous to any of our fellow-creatures," continuing that "this law of universal benevolence extends itself even to the *brutes,* supposing them capable of sensation, and consequently of pleasure and pain." Given this law, Doddridge concludes, "a virtuous man would be cautious how he abuses them, (especially since they are generally supposed to have sensation)."[5] In his analysis of the issue in 1780, Jeremy Bentham wrote that both human beings and other animals experienced "the pleasures of good-will, the pleasures of sympathy, or the pleasures of the benevolent or social affections." Yet he observed that because "animals . . . stand degraded into the class of *things,*" they were treated without sympathy or kindness. As he remonstrated, "the question is not, Can they *reason?* nor, Can they *talk?* but, Can they *suffer?*"[6] Thomas Young's *Essay on Humanity to Animals* in 1798 cast his argument in the language of natural law by calling for the recognition of "the *Rights* of Animals" derived from their "capability of perceiving pleasure and pain."[7] In May 1809, Thomas Erskine's *Bill for More Effectually Preventing Malicious and Wanton Cruelty to Animals,* legally enforcing this new sensibility against suffering, was passed in the House of Lords, and although it failed in the Commons at this attempt, was finally passed in 1822.[8] This line of reasoning has been duly celebrated as the origin of the animal ethics debate now so fiercely fought between animal liberationists and the interests of research science.[9]

The coexistence and inter-reliance of the campaigns against animal cruelty and the slave trade—and the role of the discourse of sentimentalism in the emergence of both movements—has been the focus of much work in recent decades.[10] As Laura Brown has argued, "animals helped Europeans imagine Africans, Native Americans and themselves" by raising questions about what it is to be human.[11] The animal cruelty debate was not only interleaved with but reliant upon abolitionist debate on human cruelty in slavery. A central plank of the abolition campaign was a rethinking of the equation of slave and thing, and a concomitant redefinition of the slave as human being. Slaves, like animals, were degraded to the status of things, considered as property, and as such, not human—or at least, not human in the same way as the master.[12] Encouraging readers to imagine what it was like to be a slave was central to this abolitionist campaign. The motto of the Society for Effecting the Abolition of the Slave Trade, famously cast by Wedgwood in a medallion in 1787, advertised this thinking process, depicting a kneeling African slave asking, but not stating, "am I not a man and a

4. "Am I Not a Man and a Brother?" [engraving of the design for a cameo manufactured by Josiah Wedgwood at Etruria, derived from the seal of the Anti-Slavery Society, 1787], in Erasmus Darwin, *The Botanic Garden* (London: J. Johnson, 1791), part 1, opposite p. 87. © The British Library Board (448.f.16).

brother?"[13] The poetry, letters, and narratives of former slaves, such as those published by Phyllis Wheatley, Ignatius Sancho, and Olaudah Equiano, further served to demonstrate that slaves possessed human feeling.[14] The histories they narrated in these writings provided much evidence of the cruelty and suffering of the slave trade. In addition, the literary writing of former slaves bore eloquent witness to the essential inhumanity of the slave trade, testifying that it degraded human beings to the status of commodities and things, and treated them as such. As Henry Louis Gates, Jr. argues, writing was a complex "certificate of humanity," and many slaves literally wrote their way to freedom through the acquisition of literacy.[15] It is telling that the late-eighteenth-century slave narrative is considered a form of biography or life writing, and not an it-narrative.

This essay focuses on a strange loop in this Whiggish teleology of the emergence of human tenderness toward animals in the eighteenth century, exploring a complex knot of passages in literary writings that negotiate the appropriate quality of sympathy for animals and slaves, passages in which the status of both animals and slaves as things and commodities is central. As Bentham noted, animals were considered as members of "the class of things": it was this status, he argued, that allowed them to be treated cruelly. The first set of examples centers on lapdogs, especially a particular trope which depicts an animal being lavished with sympathy while humans suffer nearby: an example of what I call here "counter-sensibility." In this case, evidence of animal suffering or feeling is offered in pursuit of arguments about the sentimental value of human beings, about their moral and political status. Maximum ideological force is extracted from this trope when the treatment of the lapdog is conjoined with the treatment of the slave. Here the status of the lapdog, as that seeming oxymoron a feeling thing, is used to prize open the status of another oxymoron, the slave, or human thing.

I

Among the diverse schemes for the reformation of public manners encompassed in Jonas Hanway's epistolary travel account *A Journal of Eight Days Journey from Portsmouth to Kingston Upon Thames* of 1756 are his "Remarks on Lap-Dogs."[16] Observing the exaggerated grief of a woman in his traveling party over the death of her pet monkey, he finds evidence of what he calls "false tenderness," a condition he analyzes as symptomatic of the practice of sympathy among women of the higher stations of life.[17] Hanway allows that "a woman of sense may entertain a certain DEGREE of affection for a BRUTE" such as a dog, for the spe-

C-1. Paul Klee (1879–1940), *Die Büchse der Pandora als Stilleben* (Still Life of Pandora's Box), 1920. Oil and watercolor on paper, 16.8 × 24.1 cm. Photo by Jens Ziehe. Courtesy of the Berggruen Collection, the National Museums of Berlin. © 2022 Artists Rights Society (ARS), New York. See p. 46.

C-2. Jan Weenix, *Port de Mer*, 1704. Oil on canvas, 139 × 117 cm. Photo by Herve Lewandowski, Réunion des Musées Nationaux / Art Resource, New York. Courtesy of the Louvre, Paris. See p. 47.

C-3. Thomas Gainsborough, *Two Shepherd Boys with Dogs Fighting*, 1783. Oil on canvas, 223.5 × 157.5 cm. © Historic England Archive. See p. 93.

cies has some redeeming qualities: "Most dogs are SYCOPHANTS, but they are FAITHFUL." Even lapdogs, which do not have the utility of the shepherd's dog, might with "PROPER DISCIPLINE" be "instrumental to the FELICITY of fine ladies." But too often the "kind intentions of providence are perverted," and we see

> a fine lady act as if she thought the DOG, which happens to be under her precious care, is incomparably of more value, in her eyes, than a HUMAN creature, which is under the care of any other person, or peradventure, under no care at all. From hence we may conclude, that an immoderate love of a brute animal, tho' it may not destroy a charitable disposition, yet it often weakens the force of it.[18]

A wealthy merchant and a noted philanthropist, Hanway condemns "immoderate grief for trifles," thereby placing his discourse on lapdogs within the broader purview of his central concern, the critical analysis of public morals. He laments that the extraordinary care lavished on pet animals does not seem to lead to an increase in public benevolence: "The costly chicken is ordered for the CAT or DOG, by her who never thinks of giving a morsel of bread to relieve the hunger of a man."[19] Hanway urges that the quality of sympathy should in some sense be matched to the worth of the sufferer's suffering. "To estimate things as they really are, is a lesson few ever learn . . . for whatever the object is, the concern should be in proportion to the suffering."[20] Although Hanway is distinguished by the unusual length of his examination of the trope, he is keying into a historically enduring discussion of lapdogs.[21]

Lapdogs had long been a special case among domesticated animals. Without obvious utility, they were ineluctably identified with luxury and the corrupting influences of modern commercial society. They were, moreover, closely associated with the domestic and the feminine. Since the seventeenth century at least, the lapdog had been a misogynist trope of female venereal concupiscence, repeatedly described as one of the *artes amatoria* of the modern woman by libertine writers.[22] Echoes of this misogynist libertine lapdog trope can be found in the suggestive ambiguities of Belinda's relation to her lapdog Shock in Alexander Pope's *Rape of the Lock* (1714).

The semiotic confusion inspired by the lapdog was intensified by the difficulties eighteenth-century science had in classifying the animals. Natural historians considered the dog in general to be difficult to classify, as the "varieties of this animal" were "too many for even the most careful describer to mention."[23] As they recognized, the various kinds of dog did not cohere around stable breed categories, as all kinds of dog could and did interbreed. "That all these [breeds], however divided, compose one general family, is apparent, from the facility with which they intermix, produce, and re-produce."[24] Nonetheless, naturalists proposed various typologies of the breeds of the dog along the lines suggested by their systems of classification. In 1756, Linnaeus identified nine species of dog, of which the lapdog was included under the term "Pet Dog" or Maltese and given the name *Canis melitæus*. By 1792, Johann Friedrich Gmelin of Gottingen, in his new edition of the *Systema Naturae,* had extended the Linnaean classification to thirty-seven distinct species, dividing the "Pet Dogs" into four: Pyrame (*Canis brevipilis*), Shock-Dog (*Canis melitaeus*), Lion-Dog (*Canis leoninus*), and Little Danish Dog (*Canis variegatus*).[25] Working in the more impressionistic tradition of Buffon's natural history, Beilby's *General History of Quadrupeds* (1790) identified thirty different varieties of dog before giving up in exhaustion at the prospect of the "numberless variety of Messets, Lap-Dogs, Waps, Mongrels, and compounds without end."[26] As noticed above, each of Beilby's thirty kinds of dog was accompanied by a Bewick woodcut that depicted its distinct features and showed each in its appropriate context. Thus, the shepherd's dog was shown against the backdrop of a mountain fell dotted with sheep. The lapdog was no exception. Beilby described "*The Comforter*" as "a most elegant little animal, [that] is generally kept by the ladies as an attendant of the toilette or the drawing-room."[27] In the second edition, he added, "it is very snappish, ill-natured, and noisy."[28] In Bewick's woodcut the lapdog is shown in an interior, next to an ink pot and quill, suggesting a domestic setting. In a vignette below, an even smaller lapdog is depicted sitting on a table next to a bottle and pipe. Most clearly associated with the domestic and the private, the lapdog was far removed from the scene of work and utility.

The anomalous status of the lapdog in systems of knowledge perhaps informs the decision taken by dog-breeding organizations in the late nineteenth century to rename the "lapdog," using instead the term "toy dog." The Kennel Club of Great Britain, founded in 1873 to regulate canine pedigree breeding, identified toy dogs as one of its seven groups of breed (the others being Hound, Working, Terrier, Gundog, Pastoral, and Utility), and today there are twenty-three acknowledged toy-dog breeds amongst the 196 breeds currently recognized in the Kennel Club Stud Book.[29] These "groups" are typologically convenient but biologically incoherent: some reflect a utilitarian purpose, others a morphological similarity. Toy dogs are a miscellaneous group huddled together in this category simply according to their size.

As this quick survey underscores, the variety of dog known as the lapdog was primarily a social construction, not a product of natural history or zoology. Although all lapdogs could be located within a zoological classification, the lapdog does not lend itself to the classificatory nomenclature of science. Modern zoology finds all dogs to be the same species, all descended from and zoologically indistinguishable from the wolf, and toy dogs are merely breeds or subspecies of dog (or more radically, wolf).[30] Historical zoology avoids the use of the term "breed" when denoting specimens before the knowledge of genetics, using the term "variety" instead.[31] The lapdog was not a new variety in the eighteenth century; remains of dwarf or *brachymel* dogs have been identified in archaeological excavations from the Roman period in Italy and in the Roman provinces, and there are numerous visual records in Roman vases and wall paintings.[32] The intensity of the struggle over the meanings of the lapdog in the mid-eighteenth century, however, suggests that more was at stake than simply representing dogs and their varieties. In the examples that follow, the lapdog is a trope associated with some particular ideas about the feminine realm.

In the final volume of Sarah Fielding's *David Simple* (1753), a lapdog scene helps to elaborate the satiric portrait of Mrs. Orgeuil, a wealthy and powerful woman dominated by the envy and malevolence she feels for David and his "little Family of love." Like most of these examples, the lapdog trope is a concise bundle of received ideas and commonplace associations. Mrs. Orgeuil (her name means *pride* in French) is consistently selfish, hypocritical, and cruel, yet she is also proficient in affecting demonstrations of refined sensibility; the lapdog is shorthand for her character. When her husband falls ill, she enthusiastically takes up the role of the grieving widow, despite the fact that her husband is not yet dead. When he recovers, her grief nonetheless finds an outlet in a replacement activity:

> A most fatal Catastrophe befel her [Mrs Orgeuil]; and this Catastrophe was no other than the Loss of a little Lap-dog, which had reigned so long in her Favour, for it bit and snarled at every one it came near, except for herself and her poor little Thing, and on them it was remarkable for fawning . . . and this Lap-dog Mrs *Orgeuil* lamented in full as pathetic Terms as she had before done the imagined Death of her Husband.[33]

In finding an equivalence between husbands and lapdogs, Fielding deftly shows the confusion of values inherent in the figure of the worldly woman. Many other mid-eighteenth-century writers followed Fielding's rewriting of the lapdog. In *Lady Julia Mandeville* (1763), Frances Brooke also drew this equation: "a lover and a lapdog have a dreadful life," as both can be used "ill with impunity."[34] Brooke's lines recall Pope's zeugmatic equation between lapdogs and husbands in *The Rape of the Lock* (1714): "Not louder shrieks to pitying heav'n are cast, /

When husbands or when lapdogs breathe their last."[35] Coleridge's juvenile poem "Julia" (1789) covers similar ground in a ridiculous mode: the heroine's lover Florio accidentally crushes Julia's lapdog to death when falling to his knees to propose, and her immoderate grief for the puppy drives her lover away. Eliza Haywood's matrimonial conduct manual *The Wife* (1756) gave several examples of wives whose preference for their lapdogs, monkeys, and squirrels made it "hardly possible for a man to have any real regard" for them.[36] These cases of women "being over-fond of animals," as Haywood has it, read the expression of tenderness between humans and animals as an excessive regard for things.

A more elaborate version of the lapdog trope occurs in Sarah Scott's *Sir George Ellison* (1766). Here the context is a slave plantation that the sentimental hero has acquired through his marriage to a wealthy Anglo-Jamaican widow. From his sentimentally valorized principles of fellow feeling, George Ellison has proposed a reformation in the regime of violence and coercion endemic to the slave plantation, remonstrating with his wife that the slaves are human and ought to be treated as such. The lapdog scene here demonstrates Mrs. Ellison's insensitivity, her lack of fellow feeling with her human property. Scott relates that

> a favourite lap-dog, seeing her approach the house, in its eagerness to meet her jumped out of the window where it was standing; the height was too great to permit the poor cur to give this mark of affection with impunity; they soon perceived that it had broken its leg, and was in a good deal of pain; this drew a shower of tears from Mrs. Ellison's eyes, who, turning to her husband, said, "You will laugh at me for my weakness; but I cannot help it."

Here the injured lapdog induces Mrs. Ellison's sentimental response. Mr. Ellison explains that a "token of sensibility" is appropriate response to seeing the "affecting sight" of the "poor little animal." However, he goes on to say, "I confess I am surprized, though agreeably, to see such marks of sensibility in a heart I feared was hardened against the sufferings even of her fellow creatures." The trap is now sprung; an indignant Mrs. Ellison stops crying over her lapdog and asks her husband, "Sure, Mr. Ellison, you do not call negroes my fellow creatures?" Ellison responds that he "must call them so, till you can prove to me, that the distinguishing marks of humanity lie in the complexion or turn of features." With that, the couple return to the house to bandage the injured leg of the "poor little sufferer."[37] Here the lapdog allows contrasting kinds of compassion to be evaluated: despite her effusive response, Mrs. Ellison's compassion is shown to be shallow and unfeeling, as it does not extend to the genuine objects of compassion that lie within her power to help, the slaves whom she does not regard even as fellow human beings.

Other examples of lapdogs as subjects of immoderate sympathy proliferate in late-eighteenth-century fiction. In each case, as the recipient of excessive human regard, the lapdog is constructed both as inhuman and as a thing. In Oliver Goldsmith's *Vicar of Wakefield* (1766), the eponymous clergyman complained of the fashion for sentimentalizing lapdogs through tales of affected sensibility in modern elegies. The "great fault" of these sentimental poetasters, the Vicar remarks, is "that they are in despair for griefs that give the sensible part of mankind very little pain. A lady loses her muff, her fan, or her lap-dog, and so the silly poet runs home to versify the disaster."[38] In the first chapter of Henry Mackenzie's *Man of Feeling* (1771), the hero Harley finds a "young lady's favourite lap-dog" occupying the seat of his departed childhood friend Ben Silton. While Harley suggests that Silton was worthy of a tear—"the cordial drop that falls to your memory now"—he is outraged to find his friend's memory erased by the excessive attention paid to the lapdog. In response, "in the bitterness" of the moment's reflection, Harley pinches its ear, causing the animal to howl and run to its mistress. Soothing her distraught hound, the young lady "bewailed" the lapdog "in the most pathetic terms; and kissing it on its lips, laid it gently on her lap, and covered it with a cambric handkerchief."[39] Mary Wollstonecraft's *Vindication of the Rights of Woman* (1792) is imbued with the trope of the lapdog, using it to attack the systems of behavioral and moral slavery that subjugate women.[40] In Fanny Burney's late novel *The Wanderer* (1814), Mrs. Ireton is so indulgent of her lapdog that she forces her family to accompany her to Brighthelmstone for the benefit of the lapdog's health. Throughout the novel, Mrs. Ireton's indulgence of the lapdog encodes the novel's critique of the excessive regard for fashion and luxury commodities among the higher stations. In one scene, Mrs. Ireton's excessive kindness to the lapdog is contrasted with the threat she makes to her black servant that she will return him to slavery in the West Indies if he continues to disobey her whims and wishes.[41]

As these examples clarify, the trope of the lapdog was increasingly deployed in attacks on the corrupting influence of luxury and fashion, and, as such, imbricated in a discourse on things. In these cases, lapdogs are the avatar of what I want to call "counter-sensibility" because they emblematize the malevolent, spiteful, and hypocritical quality of their female owners, who demonstrate an "unfeeling" nature. Their canine bodies are luxurious in themselves (expensive commodities consuming expensive commodities), and in their snappy biting ways they literalize the cruel violence of their owners, even as they are shown to be the recipients of misdirected sentimental feeling, inordinate caresses, excessive affection and grief. It is in this disparity between absent feeling and excessive feeling that the discourse of counter-sensibility is forged. In this way, counter-sensibility is not the same as lack of sensibility or insensibility—rather, it uses the rhetoric and resources of sensibility against itself.

II

The animadversions of these writers from Hanway to Wollstonecraft point to a particular problem that the lapdog identifies in the theory of sympathy in mid-eighteenth-century philosophy. The trope of the lapdog occupies a curious and fragile space within both the discourse on things and the discourse on sympathy. Sympathy, of course, was subject to intense analysis in this period by moral philosophers. Both David Hume and Adam Smith proposed that sympathy, rather than self-interest, was the "spring" or "movement" of human endeavor, as Hume put it.[42] Hume argued that "no quality of human nature is more remarkable, both in itself and its consequences, than that propensity we have to sympathize with others, and to receive by communication their inclinations and sentiments, however different from, or even contrary to, our own."[43] In *The Theory of Moral Sentiments* (1759), Smith observes that, "as we have no immediate experience of what other men feel, we can form no idea of the manner in which they are affected, but by conceiving what we ourselves should feel in the like situation."[44]

In Smith's account of sympathy, imagination gets us inside the experience of the suffering other. Our senses, he explains, never "carry us beyond our own person, and it is by the imagination only that we can form any conception" of the sensations of the sufferer: "By the imagination we place ourselves in his situation, we conceive ourselves enduring all the same torments, we enter as it were into his body, and become in some measure the same person with him, and thence form some idea of his sensations, and even feel something which, though weaker in degree, is not altogether unlike them" (9). Sympathy, an act of imagination in which we project ourselves into the place of another, produces in the sympathizer a kind of pleasure. This sympathetic pleasure is only possible if the sufferings of the object do not press too nearly: Smith describes the delicate maneuverings and recalculations of self-presentation necessary to achieve a double sympathy, where the sufferer receives a kind of pleasure from the perception of the other's sympathy.[45] In this way, we share our disagreeable passions with our friends, because we receive more satisfaction from their sympathy with our grief than with our joys: "How are the unfortunate relieved when they have found out a person to whom they can communicate the cause of their sorrow? Upon his sympathy they seem to disburthen themselves of a part of their distress: he is not improperly said to share it with them." Sharing a misfortune with a friend reawakens the "memory of the circumstance which occasioned their affliction":

> Their tears accordingly flow faster than before, and they are apt to abandon themselves to all the weakness of sorrow. They take pleasure, however, in all this, and, it is evident, are sensibly relieved by it; because the sweetness of his sympathy more than compensates the bitterness of that sorrow, which, in order to excite this sympathy, they had enlivened and renewed. (15)

Sympathy is founded on the spectator's ability to make a momentary but complete imaginary change of situation with the person principally concerned, although the spectator's emotions will be less violently felt (21–22).

Where Smith proposes that propriety is the measure of sympathy (achieved by a process of negotiating feelings in the sympathetic exchange and leading to the moment of double sympathy), Hanway reverts to a less complex sentimentalist scheme in which the proper level of sympathy is simply expressed in the signifying body language of tears and blushes. Whether one has achieved the "certain measure of grief," Hanway claims, will be ascertained by the sentimental index of the feeling body: it "adds a lustre to the brightest eyes, which have most power to charm, when bathed in tears." Hanway adds, however, that some things are not worthy of our fellow feeling: "We must mourn that rational beings, subject to so many real calamities, can act so irrationally as to waste their grief, and torment themselves for objects of so little value."[46]

Are animals appropriate objects of sympathy? The central problem posed by animals for Adam Smith's theory of sympathy is their liminal status as feelers. Smith noted that "animals are not only the causes of pleasure and pain, but are also capable of feeling those sensations" (95). In this way, we might suppose them proper objects of sympathy. But there is a problem with reciprocity, for in Smith's estimation it is not at all clear that animals are capable of feeling sympathy for humans in the same way that humans can feel sympathy for them. And this double sympathy—this potential for reciprocated sympathy—is central to Smith's theory of moral sentiments and the virtuous society it proposes. Feeling sympathy for animals, then, is dogged by the doubt that the animal is not capable of estimating the propriety of that sympathy. "What gratitude chiefly desires," Smith writes, "is not only to make the benefactor feel pleasure in his turn, but to make him conscious that he meets with this reward on account of his past conduct, to make him pleased with that conduct, and to satisfy him that the person upon whom he bestowed his good offices was not unworthy of them" (95). In Adam Smith's account, sympathy does not extend to animals because one cannot imagine what it is like to be a dog in the same way that one can imagine what it is like to be another human. Here the difference between the status of the slave and the animal comes into play. Even if animals are accorded sentience, the capacity to suffer, or various kinds of mental status, it is still the case that one cannot imagine the experience of an animal.[47] This conclusion has been reiterated by the animal behaviorist Frans de Waal in his study of bonobo monkeys entitled *Chimpanzee Politics* (1981), wherein he proposes that although the faculty of sympathy is evident in monkeys and apes, this sympathy only extends between members of their own species. By contrast, numerous abolitionists and sentimentalists identified the suasive power of the capacity to understand the suffering of a slave as a human.

Techniques for the representation of things thinking and feeling—whether slaves, dogs, animals, toys, or banknotes—are central to mid-eighteenth-century enquiry about this difference. As Liz Bellamy argues in this volume, when the it-narrative first emerged in the early eighteenth century, it was typically narrated in the third person, using the circulation trope to occasion a quasi-picaresque satire of greater or lesser extent. But by the end of the century, or more precisely after about 1780, writers using the genre of the it-narrative began to adopt a nonhuman narrative voice, a technique also known as an object-narrator. Among the first of these experiments is *The Adventures of a Whipping-Top* (1780?), a brief children's chapbook published by John Marshall in Aldermary Churchyard, which declares on the title page that it is "written by itself," although this is inconsistently maintained by the text itself.[48] The chapbook it-narratives of Dorothy and Mary Ann Kilner in the 1780s, such as *The Memoirs of a Peg-Top* (1785?) and *The Life and Perambulation of a Mouse* (1785?), further claim to be narrated by a thing or animal—"the following history . . . is *made believe* to be related by a mouse"—as do many others, such as *Memoirs of Dick, the Little Poney, Supposed to be written by himself* (1800) or *The Dog of Knowledge; or, Memoirs of Bob, the Spotted Terrier: Supposed to be written by Himself* (1801).[49] In narratological terms, such narrators are said to be present in the story they themselves narrate, and so, using Gérard Genette's terminology, are called overt homodiegetic narrators (they can hardly be called "first-person narrators").[50] Of course, despite the adoption of a homodiegetic narrator, such texts no more try to think and feel like a dog or a pony than they do a wooden toy or a pincushion. In fact, such narrators think and feel like humans, asking their readers to think and feel what it is like to be a human. Such stories depend for their narrative energy on an essential incompatibility between the narrator's animal (or even inanimate) point of view and its human comprehension of the things around it (the peg top is not only human but English, Christian, pious, and so forth).

None of the literary examples discussed above constitute attempts to think like a dog or to fully inhabit the mind of an animal. Even the immersive animal sympathy imagined by Sterne, where Yorick claims to enter fully into the feelings of the beast, is narrated from the human point of view, and the experience it describes is solely related to human feelings and emotions. As these attempts reveal, the project of writing as a dog is absurd, a contradiction in terms, a fictional construction, as the supposed act of translation between dog-think and human language is not possible, no more possible than it would be to understand how a piece of wood thinks.[51] That this is an uncrossable abyss is clear, even though it is equally clear that dogs think, feel, and emote, that they may even have self-awareness, memory, and language (the key indicators of higher mental activity according to the animal-ethics theorist David DeGrazia).[52] The case with a slave narrative is essentially different. *The Interesting Narrative of the Life of Olaudah Equiano, or Gustavus Vassa, the African* (1789) also claims on the title page to be "Written by Himself."[53] When a reader encounters a slave narrative written in the voice of the slave, a reciprocal sympathy can be imagined, and the essential humanity of the slave is made apparent, even when the narrator explains how he or she has been degraded to the status of a thing.

III

The lapdog moments surveyed here point to an interesting problem for mid-eighteenth-century ethics. By comparing and contrasting the kinds of excessive sympathy sentimental characters feel for their lapdogs with the real human misery they ignore around them, writers expose a significant impasse in sympathy theory. Adam Smith did not include animals in his account of sympathy because, as he imagines that activity, it is not possible to sympathize with them. Following Adam Smith's account, those like Mrs. Ellison in Scott's novel who lavished excessive pity on their lapdogs were doing something categorically autologous, isolated within their own imagination. But whereas it is not possible to imagine what it is like to be a dog, it is quite possible to imagine what it is like to be a slave, for a slave is ineluctably human. In fact, Mrs. Ellison's failure to identify with the slaves as she does with her lapdogs shows not her belief that they are not human, but rather her failure to imagine herself as human.

An intriguing and productive examination of this problem is undertaken in Stanley Cavell's *Claim of Reason* (1979), in a section that discusses apparently irrefutable claims that are not in fact believable as assertions. Cavell examines a claim made by slave owners in defense of their property in men—that their slaves are not fully human.[54] In Cavell's estimation, for example, Mrs. Ellison's judgment that her slaves are not her fellow humans "cannot fully be meant."[55] As Cavell reasons, slave owners know what it is to be human, yet they consider some human beings slaves, and seeing them as slaves, treat them as animals. As Cavell says (he imagines all slave owners are men), "everything in his relation to his slaves shows that he treats them as more or less human—his humiliations of them, his disappointments, his jealousies, his fears, his punishments, his attachments."[56] The slave owner has power over his slaves, but must deny that his slaves perceive him as he perceives them.

The negotiation of a practical sentimental ethics in the late eighteenth century saw simultaneous campaigns for the relief of the poor, chimney sweeps, debtors, writers, emigrants, and prostitutes, as well as the emergence of the abolitionist campaign. Nonetheless, slavery is the paradigmatic controversy for sentimentalism because only in the case of slavery did the sentimental strategy of demonstrating the human suffering of the slave fundamentally change the construction of the slave from animal to human, from nonsocial to social being, from social death to social life. Scenes in sentimental novels depicting displays of sympathy between master and slave reveal the shifting and complex dynamics of power in the master-slave relationship. Abolitionist discourse made much of such scenes, trusting to their sentimental rhetoric the work of persuading their readers that slaves were human like them. By depicting the slaves as feeling, and thinking, like humans, such scenes reveal the essential inhumanity of the state of slavery. Such scenes, then, imply an implicit revolt against the social condition of slavery. By contrast with the slave, the lapdog cannot reciprocate the act of sympathy: there is no mutual understanding to the sympathetic scene. The dog's sympathetic look or extended paw simulates but does not manifest sympathy. The lapdog trope depicts an extreme example of this sympathetic failure by instancing an animal lavished with benevolent care and sympathy but neither interested in nor capable of reciprocation.

Nonetheless, the campaigns against slavery and animal cruelty remained intertwined in the public imagination. Just as the lapdog trope had helped uncouple the equation between slaves and animals as moral subjects, so too in the animal cruelty debate a slave trope allowed the feelings of animals to be taken seriously on moral grounds. Having first been introduced into Parliament in 1789, the Act for the Abolition of the Trade in Slaves was finally passed in the session of 1807.[57] By this Act, African slaves traded between Africa and the Americas were deemed humans rather than things, and as such, accorded certain rights within the British jurisdiction. The controversy over slavery caused by the abolition debate focused attention on the question of the boundary between animals and humans, things and not things. The example of the campaign against the slave trade motivated other active citizens to mount a campaign against cruelty to animals. The English Jacobin and radical vegetarian John Oswald had made the connection between slavery and animal cruelty in his tract *The Cry of Nature* (1791), in which he cited slavery as an example of the ways man "disclaims the ties of kindred."[58] Just as the abolitionists sought to reposition Africans as thinking and feeling people, the animal-cruelty campaigners sought to refigure the cultural construction of the brute creation, showing them to be not things but animals possessed with feeling and thus endowed with certain rights. Proponents for the Prevention of Animal Cruelty Bill in the early nineteenth century produced a series of texts celebrating instances of canine sagacity and benevolence, such as Joseph Taylor's *Canine Gratitude* (1808), imagining human emotions in a canine register.[59] The Prevention of Cruelty campaign reverberated with the new sensibilities of Shaftesburian ethics and philanthropic reform, just as the Abolition campaign had.

In his *Introduction to the Principles of Morals and Legislation* (1789), Jeremy Bentham argued that the art of government ought to take into account both "other human beings who are styled persons" and "other animals, which . . . stand degraded into the class of *things*."[60] In the famous footnote cited in the introduction to this essay, Bentham asked, "is there any reason why we should be suffered to torment them?" His answer was that as they feel and suffer, so must they be included within the realm of sympathy. His reasoning, however, was by way of an analogy with slavery:

> The day has been, I grieve to say in many places it is not yet past, in which the greater part of the species, under the denomination of slaves, have been treated by the law exactly upon the same footing, as, in England for example, the inferior races of animals are still. The day *may* come, when the rest of the animal creation may acquire those rights which never could have been withholden from them but by the hand of tyranny. The French have already discovered that the blackness of the skin is no reason why a human being should be abandoned without redress to the caprice of a tormentor.

When these lines were published in 1789, slavery was illegal in metropolitan England but not in its West Indian colonies—nor for that matter in most of the states of the United States. Invoking the abolitionists' image of a humanity incorporated in rather than divided by the corporeal marker of complexion, Bentham concludes that "the number of the legs" and "the villosity of the skin" (the state of being covered in long shaggy hairs) were "reasons equally insufficient for abandoning a sensitive being to the same fate" of slavery.[61]

In *The Dog of Knowledge* (1801), the homodiegetic thing-narrator Bob the Spotted Terrier, having been stolen by a soldier, is taken to Jamaica, a journey that ironically mimics the Middle Passage. In the sugar colony, Bob is moved by the observation of "many apparently human beings, who were doomed to the severest daily toils." From such a spectacle, the narrator "turned away in horror":

> I felicitated myself on being born a dog, and not a negro, as these poor creatures are called. To be sure, they had not the complexion of Europeans, and perhaps possessed none of the same delicate sensibilities; yet they walked on two legs like the rest of the species, and seemed to me to differ in nothing but in the colour of their skin and the contour of their face.
>
> However, there must certainly be a fallacy in appearances; and these can only be a particular, though singular kind of animals, that are born to subjection, the same as dogs or horses. Man surely could never tyrannize over his fellow-man without compunction, nor dare to injure him with impunity.[62]

Bob's narration obscures—yet somehow underlines—the difference between the ethical status of humans and animals, even as it highlights and clarifies the ubiquity of their suffering. Such distinctions between dog thinking and dog sympathy continue to be dramatized when Bob professes not to understand when his master repeats a couplet from Hannah More's abolitionist verses *Slavery:* "Say, does th'eternal principle within / Change with the casual colour of the skin."[63] Bob's master, Hannah More, and Sarah Scott all perform the same kind of sentimental calculus: complexion is found wanting when weighed against the common humanity of the human species.

Nonetheless, the link between abolition and animal sympathy continued when Lord Erskine introduced his Prevention of Cruelty to Animals bill into the House of Lords in 1808. In his passionate speech, Erskine argued for the benevolent treatment of animals as our fellow creatures: "Animals are considered as *property* only—To destroy or abuse them, from malice to the proprietor, or with an intention injurious to his interest in them, is criminal—*but the animals themselves are without protection*—the law regards them not *substantively*—they have no

RIGHTS!"[64] In this way, his rhetoric and frame of reference argued that the same sentimental calculus that drove the abolition-of-slavery debate ought to drive the vote against cruelty to animals. His legislation made clear his debt to the Act for the Abolition of the Trade in Slaves. But Erskine could not marshal the same repertoire of arguments about sympathy to his cause: animals remained things, even if, as he urged, they should be treated with the kindness and compassion known as human.

Notes

I am grateful to John Barrell, Becky Beasley, Mark Blackwell, Vincent Carretta, James Chandler, Harriet Guest, Richard Hamblyn, Ian Haywood, Claudia Johnson, Jonathan Lamb, and James Watt for their comments on this essay.

1. Ralph Beilby and Thomas Bewick, *A General History of Quadrupeds. The figures engraved on wood by T. Bewick* (Newcastle upon Tyne, UK: S. Hodgson, R. Beilby, and T. Bewick, 1790), 281–82, 274. In different editions the location of the tailpieces varies.

2. William Hogarth, "First Stage of Cruelty," in *The Four Stages of Cruelty* (London, 1751).

3. Christine Riding and Michael Rosenthal, "60. Shepherd Boys with Dogs Fighting," in *Gainsborough*, ed. Michael Rosenthal and Martin Myrone (London: Tate Publishing, 2002), 142; Michael Rosenthal, *The Art of Thomas Gainsborough: 'A Little Business for the Eye'* (London: Yale University Press for the Paul Mellon Centre for Studies in British Art, 1999), 108–10.

4. Dix Harwood, *Love for Animals and How It Developed in Great Britain* (New York: Faculty of Philosophy, Columbia University, 1928), 235.

5. Philip Doddridge, *A Course of Lectures on the Principal Subjects in Pneumatology, Ethics, and Divinity: with References to the most considerable Authors on each subject*, ed. Samuel Clark (London: J. Buckland, J. Rivington, R. Baldwin, et al., 1763), 129–30. Pneumatology is the medieval theory of the spirit world, used in the eighteenth century to refer to philosophy of mind, or psychology.

6. Jeremy Bentham, *Introduction to the Principles of Morals and Legislation* (printed 1780, first published 1789), ed. J. H. Burns and H. L. A. Hart (Oxford: Clarendon Press, 1996), 282 n.

7. Thomas Young, *An Essay on Humanity to Animals* (London: T. Cadell and W. Davies, and W. H. Lunn; Cambridge: J. Deighton, 1798), 8.

8. 3. Geo. IV. c.71 (1822). Thomas Erskine, *Cruelty to Animals. The Speech of Lord Erskine, in the House of Peers, on the Second Reading of the Bill for Preventing Malicious and Wanton Cruelty to Animals* (Edinburgh: Alex. Lawrie, 1809). Acts of Parliament were passed against cruelty to horses and cattle in 1822, against cruelty to dogs in 1839 and 1854, and against baiting and cock-fighting in 1835 and 1849. The Society (later Royal Society) for the Prevention of Cruelty to Animals was founded in 1824. See Keith Thomas, *Man and the Natural World: Changing Attitudes in England 1500–1800* (1983; Oxford: Oxford University Press, 1996), 149–50; and Brian Harrison, "Animals and State in Nineteenth-Century England," *English Historical Review* 88.349 (1971): 787–820.

9. The debate is surveyed in David DeGrazia, *Taking Animals Seriously: Mental Life and Moral Status* (New York: Cambridge University Press, 1996), 1–9; and John Gluck, Tony DiPasquale, and Barbara Orlans, *Applied Ethics in Animal Research: Philosophy, Reg-*

ulation, and Laboratory Applications (West Lafayette, IN: Purdue University Press, 2002), 1–10. Tom Regan, *The Case for Animal Rights* (Berkeley and Los Angeles: University of California Press, 1983), and Peter Singer, *Animal Liberation: A New Ethics for Our Treatment of Animals* (New York: New York Review, 1975), argued that the feelings of animals should be taken into account in ethical questions. In "The Case for the Use of Animals in Biomedical Research," *New England Journal of Medicine* 315 (1986): 865–70, Carl Cohen argued that animals were not capable of higher reasoning and the notion of rights could not be extended to them.

10. Markman Ellis, *The Politics of Sensibility* (Cambridge: Cambridge University Press, 1996), 47–114; Brycchan Carey, *British Abolitionism and the Rhetoric of Sensibility: Writing, Sentiment, and Slavery, 1760–1807* (Basingstoke, UK: Palgrave Macmillan, 2005).

11. Laura Brown, *Fables of Modernity: Literature and Culture in the English Eighteenth Century* (Ithaca, NY: Cornell University Press, 2001), 221–65, 262. A connection between Abolition and the Prevention of Cruelty to Animals Campaign is made repeatedly by Keith Thomas in *Man and the Natural World* (44–45, 184–87, 291–95), although he does not make the relation between the former and the latter causal: rather, they both represent examples of a general rise in sentimentalism.

12. Abolitionist rhetoric sharpened legal definitions of slavery as perpetual labor—"an absolute and unlimited power . . . given to the master over the life and fortune of the slave," according to William Blackstone (*Commentaries on the Laws of England*, 4 vols., [Oxford: Clarendon Press, 1765–69], 1:410)—so as to liken the slave to a commodity or thing. A "cargo of slaves" is the equivalent of a "cargo of lumber" in Africanus, *Remarks on the Slave Trade, and the Slavery of the Negroes* (London: J. Phillips, 1788), 2.

13. Wedgwood and Sons Ltd., "Am I Not a Man and a Brother?" Wedgwood medallion derived from the seal of the Anti-Slavery Society, 1787, Trustees of the Wedgwood Museum, Barlaston, Staffordshire, England.

14. *"Genius in Bondage": Literature of the Early Black Atlantic*, ed. Vincent Carretta and Philip Gould (Lexington: University Press of Kentucky, 2001).

15. Henry Louis Gates, Jr., "Editor's Introduction: Writing 'Race' and the Difference It Makes," in *"Race," Writing, and Difference*, ed. Henry Louis Gates, Jr. (Chicago: University of Chicago Press, 1986), 1–20.

16. Jonas Hanway, "Remarks on Lap-dogs," *A Journal of Eight Days Journey from Portsmouth to Kingston Upon Thames; through Southampton, Wiltshire, etc. With Miscellaneous Thoughts, Moral and Religious; . . . To which is added, an Essay on Tea . . . With Several Political Reflections; and thoughts on Public Love* (London: H. Woodfall, 1756), 65–85.

17. John Pugh, *Remarkable Occurrences in the Life of Jonas Hanway, Esq. Comprehending an Abstract of such Parts of his Travels in Russia, and Persia, as are the most Interesting; a Short History of the Rise and Progress of the Charitable and Political Institutions Founded or Supported by Him; Several Anecdotes, and an Attempt to Delineate his Character* (London: J. Davis, 1787).

18. Hanway, *Journal*, 69–70.

19. Ibid., 70.

20. Ibid., 72.

21. *OED2*. First use is recorded as John Evelyn's *Diary*, May 1645.

22. [Robert Gould], *Love Given Over: or, a Satyr against the Pride, Lust, and Inconstancy, &c. of Woman* (London: R. Bentley and J. Tonson, 1690); *A Voyage to Lethe; by Captain Samuel Cock; sometime commander of the Good Ship, the Charming Sally* (Glasgow: Mrs. Laycock at Mr. Clevercock's, 1756).

23. Oliver Goldsmith, *An History of the Earth, and Animated Nature*, 8 vols. (London: J. Nourse, 1774), 3:278.

24. Beilby, *General History of Quadrupeds,* 317.

25. *The Animal Kingdom of the celebrated Sir Charles Linnæus; Class I. Mammalia: containing a complete systematic description, arrangement, and nomenclature, of all the known species and varieties of the mammalia, or animals which give suck to their young; being a translation of that part of the Systema Naturæ, as lately published with great improvements by Professor Gmelin of Gottingen,* trans. Robert Kerr (London: J. Murray and R. Faulder, 1792), 131–32.

26. Beilby, *General History of Quadrupeds,* 312.

27. Ibid., 312.

28. Ibid., 332. Bewick's animal vignettes further suggest a complex allegorization of the relationships of dependence, pleasure, and pain between man and animals. Other vignettes depict a performing bear and monkey (256), a dog being ridden by a child (342), a rat caught in a trap (356), a boy releasing a mouse from a trap for a cat to play with (364), and a pet monkey playing with a razor on a dressing table (414).

29. See *The Kennel Club's Illustrated Breed Standards: The Official Guide to Registered Breeds* (London: Ebury, 1998) and "Kennel Club Breed Standards," http://www.the-kennel-club.org.uk (accessed November 11, 2002). The Toy Dog Show Society was registered by the Kennel Club in 1899; see Edward William Jaquet, *The Kennel Club: A History and Record of its Work* (London: The Kennel Gazette, 1905), 248–49.

30. According to Juliet Clutton-Brock, *A Natural History of Domesticated Mammals,* 2nd ed. (Cambridge: Cambridge University Press, 1999), a species is "a group of actually or potentially interbreeding natural populations that is genetically isolated from other such groups as a result of physiological or behavioural barriers" (41–42). "A subspecies is a distinctive, geographical segment of a species, that is, it comprises a group of wild animals that is geographically and morphologically separate from other such groups within a single species" (42). "A breed is a group of animals that has been selected by humans to possess a uniform appearance that is inheritable and distinguishes it from other groups of animals within the same species" (41). In this sense, though subspecies and breed are broadly similar, breed is preferred for living domesticated animals.

31. The term "breed" should properly be used only for modern dogs, where reproduction is controlled by humans with the knowledge of genetics. The word "variety" is used for populations of dogs in earlier times. Juliet Clutton-Brock, "Introduction," in Susan Janet Crockford, ed., *Dogs Through Time: An Archaeological Perspective: Proceedings of the 1st ICAZ Symposium on the History of the Domestic Dog: Eighth Congress of the International Council for Archaeozoology (ICAZ98), August 23–29, 1998, Victoria, B.C., Canada,* BAR International Series 889 (Oxford: Archaeopress, 2000), 3–10.

32. Jacopo De Grossi Mazzorin and Antonio Tagliacozzo, "Morphological and Osteological Changes in the Dog from the Neolithic to the Roman Period in Italy," in Crockford, *Dogs Through Time,* 141–61.

33. Sarah Fielding, *The Adventures of David Simple,* ed. Linda Bree (London: Penguin, 2002), 394 (bk. 7, chap. 8). See Linda Bree, *Sarah Fielding* (New York: Twayne, 1996), 80–90.

34. Frances Brooke, *Lady Julia Mandeville,* 2 vols. (London, 1763), 2:35. Samuel Taylor Coleridge, *The Complete Poems,* ed. William Keech (London: Penguin, 1998), 7–8.

35. Alexander Pope, *The Rape of the Lock* (1714), in *The Poems of Alexander Pope,* ed. John Butt (London: Methuen, 1963), 231 (3.158).

36. Eliza Haywood, *The Wife* (London: T. Gardner, 1756), 187–94.

37. Sarah Scott, *The History of Sir George Ellison,* 2 vols. (London: A. Millar, 1766), 25–28 (1.2). See also Ellis, *The Politics of Sensibility,* 87–114; Brown, *Fables of Modernity,* 254–56.

38. Oliver Goldsmith, *The Vicar of Wakefield,* ed. Stephen Coote (1766; London: Penguin, 1982), 106.

39. Henry Mackenzie, *The Man of Feeling,* ed. Brian Vickers (1771; Oxford: Oxford University Press, 2001), 8.

40. Mary Wollstonecraft, *A Vindication of the Rights of Woman: An Authoritative Text, Backgrounds, The Wollstonecraft Debate, Criticism,* A Norton Critical Edition, 2nd ed. (New York: Norton, 1988), 100, 155, 221–22, 251, 258–59.

41. Fanny Burney, *The Wanderer; or, Female Difficulties,* ed. Margaret Anne Doody, Robert Mack, and Peter Sabor (1814; Oxford: Oxford University Press, 1991), 233 (3.6.51–52). See also Hannah More, "Sensibility: An Epistle to the Honourable Mrs. Boscawen," *Sacred Dramas,* (London, 1784), lines 279–84.

42. David Raynor, ed., "Hume's *Abstract of Adam Smith's Theory of Moral Sentiments* (May 1759)," *Journal of the History of Philosophy,* 22.1 (1984): 65–79.

43. David Hume, *Treatise of Human Nature,* ed. L. A. Selby-Bigge, 2nd ed., rev. P. H. Nidditch (Oxford: Clarendon Press, 1978), 316 (3.40).

44. Adam Smith, *The Theory of Moral Sentiments,* ed. D. D. Raphael and A. L. Macfie, vol. 1 of *The Glasgow Edition of the Works and Correspondence of Adam Smith* (1759; Oxford: Clarendon Press, 1976), 9. All further references will be cited parenthetically.

45. Sympathy "alleviates grief by insinuating into the heart almost the only agreeable sensation which it is at that time capable of receiving" (Smith, *Theory of Moral Sentiments,* 14). Grief is measured in tears (15), in a kind of sentimental calculus whose index is hydroptics.

46. Hanway, *Journal,* 72.

47. See Frans B. M. de Waal, *Chimpanzee Politics* (Baltimore: Johns Hopkins University Press, 1982).

48. *The Adventures of a Whipping-Top* (London, [1780?]). The dating of this text, and all these so-called chapbooks, is conjectural. An earlier example, albeit an anomalous hybrid of the spy-satire and it-narrative, is the *History of a French Louse* (London: T. Becket, 1779), a translation of Delauney, *Histoire d'une Pou François* (Paris: L'Imprimerie Royale, 1779).

49. Mary Ann Kilner, *The Memoirs of a Peg-Top* (London: John Marshall, [1785?]); M. Pelham [Dorothy Kilner], *The Life and Perambulation of a Mouse,* 2 vols. (London: John Marshall, [1785?]), 1.[iii]; *Memoirs of Dick, the Little Poney* (London: J. Walker and E. Newbery, 1800); *The Dog of Knowledge, or, Memoirs of Bob, the Spotted Terrier* (London: J. Harris [successor to E. Newbery], 1801).

50. Gérard Genette, *Narrative Discourse,* trans. Jane E. Lewin (Oxford: Blackwell, 1980), 244–45. Genette briefly discusses the it-narrative (not his term) as an example of a narrative posture where the story is told by a nonhuman character.

51. See Thomas Nagel, "What Is It Like to Be a Bat?" *Mortal Questions* (Cambridge: Cambridge University Press, 1979). Although the dominant account in recent ethical philosophy insists on a radical divide between human and animals—so that animals are not persons who enjoy legal rights—there is an important stream of speculative and radical philosophy interested in rethinking this question. See J. M. Coetzee, *The Lives of Animals,* ed. Amy Gutman (Princeton, NJ: Princeton University Press, 1999); John Gray, *Straw Dogs: Thoughts on Humans and Other Animals* (London: Granta, 2002).

52. David DeGrazia, *Taking Animals Seriously: Mental Life and Moral Status* (Cambridge: Cambridge University Press, 1996), chap. 7.

53. Olaudah Equiano, *The Interesting Narrative of the Life of Olaudah Equiano, or Gustavus Vassa, the African,* ed. Vincent Carretta (New York: Penguin, 1995), 3.

54. Stanley Cavell, *The Claim of Reason: Wittgenstein, Skepticism, Morality, and Tragedy* (Oxford: Oxford University Press, 1979), 376–77. See also Craig Taylor, *Sympathy: A Philosophical Analysis* (Basingstoke, UK: Palgrave Macmillan, 2002), 127–30 (128), which drew this section of Cavell to my attention.

55. Cavell, *Claim of Reason,* 373. Cavell does not discuss Scott's novel.

56. Ibid., 376.

57. The bill abolishing the slave trade passed the Lords (100 to 34) and Commons (283 to 16) in 1807, but the bill did not come into force until 1808. The domestic ramifications of the act were widely felt: E. P. Thompson describes the powerful influence of the abolition campaign on the campaigns against the traditional customs of trade and restrictive practices of labor (*The Making of the English Working Class* [New York: Vintage, 1963], 529). See also David Brion Davis, *The Problem of Slavery in the Age of Revolution 1770–1823* (Ithaca, NY: Cornell University Press, 1975), 442–68.

58. John Oswald, *The Cry of Nature; or, An Appeal to Mercy and Justice, on behalf of the persecuted animals. By John Oswald, Member of the Club des Jacobines* (London: J. Johnson, 1791), 5. Oswald's tract, and especially the prospect of understanding dog language, was satirized in Thomas Taylor's *A Vindication of the Rights of Brutes* (London: Edward Jeffrey, 1792), 80. Thomas Taylor was notorious for the number of pets he kept, and his Platonic metaphysics were popular with later romantic writers, including his theory of metempsychosis (see Kathleen Raine, "Thomas Taylor, Plato and the English Romantic Movement," *British Journal of Aesthetics,* 8.2 [1968]: 99).

59. Joseph Taylor, *Canine Gratitude; or, a Collection of Anecdotes, illustrative of the faithful attachment and wonderful sagacity of dogs* (London: T. Hughes, 1808). This was a continuation of Joseph Taylor, *The General Character of the Dog* (London: Darton and Harvey, 1804). See also Mrs. C. Matthews, *Mornings' Amusement; or Tales of Quadrupeds,* 3rd ed. (York, UK: T. Wilson, 1809).

60. Bentham, *Principles of Morals,* 282.

61. Ibid., 282 n. As Bentham clarifies in a footnote to his footnote, since 1685 the French *Code Noir* of Louis XIV had ascribed certain rights to slaves and manumitted slaves as human beings.

62. *The Dog of Knowledge,* 70–71.

63. *The Dog of Knowledge,* 72. Hannah More, *Slavery, A Poem* (London: T. Cadell, 1788), 5, lines 63–64, where the final line reads "casual colour of a skin."

64. Erskine, *Cruelty to Animals,* 3.

II
Approaching It-Narratives

It-Narrators and Circulation: Defining a Subgenre

Liz Bellamy

THE CORPUS OF WORKS KNOWN VARIOUSLY AS IT-NARRATIVES OR novels of circulation raises a number of problems of generic definition. It is clear to the casual reader that these books have something in common with one another, and that they are different from the canonical texts of both the epistolary and the picaresque tradition. They are characterized by a looseness of structure and an avoidance of thematic coherence, but this distinctive narrative principle has been the cause of critical neglect or dismissal until relatively recently. In a 1781 account of Helenus Scott's *The Adventures of a Rupee,* the *Critical Review* commented on the recent fashion for this kind of narrative, suggesting that "it is indeed a convenient method to writers of the inferior class, of emptying their commonplace books, and throwing together all the farrago of public transactions, private characters, old and new stories, every thing, in short, which they can pick up, to afford a little temporary amusement to an idle reader."[1] Nearly two hundred years later the *Oxford History of English Literature* described a definitive work of the genre, Charles Johnstone's *Chrysal; or, The Adventures of a Guinea,* as "almost indistinguishable from a panoramic miscellany," and in the preface to Francis Coventry's story of a Bologna lapdog, *The History of Pompey the Little,* Robert Adams Day suggested that the work should not be considered as a novel, but rather as "a string on which the satiric episodes can be threaded."[2] In the last twenty years or so, this episodic and panoramic aspect has been reappraised and identified as characteristic of a certain kind of fiction which presents a particular vision of the social system. Yet while the tradition may be distinctive and recognizable, it is more difficult to establish its essential features and its boundaries with other literary subgenres, especially as its character and audience gradually change over time.

Some critics have identified the character of the narrator or protagonist as a defining element, focusing on these works as it-narratives, novels about nonhuman characters, and "speaking object" narratives.[3]

Christopher Flint has argued that "the eighteenth-century speaking object is almost always a product of manufacture rather than a part of nature, and its satiric vision of the world arises from its particular experience of human commerce."[4] In general an object narrates its story by recounting its adventures to a human amanuensis, or by inspiring the hand of the author through some mystical process. The experiences therefore tend to be conveyed indirectly, and this distancing of the narrative voice is further complicated by the use of prefatory stories to explain how the manuscript came into the hands of the "editor." The voice of the object is therefore mediated by a range of humans who may influence the telling of the tale.

Other commentators on the genre have identified the mechanism of distribution of the narrator/protagonist as its definitive characteristic. The works are described as "novels of circulation," for although they fulfill a range of different social and ideological functions, what they have in common is the use of a plot that focuses on the way that an object passes through a diverse range of hands.[5] The protagonist can be sold, lost, found, given, and exchanged and thus come into contact with very different social groups. In *The Adventures of a Rupee,* the rupee encounters the full spectrum of society, from an impoverished sailor to a princess in the royal family.[6] The eponymous hero of *The Adventures of a Bank-Note* passes within the space of five pages from a milliner, to a bishop's wife, to the bishop, to a bookseller, to a printer, to a pastry cook, and to a seller of dead dogs.[7] "Who would not be a banknote to have such a quick succession of adventures and acquaintance?" the banknote exclaims, indicating the tendency of object-narrators to celebrate the mechanisms of exchange and the rapidity of circulation.[8]

There are, however, problems with both forms of generic definition. In the case of the object-narrator, it can be argued that while many narratives describe the adventures of inanimate objects, others focus on a living narrator/protagonist. As well as Coventry's lapdog, there are fleas, cats, a post horse, a louse, mice, a fly, and a jackdaw which all have their tales transcribed in the eighteenth century, and in the nineteenth century the animal narrative becomes a significant subsection of the form.

Flint has argued that animal or vegetable narrators necessarily differ from manufactured objects in being substitutes for human figures rather than satiric observers of them.[9] Yet this seems rather too neat a formulation. From the eighteenth century to the present, readers have identified works such as *Pompey the Little,* or John Hawkesworth's account of the transmigrations of the soul of a flea in *Adventurer* 5, as part of the same tradition of object narratives as *Chrysal* or *The Adventures of a Bank-Note.* Dorothy Kilner's *The Life and Perambulations of a Mouse*

(1785) uses a narrative technique similar to that employed in her earlier definitive object tale, *The Adventures of a Hackney Coach* (1781), and the much quoted critique of *The Adventures of a Rupee* in the *Critical Review* lists the "Adventures of a Cat, a Dog, a Monkey, a Hackney-coach, a Louse, a Shilling, a Rupee, or—any thing else" as examples of the form, indicating that animal adventures were regarded as a significant component of the genre.[10] Moreover, anthropomorphism is no more the exclusive province of the animal or vegetable narrative than satire is of the manufactured object. The essence of the genre is its flexibility, and just as the narrator of *Pompey the Little* uses Pompey as both a metaphorical embodiment of his human masters and an instrument for their satiric deflation, so one of the earliest specie narratives, Addison's "Adventures of a Shilling," establishes the anthropomorphic conventions that come to define this type of fiction. After his arrival in England, the shilling is taken out of its Indian "habit" and put into "the British mode," establishing the equation of coining and clothing. The shilling's desire to circulate is represented as "a wonderful inclination to ramble," and failure to circulate is resented as "imprisonment."[11] These images recur in specie narratives throughout the century, but they derive from the personification of the narrating object. Just as books of real or fictional travels in the eighteenth century can use foreign or imaginary nations to present at once a metaphorical indictment of the British State and a positive alternative to it, so the animal- or object-narrators can be both parodic versions and satirical observers of human behavior.

There are comparable problems with the generic definitions that focus on the mechanism of distribution. For while the majority of narratives describe objects or animals that circulate, there are a number of works which tell the stories of static features. Some of these focus on buildings, such as the *Memoirs of the Shakespear's Head in Covent Garden* (1755) and *The Life and Adventures of the Old Lady of Threadneedle Street* (1832), an economic tract that recounts the story of the Bank of England. Others deal with natural features, particularly trees, either collectively, as in *The Adventures of a Sugar-Plantation* (1836), or individually, as with *The Adventures of a Cotton-Tree* (1836). These works have the loose, inclusive, episodic format that invites admittance within the it-narrative genre, and *Shakespear's Head* was included in Meeker's early checklist of the form.[12] The difference is that in these static narratives, the diverse individuals whose tales are recounted come to the narrating object, instead of the narrating object coming to them. So there is circulation, but of the characters rather than the narrator.

Other works that ostensibly employ the circulation format also include substantial passages in which the central character is relatively static. Although in many respects Scott's *Adventures of a Rupee* is a classic specie narrative, for much of the text the rupee is not circulating within society, but is confined within a pawnbroker's shop.[13] This does not lead to a suspension of interpolated narrative, for the exchange mechanism is replaced by a series of portraits of visitors to the pawnshop, whose stories are conveyed to the rupee by the spirits of gold. This maintains the image of an atomized society in which the characters have no direct connection with one another, but it focuses not on those who are united by their access to specie or a particular possession, but rather on those individuals who have failed to survive within the commercial state. What they have in common is attendance at a pawnshop, which represents a significant reversal of the commercial principle. Instead of parting with money to obtain goods, these people are parting with goods to obtain cash. As the rupee comments, "this is not a temple where wealth has deposited its superfluities; it is a cell loaded with the spoils of the afflicted, and the very necessaries of necessity."[14] So while Scott's novel departs from the circulation format, it nonetheless develops a narrative strategy that works like circulation to present indirect and economic relationships and avoid the prioritization of affective ties as a plot mechanism. The visitors to the pawnbroker's shop are alienated from one another, connected only by a shared failure to survive within the economic system.

Smollett's adventuring atom gives a brief account of how it was "enclosed in a grain of rice, eaten by a Dutch mariner at Firando, and becoming a particle of his body, brought to the Cape of Good Hope." There it was,

> Discharged in a scorbutic dysentery, taken up in a heap of soil to manure a garden, raised to vegetation in a sallad, devoured by an English supercargo, assimilated to a certain organ of his body, which . . . being diseased in consequence of impure contact was again separated, with a considerable portion of putrefied flesh, thrown upon a dunghill, gobbled up and digested by a duck.

This duck was eventually eaten by the father of Nathaniel Peacock, in whose pineal gland the atom has become lodged. This passage is frequently quoted in accounts of the novel of circulation, yet in fact it is extremely atypical of the novel as a whole. For most of the narrative the atom simply describes the corruption and depravity of the Japanese court, in the manner of a roman à clef or fictitious traveler's tale. This is witnessed by the atom from his position initially under the big toe of the Dairo or hereditary monarch, and subsequently in the gut of the Cuboy or Prime Minister, the transition having been made following a too enthusiastic performance of the ceremony of kicking the minister's posteriors. So although the *Adventures of an Atom* is one of the best known and most nearly canonical narratives of this kind, in practice it makes little use of the circulation/object-narrator gimmick. The popularity of the genre is exploited as a mechanism for the thinly veiled allegory of the atom's "political anecdotes . . . for the instruction of British ministers."

The narratives that comprise this subgenre can therefore be identified as having one or both of the two definitive components. The first is a narrator that, whether animal, vegetable, or manufactured object, lacks independent agency. As I have observed elsewhere, although Pompey the Little is a dog, it is stressed by the third-person narrator, and made clear in his name, that he is a very small dog, and he is therefore deprived of volition. He is carried about like an object, and although he gets lost on one occasion, he does not run away from his owners or move of his own accord.[15] He is therefore able to circulate through society, binding together the narratives of otherwise disparate individuals and subject to the mechanisms of exchange. In this respect he fulfills a function very similar to that of the watches, coins, sedan chairs, etc. This highlights the second definitive aspect of the genre, which is the transference of the narrator or protagonist between otherwise unconnected characters, or, in the case of narratives of static objects like buildings, the movement of unconnected characters within the precincts of the protagonist. Above all, these works are different means of accumulating stories, which gives them their distinctive looseness of form. They are, to use the words of the *Oxford History of English Literature,* a particular kind of panoramic miscellany, and this is not their failing or weakness, but rather their defining feature.

Circulation does not invariably involve economic exchange, although it often does. A significant subsection of the genre focuses instead on metempsychosis and the transmigration of the soul, drawing on the classical tradition of transformation narratives. In John Hawkesworth's "Remarks on Dreaming: Various Transmigrations related by a Flea" in *Adventurer* 5, the flea dictates his adventures to the author, describing the various states through which his soul has passed.[16] His spirit starts off in the son of a country gentleman, who is killed in a fall while hunting. It then passes into a mongrel puppy, which is tortured for sport and driven to such a state of frenzy that he is killed by "peasants" who believe he is mad. The spirit then migrates into a bullfinch, which is captured and blinded to improve his song, before being eaten by a cat, at which point the spirit moves into a cockchafer. This beetle is impaled upon a pin to make a toy for a child, and is squashed when it can no longer fly. It becomes a worm used as fishing bait, a cock, a lobster, and a pig. The essay becomes an exposition of the routine cruelty of mankind towards the animal world as the flea recounts how, in his various forms, "I suffered the same kind of death with those who are broken upon the wheel, I was roasted alive before a slow fire, and was scourged to death with small cords, to gratify the wanton appetite of luxury, or contribute to the merriment of a rabble."[17] This message is reinforced when the author, unaware of the origin of the mysterious narrating voice, notices the flea and crushes it. The spirit is then translated into a "young lady of exquisite beauty" who attacks the author for his thoughtless cruelty in killing his "monitor." She tells him, however, to "publish . . . what I have communicated" on the grounds that "if any man shall be reclaimed from a criminal inattention to the felicity of inferior beings, and restrained from inflicting pain by considering the effect of his actions, I have not suffered in vain."[18] By revealing the barbarity of the human exploitation of the animal world and the implications of commodification, this narrative contributes to the tradition of anti-luxury discourse. But it also represents an early manifestation of the appropriation of the circulation format for an explicitly didactic and humanitarian purpose. This aspect was to be developed in nineteenth-century adaptations of the genre.[19]

Whether moved by transmigration or economic exchange, the circulating object is able to transgress social barriers to an even greater degree than picaresque human protagonists with their characteristically ambiguous social status. It is also able to present stories that lack narrative closure. The soul of Hawkesworth's flea moves on only after the death of his host, but in other tales the interpolated narratives terminate when the character is no longer in possession of the central object, as the penny or pen or puppy or whatever is lost, stolen, or exchanged. This point is often reached both abruptly and arbitrarily. Johnstone's *Chrysal,* for example, is composed of a series of largely unresolved narratives. In one episode a servant tricks his pedophile master into gaining preferment for a deserving old soldier, in the expectation that this will enable him to seduce the man's ten-year-old niece. We are informed that in fact the soldier "had no such neice [*sic*] in the world," but we do not witness the outcome of the deception, as the guinea passes on to another hand and another tale.[20] This aspect of the form was condemned in a review of *The Adventures of a Hackney Coach* in the *Critical Review.* The reviewer complains that "our coachman's fares . . . are too short; and before any interesting story can be told, or any good character drawn of one person, he stops on a sudden and takes up another."[21]

Chrysal ends when the spirit of gold vanishes in disgust as the alchemist to whom he narrated his tale "emitted an explosion that filled the room with a fetid steam."[22] The narrative of *Pompey the Little* ends with the sad death of the eponymous hero, but this conclusion is only really possible in the small minority of tales that have a third-person narrator. The majority of works in this tradition use the first-person narrative format and avoid resolution of the central story, as well as of the individual episodes. The protagonist terminates rather than concludes the sequence of adventures, leaving the way open for the production of subsequent volumes.[23]

In the canonical novels of the eighteenth and nineteenth centuries, narrative resolution is occasionally achieved by the death of the protagonist, but is usually a consequence of the marriage of the central characters. Society is presented as a series of discrete individuals seeking to combine with one another to form marital units. The substitution of the object for the individual, and of the economic for the affective mechanism, means that such narrative closure is not possible or necessary. Society is conceived as one long succession of commercial relationships or mini-narratives which only end when the object passes into other hands, when the character leaves the shop, or when the spirit passes into another creature. Elements of this more diverse structuring can be found within the interpolated narratives of canonical works, but in novels like *Tom Jones* the stories of minor characters like the Man of the Hill are contained within the dominant framework of the narrative of the eponymous hero and can be seen as parallel or contrasting tales. In circulation novels the narrative is almost entirely comprised of an accumulation of interpolated accounts. So while canonical texts are primarily structured around a plot that culminates in the establishment of permanent bonds between individuals, the relationships within circulation and object novels are inherently transitory as well as often economically motivated. They are narratives of irresolution.

The loose, discursive narrative form is further validated in a number of late-eighteenth-century texts by invocation of the Sternean idiom.[24] The *Critical Review* describes *The Adventures of a Hackney Coach* as "a servile copy of Sterne's peculiarity of expression, his sudden transitions, exclamations, &c., without his force, spirit and sensibility."[25] The banknote draws on a Shandean range of authorities to support his contention that Adam's hobbyhorse was a different color from Eve's:

> HUGO GROTIUS, in his Treatise de Jure Belli ac Pacis says,—hold, I believe I am wrong, it could not be Hugo Grotius, he was too grave a writer for such an expression; and yet if it was not him, it must be somebody else, for I could never invent it myself; however, whether it was him or Puffendorf, or Heliodorus, or Theocritus, or Homer, or Virgil, or Horace, or Ovid, or Claudian, or Lucretius, or Tasso, or Spinone Speroni, or Demosthenes, or Juvenal, or Catullus, or Aristotle, or Quintilian, or Petronius, or Longinus, or Democritus, or Pythagoras, or Heraclitus, or Plato, or Epicurus, or

> Panaetius, or Polybius, or Thomas Aquinas, or one of the ten thousand more, whose names I cannot recollect, (though I have carefully perused them all) I cannot positively assert; but let it be which of them it will, I know he says that Noah, when he preserved a pair of all kinds of animals, took particular care to ship a pair of hobby-horses on board his swimming house.[26]

The banknote's assertion that he could not have invented such a tale himself appears to reinforce his role as a truthful retailer of facts, rather than a contriver of fictions, and therefore suggests that he is an appropriate figure to be narrating a story. He can be taken at face value. But the passage is rendered ironic when we remember that the banknote is claiming to have carefully perused all these weighty authorities. In raising the question of his sources, the banknote draws attention to the issue of his own creditworthiness. Such references enhance the anthropomorphism of the narrative, but also make it rather ludicrously comic and suggest a satire on the credulity of those in both the reading and the commercial public who are prepared to put their trust in paper money.

The combination of the absence of closure and the often hectic accumulation of very diverse and unresolved interpolated narratives has encouraged the critical dismissal of the form on the grounds of its lack of character development and structural coherence, as has been indicated above. Yet these works should not be seen as texts that tried and failed to achieve the kind of coherence that came to characterize the fictional traditions established by writers such as Richardson and Fielding. They are aiming for a different, more diffuse, form, which is crucial in the construction of their distinctive vision of the social system. The world of these novels is by no means an ordered framework in which characters and narrative gradually unfold. It is an atomized and fragmented society, full of diverse individuals whose narratives occasionally and fortuitously coincide and then diverge. By refusing to enclose individual stories within a structure of fictional containment, these works are able to explore the social system from a range of ideological positions and with a satirical vision that avoids the reassertion of hegemony and negation of subversion that tends to be implicit within narrative resolution. The structural and metaphorical significance of circulation within the narratives does not, therefore, necessarily entail endorsement of the economic system and commercial values, but rather the presentation of them as definitive of relationships within contemporary society.

The satirical purpose of Thomas Bridges's *Adventures of a Bank-Note* is signaled in the epigram:

> When I've held up a proper number
> Of fools and knaves, and such-like lumber,

To public view, and public scorn,
Contented I'll to dust return.

The verse is followed by a reference to the corruption of Robert Walpole.[27] This is hardly cutting-edge contemporary political comment, since Walpole had been dead for thirty-five years by the time the banknote's *Adventures* were published. But the familiarity of the allusion to "Bobby" suggests the location of the work within the satirical tradition of the periodical and pamphlet literature of the early eighteenth century, and thus within an anti-luxury, anticommercial discursive framework associated with an earlier era of civic humanist rhetoric.

In practice, however, the book presents a more complex vision of the economic system, not least because it is narrated by a character dependent for his existence on the maintenance of credit. In his first volume the banknote presents a series of satirical stereotypes, such as the henpecked husband (97–101), the "scoundrel baronet" (148), the corrupt, Epicurean churchwarden (172), and the naive country gentleman (190). Far from seeking greater structural coherence and more developed characters, the banknote celebrates the range of "friends" whom he encounters, and the rapidity with which he passes from hand to hand. When he asks, "who would not be a bank note?" towards the start of the second volume, he anticipates a negative response from "a custard-eating alderman," a symbol of peculation but also of self-indulgent and parasitic inactivity.[28] The alderman suggests that banknotes are not to be envied because of the brevity of their life expectancy, since "few survive the year, but not one in fifty live to be two years old." The banknote responds by suggesting that two banknote's years are equal to 200 human ones:

> Time is measured only by the slower or quicker succession of ideas. A sparrow that dies of old age at the end of four or five years, performs some particular feats oftener than any man that lives to the age of four-score, and has been as useful to his generation.[29]

The joke is typical of the Sternean bawdy of the *Adventures,* but it reinforces the importance of the pace rather than the duration of life. For the banknote, rapidity of circulation is the key to vitality, and he shares the "wonderful inclination to ramble" that characterized the hero of "Adventures of a Shilling."[30] Both the banknote and the shilling represent possession by a miser in metaphors of incarceration. The shilling recounts how, "in the beginning of my sixth year, to my unspeakable grief, I fell into the hands of a miserable old fellow, who clapped me into an iron chest, where I found five hundred more of my own quality who lay under the same confinement."[31] The banknote describes the miser he encounters as "the most sordid, ill-tempered, envious creature that nature ever formed."[32] In both narratives, the restriction of circulation is identified as unnatural, although the banknote sees this disruption of the natural flow of trade as a consequence of the intervention of providence, which uses it as a means to punish the "wretch who took pains to render his own life both miserable and contemptible."[33]

Yet although the specie narrators celebrate circulation, this does not necessarily mean that this view is endorsed by our reading of the narrative. The roman à clef origins of the form ensure that the majority of specie narratives tend to include numerous transactions that are less than respectable. Some of these involve various forms of cheating and sharp practice which the banknote identifies as endemic within the economic system: "Thus the world goes round, the jockey cheats the coal-merchant and the coal-merchant, to make it up, robs all his customers by short measure.—What numbers of rogues in this world say you! What numbers indeed I reply."[34] *Chrysal* likewise functions as a detailed exposition of the extent of corruption in the administration of society. The guinea is exchanged through transactions involving gambling, bribery, prostitution, and peculation, the corrupt supply of damaged and overpriced goods to the armed forces, and the misappropriation of charitable funds. It is hardly ever passed on through a straight commercial exchange.

Chrysal expresses a conventional specie anxiety when he is conveyed from the Royal Mint to the Bank of England, and thrown onto a heap of coins,

> where the pleasure I had felt at the beauty and convenience of my new figure was considerably cooled, at my being thrown into so large a heap, as took away all my particular consequence, and seemed to threaten a long state of inactivity, before it might come to my turn to be brought into action. But I soon found myself agreeably mistaken, and that the *circulation* there was too quick to admit of such delay: for I was that very day paid out to a noble lord, in his pension from the ministry.[35]

Chrysal is like a newly enlisted soldier, impressed by the sight of himself in his uniform and boldly anxious to be "brought into action" as soon as possible. But the celebration of circulation implicit in this martial imagery is satirically undermined by the connection of circulation with the ministerial corruption associated with "pensions." Chrysal is not brought into action to facilitate the free flow of trade, but to perpetuate the institutionalized bribery embodied in the system of government appointments.

Prostitution is one of the most common forms of exchange portrayed within specie narratives, and also features in other kinds of circulation novel.[36] This involves both the depiction of established brothels, and stories concerning the seduction of innocence. Chrysal exploits the sentimental potential of such accounts in the portrait of a virtuous widow who is deceived by a bawd, only to discover that the man for whom she has been procured is her long lost father.[37] The banknote is less overtly judgmental in his casual references to the sexual predation he witnesses. He describes the doctor whose treatment of a beautiful young girl for greensickness produced another disorder that resulted in "a swelling in the waist" and a sugar baker who "never went to any wicked bawdy-houses, but commonly hired a good stout country wench to be a maid of all work, viz. to dress his victuals, make his bed, and sleep with him &c."[38]

Pompey the Little is frequently given as a token of love—for example, by a courtesan to Hillario, and then by him to Lady Tempest. The speed with which he circulates indicates the transience of love in a decadent, modern society. The scandalous events witnessed by Mopsey the cat and recounted in "The Adventures of a Cat," which appeared in *The Westminster Magazine* in 1774, were probably read by contemporaries as thinly disguised versions of current scandal tales.[39] Mopsey's account of the extracurricular liaisons of the kept mistress of the impotent Lord C— — —e is very similar to the account in *Chrysal* of the mistress maintained by a man "remarkable for the coolness of his constitution."[40]

These works draw on an element of *chronique scandaleuse* not uncommon in the circulation genre and evident in such early examples as Crébillon's *The Sopha*. But the portrayal of prostitution and sexuality has a narrative significance beyond its function as contemporary scandal or titillation. Prostitution becomes a metaphor for the mercenary and transitory nature of relationships within a society based on circulation and rapidity of exchange, and thus reinforces the disjunction between the celebration of circulation by the narrator/protagonist and the reader's interpretation of the economic message of the text.

In the absence of an affective resolution and a structurally significant marriage plot, circulation narratives and object tales portray instead the commodification of sexuality. By focusing on all relationships as commercial transactions, because only such transactions come to the attention of the narrator, the novels necessarily present a negative image of contemporary society that accords with the satirical function of the form. The elevation of economic evaluation into a system of moral and social values emphasizes the mercenary outlook of the object-narrators and their exclusion from more human ethical codes. These narratives therefore invite an ironic interpretation, as readers recognize the disjunction between the anthropocentric and anthropomorphic social vision.

It would be wrong, however, to assume that the novels within this genre necessarily share a common political or economic perspective. The narrative structure provides a particular image of commercial society, but narratives vary in the extent to which that image serves a critical purpose. In *The Adventures of a Rupee* the experiences of the customers in the pawnbroker's shop indict a commercial system that leaves so many individuals unable to cope. Yet elsewhere in the novel the commercial and political status quo are celebrated by the rupee.

Helenus Scott, the author of the *Rupee,* was a doctor in the service of the East India Company.[41] This may help to explain the extravagant praise that the rupee heaps upon "that great East India Company, which can keep black men in such good order at so great a distance."[42] This view is endorsed in the interpolated narrative of Miss Melvil, who recounts her father's parting words to her brother as he leaves to join the East India Company:

> Your particular province is to protect the trade of our country, against the insults of European powers, or of the India nations, who ignorant of the blessings that commerce diffuses even to themselves, are often disposed to interrupt its equitable course. The prosperity therefore of trade, is what you have in view, not the extension of settlement, and much less your private advantage.[43]

The expansion of trade is represented as a form of public virtue that can make the individual "a benefactor of mankind."[44] As such, it is contrasted with personal aggrandizement but also with colonial settlement. Commerce is portrayed as a civilizing and stabilizing force, but is juxtaposed with a rapacious and imperialistic colonialism, which seeks political power rather than economic advantage. Later in the novel, a soldier contrasts the corruption in the army, where promotion is based on bribery or connections, with the meritocratic organization of the East India Company, where "it is known abilities and former services that entitle [a man] to a distinguished rank."[45]

The rupee passes for a time into the hands of one of the "lovely children of the greatest king."[46] The court of George III is celebrated as a haven of happiness and virtue, leading the rupee to exclaim: "Happy sovereign, you are not only exalted above all your people in dignity but in merit. You are the favourite of a nation that values itself above every other, with the disadvantage of not being even a native of it. There is no rank of life that does not admire your virtues; you have not a good subject who does not wish to imitate them."[47] Such is the extravagance of the eulogy of the status quo that the reader is initially inclined to question the sincerity of the rupee and suspect that the book shares the satirical impulse of so many other circulation—and particularly specie—narratives. Yet further reading makes it clear that this is not the case. The interpolated narratives of characters such as the impecunious curate and the chimney sweep whose mother has sold his teeth reveal that poverty and injustice exist within society. But the solution to such problems is clearly located in the expansion of trade and commerce, combined with the pursuit of virtue and liberty, through the good offices of the monarch and the East India Company.

The celebration of economic liberty is embodied in the loose and inclusive structure of the circulation narrative, while the price of this freedom is simultaneously recognized in the sympathetic portrait of the casualties of commerce. Yet the development of the novel in the eighteenth century increasingly led to the critical dismissal of the episodic form. As the concept of a distinct fictional tradition developed and as structural coherence became a definitive element of the novel, those narratives that presented a more diffuse picture of the social system tended to be marginalized.

As the table in Appendix A indicates, there were significant changes in the distribution of circulation narratives over the eighteenth and nineteenth centuries. The data used to generate these figures are by no means complete, for they are based on an extensive but not exhaustive trawl through the British Library Catalogue and the Cambridge University Library Catalogue. Appendix B contains the resultant list of all the circulation narratives that I have been able to trace that were published in Britain between 1701 and 1900. There are, no doubt, many omissions, and also some texts the admissibility of which within the circulation genre may well be called into question. I have, however, no reason to believe that these limitations constitute any systematic bias, so that while particular figures should not be considered reliable, the data as a whole can be used to identify general trends. These can be discerned both in the total number of circulation narratives produced, and in the kind of narrative that makes up that total. Appendix A indicates the total number of circulation/it-narratives identified for each of the decades from 1701 to 1900; the number of object narratives; the number of specie narratives (a subset of the object narratives); and the number of animal narratives. The numbers in columns 2 and 4 do not invariably add up to the figure in column 1, because there are some narratives, such as the *Adventures of an Atom* or *Memoirs of a Stomach,* which do not fit neatly into either category.

These figures indicate that while object narratives continued to be produced through the eighteenth and nineteenth centuries, there were significant changes in their distribution when represented as a proportion of total circulation works. In the first half of the eighteenth century, object narratives made up 100 percent of circulation/it-narratives. This declined to 71 percent in the second half of the century, making 75 percent for the century as a whole. In the first half of the nineteenth century, the figure fell to only 51 percent, rising to 59 percent in the second half of the century, making 57 percent for the century as a whole. Of these, specie narratives declined from 29 percent of all circulation narratives in the first half of the eighteenth century, to 18 percent in the second half, 17 percent in the first half of the nineteenth century, and only 9 percent in the second, although the numbers produced in each half century remained relatively stable after 1750, at around 10 (10, 9, 12). In contrast, while there were no animal narratives in the first half of the eighteenth century, these made up 27 percent of the total in the second half, rising to 45 percent between 1801 and 1850, and declining to 37 percent from 1851 to 1900.

These figures may be distorted by a number of factors, apart from the lack of a complete data set. For example, the apparently large number of works produced in a particular decade may reflect the activities of a prolific individual who, having hit on a winning formula, generated a series of works. In the 1790s and 1800s, Edward Kendall produced a series of stories about various varieties of bird, and in the 1850s, Alfred Elwes the Elder published a number of animal adventures. As discussed above, the boundaries of the genre can become blurred, as circulation narratives impinge on other forms so that there may be some debate over whether particular works should be included in the figures. In the late Victorian period, for instance, the circulation format was increasingly adopted for scientific books. The "Adventures of a Quire of Paper," published in the *London Magazine* in 1779, seems to have initiated this format, using the story of the quire to provide an insight into the process of paper manufacture. In the 1880s Alexander Watt published a series of works exploring the history of a lump of coal (1882), a lump of chalk (1883), a lump of iron (1884), and a lump of gold (1885). Michael Faraday's "Lectures delivered before a Juvenile Audience at the Royal Institution" traced *The Chemical History of a Candle* (1886).

On the other hand, the format overlaps with the adventure story in works such as R. M. Ballantyne's *The Dog Crusoe and his Master* (1861), which follows the life of a Newfoundland dog in the wilds of the American West. It is difficult to ascertain the point at which animal narratives cease to be a subsection of the circulation genre and become a distinct form, leading, for example, to the works of Beatrix Potter in the twentieth century. Finally, it is important to bear in mind that the total number of books published per annum increased in the course of the eighteenth and nineteenth centuries. As a result, the fourteen object narratives produced in the 1780s represent a greater proportion of total publishing output than the fourteen animal narratives produced in the 1870s.

The increasing popularity of animal narratives in the late eighteenth and early nineteenth centuries is associated with a more general change in the purpose and apprehended audience of circulation narratives as a whole. For much of the eighteenth century, up until around 1780, the circulation format was largely used in satirical works addressed to an adult audience. In the last twenty years of the eighteenth century, a number of works were produced that adapted the circulation structure to produce moral and didactic stories for children. At least three such books appeared in or around 1780 (the publication dates are not always precise): Mary Kilner's *The Adventures of a Pincushion: Designed Chiefly for the Use of Young Ladies; The Adventures of a Whipping-Top. Illustrated with Stories of Many Bad Boys . . . and of Some Good Boys . . . Written by Itself;* and Mr. Truelove's *The Adventures of a Silver Penny: Containing much amusement and many characters with which young gentlemen and ladies ought to be acquainted . . . For the benefit of all good children, who love to be merry and wise.* Works of this kind continued to be produced in significant numbers in the 1780s and '90s, many of them published by Elizabeth Newbery of Ludgate Hill (widow of Francis Newbery, the nephew of pioneer children's publisher John Newbery) and John Marshall of Aldermary Churchyard. These two individuals were the leading producers of didactic moral tales for children in the late eighteenth century.[48] The works describe the adventures of objects with which children would be familiar, such as coins or toys and also pets and other animals that have close contact with humans.

Instead of witnessing scandalous sexual liaisons, the heroes of these circulation novels describe morally improving scenes of virtue rewarded and vice detected. Mary Kilner's peg top assures his "Young Gentlemen" readers that "however vice may triumph for a time, it is generally discovered in the end, and meets with its deserved retribution."[49] The peg top provides an edifying lecture on the importance of always telling the truth, but the narrative draws attention to the incongruity of this lesson being placed in the mouth of a wooden toy.[50] It assures us that "when a story is written or told where things inanimate are represented as talking or acting, it must be known to be only supposition; as in reality *wood* cannot *feel,* nor iron *think.*" This highlights the tension between the didactic emphasis on truthfulness and the fictional convention of the it-narrative.

Animals provide an ideal vehicle for a circulation narrative because they can be endowed with thoughts and feelings with less violation of probability than was the case with object-narrators. Dorothy Kilner's popular *The Life and Perambulation of a Mouse* (1785?) recounts the adventures of Nimble, supposedly dictated to the author. The author's introduction assures the readers that "*in earnest* I never heard a mouse speak in all my life," but Nimble's tale provides a vivid account of the dangers facing small animals in a world dominated by cruel or thoughtless humans. Some animal tales are used to inculcate conventional moral and didactic lessons, such as *The Life of Bushtail the Squirrel, that could play and not quarrel* (1806). But many draw on the polemical element of earlier circulation narratives, such as Hawkesworth's "Adventures of a Flea," in exposing the sufferings of the animal world and appealing for more compassion and consideration from their youthful readers. This was a feature of the classic animal narrative of the nineteenth century, Anna Sewell's *Black Beauty* (1877).

Beauty recounts his gradual decline in the world, from carriage horse to hired hack to cab horse before his final happy retirement. In the process he exposes the cruelty to which horses are routinely subjected, most notably through the use of the bearing rein. This was a device to pull a horse's head back when harnessed to a carriage, and was used to create a fashionable appearance. Beauty describes how, when using the bearing rein,

> The action of the sharp bit on my tongue and jaw, and the constrained position of my head and throat always caused me to froth at the mouth . . . Besides this, there was a pressure on my windpipe, which often made my breathing very uncomfortable; when I returned from my work, my neck and chest were strained and painful, my mouth and tongue tender, and I felt worn and depressed.[51]

As this account has indicated, for most of the eighteenth century the circulation format was primarily used to provide a satirical vision of the atomized and mercenary nature of society within a commercial state. From the 1780s it began to be adopted as a vehicle for moral didacticism in works aimed at a juvenile readership. This trend continued so that by the end of the nineteenth century the majority of circulation novels were directed towards child readers, fulfilling a range of functions, including the presentation of scientific information, the inculcation of humanitarian philosophy, and the provision of comic tales for entertainment.

Within adult fiction the loose discursive form of the circulation novel, with its evasion of narrative closure, presented a world that was diverse and inconsequential, lacking any structural or thematic coherence. But this image was increasingly measured against a fictional tradition that emphasized a narrative form that could present an ordered and meaningful picture of the social system and contain the elements of ideological critique. So while adults sought refuge in the social myths of more structured narratives that presented the world as ultimately comprehensible, the disconnected and episodic form of the circulation narrative was adapted for children. While the didactic and moralizing tone of many of these stories reveals the patriarchal and controling aspirations of their writers, the structural incoherence that constitutes the essence of the circulation format can be seen as having a less coercive effect.

The dolls and dogs that narrate so many circulation tales are marginalized figures that are characterized by their inability to control events. They encounter a series of different people (owners) and experience different incidents, but can perceive only temporal and not causal links between the diverse scenes. This evocation of a disordered and uncontrollable universe, devoid of structures of closure and ideological containment, perhaps reflects an image of the world peculiarly appropriate for children, yet has a subversive potential that may undermine the didactic aspirations of the authors.

APPENDIX A
Temporal Distribution of Circulation Narratives 1701–1900

Decade	total number of circulation narratives	object narratives	specie narratives	animal narratives
1701–10	2	2	2	0
1711–20	0	0	0	0
1721–30	0	0	0	0
1731–40	2	2	0	0
1741–50	3	3	0	0
total number per half century	7	7	2	0
% of total narratives		100%	29%	0%
1751–60	11	8	1	3
1761–70	3	2	1	0
1771–80	12	10	3	2
1781–90	16	14	3	2
1791–1800	14	6	2	8
total number per half century	56	40	10	15
% of total narratives		71%	18%	27%
1801–10	12	3	1	9
1811–20	16	10	4	6
1821–30	8	4	2	4
1831–40	8	4	1	2
1841–50	9	6	1	3
total number per half century	53	27	9	24
% of total narratives		51%	17%	45%
1851–60	30	16	2	12
1861–70	25	14	3	11
1871–80	25	11	0	14
1881–90	28	22	4	3
1891 –1900	24	15	3	9
total number per half century	132	78	12	49
% of total narratives		59%	9%	37%

APPENDIX B
Chronological Catalogue of Circulation Narratives (Divided by Decade)

1. Charles Gildon, *The Golden Spy* (London, 1709).
2. Joseph Addison, "Adventures of a Shilling," *Tatler* 249 (1710).

---

3. *The Secret History of an old Shoe* (London, 1734).
4. *The Genuine and Most Surprizing Adventures of a Very Unfortunate Goose-Quill* (London, 1734).

---

5. Claude Crébillon, *The Sopha, a Moral Tale* (London, 1742).
6. *The Settee; or, Chevalier Commodo's Transformation* (London, 1742).
7. Edward Philips, *The Adventures of a Black Coat: Containing a Series of Remarkable Occurrences and Entertaining Incidents . . . As Related by Itself* (Edinburgh: Alex M. Caslan, [1750]).

---

8. Francis Coventry, *The History of Pompey the Little; or, The Life and Adventures of a Lap-Dog* (London, 1751).
9. *The Memoirs and Interesting Adventures of an Embroidered Waistcoat,* 2 vols. (London, 1751).
10. John Hawkesworth ["flea"], *The Adventurer* 5 (1752).
11. Susan Smythies, *The Stage-Coach* (1753).
12. *Travels of Mons. le Poste-Chaise: Written by Himself* (London, 1753).
13. *The History and Adventures of a Lady's Slippers and Shoes* (London: M. Cooper, 1754).
14. *Memoirs of the Shakespear's Head in Covent-Garden. In which are introduced many entertaining adventures, and several remarkable characters. By the Ghost of Shakespear* (London, 1755).
15. *The Adventures and Metamorphose of Queen Elizabeth's Pocket-Pistol, late of Charles-Fort near Kinsale. By a matross of said Fort* (Dublin, 1756).
16. *The Sedan: A Novel: In Which Many New and Entertaining Characters are Introduced* (London, 1757).
17. [William Guthrie?], *The Life and Adventures of a Cat* (London: Willoughby Mynors, 1760).
18. Charles Johnstone, *Chrysal; or, The Adventures of a Guinea,* 2 vols. (1760); expanded ed. 1761; 4 vols. (London, 1764).

---

19. Charles Perronet, *A Dialogue between the Pulpit and Reading Desk* (London, 1767).
20. Tobias Smollett, *The History and Adventures of an Atom* (1769).
21. Thomas Bridges, *The Adventures of a Bank-Note,* 2 vols. (London, 1770–71).

---

22. *The Birmingham Counterfeit; or, The Invisible Spectator: A Sentimental Romance* (London, 1772).
23. Edward Thompson, "Indusiata, or, the Adventures of a Silk Petticoat," *Westminster* 1 (June–December 1773), 7 parts.
24. "Mopsey" [Edward Thompson?], "The Adventures of a Cat," *Westminster* 2 (August–September 1774), 2 parts.
25. Edward Thompson, "Adventures of a Six-and-Nine-Pence, comprehending Anecdotes of Living Characters" (incomplete), *Westminster Magazine* 2 (November 1774): 583–86.
26. *The Adventures of a Cork-Screw in which . . . the vices, follies, and manners of the present age are exhibited* (London: T. Bell, 1775).
27. Laurence Sterne, "The History of a Good Warm Watch-Coat," *Westminster Magazine* 3 (July 1775), 1 part.
28. "Adventures of a Quire of Paper," *London Magazine* 48 (August–October 1779), 3 parts; *Edinburgh Weekly* 46 (October 20–November 17, 1779), 3 parts; *Gentleman's and London* (October–December 1779), 3 parts.
29. *History of a French Louse; or, The Spy of a New Species, in France and England* (London, 1779).
30. *The Adventures of a Kite* [London, 1780?].
31. Mary Ann [Jane?] Kilner, *The Adventures of a Pincushion: Designed Chiefly for the Use of Young Ladies* (London, [1780]).
32. *The Adventures of a Whipping-Top. Illustrated with Stories of Many Bad Boys . . . and of Some Good Boys . . . Written by Itself* (London: [J. Marshall], [1780]).
33. Mr. Truelove, *The Adventures of a Silver Penny: Containing much amusement and many characters with which young gentlemen and ladies ought to be acquainted . . . For the benefit of all good children, who love to be merry and wise* (London: W. Nicoll, [ca. 1780]).

---

34. Dorothy Kilner, *The Adventures of a Hackney Coach* (London, 1781).
35. Richard Johnson, *The Adventures of a Silver Penny, including many secret anecdotes of little misses and masters both good and naughty* (London, [1782]).
36. Helenus Scott, *The Adventures of a Rupee* (London, 1782).
37. "History of a Perriwig, from its First Origin in a Barber's Shop, till it Landed at Dipping-Row, Holborn," *Westminster Magazine* (April–May 1782).
38. "The Adventures of a Gold Ring," *Rambler's Magazine* 1 (March–July 1783), 5 parts.
39. Theophilus Johnson, *Phantoms; or, The Adventures of a Gold-Headed Cane* (London, 1783).
40. "The History and Adventures of a Bedstead," *Rambler's Magazine* 2–5 (December 1784–April 1787), 28 parts, uncompleted.
41. Dorothy Kilner, *The Life and Perambulation of a Mouse* [1785?].
42. Mary Ann Kilner, *The Memoirs of a Peg-Top* (London, 1785).
43. *The Comical Adventures of a Little White Mouse; or, A Bad Boy happily changed into a Good Boy. A Useful Lesson to all Young People* (London: H. Turpin, [1786]).

44. "Adventures of a Sopha," *Rambler's* 4–8 (Supplement, 1786–June 1790), 45 parts.
45. *The Adventures of a Watch* (London, 1788).
46. "The Adventures of a Shilling," *New Ladies* 3–4 (August 1788–November 1789), 16 parts.
47. "Adventures of a Stage Coach," *Rambler's* 6–7 (July–December 1788–April 1789), 7 parts.
48. *The Adventures of a Pin* (London, 1790).
49. *The Adventures of a Whipping-Top* (London, 1790).

---

50. "The Adventures of a Mirror," *Lady's* 22 (January, February, May, 1791), 3 parts, uncompleted.
51. *Argentum; or, The Adventures of a Shilling* (London: J. Nichols, 1794).
52. *The Adventures of the Guildford Jack-daw. Interspersed with anecdotes of some little good and bad boys. For the use of children* (London, 1795?).
53. J. Hunt, "The Adventures of a Pen," in *The Miscellany* (Stony Stratford, UK: 1795).
54. *The History of a Pin, as related by itself* (London: E. Newbery, 1798).
55. *The Silver Thimble* (London: E. Newbery, 1799).
56. Edward Augustus Kendall, *Keeper's Travels in Search of his Master* (London: E. Newbery, 1799).
57. Edward Augustus Kendall, *The Crested Wren* (London: E. Newbery, 1799).
58. Edward Augustus Kendall, *The Canary Bird: A Moral Fiction, interspersed with poetry* (London: E. Newbery, 1799).
59. *The Hare, or, Hunting Incompatible with Humanity* (London: Vernor and Hood, 1799).
60. Mr. Truelove, *The Adventures of a Silver Three-Pence* (London: E. Newbery, [1800]).
61. [Stephen Jones], *The Life and Adventures of a Fly* (London: E. Newbery, [1800]).
62. *Memoirs of Dick, the Little Poney supposed to be written by himself, etc.* (London: E. Newbery, 1800).
63. *The Life of a Bee. Related by herself* (London: John Marshall, [1800]).

---

64. *The Dog of Knowledge: Or, Memoirs of Bob, the Spotted Terrier: supposed to be written by himself . . . By the author of Dick the Little Poney* (London: J. Harris, 1801).
65. Mary Pilkington, *Marvellous Adventures; or, The Vicissitudes of a Cat* (London: Vernor and Hood; J. Harris, 1802).
66. "The Adventures of a Lady's Lap-Dog," *Lady's Monthly Museum* 8–9 (March 1802–December 1802), 9 parts.
67. Guillame Charles Antoine Pigault-Lebrun, *The History of a Dog. Written by himself, and published by a gentleman of his acquaintance* (London: Lane and Newman, 1804).
68. *Biography of a Spaniel. To which is annexed The Idiot. A Tale* (London: Lane and Newman, 1804).

69. "The Adventures of a Bad Shilling, in the Kingdom of Ireland," *Ireland's Mirror* 2–3 (June 1805–April 1806), 11 parts.
70. *The History of a Religious Tract, supposed to be written by itself* (London: T. Williams, [1805]).
71. "Adventures of a Pen," *European* 50 (July–October 1806), 3 parts; and *Hibernian* (August–November 1806), 3 parts.
72. *The Life of Brushtail the Squirrel that could Play and not Quarrel* (1806).
73. Edward Kendall, *The History of a Goldfinch* (1807).
74. Elizabeth Sandham, *The Adventures of a Bullfinch* (London: J. Harris, 1809).
75. Elizabeth Sandham, *The Adventures of Poor Puss* (London: J. Harris, 1809).

---

76. Ann Hamilton, *The Adventures of a Seven-Shilling Piece* (London, 1811).
77. *Felissa; or, The Life and Opinions of a Kitten of Sentiment* (London: J. Harris, 1811).
78. *The Origin and Adventures of a Hull Eighteen-Penny Silver Token* (Hull, UK: [1811]).
79. "The History of an Old Pocket Bible," *Cottage* 1–2 (March 1812–December 1812), 6 parts.
80. Mary Pilkington, *The Sorrows of Caesar, or, The Adventures of a Foundling Dog* (London: G. and S. Robinson, 1813).
81. "The Adventures of a Three-Shilling Bank Token," *Town Talk* 5 (November 1, 1813), 1 part.
82. *Tell-Tale Sophas, an Eclectic Fable, in Three Volumes* (London, 1814).
83. "Memoirs of a Wig," *Scourge* 7–8 (June 1814–July 1814), 2 parts.
84. Arabella Argus (pseudo.), *The Adventures of a Donkey* (London: William Darton, 1815).
85. Henry Beauchamp, *The Interesting Adventures of a Hackney Coach* (London: S. Hood, 1815).
86. Mary Mister, *The Adventures of a Doll* (London: Darton and Harvey, 1816).
87. *Cato, or Interesting Adventures of a Dog of Sentiment, interspersed with . . . anecdotes* (London: J. Harris, 1816).
88. *Domestic Scenes, or, The Adventures of a Doll* (Burnham, 1817).
89. *The History of a Tame Robin, supposed to be written by himself* (London: Darton and Harvey, 1817).
90. *The Adventures of the Grey Mare, or, The Answer to the Grey Horse* (Dublin, 1820).
91. *A Month's Adventures of a Base Shilling* (Bristol, UK: J. Wansbrough, [1820]).

---

92. Mary Belson (Elliott), *Confidential Memoirs: Or, Adventures of a Parrot, a Greyhound, a Cat and a Monkey* (London: William Darton, 1821).
93. Arabella Argus, *Further Adventures of Jemmy Donkey; interspersed with biographical sketches of the horse* (London: William Darton, 1821).

94. Susanna Moodie, *Little Downy, or, The History of a Field-Mouse, a Moral Tale* (London: Dean and Munday, 1822).
95. *Aureus; or, The Life and Opinions of a Sovereign* (London, 1824).
96. *Adventures of a Bible; or, The Advantages of Early Piety* (London: Dean and Munday, [1825]).
97. Ann Oulton, *The Adventures of a Parrot, named Poll Pry . . . including her birth, education, adversity, prosperity and death* (London: W. Cole, 1826).
98. *The Life, Adventures and Serious Remonstrances of a Scotch Guinea* (Edinburgh, 1826).
99. Henri L. Dubois, *The History of a French Dagger; an Anecdote of the Revolution. From the French* (London, 1828).

---

100. Eliza Grey, *The Adventures of a Marmotte* (London: Simpkin and Marshall, 1831).
101. *The History of a Geranium* (London: Simpkin and Marshall, 1831).
102. [W. Reid], *The Life and Adventures of the Old Lady of Threadneedle Street . . . written by herself* (London, 1832).
103. H.H., Esq., *Birth, Parentage, Life and Adventures of a Loaf of Bread* (London: Marshall, [1834]).
104. *The Adventures of a Halfpenny, commonly called a Birmingham Halfpenny, or Counterfeit, as related by itself* (Banbury: J. G. Rusher, [1835]).
105. *The History of a Banbury Cake* (Banbury: J. G. Rusher, [1835]).
106. Henry Harcourt, *The Adventures of a Sugar-Plantation* (London: Westley and Davis, 1836).
107. *The Interesting Adventures of a Little White Mouse* (Birmingham, UK: T. Bloomer and A. Carvalho, [1840]).

---

108. Douglas Jerrold, *The Story of a Feather* (London, 1844).
109. G. Herbert Rodwell, *The Memoirs of an Umbrella* (London, 1845).
110. Richard Hengist Horne, *Memoirs of a London Doll, written by herself* (London, 1846).
111. *The Adventures of a Fly* (London: James Burns, 1847).
112. Mrs. Henry Glassford Bell, *The History of a Sandal Wood Box, written by itself* (Glasgow, [1848]).
113. Edward Phipps, *The Adventures of a £1000 Note; or, Railway Ruin Reviewed* (London, 1848).
114. John Mills, *The Life of a Foxhound* (London, 1848).
115. Hannah Mary Rathbone, *The History of a Prayer Book* (London, 1849).
116. L. G. B., *The History of a Hare. A True Story* [1850].

---

117. *The Life of a Bird* (1851).
118. [W. Ayrton], *The Adventures of a Salmon in the River Dee, by a friend of the family; together with Notes for the fly-fisher in North-Wales* (London: W. Pickering, 1853).
119. Alfred Elwes the Elder, *The Adventures of a Bear, and a Great Bear too* (London, 1853).

120. Edward Thompson, *The Adventures of a Carpet Bag,* illustrated by R. Cruikshank (London, 1853).
121. S. Whiting, *Memoirs of a Stomach. Written by Himself, that all who eat may read. With notes critical and explanatory, by a Minister of the Interior* (London, 1853).
122. Alfred Elwes the Elder, *The Adventures of a Dog, and a Good Dog too* (London, 1854).
123. Jane Besset, *Memoirs of a Doll, written by Herself . . . adapted from the French by Mrs Besset* (London: G. Routledge, 1854).
124. John Mills, *The Life of a Race-Horse* (London, 1854).
125. Napoleon Roussel, *The History of a Piece of Wood, from the French* (London, [1854]).
126. Julia Pardoe, *Lady Arabella, or, the Adventures of a Doll* (London, [1856]).
127. Lady Catharine Long, *The Story of a Drop of Water* (London, 1856).
128. Alfred Elwes the Elder, *The Adventures of a Cat* (London, 1857).
129. T. Miller, *The Life and . . . Adventures of a Dog* (London, [1857]).
130. *Adventures of a Sixpence in Guernsey* (London, 1857).
131. *The Life of a Ship, from the Launch to the Wreck* (London, 1857).
132. [J. A. Winscom], *Pleasure and Profit: The Story of a Christmas Tree* (London, 1857).
133. Mrs. E. Perring, *The Story of a Mouse, for the Amusement and Benefit of Little People* (London, 1858).
134. *Memoirs of a Ring* (Guernsey, UK, 1858).
135. *Spare Well, Spend Well: Or, The Adventures of a Five Franc Piece* (London: T. Nelson and Sons, 1858).
136. Sir Archibald Geikie, *The Story of a Boulder; or, Gleanings from the Note-Book of a Geologist* (Edinburgh, 1858).
137. Julia Attersoll, *The Life and Adventures of a Doll, told by herself* (London: Darton, [1858]).
138. *The Adventures of a Cat, written by herself, translated from the French by E.T.* (London, [1858]).
139. *The Life of a Plant* [1858].
140. A.L.O.E. [Miss C. Tucker], *The Story of a Needle* (London, 1858).
141. *The Story of a Pocket Bible* (London, [1859]).
142. *Adventures of a Horse: In Peace and War* (London: Ward and Lock, [1859]).
143. *Rana; The Story of a Little Frog. By a Friend of the Family* (London, 1860).
144. R. M. Ballantyne, *The Dog Crusoe and his Master: A Story of Adventures in the Western Prairies* [1860].
145. M.E.F., *George d'Amboise; or, the Story of a Bell* (London: Cheap Repository Series, 1860).
146. L. A. Hall, *The Story of a Pebble* [1860].

---

147. Emma M. Stirling, *The History of a Pin* (Edinburgh: Alexander Strahan, 1861).
148. [Matilda Horsburgh], *The Story of a Red Velvet Bible* (Edinburgh: Johnstone, Hunter, 1862).

149. *Sarah's Present; or, the Story of a New Testament* (Edinburgh, 1862).
150. Catherine Crowe, *The Adventures of a Monkey* (London: Dean and Son, 1862).
151. Clara Lucas Balfour, *Passages in the History of a Shilling* (London: S. W. Partridge, [1862]).
152. Mrs. Richardson, *The Story of a Bee and her Friends. Told by herself.* (London: Wertheim, Macintosh, and Hunt, [1862]).
153. Mrs. E. Perring, *The Adventures of a Penny* (London, 1863 [1862]).
154. *The History of a Cotton Bale* (London, [1863]).
155. Edmund Routledge, *The Adventures of a Sporting Dog,* adapted from the French (London, 1863).
156. Harriet Parr, *The True Pathetic History of Poor Match* (1863).
157. *The Story of a Troublesome Young Monkey who would see the world, with his tricks . . . written down from the Monkey's own dictation by Doctor Gore-illa* (London, [1863]).
158. Julie Gouraud, pseudo. [i.e., Louise d'Aulnay], *The Adventures of a Watch,* trans. from the French (London, [1864]).
159. Lucy Guernsey, *Tabby's Travels: Or, The Holiday Adventures of a Kitten* (Edinburgh: Andrew Elliot, 1864).
160. Jean Macé, *The History of a Bit of Bread,* trans. and ed. by Mrs. A. Gatty (London, 1864).
161. Mrs. Matthew Hughes George Buckle, *Fifi; or, Memoirs of a Canary Bird* (London: Edward Bumpus, [1865]).
162. *Jessie and her Friends, with the History of a Lost Purse* (London: Religious Tract Society, [1865]).
163. Mrs. E. Perring, *The Story of a Cat* (London, 1865).
164. Mrs. E. Perring, *The Story of a Dog* (London, 1866).
165. W. P. Nimmo, *The History of a Picture,* vol. 9 of *Nimmo's Popular Tales* [1866].
166. Charles F. Kirby, *The Adventures of an Arcot Rupee* (London, 1867).
167. C. H. Ross, *The Extraordinary Adventures of a Young Lady's Wedding Bonnet, up the Rhine, over the Alps* (London, [1867]).
168. *The Whale's Story: Passages from the Life of a Leviathan* (London, 1868 [1867]).
169. Eugene Froment, *The Story of a Round Loaf* (London, 1868).
170. Emma Marshall, "The Story of a Basket," in *Little May's Legacy and the Story of a Basket* (London, 1869).
171. *Clever Jack, or, The Adventures of a Donkey. Written by himself* (London: Ward, Lock and Tyler, [1870]).

---

172. M.K.M., *The History of a Stone* (London: Christian Knowledge Society, [1871]).
173. *Little Fan; or, The Story of a Pet Dog* (The Tiny Library, [1871]).
174. William Black, *The Strange Adventures of a Phaeton* (London, 1872).
175. John Watts, "The Life and Adventures of a Little Bird," in *The Life and Adventures of a Little Bird and other Tales* (London, [1872]).

176. Mary Atteridge, *The Story of a Picture* (1872).
177. *Snowdrop, or, the Adventures of a White Rabbit related by himself* (London, 1873).
178. Annie Carey, *The History of a Book* (London: Cassell, Petter and Galpin, [1873]).
179. *The Life of a Bear. His Birth, Education and Adventures,* trans. from the French (London, 1874).
180. Alexander Watt (Versatilius), *The Vagaries of a Pen* (London, [1874]).
181. *The Life of an Elephant* (London, 1875).
182. *Poor Blossom: The Story of a Horse* (London: S. W. Partridge, [1876]).
183. Alexander Watt, *'This Side Up!' or, The Adventures of a Christmas Hamper* (London, [1876]).
184. Francis Bret Harte, *The Story of a Mine* (London, [1877]).
185. Mrs. Sale Barker, *Memoirs of a Poodle,* trans. from *Memoires d'un caniche* by Julie Gourand (London: G. Routledge and Sons, 1877 [1876]).
186. Anna Sewell, *Black Beauty* (London, 1877).
187. Sarah Mores, *Pretty Polly; or, The History of a Cockatoo* (London, [1877]).
188. *The Story of a Pie* (London: Religious Tract Society, [1877]).
189. Richard Rowe, *The History of a Lifeboat* (London, 1878).
190. Ernest Charles Auguste Candèze, *The Curious Adventures of a Field Cricket,* trans. by N. D'Anvers (London: Sampson Low, 1878).
191. *Passages from the Life of a Church Owl. Related by Herself* (London: Griffith and Farran, 1878).
192. *Little Speckly, or, the Adventures of a Chicken, told by herself* (London, 1879).
193. Henrica Frederic, *The Story of a Paper-Knife* (London, 1879).
194. Lady Florence Elizabeth King, *Passages from the Life of a Fox Terrier* (London, [1879]).
195. Lady Louise Mary Caroline Lamb, *The Veracious History of a Black-and-Tan Terrier, told by himself* (London: Newman, 1880).
196. Nellie Hellis, *The Story he was told; or, The Adventures of a Teacup* [1880].

---

197. *The History of a Pink* (London: Griffith and Farron, [1881]).
198. John Ross Macduff, *The Story of a Dewdrop* (London: Ward, 1881).
199. James Yeames, *Gilbert Guestling; or, The Story of a Hymn-Book* (London, Edinburgh: Wesleyan Conference Office, [1881]).
200. Alexander Watt, *The History of a Lump of Coal, from the pit's mouth to a bonnet-ribbon* (London: A Johnstone, 1882).
201. *Little Kittiwake; or, The Story of a Life-Boat* (London: Religious Tract Society, [1882]).
202. Mary E. Gellie, *Dolly Dear, or, The Story of a Waxen Beauty* (London: Griffith and Farran, 1883 [1882]).
203. Talbot Baines Reed, *The Adventures of a Three Guinea Watch,* reprinted from *The Boys Own Paper* (1883).
204. A. C. Lambert, *The Story of a Pillow* (London: T. Woolmer, 1883).
205. Alexander Watt, *The History of a Lump of Chalk* (London: A. Johnston, 1883).

206. *Johnnie Tupper's Temptation; or, The Story of a Top* (London: Blackie and Son, 1884 [1883]).
207. Alexander Watt, *The History of a Lump of Iron* (London: A. Johnston, 1884).
208. *Jack; or, the Story of a Pocket-Book* ([London]: Religious Tract Society, [1884]).
209. Alexander Watt, *The History of a Lump of Gold* (London: A. Johnston, 1885).
210. G. R. Henderson, *The Story of a Moorish Knife* (London: London Literary Society, [1885]).
211. Richard Le Free [Richard William Free], *The History of a Walking-Stick. In Ten Notches* (London: Sonnenschein, 1886).
212. Michael Faraday, *The Chemical History of a Candle. A Course of Lectures delivered before a Juvenile Audience at the Royal Institution,* ed. William Crookes (1886).
213. Maurice Noel, *Buz; or, The Adventures of a Honey Bee* (Bristol: J. W. Arrowsmith, [1886]).
214. Jesse Page, *The Story of a Yellow Rose told by Itself* ([London]: Religious Tract Society, [1886]).
215. Robina F. Hardy, *The Story of a Cuckoo Clock* (Edinburgh: Oliphant, 1887).
216. William Black, *The Strange Adventures of a House-boat* (London: Sampson Low, 1888).
217. Beatrice Stebbing (Batty), *The Life and Adventures of a Very Little Monkey* (London: Sonnenschein, 1888).
218. Harriett Boultwood, *The Adventures of a Sixpence* (London: J. Shaw, [1888]).
219. John G. Sowerby, *Jimmy: Scenes from the Life of a Black Doll* (London: G. Routledge and Sons, [1888])
220. Lucy D. Thornton, *The Story of a Poodle* (London: Sampson Low, 1889).
221. R. J. Irish, *The Story of a Missionary Penny* (London: Church Missionary Society, [1889]).
222. P. H. Emerside and T. F. Goodall, *Wild Life and Tidal Water: The Adventures of a House Boat and Her Crew* (London: Sampson, Low, 1890).
223. Dora Havers, *The Story of a Coin* [1890].
224. Emma Leslie, *The Story of a Christmas Sixpence* (London: Religious Tract Society, [1890]).

---

225. Ada Hityer, "Frolic, or, the Adventures of a Water Spaniel: A Tale," in *Stories of Pets* [1891].
226. Jeanie Hering (Acton), *Adventures of a Perambulator* (London: G. Routledge and Sons, 1894).
227. Emma Leslie, *How Rosie Helped Mabel; or, The Story of a Birthday Doll* [1894].
228. Uncle Oldman, *Ted: The Story of a Cart Wheel* (Manchester. UK: J. Heywood, [1894]).

229. Bertha Upton, *The Adventures of Two Dutch Dolls and a 'Golliwogg'* (1895).
230. William Gordon Stables, *Shireen and Her Friends. Pages from the Life of a Persian Cat* (London: Jarrold and Sons, 1895).
231. Catharine Jane Hamilton, *From Hand to Hand, or, the Adventures of a Jubilee Sixpence* (London: S. W. Partridge, [1895]).
232. W.H.H., *The Life and Adventures of a Penny* (London: Skeffington and Son, 1895).
233. Ascott Robert Hope, *Ups and Downs; or, the Life of a Kite* (London: Christian Knowledge Society, 1895).
234. Thomas Smith, *The Life of a Fox. Written by himself, and Extracts from the Diary of a Huntsman* (1896).
235. Mary Seymour, *Here, There and Everywhere: Or, The Strange Adventures of a Penny* (London: Blackie and Son, [1896]).
236. Edward Martin, *The Story of a Piece of Coal: what it is, whence it comes and whither it goes* (London: G. Newnes, 1896).
237. John William Fortescue, *The Story of a Red Deer* (London: Macmillan, 1897).
238. Mary Seymour, *The Adventures of a Leather Purse* (London: Blackie and Son, [1897]).
239. Helen Burnside, *The Last Letter, or, The Adventures of a Postage Stamp. A Story of the Relief of Lucknow* (London: T. Nelson and Sons, 1898 [1897]).
240. Agnes Underwood, *The Story of a Robin* (London: T. Nelson and Sons, 1898 [1897]).
241. M.C.H., *Adventures of a Cat* (London: T. Nelson and Sons, 1898 [1897]).
242. Jennie Chappell, *The Story of a Persian cat* (London: T. Nelson and Sons, 1898 [1897]).
243. Mrs. Rouquette, *Our Polly: The Adventures of a Parrot,* ed. S. E. Hubbard (London: Gardner, Darton, 1898 [1897]).
244. George Firth, *The Adventures of a Martyr's Bible* (London: John Lane, 1898).
245. A. G. Butler, *Gracie; or, The History of A Stair-Carpet* (London: Simpkin, Marshall, 1898).
246. *From Hand to Hand, or, The Story of a Hymn-Book* (London: Christian Knowledge Society, [1898]).
247. Tertia Bennett, *Tiptail: The Adventures of a Black Kitten* (London: Lamley, 1900 [1899]).
248. Helen Atteridge, *The Bravest of the Brave, and The Story of a Soldier, a Donkey and a Doll* (London: Cassell, 1900).

Notes

1. Review of *The Adventures of a Rupee,* in *The Critical Review: or, Annals of Literature* 52 (1781): 477–78.

2. John Butt and Geoffrey Carnall, *The Mid-Eighteenth Century,* vol. 8 of *The Oxford History of English Literature* (Oxford: Clarendon Press, 1979), 458; Robert Adams Day,

introduction to Francis Coventry, *The History of Pompey the Little; or, The Life and Adventures of a Lap-Dog* (1751; Oxford: Oxford University Press, 1974), xxi.

3. Aileen Douglas, "Britannia's Rule and the It-Narrator," *Eighteenth-Century Fiction* 6.1 (1993): 65–82; Richard K. Meeker, "Bank Note, Corkscrew, Flea and Sedan: A Checklist of Eighteenth-Century Fiction," *Library Chronicle* 35 (1969): 52–57; and Toby Olshin, "Form and Theme in Novels about Non-Human Characters, a Neglected Sub-Genre," *Genre* 2.1 (1969): 41–53; Christopher Flint, "Speaking Objects: The Circulation of Stories in Eighteenth-Century Prose Fiction," *PMLA* 113.2 (1998): 212–26. Versions of Aileen Douglas's and Christopher Flint's essays appear in this volume.

4. Flint, "Speaking Objects," 212.

5. Liz Bellamy, "Private Virtues, Public Vices: Commercial Morality and the Novel, 1740–1800," (Ph.D. diss., University of Cambridge, 1988), 258–64, and *Commerce, Morality, and the Eighteenth-Century Novel* (Cambridge: Cambridge University Press, 1998), 119–28; Markman Ellis, *The Politics of Sensibility: Race, Gender and Commerce in the Sentimental Novel* (Cambridge: Cambridge University Press, 1996); Ava Arndt, "Pennies, Pounds and Peregrinations: Economic and Social Circulation in Eighteenth-Century Literature and Culture," (Ph.D. diss., University of London, 1999).

6. Helenus Scott, *The Adventures of a Rupee* (London, 1782), 92–93, 223–40.

7. Thomas Bridges, *The Adventures of a Bank-Note,* 4 vols. (1770–71), 1:158–63.

8. Ibid., 2:25.

9. Ibid., 2:224 n. 1.

10. *Critical Review* 52 (1782): 477.

11. [Joseph Addison], "Adventures of a Shilling," *Tatler* 249 (November 11, 1710), rpt. in James Ferguson, ed., *The British Essayists* (London, 1819), 5:177.

12. Meeker, "Checklist," 54.

13. Scott, *Adventures of a Rupee,* 139–215.

14. Ibid., 138.

15. Bellamy, *Commerce,* 120.

16. John Hawkesworth, "Remarks on Dreaming: Various Transmigrations related by a Flea," *The Adventurer* 5 (November 21, 1752), rpt. in Ferguson, *British Essayists,* 23:22–30.

17. Hawkesworth, "Remarks on Dreaming," 28–29.

18. Ibid., 29.

19. See Lynn Festa's essay in this volume.

20. Charles Johnstone, *Chrysal; or, The Adventures of a Guinea,* 2 vols. (London, 1760), 1:143.

21. *Critical Review* 51 (1781): 284.

22. Johnstone, *Chrysal,* 2:274.

23. For example, Johnstone, *Chrysal,* 2 vols. (1760), expanded edition (1761), 4 vols. (1764); Bridges, *Bank-Note,* 2 vols. (1770), expanded edition, 4 vols. (1771).

24. See Mark Blackwell's essay in this volume.

25. *Critical Review* 51 (1781): 286.

26. Bridges, *Bank-Note,* 1:110–11.

27. Ibid., 1:2.

28. Ibid., 2:25.

29. Ibid., 2:26.

30. [Addison], "Adventures of a Shilling," in Ferguson, *British Essayists,* 5:177.

31. Ibid.

32. Bridges, *Bank-Note,* 2:54.

33. Ibid., 2:57.

34. Ibid., 2:39.

35. Johnstone, *Chrysal,* 94.
36. See Bonnie Blackwell's essay in this volume.
37. Johnstone, *Chrysal,* 163–79.
38. Bridges, *Bank-Note,* 1:42; 2:28.
39. [Edward Thompson?], "The Adventures of a Cat," *Westminster Magazine* 2 (August–September 1774): 393–97, 459–63.
40. Johnstone, *Chrysal,* 1:149.
41. "Memoir of the Author," prefixed to the 1783 second edition of Scott, *Adventures of a Rupee,* i–x.
42. Scott, *Adventures of a Rupee,* 13.
43. Ibid., 59.
44. Ibid., 60.
45. Ibid., 244.
46. Ibid., 223.
47. Ibid., 228.
48. Mary F. Thwaite, *From Primer to Pleasure in Reading: An Introduction to the History of Children's Books in England from the Invention of Printing to 1914* (London: The Library Association, 1972), 71.
49. Mary Kilner, *Adventures of a Peg-Top* (London: [1785]), 31.
50. Ibid., 64–69.
51. Anna Sewell, *Black Beauty* (Harmondsworth, UK: Puffin, 1994), 116.

Britannia's Rule and the It-Narrator

Aileen Douglas

IN A VOLUME PUBLISHED IN 1781, A GIRL STEPS INTO A HACKNEY COACH and remarks:

> 'Tis surprising some of these literary beings do not give us *The Adventures of a Hackney Coach;* I am sure there is an extensive field for a fertile genius, and no contemptible one: we have the *Adventures of a Guinea,* a most entertaining work; and similar adventures, full of fancy and instruction.[1]

The hint, as the existence of such a volume testifies, was not wasted; the hackney coach joined those literary objects (among them the guinea, black coat, and corkscrew) who had already taken their turn at delighting and instructing the eighteenth-century public. The vogue for it-narration was initiated by Charles Johnstone, when he had a gold guinea narrate *Chrysal; or, The Adventures of a Guinea* (1760). Within two years of its publication the novel was in its third edition. When in 1765 Johnstone presented the public with an expanded, four-volume version he could justifiably speak of the "uncommon favour" with which his work had met—favor that extended to the derivative works of Johnstone's successors.[2] *Adventures of a Hackney Coach,* published in 1781, was in its fifth edition two years later, and, like *Chrysal,* this novel also produced a sequel, published with the author's "warmest effusion of gratitude" to the book-buying public (2:n.p.). From the 1760s on, enthusiastic public response to novels like *The Adventures of a Guinea, The Adventures of a Black Coat, The Adventures of a Cork-Screw,* and *The Adventures of a Hackney Coach* ensured a steady supply of works narrated by inanimate objects.[3] The great popularity of these works, so often independent of literary merit, was a cause for complaint in contemporary reviews:

> This mode of making up a book and styling it the *Adventures* of a Cat, Dog, a Monkey, a Hackney-Coach, a Louse, a Shilling, a Rupee, or—anything else, is grown so fashionable, that few months pass which do not bring one of them under our inspection. It is indeed a convenient method to writers of

> the inferior class, of emptying their commonplace books, and throwing together all the farrago of public transactions, private characters, old and new stories, everything, in short, which they can pick up, to afford a little temporary amusement to an idle reader.[4]

It will be noted that not all of the narrators this disgruntled critic lists are inanimate. In fact, it-narratives were part of a broader subgenre that included eccentric narratives of various sorts, usually by animals. When the reviewer for the *Critical Review* denigrates the "method" of such works, and castigates their authors for jumbling materials that should be kept apart, he actually intimates the shared appeal of eccentric narratives: their lack of discrimination.[5] Such narratives did not respect the boundaries and limits that organized eighteenth-century society. Corkscrews and lapdogs could move among classes and ranks in a way no human subject could. To readers locked within particular social roles such movement must have been both engrossing and refreshing. Moreover, the "farrago" that the reviewer deprecates is a literary version of a very real, and earnestly discussed, social threat. The it-narrators of later eighteenth-century fiction are emblematic of a burgeoning consumer culture that seemed, to contemporaries, to dissolve the marks of social class and to render the barriers between social orders frangible and vulnerable.

The expressed and shared ambition of these diverse works is to "excite virtue, depress vice, and ridicule folly," or to "prove an incitement to virtue, rectitude, and benevolence."[6] Their moral intentions, however, contributed less to their contemporary success than did the facility with which they exploited and strengthened an emerging consumer culture. Indeed, it would be difficult to imagine another literary genre more thoroughly determined by the logic of consumerism. Not only are these it-narrators commodities speaking within the commodity form of the book, but one of their major attractions is the commodification of the rich and famous. When the Hackney Coach (the most ostentatiously literary of these objects) prefaces his adventures with a warning from Shakespeare: "Tremble thou wretch / That hast within thee undivulged crimes / Unwhipt of justice," the reader familiar with the genre knows that the wretch will not be an anonymous individual. The Corkscrew more subtly promises striking anecdotes, characters, and actions of "Persons in Real Life."[7] As the first, and most outrageous, of the it-narrators, Johnstone's Guinea is privy to conversations between George II and his first minister of state, William Pitt, and attends an initiation ceremony of the Monks of Medmenden—a notorious group of libertines dedicated to devil-worship. "Persons in Real Life" had appeared—in their own names—in novels before Johnstone's, but it-narrators created the illusion that readers shared the lives of wealthy, powerful, and distinguished individuals. In providing an opportunity to overhear the conversation of a king, see Samuel Johnson dispense charity, or take a coach-ride with Oliver Goldsmith, it-narrations supposedly gave their readers access to the casual, intimate, and mundane acts of public figures. Such creative opportunism blurred the distinction between private and public, and given that the personal information purveyed was sometimes entirely fictional, it separated the historical individual from the commercial use of his or her name and actions. It-narrations hit on a new product, the development of which, in our own day, sustains a lucrative industry.

Even more central to the popularity of these texts is their ability to mediate the consumerism they exploit. They whimsically register England's transformation into a consumer society, turning a troubling, if exciting, phenomenon into a harmless game. It is worth remarking that Johnstone's *Chrysal* was composed and published during the Seven Years' War (1756–1763). Virtually global in scope, the war saw English victories over the French in Canada, the West Indies, Africa, and India, which laid the foundations of the British Empire and strengthened trade and commercialism as vital elements in English national identity. As trade flourished, new goods became available. Such availability (for example, of cheap calico and muslin from India) stimulated demand and consumption. As Peter Mathias remarks, "the expansion of foreign trade was intimately associated with the extension of internal demand."[8] During the last fifteen years of the century, the consumption of tobacco, soap, candles, printed fabrics, spirits, and beer was "increasing more than twice as fast as population."[9] While moralists often singled out the tea-drinking of the lower classes as a particularly blatant symptom of luxury, the consumption of more substantial articles was also on the rise. Examining wills from the period, D. E. C. Eversley finds confirmed "the general impression that the number of people possessing goods they must have bought in their lifetime, rather than inherited, grows steadily," and observes that "the new products are striking."[10] Horrified moralists, confronted with a "convulsion of getting and spending" which, historians have argued, represented nothing less than the "birth of a consumer society," denigrated consumption as luxury and listed its enervating effects.[11] Of course, the association of trade and vice was not new; Bernard Mandeville's *The Fable of the Bees* (1714) had habituated at least some readers to the notion that a thriving commercial society depended on individual vice. It will be remembered that in Mandeville's hive moral reformation has disastrous effects on commerce:

As Pride and Luxury decrease,
So by degrees they leave the Seas.
Not Merchants now; but Companies
Remove whole Manufacturies.[12]

Finally, the rise of virtue causes complete social collapse, as the bees, unable to defend themselves "against th' Insults of numerous Foes," abandon the hive. As the century wore on, imagined relationships between trade and vice became even more sinister, writers now arguing that trade directly caused vice. Speaking of the "moral Evils introduced by Trade," and with his eye especially (but not exclusively) on the "lower Sort," Henry Fielding observed: "The Narrowness of their Fortune is changed into Wealth; the Simplicity of their Manners into Craft; their Frugality into Luxury; their Humility into Pride, and their Subjection into Equality."[13] Fielding's views on this topic were shared by John Brown, author of an enormously popular jeremiad, *An Estimate of the Manners and Principles of the Times*. Brown argued against the "ruling maxim of this Age and Nation, that if our Trade and Wealth are but increased, we are powerful, happy, and secure." On the contrary, Brown asserted that commerce eventually "brings in superfluity and vast wealth; begets Avarice, gross Luxury, or effeminate Refinement among the higher Ranks, together with general loss of Principle." According to Brown, the "exorbitant Trade and Wealth of *England*" sufficiently accounted for its "present effeminacy."[14] At mid-century then, there was a well-beaten rhetorical path between trade and vice. Vice might spur trade, or trade might engender vice. At any rate, social commentators managed, without much argumentative armature, to get from one to the other.

Even proponents of commercialism caught a whiff of something disquieting in stiffening trade winds. Boswell, for example, took pride in the "great commercial country" in which he lived but expressed anxiety that the commercial spirit "tends to lessen the value of that distinction by birth and gentility, which has ever been found beneficial to the grand scheme of subordination."[15] Ever-widening, ever-quickening, systems of trade and exchange threatened traditional order and hierarchy. Britons, even as they expressed satisfaction in their evolving commercial empire and their rule of the waves, anxiously associated trade with moral deterioration and suspected its effects on social organization.

The technique of it-narrations subordinates the individual (and that individual's moral or immoral acts) to impersonal patterns of circulation. What the writer for the *Critical Review* denigrated as a "convenient method" for "writers of an inferior class" also mirrors a new "method" for connecting individuals in society. The very notion that objects have adventures, and that society is integrated through the transmission of objects from hand to hand, is itself a novel way of thinking. The displacement of the human voice in this later eighteenth-century fiction expresses fear and excitement particular to the times. The fear is that people have become enthralled to things and that therefore objects can explain society as it really is; the excitement comes from the unfamiliarity and novelty of the society the objects reveal.

As one would expect, these novels chiefly unfold in a world of commerce. Mostly set in London, they occasionally use Jamaica or India to add a dash of colonial exotic. In the population of these novels, merchants and their families are overrepresented. Aristocrats intrude now and then (mainly to get their fortunes repaired through marriage to a merchant's daughter), but they are exceptional presences. Patterns of circulation in these novels almost completely exclude agricultural England, thereby suggesting an irrelevance that was far from the case. The symbolic weight carried by the country house in the novels of Fielding and Smollett is here borne by the debtor's prison and the pawnshop. As satires, it-narrations dwell on those unable to pay for goods they have already consumed, and those forced to part with the few goods they possess. Technique, locations, and characters combine to impress upon the reader that commercialism is both prevalent and dangerous.

On the title page of *Chrysal,* Charles Johnstone, again quoting Shakespeare, promises that through the medium of the Guinea he will

> —Hold the Mirror up to Nature
> To shew Vice its own Image, Virtue her own Likeness
> And the very Age and Body of the Times
> His Form and Pressure.

Yet, the "Form and Pressure" of the Times (as Chrysal explains) delimit the usefulness of "vice" and "virtue" in talking about humans in society. In fact, they make human nature itself seem an outmoded idea. As the Guinea explains, "When the mighty spirit of a large mass of gold takes possession of the human heart, it influences all its actions, and overpowers, or banishes, the weaker impulse of those immaterial, unessential notions called *virtues*" (1:7). The impulses that govern society are no longer those of the human heart; virtue, being "immaterial," becomes irrelevant. Human nature is overpowered, or banished, by the material world.

One of the first lessons these objects teach about their consumer society is its instability. There is something ephemeral about trading fortunes. The Hackney Coach, for example, started life in the home of an honest merchant bankrupted, like so many others, by the fall of the banking firm of Fordyce in 1772.[16] Castigating Fordyce as a "plunderer" (5), the family meets calamity by vowing: "We will retrench all our superfluities and live like our primitive parents, when there were no F— — —s" (7). Credit, which facilitates trade, also encourages "superfluities." In deciding to live like their "primitive parents" the merchant's family reject the consumer society in which they had been temporarily successful. Of course, the incident is related to us by one of the first victims of retrenchment: the family coach.

Representing trading fortunes as precarious in and of themselves, it-narrators also try to shore up the "grand scheme of subordination" which Boswell saw as particularly threatened in a commercial society. Significantly, these objects tend not to attack merchants or tradesmen directly; instead, they implicate the female members of trading families in scandal. Such narrative developments are based on a widely held (or at least frequently expressed) belief that women particularly are given to luxurious consumption. In a fairly typical anecdote, the Black Coat tells us the story of one Susan Sirloin, daughter of a "plain decent looking tradesman" (67). Emulating her social betters rather than her frugal father, Susan is allowed to dress as a lady. In doing so, she exemplifies the way in which "the different stations of Life so run into and mix with each other, that it is hard to say, where the one ends, and the other begins."[17] Lower-class stylishness, and the consequent difficulty of using dress to distinguish among classes, was a frequent subject of comment by foreign visitors to England. In fiction, however, the lines could be clearly redrawn. Susan's indulgence in frippery leads eventually to a rapid social descent and she ends her days as an "abandoned prostitute" (164). While the Black Coat is not the most inventive of eighteenth-century storytellers, it does render in dramatic form the society's fear that confusion of dress standards leads inevitably to social and moral confusion. Even "decent looking tradesmen" are made vulnerable by a conspicuous consumption on the part of their daughters which, in fact, advertises incipient vice.

At certain points in these narratives, however, the language of virtue and vice begins to seem both obstinate and desperate. Virtue and vice, after all, only make sense in terms of moral agency, and in these novels people have become objects. Women, especially the daughters of tradesmen, are particularly likely to become commodities in circulation. In *Adventures of a Cork-Screw* Lucy Lightairs, "daughter of a very eminent tradesman in the city of London" (42), becomes "at different times the property of the peer, the squire, the tradesman and others" (76). In Johnstone's *Chrysal,* a kept mistress receives her adulterous lover. No sooner has he fallen into a drunken stupor than she calls her maid to take her place by his side. The substitution effected, the mistress goes "directly to an house, where she used to piddle away her leisure hours with any chance customers, rather than be idle" (1:151). Even this novel's happier episodes are permeated by an economy of prostitution. In one, a young widow is accosted in church by an older woman, who is, unknown to the widow, seeking to supply a client with a prostitute. We learn that the widow married against her father's will and is now destitute. That father (who is, of course, the client) had promised the bawd "the paultry reward of 50 l . . . little imagining that [he] was bargaining for the seduction of [his] own innocent child" (1:176). While in this instance natural ties are repaired ("From henceforth you are *my* child, and I will be *your* father" [1:175]), the reader knows such an outcome depends upon the momentary identification of father and daughter with the commercial relationship of prostituter and prostituted. Nor is the commercial potential of the human body limited to sex. One it-narrative features a chimney sweep whose mother has sold his front teeth to transplant them "into the head of an old lady of quality."[18] The sweep is, however, better off than his sister, entirely toothless and living on slops. If even the teeth in one's head are not safe from circulation, neither are the dead. An incident the Hackney Coach finds especially distasteful is its use in a grave-robbing incident undertaken by "Resurrection Thieves" (43).

The logic of these texts is the logic of consumerism and their most pointed irony is that the objects for which human beings have sacrificed virtue and nature become the last refuge of both. For example, the scenes it witnesses cause the Black Coat to reflect that although men have been given the power of reasoning to "distinguish the true road to happiness," it is, in fact, "of little or no service to them in their pursuit," for "the present gratification of the passions and senses, seems to be the chief consideration and stimulator of all their actions" (106). Immersed in luxury, men leave philosophy to their garments. The soul of this society is invested in its commodities, and there, these texts tell us, it has found a surprisingly safe home: "Good Heaven! [thinks the Hackney Coach] what a world of extravagance we live in!—how thoughtless of past indigence, and how madly vain in the sun-shine of prosperity" (89).

Loose connections between trade, consumerism, and vice are common in these narratives, but their treatment of trade has a more extensive, paradoxical aspect. Many also propagate the notion that trade is virtuous, and develop a rhetoric whereby commerce, far from defeating human virtue, actually replenishes and strengthens it. This seeming inconsistency can be explained by reflecting that while domestic consumption in one aspect of trade, another is that of imperial expansion. As far as it-narrators are concerned, empire cleanses trade.

We see this process at work in Charles Johnstone's *Chrysal*, where it contrasts strangely with the novel's scenes of human depravity. Once past the novel's framing device, we are introduced to the story of one Traffic. The only son of a wealthy merchant, Traffic's life has brought him from London, to Jamaica, to a Peruvian gold mine. The prominent position of this story at the beginning of the novel, and the name Johnstone gives his character, suggest that this tale is in some sense the story of commerce itself. In fact, the story turns out to be about the end of commerce—both literally and metaphorically. Against "received opinion," Traffic's father is convinced that "though trade adds to the wealth, yet too eager a pursuit of it, even with the greatest success, diminishes the strength of a nation . . . The real strength of a nation consists in the prevalence of a disinterested spirit, which, regardless of *self*, throws its weight into the public fund" (1:15). The fortune Traffic's father has acquired has removed "all necessity of labour" (1:14) from his son, whom he therefore advises to leave off trade, enjoy his riches, and "employ the super-plus in acts of private benevolence and public spirit" (1:14). If Traffic chooses to continue in trade, he should be governed by an injunction which his father would have written "on the heart of every merchant": "that he should never let private interest tempt him to engage in any trade or scheme that can interfere with the publick interest, or is forbidden by the laws of his country" (1:20). Johnstone starts his novel with a homily on the regulation of traffic—both the person and abstraction. He offers us a view of society in which trade is subjected to moral and public considerations.

The received opinion against which the father speaks is obviously Mandevillian. Whereas Mandeville argued that the "eager pursuit" of trade—even vicious trade—contributed to the health of society as a whole, Traffic's father emphasized the point at which the public interest requires the sinking of the "spirit of commerce." Moreover, he imagines that the dictates of the public interest can be inscribed on the heart of the individual. According to Traffic's father, trade can be conducted virtuously: successful trade results in a "super-plus" which can be devoted to benevolence; and the final reference of trade should be the public interest.

Traffic's refusal to unite virtue and commerce as his father desires is the catalyst for the entire novel. The hundreds of pages in which Chrysal passes from hand to hand—through bribery, corruption, and prostitution—present us with a vicious and perverse society. After various kinds of illegal trading, which serve only to dissipate his fortune, Traffic reaches his nadir by entering "into measures the most injurious to my country, which was then engaged in a just and extensive war" (1:22). Traffic's filial disobedience recalls that of another, more famous merchant. Robinson Crusoe rejects his father's advice to stay home, comfortable in the middle stations of life, and goes to sea, an act that leads both to his long sojourn on the island and to his ultimate prosperity. This act he will later identify as his "original sin," a flouting of providence.[19] Although, in *Chrysal,* Traffic's model of trade claims most of our attention, the novel suggests it is aberrant. Traffic too can be read as a prodigal son who acts against the course of providence. The difference between Traffic and Crusoe in this respect is that Crusoe sins against a providence connected to his personal salvation, and Traffic sins against a providence connected to national destiny. Significantly, the year in which Johnstone published Traffic's story was also that in which Lord Egremont, addressing his new King, attributed the "signal successes" of the English at war to the "goodness of Providence."[20]

Finally, the novel does find a way to unite virtue and commerce and enact the vision of Traffic's father. Despite all its vicious episodes, the novel reserves a place for the practice and theory of charity, a virtue that the spirit of gold regards as the "most exalted of human virtues" (1:215). The Guinea asserts further that there can be no "stronger proof of the beneficence of the author of human nature, that his placing this virtue, which is the perfection of it, within the reach of every individual" (1:215). Given that the very concept of human nature is more or less emptied out in the novel, Chrysal's praise of charity as the perfection of human nature seems beside the point. It receives support, however, from an unexpected source: the building of England's "mighty empire" (1:vi). In the rhetoric of the novel, the public interest, now the imperial interest, nurtures benevolence. The novel suggests that empire-building puts charity within "the reach of every individual." If private life is mostly unedifying, public life is both benevolent and noble; the public interest and the individual heart do, as Traffic's father wished, come together, and this notwithstanding the considerable satire of public life the novel contains. In the manner of Fielding and Smollett, Johnstone satirizes both the law and the navy as institutions riddled with corruption and inhospitable to individuals of merit. Also, especially in the later volumes, he devotes much satiric attention to controversial contemporary events, most obviously the execution of Admiral Byng for his failure to support Minorca in 1756.

It is all the more surprising, then, that the novel can imagine the "just and glorious" war in which England is engaged, and the empire that that war founded, as innocent, even benevolent phenomena. Johnstone dedicates his novel to William Pitt, as one on whom "the welfare, not only of this mighty empire, but also of the greater part of *Europe,* do now so eminently depend" (vi). Throughout the novel's original two volumes, the author's allegiance to Pitt, and the "necessary and just war" (2:81) which he prosecutes, is unmistakable. The country's "glory" and "interest" (2:68, 2:91) are at stake.

The novel additionally claims that Pitt's handling of the war has led to a new, mutual confidence between rulers and ruled and that it has restored national vigor and initiated a decisive change in the English character. In an exchange between Frederick of Prussia and one of his advisers, Pitt features as one newly in power who has "always been against dealing with your highness" (2:140). The portrayal is accurate enough—Pitt had first won popular favor for his demands that England should not become embroiled on the Continent to serve the interests of George II's native Hanover, and more specifically for his opposition to the German subsidy (funds paid by England to Prussia to protect Hanover). Instead, Pitt wished to assign the navy the primary role in national defense. Endorsing Pitt's foreign policy, Johnstone has the advisor draw the attention of Frederick to the renovation of English spirit and prophesy the growth of the English empire:

> I fear your highness does not attend to the change which has lately been in *England* . . . the people begin to see their own strength, and their governors to exert it properly, and shew them that they want no foreign assistance . . . they have actually sent a powerful body of their troops abroad, and are carrying on the war with vigour and success in every quarter of the world. (2:140–41)

Chrysal, then, is very much concerned with, and offers partial views on, a war in which "the main lines of the British Empire were finally laid down."[21] Nor is the defense of the English war effort confined to England's citizens and allies. Perhaps the most extraordinary apologist for the English cause is a "noble" Spaniard. Taken prisoner in battle, the Spaniard is treated with "that generous tenderness which brave men feel for each other." Struck with conduct so different from what he expected—for he had "been taught to look upon the *English* as enemies to mankind"—the soldier asks to be ransomed so that he can "faithfully remove the prejudices" of his people (3:42). The prejudice of which the Spaniard speaks, and the lies he had been taught, point to very specific agents: the Roman Catholic church, particularly the Jesuits, who are satirized throughout the novel. In fact, as the novel unwinds, the vices of various international groups, most notably the Jesuits and the Jews, serve increasingly as foils for English national virtues.[22] In fighting a global war, the English are not merely acquiring trading routes and colonies, but are also combating superstition and dispensing enlightenment.

In this novel, virtue, particularly benevolence, has a political cast. An unfortunate Bulgarian, who has received charity from an Englishman, attributes this charity directly to the English system of government and (by implication) to its colonial ambitions:

> Such (said he) is the noble benevolence that distinguishes the sons of liberty! Such the generosity of heart, that always extends the ready hand of a *Britain,* with relief to the distressed. May heaven preserve to your happy nation the blessings which enable it to exert its virtues, to make them a blessing to all who want their assistance. (2:126–27)

Notable in the Bulgarian's apostrophe is the shift from private to national benevolence, from individual generosity to the virtues of a nation. The reader is led to understand that the English are charitable because they are the "sons of liberty." Indeed, even dour commentators on English manners, such as John Brown, were willing to attribute what he called "the few remaining virtues we have left" (17) to the English political system. Public life ensures private virtue. Moreover, the language of moral discrimination provides a way of discussing conquest and colonization. In the Bulgarian's speech English commercial expansion is represented as "relief to the distressed," and a commercial war is equated with the exertion of English virtues.

The elevation of the English war effort into a species of virtue is neatly expressed by the King of Bulgaria, when he comes into possession of a pile of coin, among which Chrysal lies. At first, the King addresses the money as the "source of every evil which distracts this wretched world." In his distaste we hear the cadences of traditional morality: money is the root of all evil. Then, however, the eye of the King is caught by the English guinea and his attitude changes completely:

> Happening to observe *my* shape, he took me up, and looking attentively at me, "Is there no corner of the earth (said he) where the wealth of Britain is not dispersed? If its commerce collects the produce of every climate under heaven, its munificence does also diffuse its riches as far. Great and happy nation!" (2:167–68)

Filthy lucre is cleansed if it circulates in the interests of empire. What makes Britain a "great and happy nation" is not only the extent of its commerce, but also the "munificence" through which it disperses not only material coin, but also the immaterial "riches" of custom and habit.

There are two distinct patterns of circulation at work in this novel. In the first, the coin's progress serves to expose venality and vice of all kinds, the "evil" for which the King of Bulgaria blames money itself. Typical here is the pattern in which Chrysal is disposed of by one master who "gave me to a pimp, who gave me to a whore, who gave me to a bully, who gave me to a pawn-broker, who gave me to a beaux, who gave me to a tavern-keeper, who paid me into the bank, from whence I was sent, in the change of a note, to the first minister of state" (2:73). At first glance, the inclusion of the "minister of state" in such a list seems satiric, and indeed Chrysal expresses "reluctance" at entering such a service. From William Pitt's possession, however, Chrysal enters on the novel's second and contrary pattern of circulation in which British war aims are associated with benevolence and moral action. Having carried the coin off to an interview with George II—where the latter appears to great advantage—Pitt disposes of it in a charitable act. Observing a group of disabled soldiers outside his door, he opines: "*The Man who does not use, to the best advantage, the means entrusted to him by his country, to destroy its enemies, is guilty of all the evils, which those enemies may afterwards do to his country*" (2:83). Then, turning to his companion, Pitt asks, "Shall I beg a favour of my friend; distribute this money." The minister, right at the center of power, supports and enables the "munificence" of which the King of Bulgaria speaks. Vigorously using the "means entrusted to him by his country, to destroy its enemies" and increase English possessions abroad, the minister protects trade in the interests of England. Such use of the country's "means" is endorsed, and represented in little, when Pitt follows his argument in favor of war with an act of private charity.

The notion that the colonies are blessed in their trading relationship with the mother country, and that trade can be identified with virtue and moral good, also emerges very clearly in *The Adventures of a Rupee.* This narrator, lying around in the mountains of Tibet, is somewhat improbably seized with the desire that fortune will carry it to England. When the Rupee eventually gets there, it ends up in a pawnshop from which it surveys a fairly standard sample of miserable people and justifiably reflects that the pawnshop is "not a temple where wealth has deposited its superfluities; it is a cell loaded with the spoils of the afflicted, and the very necessaries of life" (122). The pattern of circulation centered on the pawnshop parodies the pattern of trade which has brought the Rupee from India to London. If English commerce "collects the produce of every climate under heaven" (*Chrysal,* 2:168), the pawnshop is a "cell loaded with the spoils of the afflicted." At the same time, however, the novel explicitly limits the scope of the parody and makes it impossible to argue that London itself is a cell loaded with spoils. It does this by dissociating imperial trade from any notion of self-interest or private advantage. In this novel, as in *Chrysal,* trade is associated with sublime virtue.

As with *Chrysal,* the *Rupee* is published against the backdrop of a war which becomes the subject of direct narrative comment. The Rupee finds itself in the Royal Nursery where the nonappearance of George III is explained by his involvement in the war effort: "Almost all the nations in the earth had taken up arms against his sea-surrounded land." The narrator is, however, assured that "their impotent efforts will expose them to contempt, while Britain shall remain the admiration of future times—Great monarch, into whatever country your free born subjects move, they shall carry in their hands both victory and law" (207). English victory will allow greater scope to English munificence, as "law" is carried into "whatever country" her freeborn subjects move. In the novel's richest example of the rhetorical elevation of trade, a young officer in the East India Company is advised by his father:

> Your particular province is to protect the trade of your country against the insults of European powers, or of the Indian nations, who ignorant of the blessings that commerce diffuses, even to themselves, are often disposed to interrupt its equitable course. The prosperity therefore of trade, is what you are to have in view, not the extension of settlement, and much less your private advantage. Your profits will be sufficient to your wants, and if your good behaviour allows you to advance to a high rank, they may even enable you to return to your own country with honourable wealth. In this station in India, my son, you may enjoy the glorious honour of rectifying particular abuses, you may be blessed by those nations, that have so often cursed our rapacity, and the heart of your old father may beat high with the idea of having given life to a benefactor of mankind. (52)

The father's exhortation dissociates trade—clearly represented as national—from both "extensive settlement" and "private advantage." Trade is an absolute good, from which everyone benefits, although the Indian nations may be "ignorant" of the blessing it diffuses. While there is some suggestion of past misconduct and rapacity, the son goes to India to rectify abuses, and it is "good behaviour" on his part that may make possible an eventual return to England as a wealthy man.

Over the course of a quarter-century, it-narrators offered two distinct perspectives on commercialization, and the more sophisticated efforts in the genre tend to offer both together. The first perspective is a satiric one in which it is left to an inanimate object, supposedly outside the realm of morality and nature, to enunciate a moral code that the citizens of the commercial order have abandoned. The second perspective, demonstrated in both *Chrysal* and the *Rupee,* is to rehabilitate trade. These works paradoxically suggest that the damage done to human nature by trade can be repaired once trade is understood in terms of empire. It seems fitting that Johnstone, who was born in Ireland and spent his writing career in London, ended his life in Calcutta. Certainly, *Chrysal,* written as Britannia really was beginning to rule the waves, uses its inanimate narrator not only to castigate human vice but also to suggest that the burgeoning empire is the arena of virtue.

Notes

This essay originally appeared in *Eighteenth-Century Fiction* 6.1 (1993): 67–82.

1. Anon., *Adventures of a Hackney Coach* (London, 1781), 2. References are to this edition. An additional volume was also published in 1781.

2. Charles Johnstone, *Chrysal; or, The Adventures of a Guinea* (London, 1765), 3:a. Actually, what Johnstone published in 1765 were two additional volumes. These volumes were not a sequel in the usual sense, as they contained material that the industrious reader was to insert into the work as first published. Volumes 3 and 4 contain elaborate instructions for these mental insertions. This essay refers to volumes 1 and 2 as published in 1760, and volumes 3 and 4 as published in 1765.

3. In his bibliographic article, "Banknote, Corkscrew, Flea and Sedan: A Checklist of Eighteenth-Century Fiction," *Library Chronicle* 35 (1969), 52–57, Richard K. Meeker records at least sixty eighteenth-century works written from a nonhuman point of view.

4. *Critical Review* (December 1781), quoted in J. M. S. Tompkins, *The Popular Novel in England* (1932; rpt. Lincoln: University of Nebraska Press, 1961), 49.

5. This statement seems as true of works like Francis Coventry's *The History of Pompey the Little; or, The Life and Adventures of a Lap-dog* (1751), or Tobias Smollett's *The History and Adventures of an Atom* (1769), as it does of it-narratives properly speaking. Of all the works in this genre, Smollett's most consummately exploits the philosophic, political, and satiric potential of a fully miscible world. The narrating atom of the tale is animate and inanimate by turns and fully self-conscious about its ability to render the most basic discriminations meaningless. In addition to their narrative method, both Smollett's *Atom* and Johnstone's *Chrysal* share material provided by the Seven Years' War. In the main, however, Smollett's eccentric narrator does not show that concern for issues of trade and consumerism displayed by its purely inanimate fellows. As this essay focuses on these issues, it is restricted to works narrated by objects.

6. *Adventures of a Black Coat* (London, 1760), vi (references are to this edition); *Adventures of a Hackney Coach,* 149. Toby A. Olshin, arguing for modern critical consideration of these works, read them in moral terms ("Form and Theme in Novels about Non-Human Characters, a Neglected Sub-Genre," *Genre* 2.1 [1969]: 43–56). J. M. S. Tompkins offered a suggestive view of them as an extension of the picaresque (*Popular Novel,* 47, 49).

7. *Adventures of a Cork-Screw* (London, 1775). References are to this edition.

8. "Leisure and Wages in Theory and Practice," in *The Transformation of England: Essays in the Economic and Social History of England in the Eighteenth Century* (New York: Columbia University Press, 1979), 154.

9. Ibid., 162. According to Mathias, population in England and Wales rose by 14 percent between 1785 and 1800, whereas the demand for printed fabrics (the most dramatic example) rose by 141.9 percent.

10. "The Home Market and Economic Growth in England 1750–80," in *Land, Labour and Population in the Industrial Revolution,* ed. E. L. Jones and G. E. Mingay (London: Edward Arnold, 1967), 238.

11. Neil McKendrick, "The Consumer Revolution of Eighteenth-Century England," in *The Birth of a Consumer Society,* ed. Neil McKendrick, John Brewer, and J. H. Plumb (Bloomington: Indiana University Press, 1985), 9. For the conservative anxieties on

this score see John Sekora, *Luxury: The Concept in Western Thought, Eden to Smollett* (Baltimore: Johns Hopkins University Press, 1977). See also Roy Porter, *English Society in the Eighteenth Century* (Harmondsworth, UK: Penguin, 1982), 201–31.

12. *The Fable of the Bees*, ed. Philip Harth (Harmondsworth, UK: Penguin, 1989), 75.

13. Henry Fielding, "An Enquiry into the Causes of the Late Increase of Robbers," in *An Enquiry into the Causes of the Late Increase of Robbers and Related Writings*, ed. Malvin R. Zirker (Middletown, CT: Wesleyan University Press, 1988), 70.

14. John Brown, *An Estimate of the Manners and Principles of the Times*, 6th ed. (London, 1757), 150, 153, 161.

15. James Boswell, *The Life of Dr. Johnson*, ed. G. B. Hill and L. F. Powell, 6 vols. (Oxford: Clarendon Press, 1934–50), 1:490.

16. Alexander Fordyce (d. 1789) first gained a fortune when he obtained early knowledge of the signature of the preliminaries of the peace of Paris in 1763 (the peace by which the Seven Years' War was ended), and consolidated that fortune when East India stock rose dramatically in 1764–65. His fall was the subject of a sermon by Thomas Toller.

17. Josiah Tucker, quoted in Neil McKendrick, "Home Demand and Economic Growth," in *Historical Perspectives: Studies in English Thought and Society*, ed. Neil McKendrick (London: Europa, 1974), 190. For a discussion of fashion, social emulation, and moral anxiety during the period, see also Neil McKendrick, "The Commercialization of Fashion," in *Birth of a Consumer Society*, 34–99.

18. *Adventures of a Rupee* (Dublin, 1782), 190. References are to this edition.

19. Daniel Defoe, *Robinson Crusoe* (Harmondsworth, UK: Penguin, 1985), 198.

20. *The Parliamentary History of England from the Earliest Period to the Year 1803* (London, 1813), 15:986.

21. J. S. Corbett, *England in the Seven Years' War*, 2 vols. (London: Longmans, Green, 1918), 1:7.

22. See Ann Louise Kibbie's essay in this volume.

Speaking Objects: The Circulation of Stories in Eighteenth-Century Prose Fiction

Christopher Flint

PUBLISHED IN 1709, CHARLES GILDON'S *THE GOLDEN SPY* INAUGURATED a storytelling fad—the speaking object—that influenced British fiction well into the nineteenth century. While inanimate storytellers can be traced back to Pythagoras (who described the oral capacities of rocks and trees), the eighteenth-century representation of them as both authors and commodities concentrated on how the circulation of things related to narrative practice in an age of mechanical reproduction. The eighteenth-century speaking object is almost always a product of manufacture rather than a part of nature and its usually satiric vision of the world arises from its particular experience of human commerce. In Gildon's work, for instance, a handful of quarrelsome gold coins from various countries jointly narrate the story, boasting not only of their national origins but also of their special authorial perspective. "I have had such various transmigrations thro' the World," the French sovereign remarks, "and may justly say, that I know the Transactions in all the Climates of *Europe,* and Ages of the World."[1] This extensive knowledge of human transactions stems from the coin's status as an artifact; its mobility and anonymity as a manufactured unit of exchange endow it with the authority to tell tales.[2] The object's authority, however, is complicated by the very extemporaneous nature of its experience. It-narratives are invariably picaresque; shifts in plot, subject, and locale emphasize the rapid changes of ownership that dictate the object's market value. It seeks a unified national identity but is subject to a variety of dislocations that not only disrupt its storytelling but also complicate the meaning of belonging.

While *The Golden Spy* is unusual in that several speaking objects narrate, most such works similarly align authorship, market value, and national acculturation. In this essay I argue that the appearance of speaking objects in eighteenth-century fiction foregrounds authorial concerns about circulating books in the public sphere. Object narratives, I claim, represent that sphere as a dynamic field where the author seeks public exposure but frets over its consequences. Were it not for the sympathy the objects express toward the writers of their stories, such fables might even appear to displace the human agent, portending a new economy in which the commodity serves the interests of the consumer at the expense of the producer. But like their human counterparts, inanimate narrators repeatedly express fears that printed words invest writers with a professional identity only by voiding the writer's authority. The speaking object duplicates the author's position in a print culture in explicit (though not always systematic) ways, echoing Gildon's claim that a writer is rewarded and threatened by the opportunities of print. It both reflects and addresses domestic and global pressures that constantly shifted the function of authorship, redefining the attributes of the writer with each alteration in the public existence of books.[3]

❧

Unlike Aesop's *Fables* or Apuleius's *Golden Ass,* nearly all eighteenth-century object tales are framed, usually in a preface, by an additional story that describes the convoluted process leading to their publication. They are, in other words, specifically linked to the circulation of the author's work in a modern print economy. In the preface to *The Golden Spy,* entitled "Epistle Nuncupatory to the Author of *A Tale of a Tub,*" Gildon prepares the reader for the object tale by imagining his manuscript's conversion into printed form and its gradual detachment from the history of its author. Rather than speak as writer, Gildon poses as a bookseller who has received an anonymous manuscript. He rejects conventional explanations of how *"the Author sent the following Sheets to Visit the World,"* detailing instead his vexing search for a suitable patron, necessitated by his *"Author having sent me his Copy without inscribing it to any living Creature"* (v). That the narrative itself is unattributed also contributes to the indeterminacy of textual authority, which editorial interventions must offset (*The Golden Spy* itself appeared anonymously). Gildon thus portrays the bookseller as interested more in the material than in the intellectual consequences of authorship. For one, the preface situates the professional writer within a highly unstable print economy and thus intensifies the separation of author and text. Further, in describing the effects of circulation on a manuscript that is itself about the "miraculous" circulation of a linguistic object, the so-called canting coin (iii), Gildon's bookseller addresses his letter to Jonathan Swift, whose own *Tale of a Tub* refers obsessively to the published writer's alienated identity. As Swift's "modern" author complains, "Books, like Men their Authors, have no more than one Way of coming into the World, but there are ten Thousand to go out of it, and return no more."[4] Just as

Swift ponders the uncertainty of a work's passage from author to printer and reader, Gildon speculates on the dangers of marketing one's writing. Gildon also looks for a "return" but recognizes how easily his words spiral out of control once introduced into the public sphere; before the story even begins, the book has assumed an autonomous role as an object of trade.[5]

One of the fictive bookseller's greatest fears in *The Golden Spy* is that without a dedication the book will "*look so naked and bare, as to fright all the modish Buyers,*" though he admits that his "*Customers*" are satisfied by "*a plausible* Title Page *(the Bookseller's Art) and a good* Gilt Back" (vi). Here Gildon, playing on his own name (the word *gilden* being a common contemporary variant of *golden, gilded,* or *gilt*), subtly names himself as author through his titular subject (the golden spy) and the text's material support (its gilded spine). But he regards authorship and book as entities that are compromised once the text enters the literary marketplace. As the bookseller notes, the "*Catalogue*" of his customers includes a variety of incompetent consumers from public and private domains such as "White's Chocolate House, Tom's *and* Will's Coffee House, *and the* Temple . . . *the Court, the Great Men's Studies, and the Ladies' Closets*" (vi–vii). The author's work, moreover, is subject as much to the degrading effects of other scribblers as it is to the vagaries of its readership. Like Swift, Gildon's editorial persona knows that all manner of "*Dulness*" is enriched by false "Intimacy" with writers of distinction, and he sympathizes with Swift's plight, in which lesser works are "*easily pass'd on the Town for your Productions.*" Unlike other writers, this persona has "*too much Modesty (tho' a* Bookseller), *to palm the following Treatise*" (x) as Swift's work (managing, of course, to borrow Swift's currency by simply speculating on the possibility). Using monetary language, he distinguishes between genuine and counterfeit productions yet acknowledges how easily a market society blurs them, and how easily the writer's activity becomes "*but a* Trade," turning words into things all "Light *and* Gaudy" (xii–xiii). Masking his own authorial interests in the fate of the book as the concern of an editor, Gildon manages to articulate both his writerly fears and his attraction to the vitality of the book market. He pities his own Grub Street status while positioning himself in the public sphere by having the "editor" derogate other writers.

What alarms Gildon is the slippage between author and word, or authority and possession, that increases with the text's progress through various stages from reproduction to distribution. Through this process, he fears, the document will lose much of its value as an original creation even as it reaches a wider readership. This cycle of authorial alienation and professional advancement is exacerbated in *The Golden Spy* by the peculiar narrative process in which the coins recount the story to a human interlocutor, who "writes" the book but does not "author" it. Gildon's book depicts the loss of individual storytelling power through images of continual exchange, the foremost being the canting coin itself, a linguistic object that, like a book, is repeatedly handled. The force of this repetition would have been especially pronounced at a time when legal right, originality, and literary ownership were remarkably fluid and yet ideologically compelling concepts (especially around the time of the 1710 Copyright Act, which confused as much as it clarified issues of literary property).[6] *The Golden Spy* dramatizes the complex, often unpredictable transmutation of text from manuscript (the author's provenance), to book (the concern of publisher and printer), to literary commodity (a status dictated by exchanges between bookseller and reader). Gildon's narrative variously equates authors, editors, distributors, and readers through acts of expenditure. The duplication and transfer of texts entailed in these acts erode the referential belief system, predicated on the evidential aura of an authentic manuscript, by which a fiction frames its empirical status. The bookseller, conceding that as a market agent he is "*speaking for another,*" concludes the preface to *The Golden Spy* by declaring that he will let the author "*shift for himself*" (xiv, xv). Indeed, the bookseller's act of speaking for the absent author highlights the author's absorption into a print market.[7] Gildon's preface correlates the modern author's dependence on the bookselling industry and the fluctuating status of the book as a producer of signs and an object of consumption.

Gildon's concern with the economic, legal, and social disposition of texts in a fluid public sphere is not unique. The representation of books and papers that pass promiscuously between various readers and handlers in such disparate works of fiction as Aphra Behn's *Love Letters Between a Nobleman and His Sister,* Samuel Richardson's *Clarissa,* Henry Mackenzie's *Man of Feeling,* and Maria Edgeworth's *Castle Rackrent* indicates that eighteenth-century writers frequently associated the circulation of texts with the desirable yet troubling consequences of public exposure. Gildon's work and the object narratives it inspired, however, are particularly engrossed in the textual objectification that their inanimate narrators duplicate. Articulating the author's complex relation to print culture, these stories literalize the disjunction between writer and written matter that was intensified by eighteenth-century bookselling practices.

A remarkably persistent feature in eighteenth-century fiction, the narrating object appears in a surprising number of satires published between 1709 and 1824, manifesting a particular cultural obsession with stories as things.[8] Gildon's work seems to have initiated the vogue, and later writers often show an uncomfortable awareness of the similarities between their work and his. Moreover, Gildon's endorsement of *A Tale of a Tub* suggests that Swift's conflation of story, object, and author in his title provided a conceptual foundation for later narratives. While Swift does not develop this trope, *A Tale of a Tub* alludes repeatedly to the modern author's transformation into an idioglossic object, the result, according to Swift, of society's saturation by print. Swift's modern writer, having noted that his is a "blessed Age" for "the mutual Felicity of *Booksellers* and *Authors*, whom [he] may safely affirm to be at this Day the two only satisfied Parties in *England*" (182), admits that this mutually indulgent arrangement is reflected in the writer's ultimate self-absorption: "I am now trying an Experiment very frequent among Modern Authors; which is, to *write upon Nothing;* When the Subject is utterly exhausted, to let the Pen still move on; by some called, the Ghost of Wit, delighting to walk after the Death of its Body" (208).

Such alienation, where things become narrators, is echoed in the titles of the object tales: for example, *The Genuine and Most Surprizing Adventures of a Very Unfortunate Goose-Quill; Travels of Mons. le Poste-Chaise, Written by Himself; The Adventures of a Pin, Supposed to be Related by Himself, Herself, or Itself;* and *The Adventures of a Kite.*[9] Other speaking objects include a settee, a sofa, a bedstead, a pulpit, a reading desk, a mirror, an old shoe, a smock, a waistcoat, a wig, a watch, a ring, an umbrella, a gold-headed cane, a sedan, a pincushion, a thimble, a top, a pen, an old pocket bible, and a stagecoach.[10] Often of substantial length, object narratives delineate the alarming way in which possessions inscribe the private experiences of their owners and then circulate those experiences for public consumption. In 1781 the *Critical Review* observed that "this mode . . . is grown so fashionable, that few months pass which do not bring one of them under our inspection."[11] By 1788, they were so numerous that writers rationalized adding more. The narrator of *The Adventures of a Watch* argues that "bank notes, guineas, nay even Birmingham halfpence, though of very roguish appearance, give the history of their lives. . . . [A] watch is surely as intelligent as any of the above. . . . Besides, 'tis no vulgar watch, but a watch of fashion! a gold Repeater, elegantly chased! Listen to it attentively!"[12] Such narratives not only reflect self-consciously on Gildon's work but also often attempt to increase narrative authority by enhancing the object's value.

Like *A Tale of a Tub, Clarissa,* or *Tristram Shandy,* these stories reproduce the continual circulation of text in modern print culture. One repeated structural feature is the mediated transmission of the narrative. Initially spoken to a recent owner of the object, the narrative is transcribed by the interlocutor; the resulting manuscript passes to a family member or an acquaintance, who in turn sells the work to an interested buyer; the buyer then publishes the story, sometimes to aid the family member. *The Adventures of a Cork-Screw* provides a particularly detailed example: an "incorporeal substance" that inhabits a bottle opener relates its story to a man who then dies.[13] To defray the costs of his burial, the man's wife sells the manuscript to an editor, who publishes the text as a means of assisting her. Object narratives, in other words, signal the unprofitability of writing to the original writer, though their transmission is often meant to redress inequities. They circulate by means of self-interested and frequently exploitative social transactions that tend to efface the original author. Eighteenth-century bookselling is thus postulated as a social and economic system that erodes the status of authors precisely as it requires a greater supply of them to meet increasing demand for printed literature.[14]

Literary criticism of object narratives initially focused on their limited generic, moral, or commercial function, often connecting them to British imperialism. Aileen Douglas, for example, argues that these tales seek to "repair" the damaging consequences of trade on human nature by linking such commerce to the positive effects of empire.[15] More recently, scholars have linked object tales to broader economic, social, and political issues, situating commodities in a complex signifying field that challenges international distinctions and complicates both nationhood and the public sphere.[16] The most satiric narratives, such as Tobias Smollett's *History and Adventures of an Atom,* Charles Johnstone's *Chrysal,* or Helenus Scott's *Adventures of a Rupee,* not only disparage imperial economy but also blur exotic and British locales. Indeed, object narratives typically display a capricious mobility of animate and inanimate forms that frequently disrupts a coherent sense of social order. Many of the stories abandon historical particularity in depicting the incessant movement of things across space and time, appearing to favor generality over specificity. Most were published between 1770 and 1800, and, despite the social ferment of this period, they tend to reject the distinct political allegory of earlier narratives such as Gildon's, Smollett's, Johnstone's, and Scott's. Indeed, the later resistance to political particularism is itself a significant, if an evasive, response to historical events in the century's closing decades. Relying on conventional features of the form, writers instead turned a fascinated eye toward the disquieting fluency of objects in everyday life.[17]

As items of clothing, jewelry, furniture, transportation, currency, and so on, narrating objects invariably evoke physicality, grounding their narratives in the experiences of vulnerable human bodies. The speaking object's effectiveness as a storyteller derives from its proximity to human beings, but as these objects frequently proclaim, human subjects rarely deserve their attention. As the eponymous hero of *The Adventures of a Black Coat* complains, "when I contemplate the . . . vile schemes I have been obliged to countenance in those whose sole merit and reputation arose from my close attachment to them, my very threads blush at the indignity."[18] Though widening the public sphere to incorporate (in all senses of the word) personal, communal, national, and global relations, such narratives uncover a disorganized and venal world. Either passing through the hands of human subjects or serving to transport, protect, and furnish them, the objects ostensibly mediate social and material experience. But their mediating function is always impeded by the economic conditions that generate them, and, in several cases, separate them from their cherished original owners.[19]

That the capacity to enhance the physical well-being of the human subject, which makes these commodities ideal narrators, also incites the owners of the objects to trade them for profit suggests a collusion between professional literary discourse and an acquisitive market economy. In *The Adventures of a Cork-Screw* the speaking object tries to merge its narrative function with its role as commodity. Thus it frequently defers stories at strategic moments of readerly concern: "in order to give my reader some necessary respite to draw a cork or so himself, I shall not introduce his lordship's life till the next chapter" (13). But the stories themselves deny such happy affinity between object and user. Whenever the corkscrew's owners need to complete a social transaction, they suddenly feel it in their pockets and, reminded of its economic value, exchange rather than use it. Coupling the act of narration with the object's continual displacement, the corkscrew's adventures reveal in a particularly distressing way what Marx calls the "definite social relation between men" that governs all commodities.[20]

A chief aim of object tales is, of course, simply to generate interest through the startling proposition of an inanimate narrator. But they also focus reflexively on the object's narrative motivation. Punning on *novel writing* and defending the decision to enter a saturated print market, a gold watch argues in *Adventures of a Watch* that "to handle a feeling subject properly, requires some consideration; for though numbers may speak feelingly, yet to write so is rather novel, notwithstanding there are a number of novel writers" (5). More pointedly, the narrator of *The Memoirs and Interesting Adventures of an Embroidered Waistcoat,* whose story is "as wonderful and as replete with Matter as most Part of our late Novels," extols its narrative to the interlocutor in terms of publishing and profit: "I doubt not but some of the Magazines will sufficiently reward you for a Detail of my Story."[21] The intimacy and authenticity that fiction pretends to provide the reader and that would ideally distinguish the printed book from other wares are bracketed by the power of commodities to create demand. Of course, the illusion that a book has a more personal effect on its purchaser than other commodities do is poignantly refuted by the fantastic nature of these stories and by the improbability of the storytellers. By speaking through a seemingly disinterested object, the authors veil the profit motive that in ordinary circumstances might compromise the narrative's objectivity.

The troubling impact of this public exchange is implied by the narrating object's painful awareness that its consciousness is imprisoned. The corkscrew emphasizes this condition by repeating the language of entrapment used by its interlocutor, who dies after "a long confinement" for debt (iv). The only valuable legacy left by the dead man, once particularly "fond of scribbling," is "a large parcel of paper entirely spoiled, being scribbled all over" (viii)—that is, the manuscript published by the anonymous editor. The original storyteller, the corkscrew, is a spirit similarly punished by being "confined in" a "steel imprisonment," where it is "doomed" to languish until it "should fall into the hands of some mortal, whose misfortunes were not brought on himself by his folly" (5, 4). The object's only comfort is to "relate" the "histories" of those "persons . . . in whose hands [it has] been" (5), and its bequest is the same as its interlocutor's. Both the imprisoned scribbler (the conventional designation for a Grub Street writer) and the inspirited object share the defining experience of desperately relating a story from within a "steel imprisonment." Each hopes to escape confinement through narrative production and to find freedom through the public circulation of a story. The narrator of *The Adventures of a Cork-Screw* thus exploits magical transferability of commodities while recognizing the limits of economic exchange.

Parallels between writer and speaking object are even more pronounced in *The History and Adventures of a Lady's Slippers and Shoes,* whose title page makes speaking objects the counterparts of modern scribblers who burden an already crowded public sphere:

So common now are Authors grown,
That ev'ry Scribler in the Town,
Thinks he can give delight.
If writers then are got so vain,
To think they pleasure when they pain,
No wonder Slippers *write.*

Anon.

Continuing this premise, the work ascribes even the "Preface, Introduction, Dedication, or Advertisement" to the Slippers ("*we beg leave to suscribe ourselves,* Your most devoted SLIPPERS"). The slippers not only parody the overloading of texts with prefatory material, as Swift does, they specifically liken themselves to "*many* great Authors."[22] In other works, such self-consciousness about "authorship" is reinforced when, in imitation of literary convention, the object uses its pedigree to authenticate itself as narrator and to justify the printed text it engenders, thus allying itself with the human authors it otherwise disdains. As the narrator of *The Adventures of a Cork-Screw* observes, "When an author issues his performance into the world; every one is desirous to know his name, his character, and the motives which urges him to trouble the world with such a quantity of paper" (ii). Similarly, when the hackney coach notices a customer admiring its unusually fine appearance, it feels compelled to clarify its special pedigree:

> Before I introduce any of the characters I mean to exhibit to my reader, I must beg leave to introduce my
>
> ORIGIN.
>
> I WAS made by a distinguished Coachmaker of Great Queen-Street, Lincoln's-Inn-Fields, for Mr. M— — —, a very worthy merchant in Threadneedle-Street.[23]

The coach speaks directly to its reader and, like the slippers, stresses its origins typographically, using offset capital letters that accentuate its relation to the printed page. Here the history of its manufacture confers authorial pedigree, as the coach accepts its necessary entrance into a crass commercial world and underscores its superior and inimitable condition.

This appropriation of human behavior by narrative objects for the purpose of dramatizing the plight of the author is probably best exemplified in Smollett's *The History and Adventures of an Atom.* Here the narrator actually merges with human bodies, transmigrating through various persons, animals, and bodies of base matter until it lodges in the pineal gland of the interlocutor, who then writes from dictation as its "editor." After a series of mishaps, a "publisher" acquires the manuscript, carefully validates the narrative, and decides to "present in print" what the "editor" has transcribed from the atom.[24] The story's progress exemplifies the mobility of objects, narration, and consciousness in general:

> Fate determined I should exist in the empire of Japan, where I underwent a great number of vicissitudes, till, at length, I was enclosed in a grain of rice, eaten by a Dutch mariner at Firando, and, becoming a particle of his body, brought to the Cape of Good Hope. There I was discharged in a scorbutic dysentery, taken up in a heap of soil to manure a garden, raised to

> vegetation in a sallad, devoured by an English supercargo, assimilated to a certain organ of his body, which, at his return to London, being diseased in consequence of impure contact, I was again separated, with a considerable portion of putrefied flesh, thrown upon a dunghill, gobbled up, and digested by a duck, of which duck your father, Ephraim Peacock, having eaten plentifully at a feast of the cordwainers, I was mixed with his circulating juices, and finally fixed in the principal part of that animacule, which, in process of time, expanded itself into thee, Nathaniel Peacock. (7)

The narrative impulse is literally embodied and naturalized, "assimilated" into animal, vegetable, and mineral domains by its metempsychosal passage through starches, diseases, soils, bodily discharges, leafy plants, aquatic birds, and human anatomies. Its thorough occupation of the world indicates a universal signifying power; it not only becomes an object, but also multiplies its objective state by a fantastic circulation through a variety of all known physical elements. Divided among many, it nonetheless preserves its indivisible nature. Moreover, the atom's experience encompasses Pacific and Atlantic crossings, blurring of racial types, rapid transitions in national languages, and indiscriminate passage between countries; it surpasses, in other words, all boundaries of human containment, yet is one of the most contained things on earth. Given the complex, and by Smollett's time conventional, frame by which the "writer" recounts his acquisition of the story and the "editor" justifies ownership, it is clear that the atom's tortuous route is merely a prelude to its intricate verbalization. The printed form of the story extends the narrative's strange progress through the world. Its circulation, foregrounded by the elaborate editorial frame, parallels that of the atom. The atom's absorption into such human agents in global and domestic trade as a mariner, a supercargo, and a cordwainer before lodging in an "editor" emphasizes parallels between writing and marketing that objects in other stories embody more directly. Comparing the diffusion of printed texts to the movement of money, ships, goods, vital fluids, and matter, "unauthored" narratives highlight writerly concerns about the unpredictable circulation of books in the public domain.

One explanation, then, for the popularity of these works in the eighteenth century is that they reproduced transformations in the marketing of printed literature. They assumed that Britain prospered by promoting a continual circulation of goods through highly developed networks of distribution, such as a national postal system, extensive highways and canals, provincial printing houses, circulating libraries, coffeehouses, charitable societies, a national bank, and modern international systems of credit and stocks. Indeed, some object narratives specifically align their narrators with these systems of dissemination: "Adventures of a Quire of Paper" (printing houses, stationers, and coffeehouses), *The Adventures of a Hackney Coach* (turnpikes), and various currency stories such as *The Adventures of a Bank-Note* (systems of national banking and credit).[25] If the establishment of an effective public sphere, in which each citizen participates in continuous exchange, is advanced through practical local, national, and international means such as coffeehouses, turnpikes, and banks, it is also facilitated through the encouragement of a public-mindedness that urges readers to regard literature both as an economic instrument and an aesthetic, moral, or informational resource. Jürgen Habermas has argued that the development of the public sphere in England in the eighteenth century was "rooted in the world of letters," particularly through the journal and novel reading promoted by libraries, book clubs, and reading circles, which replaced early institutions such as coffeehouses and salons. As a result of this shared reading, Habermas contends, "the public sphere appeared as one and indivisible" in the "self-understanding of public opinion."[26] This would also seem to be the ideal condition for speaking objects to encounter in circulating through the world.

But as in *A Tale of a Tub,* the public sphere described by the objectified narrators is often disrupted by an indiscriminate print industry. As the preface to the black coat's narrative scornfully, and somewhat paradoxically, proclaims, "In this age of *Magazines* and *Chronicles,* the *Cacoethes Scribendi* hath infected the town so much, that almost every *shop,* or *workroom,* harbours an author. . . . When such *gentlemen* assume the pen, I hope it will not be deeming vanity, if I decline standing as candidate for literary fame" (ix–x). Equally reluctant authors, the anonymous writer and the inanimate narrator regard themselves as suspended between the compromising aspects and demonstrable benefits of the publishing world. They deny the value of print culture as they deliberately enter into it. Indeed, the author of this story admits that the anonymity and modesty of the speaking object as a narrative trope deliberately elides original authorship: "All I shall say of the following *petit* performance is, that I have endeavoured to make the *Author* less conspicuous than the *moral*" (viii). The disjunction between object narrator and author seems, on the one hand, to enhance claims about the autonomy and disinterestedness of the literary work and free the writer from accountability; on the other hand, it dramatizes the mechanical and alienated nature of modern writing and highlights the problems of literary property and of the writer's status in an overpopulated print culture.

The narrating object serves several corrective functions, from reversing the relation between subject and object to exposing the contradictions between private and public behavior. But these effects ironically only intensify existing social discord. According to the *Critical Review,* such narratives constituted a fashionable repository for "all the farrago of public transactions, private characters, old and new stories," thrown together by "writers of the inferior class" to provide "a little temporary amusement to an idle reader" (52:478). Underscoring the connection between "public transactions" and "private characters," the *Review* recognizes, though it does not choose to commend, the creation of a heterogeneous public sphere and the consequent impact of rapidly distributed printed matter on a national audience. The *Review*'s objections, however, are already highlighted in the stories themselves. Often of irreducible form (as with Smollett's atom), speaking objects offer only fragmentary portrayals of human subjects—partial histories—that produce neither a unified plot nor a coherent social sphere. The hybridity of the narratives reinforces this discord: a single tale may incorporate satire, allegory, anatomy, picaresque, scandal chronicle, roman à clef or secret history, news, propaganda, autobiography, moral tale, sentimental romance, Aesopian fable, spy novel, travelogue, and imaginary voyage. If these texts are among the cultural technologies of eighteenth-century Britain that enabled individuals to reconcile personal and civic experience through rhetorical incorporation of the public sphere (as their educative function as satires or children's cautionary tales might suggest), they also recognize and retain notable traces of disjunction. The circulation of the objects in this respect becomes a measure of the dispersion rather than the consolidation of people and things; their polyglot nature, the rapid shifts in locale, and transfigurations in their physical status belie the unifying force of commodities while accentuating the dismantling effects of human commerce.[27]

The changes in subject that these stories exhibit are often dramatized through the commodity form of the object. In "Adventures of a Quire of Paper," originally printed in the *London Magazine,* the narrator not only embodies the fabric on which magazines, newspapers, and novels are produced; it also illustrates the essential poverty of textual embodiment, portraying its destined conversion into a printed book as a terrifying unalterable condition. Initially a thistle, it is gradually transformed into flax, woven into a large piece of cambric, and then converted into various articles of clothing that eventually become the tatters a ragpicker sells to a papermaker, who transforms them into "the sort of paper you have in your hands."[28] Here, the paper "in your hands" doubles as the sheets of text the reader of the *London Magazine* holds and the leaves of a printed sermon that the interlocutor picks up during an idle hour in a "publick coffee-room," and whose pages become, in a dream, the speaking quire of paper (355). The narrating object thus is tied specifically to two of the period's noteworthy forms of printed material—periodicals and sermons—and is associated with one of the most crucial sites of public reading—the coffeehouse. But the quire of paper's feelings about joining these other forms of public print are not entirely positive. The narrator, which is transformed into a number of texts, fears that the permanence of a book will, as it says, "hand me down in my present nature to the latest posterity, and cut me off for ever from being united to my other widely scattered and wretched parts, in my original form" (451). Lamenting the fragmented identity, scattered body, and partial consciousness that writing for a "publick" market entails, it seems aware that its existential status has been reduced to the brief, disposable magazine form in which it appears. In this story, the circulation and transformation of the commodity as printed text becomes a process of debasement and devaluation.

It is not surprising, given the emphasis on circulation in these narratives, that the dominant representative objects are pieces of money. Such figures underline the interconnection of economy, language, and possession. The monetary range of this subgroup is broad; there are stories told by banknotes and bank tokens, rupees, guineas, sovereigns, shillings, and pennies.[29] A few are short narratives, often from magazines or newspapers—the stories of a half guinea and halfpenny are appropriately presented in smaller formats than those of a full guinea or shilling. Like the quire of paper, the modest denominations adjust their narrative expectations to fit less exalted textual forms. In contrast, the most popular such work, Johnstone's four-volume *Chrysal; or, The Adventures of a Guinea,* produced a sequel in 1764 and by 1800 had reached twenty editions. Almost as long as *Tom Jones,* it follows the peregrinations of its numismatic hero in four continents, through more than twenty countries, and between over fifty people.

Whether short or long, the money tales consistently parallel currency and writing. An explicit example of this alignment, *The Adventures of a Bank-Note* accentuates the object's authorial sovereignty to validate its story. Explaining its "unaccountable" ability as "a writer," the banknote distinguishes its talents from mere transcription, and in the process, dehumanizes the human agent who tells its story:

> The inquisitive world may perhaps be curious enough to enquire, why I alone, amongst so many thousands of bank-notes, came to be possessed of such uncommon talents, as not only to recollect the particular passages of my life, but be likewise able to dictate to a secretary, or more properly speaking, to inspire knowledge into a machine, whose utmost qualification before was (like most of the quorum) just to be able to write his name, and read it when he had done.[30]

No other note, it later adds, is capable of "making a single remark, much less of arranging those remarks in so masterly a manner as I do" (1:166). Being the offspring of a Grub Street scribbler accounts for its penmanship, since, according to the note, "the person that deposits cash for a bank-note may properly be called its father" (1:6). Its subsequent orphaning occurs when its "father," unable to publish, changes the note to rent cheaper quarters. The note's suspicion of print thus arises from losing a father through the printing establishment's unreliability. Indeed, the narrator regularly attacks the publishing industry: "my bookseller rather hurries me, or more properly speaking, hurries the person I inspire with my knowledge, and whose head and hand are now fully employed in penning these adventures of mine . . . it is no unusual thing for booksellers to hurry poor devils of authors" (1:164–65). Allying itself with its Grub Street father as a "poor devil of an author," and yet distinguishing itself from its human "secretary" by turning him into "a machine," the banknote alternately disdains and endorses the market logic underlying the author function. It knows and fears that its words must undergo a sequence of uncontrollable transmissions, not unlike those of currency, before reaching their targeted audience.

Money tales, then, are particularly emblematic of eighteenth-century literary attitudes about publishing because they fuse linguistic and material exchange. The focus of this subspecies of object narratives on the nature of money parallels the textual commodification of the literary forms in which they appear. As agents of social contact that pass through various hands, speaking coins mediate between different physical bodies, but only as symbolic objects that indirectly enable the purchase of creature comforts (unlike other narrating objects, such as pens or sofas, whose use value is more directly embodied). As Marc Shell notes in *The Economy of Literature,* "coins are themselves both artful reproductions and active participants in the sum total of the relations of production." The same, he argues, may be said of the printed word: "The study of economic and verbal symbolization, and of the relationship between them, begins at the mint."[31] This relation between money and language use is intensified in *The Adventures of a Bank-Note,* where the note not only speaks directly as author but compares its right to authenticate words with Samuel Johnson's: "The author thinks he has as great a title to coin words as the great Doctor any-body; and whether he takes his degree or not, he declares he will do it whenever he pleases" (2:42). The pun on coining reinforces the analogy the "author" is drawing between monetary and verbal exchange. Moreover, as the banknote constantly asserts, deciphering the text on a note is essential to using or valuing it properly. For example, a "bookish" tavern owner is able to bilk an illiterate couple of the note by pretending it is one of his lost account receipts (2:147). The banknote's approximation of human language thus connects the individual to a treacherous body politic, grounding public experience in a dense, empirical realm of social, economic, and political transactions that stem from a compulsive need for change.

A similar relation inheres in the polyglot nature of currency tales. Repeatedly, the movement of the objects occurs in a specifically international setting. These narratives, such as Johnstone's *Chrysal* or Scott's *Adventures of a Rupee,* mix "oriental" background and English history to produce a cosmopolitan perspective. In *The Golden Spy* the "editor" transcribes a heated debate among coins of various nationalities about the merits of the countries in which they have been minted. In a parody of the conversation in coffeehouses, playhouses, pleasure grounds, and musical venues—locales Habermas celebrates as sites of transformation in the eighteenth-century English public sphere—the interlocutor finds that he is "oblig'd to interpose [his] Authority for the Preservation of the Peace" (39).[32] This internationalism both widens the boundaries of the cultural realm and indicates that national bias, competing languages, and imported ideologies substantially disrupted the sites of public discourse in Britain. One consequence of expanding the means of circulation was that the public sphere became increasingly heterogeneous as it seemed to be providing new possibilities for consensus. Although object narratives often privilege British citizenship, they also emphasize the international components of national definitions of the state. Furthermore, the authorial interposition of Gildon's interlocutor divulges a yearning for a powerful central authority that the very notion of the public seemed to displace or disguise.

This global perspective, coupled with the transformability of currency in a world market, changes the relation of writer and book in object narratives. The stories are, among other things, parables of textual and authorial objectification; the storyteller is not only transformed into inanimate form but also compelled by a system of ownership to describe the experience of others, usually at the expense of internal or personal reflection. One frustration for speaking objects is that, despite their narrative capacity, they are not adequate subjects themselves. Unlike *The Life and Strange Surprizing Adventures of Robinson Crusoe* or *The History of Miss Betsy Thoughtless,* titles of object narratives, which typically cite adventures, histories, and memoirs, refer not to the title character's "life" but to its accounts of others. The objects have little agency of their own; rather, they are repeatedly constituted as having a peculiar or magical capacity to both "intuit" (a word used frequently in these narratives) and recall the entire experience of those who possess them. Their movement through the public sphere is dependent on their debased users, for whom they rarely express any admiration. Yet their importance as objects is connected less to an investigation of their own material context than to a secret examination of human experience. The commodity, even when it is given voice, is thus still rendered as a potential aid to human self-realization.

The storyteller, in other words, gains access to subjectivity only through the impoverished subjectivities of others, gradually unfolding a vision of the national state in which identity itself is fungible. The objects are acutely aware of this double bind, owning that their powers of insight, though astonishing, depend on the structures of usage and distribution by which they circulate. The banknote, for example, is often unable to supply an "account" of an episode or to complete a given "narrative" because it has been "delivered" into the hands of a new owner (1:179, see also 1:190, 2:38, 2:74, 2:123, 2:164–67). In an innovative twist, the corkscrew links such sudden transfers to textual structure: "as I have entered into a new service, it would not be consistent to introduce my new governor, otherwise than at the beginning of a new chapter" (34). These sequences of displacements are aligned with the isolating effects of circulation: the power to tell stories is compromised by the subjection of the storyteller to systems of social, economic, and material exchange that delimit its identity. The word "circulation" is, in fact, repeatedly invoked by the objects to articulate their almost helpless physical, rhetorical, and mental transit through the world. The circumstances of the objects suggest that the authors of object narratives envisioned the cultural sphere as a hazardous field for human representation. Authorial voice is effectively prostituted by being detached from the body, circulated, exchanged, and depersonalized. To some degree, the narratives do shield the author from the kind of public vortex that necessarily envelops the text. It is, after all, the author's surrogate that experiences the full effect of exploitation in the marketplace. But the protection is nonetheless a sign of the author's vulnerability. Object narratives explicitly displace and disembody the human agent, simultaneously freeing the author of liability and exposing his or her limited cultural power.

Because of this complex negotiation of the marketplace, moreover, it is of crucial importance in all the narratives that the objects in these narratives be used constantly; this circumstance supplies one of the more salacious implications of such works as those produced by sofas, settees, and bedsteads. But the pervasively amorous content of these stories also suggests that the writers themselves aligned writing and publishing with promiscuity (in the bedstead's account politics literally makes strange bedfellows).[33] Money tales too are particularly sexualized. In Gildon's *Golden Spy,* for instance, receiving stories becomes a carnal, nearly autoerotic experience, as if the power of the narrator or story worked on the human interlocutor in terms of arousal, seduction, and intercourse. Every evening Gildon's editorial persona hurries home to repeat a ritual of narrative exchange: first, he locks the door to his "Chamber," dresses in his "Night-Gown," and picks up his four "Bed-fellows"—four garrulous coins from England, France, Italy, and Spain. He then gets beneath the sheets, fondles the coins, and holds them close to his ear one at a time as they entertain him with their "tales" (34). He is particularly "transported" by the French coin: "I took him up in my Hand, gave him a thousand kisses, and hugging him close in my Bosom, full of Pleasure as great as if I had got the beautiful CÆLIA in my Arms—*Go on,* (said I) *my Charmer, go on, and bless me with a Conversation, which sure no Man ever enjoy'd before!*" (6). Here, in a typical synthesis, the desires for sex, money, and knowledge (all marked as different forms of circulation) coalesce. Eroticizing the act of exchange at all levels, the object tale publicizes its own bodily, economic, and intellectual transformability in the details of the stories it tells about others.

Yet speaking objects invariably disdain the concrete forms they enter, and deplore the physical crudeness of the human bodies they serve or imitate, stressing the corruptible nature of somatic and linguistic being. Orality itself is compromised by its physical source, but the narrative voice nonetheless recognizes the need to assume palpable form to yield anecdotal "history," however frustrating the limits of human language. As the rupee complains in moments of intensely felt experience, "The mode that mortals have adopted of expressing ideas by words now fails me entirely."[34] Chrysal describes the problem even more specifically, yoking the hazards of language to print culture: "Whenever I comply with the ludicrous taste that prevails at present, and couch a double meaning, in a plain word, my manner of speaking will explain my sense to you, just as well as the use of different characters does in print" (2:4). Objecting to the practice of italicizing, Chrysal accuses printers of "assuming the liberty of giving any word, phrase, or sentiment, which he does not understand himself or thinks the reader may not understand, just as *he* does," a typographical emphasis that will "disfigure the appearance, and perplex the sense." "I have thought it proper to say this," it adds, "to prevent the loss of my labours, in the mistake or perversion of my words" (2:4–5). The bookseller's italics only confirm what Chrysal already suspected about human discourse, "the signification of words, in the language of men, being so unsettled, that it is scarce possible to convey a determinate sense" (2:1–2). Using italics for emphasis, the canting coin indicates exactly where the contest between the author and the bookselling establishment occurs: at the convergence of intellectual and commercial property.

Chrysal's petulance about the vagaries of printed text derives from its convictions about the transparency of language. Like most speaking objects, Johnstone's narrator boasts transcendent powers of communication that eliminate temporal, physical, and vocal distinctions: "I can see your thoughts; and will answer every doubt which may arise in your mind at the wonders of my relation, without the interruption of your inquiries, as *awful silence is the essence of my converse*" (1:4). As it goes on to explain, "Besides that *intuitive knowledge* common to all spirits, we of superior orders, who animate this universal monarch GOLD, have also a power of entering into the hearts of the immediate possessors of our bodies" (1:6). Inanimate narrators, in fact, are often emanations or spirits enclosed in the objects; they can converse as capably outside as within the material form they inhabit, and they "speak" silently, anticipating in a sense the full exploitation of free indirect discourse later in the century. They do not hear (having no suitable organs for such a task) but "intuit" the details of their owners' lives; many do not even talk (though some of the coins at least have symbolic ears and mouths). The remove from orality serves to clarify the distinction presumed to exist between speech and writing, and, further, between handwritten and printed texts.[35] The printed text, following spoken, handwritten, and typeset forms, is therefore quadruply removed from the nonverbal sphere of ideal mental speech. For object narrators, the public sphere is characterized not by a semblance of unity but by systems of metonymic displacement. If, as Benedict Anderson, Pierre Bourdieu, and Jürgen Habermas contend, the public sphere is foremost a discursive field, many eighteenth-century texts that helped shape it as such reflect an awareness of the supposed consensual effect of language.[36] By attaching the idea of narration to physical objects, which in circulation lose their prime function and identity, object narratives refute optimistic assessments of print as a mechanism for promoting public order or a sign of the nation's concerted will.

That the authors of these works needed to disguise and protect themselves by speaking in another voice, and, moreover, by attributing their words to a seemingly neutral object, often one able to move "invisibly" through the world, suggests that writing alienated the author from the work. In money tales particularly, the object chosen to emulate the writer effectively aligns authorial activities with the omnipresent circulation of currency, so that its extraordinary symbolic force becomes a measure of its dematerializing power. As Marx notes: "Since every commodity disappears when it becomes money it is impossible to tell from the money itself how it got into the hands of its possessor, or what article has been changed into it. *Non olet*" (205). The metaphoric lack of smell in money is a sign that its circulation eliminates all marks of exchange. Similarly, though the object story evokes the material world and the arduous transfer of manuscripts, it dramatizes the invisible conditions of authorship in published fiction. As the speaking object reveals, print culture demands the ostensible erasure of a conventional author; it requires that there be no body there.

The successful marketing of eighteenth-century prose fiction resulted, in part, from the mobilization of different mechanisms for distributing published work. As several scholars have shown, these mechanisms constituted forms of cultural technology that enabled productive social exchange. According to Habermas, for example, the periodicals, printed plays, and books available in coffeehouses, shops, theaters, circulating libraries, and taverns produced models of critical reasoning that allowed "the sphere of private people to come together as a public" and experience a "process of self-clarification" by "focusing on the genuine experiences of their novel privateness" (27, 29). Extrapolating from Habermas, Tony Bennett traces the process of culture, "through which artistic and intellectual practices come to be inscribed into the processes of government," to the eighteenth century: "It is only with the Enlightenment and its aftermath that artistic and intellectual practices come to be thought of as instruments capable of being utilized, in a positive and productive manner, to improve specific mental or behavioral attributes of the general population."[37]

Many object narratives, as I have noted, feature highways, international shipping routes, global banking, newspapers, and modern printing practices as their means of social exchange. Their narrative efficacy is directly associated with their capacity to use both private and public systems of circulation, and they repeatedly accentuate their access to discourse networks such as coffeehouses, booksellers' shops, circulating libraries, and taverns. By invoking these venues, however, object narratives exhibit a fissured rather than a unified cultural field, revealing breaches not only in the structures governing private and public behavior, but in national identity as well. Circulating libraries, for example, not only served to disseminate texts but also became subjects of concern in the very narratives that profited from such public exposure. These "publick places" were themselves a recognized component of a controversial process of national acculturation. For every writer who claimed, as John Bell did in 1770, that they were "justly esteemed as . . . the greatest Conveniences to this Kingdom," a host of others complained, as Edward Mangin did in 1808, that there was not "a corner of the Empire, where the English language [was] understood that ha[d] not suffered from the effects of this institution."[38]

Such means of cultural dissemination, then, produced dissension as much as they unified public endeavor. As I have shown, that divisiveness is often inscribed in the very literary texts that contributed to the transformation of the public sphere. In object tales, literary success depends—for author, publisher, and audience alike—on the very atomizing circulation of stories in a public form that many of the stories themselves eschew. Mastering narrative techniques consequently becomes a destabilizing, alienating, or falsifying experience. As remarked by the canting coin in *The Birmingham Counterfeit; or, Invisible Spectator*—a forged gilded shilling that can "pass current for a guinea"—"We live in a world, where the generality of human actions, like a great deal of our present current coin, is *counterfeit*."[39] Punning on both the temporal and dynamic aspects of the words *current* and *currency,* the narrator uses its own currency to trace the interrelated but nonetheless disruptive nature of social, economic, and textual circulation.

In object narratives, the act of storytelling is indissolubly linked to the movement of commodities and capital; they convey, in other words, an implicit theory of culture in which literary dissemination and economic exchange appear homologous. As principal narrators that represent authorship, the objects also symbolize the promiscuous movement of text, the commodification of stories, the international entanglements in the book trade, and the loss of narrative identity and authority that stem from circulation in the social sphere. Far from mediating between private and public spheres or synthesizing national and cosmopolitan values, they are often undone by such categories. The picaresque form of the object tales is commensurate with this narrative effect—the abrupt shift in subject, the fragmentary diegesis, and the multitude of characters signal the storyteller's subordination to extrinsic forces and manifest the continual exchange (literary as well as financial) that gives currency to the objects' various accounts of human behavior. On the one hand, the narratives extol the author's ability to infiltrate, observe, and reveal social customs; on the other hand, they imply that the author is merely a possession, a medium, or specie, reduced to the status of the artifact whose production is the writer's compulsory activity in a world where print commerce dictates the value of words.

Notes

An earlier version of this essay appeared in *PMLA* 113.2 (1998): 212–26.

1. Charles Gildon, *The Golden Spy; or, a Political Journal of the British Nights Entertainments of War and Peace, and Love and Politics; Wherein Are Laid Open, the Secret Miraculous Power and Progress of Gold, in the Courts of Europe* (London, 1709), 13. Subsequent quotations from this work are cited parenthetically in the text.

2. Because such objects are manufactured, the stories they relate differ from those told by animals or vegetation, such as James Howel, *The Vocal Forest* (London, 1691); Frances Coventry, *The History of Pompey the Little; or, The Adventures of a Lap-Dog* (London, 1751); and *History of a French Louse; or the Spy of a New Species, in France and England* (London, 1779), which derive from Aesop, Ovid, and Apuleius and do not equate nonhuman narration with textual circulation. These latter tend to serve as substitutes for human actors, whereas the manufactured narrators become the vehicles for judging human society, often through the transference of authorial capacities. While the animals usually parody human figures or types, the commodities are satiric observers of them.

3. For another viewpoint on this dynamic, see Jonathan Lamb, "Modern Metamorphoses and Disgraceful Tales," *Critical Inquiry* 28.1 (2001): 133–66, especially the claim that "it-narratives are surprisingly unkind to the extent that they show sympathy to be a perverse outcome of a defensive or hostile relation between species and things" (134). Lamb regards the engagement of feeling in these stories as attempts to foster sympathetic tendencies in the reader for objects and other species that might otherwise be regarded with unease. But, as he notes, the "autonomy" that sympathy "confers on things and creatures, far from mirroring a benevolent intention, generates narratives of human behaviour replete with arrant but unsuccessful selfishness, remorseless cruelty, and humiliating weakness" (166). My argument differs insofar as I see that attempted sympathy extended to the unrelieved author and complicated, furthermore, by the counteracting effects of anxieties about commodities, professional jealousy, and Grub Street economics. See also Lamb's fascinating account of lost things, storytelling, and advertising in "The Crying of Lost Things," *ELH* 71.4 (2004): 949–67, which includes comments on object narratives.

4. Jonathan Swift, *A Tale of a Tub* (1704), ed. A. C. Guthkelch and D. Nichol Smith (Oxford: Clarendon Press, 1958), 5, 36. Subsequent quotations from this work are cited parenthetically in the text.

5. Eighteenth-century developments in the British book trade are effectively summarized in John Brewer, *The Pleasures of the Imagination: English Culture in the Eighteenth Century* (New York: Farrar, Straus and Giroux, 1997), 125–97; John Feather, *A History of British Publishing* (London: Routledge, 1988), 67–105 and *The Provincial Book Trade in Eighteenth-Century England* (Cambridge: Cambridge University Press, 1985), 44–68; and J. H. Plumb, *The Birth of a Consumer Society: The Commercialization of Eighteenth-Century England*, ed. Neil McKendrick, John Brewer, and J. H. Plumb (Bloomington: Indiana University Press, 1982), 263–334, esp. 266–73. Changes included the enactment of copyright law and taxation of printed matter; the emergence of wholesale marketing, copy-owning congers, trade sales, circulating libraries, and large-scale printing firms; increased production by provincial presses; the institution of serial publication and advertising lists in magazines and books; and accelerated growth of newspapers. On increased publication of fiction, see James Raven, *Judging New Wealth: Popular Publishing and Responses to Commerce in England, 1750–1800* (Oxford: Oxford University Press, 1992), 19–60. As Raven notes, despite the demand for popular fiction, the writer's life was still mostly a matter of obscure toil, paltry remuneration, and exploitation by the bookselling establishment (58–59).

6. On the confusion over eighteenth-century copyright, see Feather, *History*, 73–83; David F. Foxon, *Pope and the Early Eighteenth-Century Book Trade* (Oxford: Oxford University Press, 1991), 39–60; Jody Greene, *The Trouble with Ownership: Literary Property and Authorial Liability in England, 1660–1730* (Philadelphia: University of Pennsylvania Press, 2005), 1–103; Benjamin Kaplan, *An Unhurried View of Copyright* (New York: Columbia University Press, 1967), 6–25; Lyman Ray Patterson, *Copyright in Historical Perspective* (Nashville, TN: Vanderbilt University Press, 1968), 180–96; Marjorie Plant, *The*

English Book Trade: An Economic History of the Making and Sale of Books (London: George Allen and Unwin, 1974), 98–121; Mark Rose, *Authors and Owners: The Invention of Copyright* (Cambridge, MA: Harvard University Press, 1993), 9–129; Martha Woodmansee, *The Author, Art, and the Market: Rereading the History of Aesthetics* (New York: Columbia University Press, 1994), 425–48. These scholars generally agree that changes in copyright (particularly as recorded in the 1710 Act for the Encouragement of Learning, or "Copyright Act" as it is now usually called) were not *principally* about recognizing authorial rights. According to Patterson, "The most significant point about the statutory copyright is that it was almost certainly a codification of the stationer's copyright" (146). Greene adds, however, that "the act was important because it conceived of an author's primary—even aboriginal—relation to his or her work as a matter of ownership . . . [even though] the nature of the proprietary relationship is never spelled out in the act" (2).

7. D. F. McKenzie, *The London Book Trade in the Later Seventeenth Century* (Sandars Lectures, 1976), notes that the rise of trade publishing led, in practical terms, to "the *dis*sociation of author, printer and bookseller from one another, and all of them from their market, turning books into mere commodities" (29).

8. On the theory of things see Arjun Appadurai, *The Social Life of Things: Commodities in Cultural Perspective* (Cambridge: Cambridge University Press, 1986), 3–91, and the special edition entitled "Things" recently edited by Bill Brown, *Critical Inquiry* 28.1 (2001).

9. See *The Genuine and Most Surprizing Adventures of a Very Unfortunate Goose-Quill* (London, 1734); *Travels of Mons. le Poste-Chaise, Written by Himself* (London, 1753); *The Adventures of a Pin, Supposed to be Related by Himself, Herself, or Itself* (London, 1790); and *The Adventures of a Kite* (London, 1790), all published anonymously.

10. Many narratives featuring such objects were published in periodicals: for example, "Adventures of a Gold Ring," "Adventures of a Mirror," "Adventures of a Pen," "Adventures of a Sopha," "Adventures of a Stage Coach," "The History and Adventures of a Bedstead," "The History of an Old Pocket Bible, Supposed to Be Written by Itself," and "Memoirs of a Wig: Presented in Two Letters Signed 'Peruke, Jun.'" (all catalogued alphabetically in Robert D. Mayo, *The English Novel in the Magazines, 1740–1815* [Evanston, IL: Northwestern University Press, 1962], 442–553). Other narratives featuring such objects include *The Settee; or, Chevalier Commodo's Transformation* (London, 1742); Claude Crébillon, *The Sopha,* trans. from the French (London, 1742); Charles Perronet, *A Dialogue between the Pulpit and Reading Desk* (London, 1767); *The Secret History of an Old Shoe* (London, 1734); *Frailties of Fashion; or, The Adventures of an Irish Smock* (London, 1782); *The Memoirs and Interesting Adventures of an Embroidered Waistcoat,* 2 vols. (London, 1751); *The Adventures of a Watch* (London, 1788); G. Herbert Rodwell, *The Memoirs of an Umbrella* (London, 1845); Theophilus Johnson, *Phantoms; or, The Adventures of a Gold-Headed Cane* (London, 1783); *The Sedan. A Novel. In Which Many New and Entertaining Characters are Introduced* (London, 1757); Mary Jane Kilner, *The Adventures of a Pincushion: Designed Chiefly for the Use of Young Ladies* (London, 1784); *The Silver Thimble* (London, 1799); *The Adventures of a Whipping-Top* (London, 1790); Mary Ann Kilmer, *The Memoirs of a Peg-Top* (London, 1785).

11. *Critical Review* 52 (December 1781): 477–78. Subsequent quotations from this work are cited parenthetically in the text.

12. *The Adventures of a Watch* (London, 1788), 3. Subsequent quotations from this work are cited parenthetically in the text.

13. *The Adventures of a Cork-Screw; in Which, Under the Pleasing Method of Romance, the Vices, Follies and Manners of the Present Age Are Exhibited and Satirically Delineated* (London, 1775), 3. Subsequent quotations from this work are cited parenthetically in the text.

14. Perhaps the most threatening aspect of this system was the possibility that authors were merely products of market forces. John Feather argues that the demand for new books increased the need for writers and observes that "literary" authors were affected by the evolution and growth of the book trade, with many of them now acknowledging the financial rewards for writing. See *A History of British Publishing* (London: Routledge, 1988), 102.

15. Aileen Douglas, "Britannia's Rule and the It-Narrator," *Eighteenth-Century Fiction* 6.1 (1993): 70–89, 81. A version of Douglas's essay appears in this volume. See also Richard K. Meeker, "Bank Note, Corkscrew, Flea and Sedan: A Checklist of Eighteenth-Century Fiction," *Library Chronicle* 35 (1969): 52–57; Toby A. Olshin, "Form and Theme in Novels about Non-Human Characters, a Neglected Sub-Genre," *Genre* 2.1 (1969): 41–53; J. M. S. Tompkins, *The Popular Novel in England 1700–1800* (1932; Lincoln: University of Nebraska Press, 1961), 49.

16. Since this essay first appeared as an article in 1998 there has been a veritable cottage industry in object narratives, to which this volume attests.

17. For a different account of how narratives from this period were unlikely to address commodity culture as such, see Wolfram Schmidgen's "*Robinson Crusoe,* Enumeration, and the Mercantile Fetish," *Eighteenth-Century Studies* 35.1 (2001): 19–39, in which he cautions those of us "who have been drawing on Karl Marx's analysis of the nineteenth-century commodity fetish to describe the representation of things in eighteenth-century literature" (20). While I certainly agree that a capitalist commodity culture or Marxian processes were not operative in 1709, my claim is that books already had a particular mode of production that anticipated the mass markets, attention to labor practices, and alienation of property that would eventually make Marxist analysis appropriate. Including its Grub Street variants, the bulk of the literary book market, in fact, comprised disposable works aimed at creating demand that would in turn fuel production. Such a system frequently rendered the author both instrumental as an intellectual laborer and alienated in relation to the work produced. As Laura Brown argues in *Fables of Modernity: Literature and Culture in the English Eighteenth Century* (Ithaca, NY: Cornell University Press, 2001), "the eighteenth-century business of bookselling displayed in a highly visible public arena the power and effects of the capitalist development of an industry: the exploitation of free enterprise, the trajectory of an expanding trade, the growth of productivity, the development of a national market, the centrality of consumer demand, the proliferation of advertising, the preeminence of profit, the commodification of the printed text, and the professionalization of the author" (142).

18. Edward Philips, *The Adventures of a Black Coat: Containing a Series of Remarkable Occurrences and Entertaining Incidents, That It Was a Witness to in Its Peregrinations through the Cities of London and Westminister, in Company with a Variety of Characters: As Related by Itself* (London, 1760), 4. Subsequent quotations from this work are cited parenthetically in the text.

19. For a sign that at least some eighteenth-century assumptions about the relationship between authors, readers, and the commodity form of the book needed to be revalued, see Lynn Festa's contribution to this volume, which provides a probing analysis of how object narratives in the nineteenth century project a more positive relation between humans and objects, especially as the genre becomes increasingly absorbed into children's literature. A work such as Sarah Trimmer's *The Silver Thimble* (Philadelphia, 1801) thus aims to restore and naturalize the relation between producer, object, and owner that would in turn serve to humanize material culture.

20. Karl Marx, *Capital: A Critique of Political Economy,* vol. 1., trans. Ben Fowkes (New York: Vintage, 1977), 165. Subsequent quotations from this work are cited parenthetically in the text.

21. *The Memoirs and Interesting Adventures of an Embroidered Waistcoat,* 2 vols. (London, 1751), 2:6, 1:5. Subsequent quotations from this work are cited parenthetically in the text.

22. *The History and Adventures of a Lady's Slippers and Shoes* (London, 1754), iv, iii. Subsequent quotations from this work are cited parenthetically in the text.

23. Dorothy Kilner, *The Adventures of a Hackney Coach* (London, 1781), 4. Subsequent quotations from this work are cited parenthetically in the text.

24. Tobias Smollett, *The History and Adventures of an Atom* (1769), ed. O M Brack, Jr. (Athens: University of Georgia Press, 1989), 3. Subsequent quotations from this work are cited parenthetically in the text.

25. See "Adventures of a Quire of Paper," *London Magazine* (August 1779): 355–58, (September 1779): 395–98, (October 1779): 448–52; Dorothy Kilner, *The Adventures of a Hackney Coach* (London, 1781); Thomas Bridges, *The Adventures of a Bank-Note,* 2 vols. (London, 1770–71). On distribution in the period, see Feather, *The Provincial Book Trade,* 44–68; Jürgen Habermas, *The Structural Transformation of the Public Sphere: An Inquiry into a Category of Bourgeois Society,* trans. Thomas Burger (Cambridge, MA: MIT Press, 1989), 14–18, 57–67, 73–79; Greg Laugero, "Infrastructures of the Enlightenment: Road-Making, the Public Sphere, and the Emergence of Literature," *Eighteenth-Century Studies* 29.1 (1995): 45–68; Plumb, *Birth of a Consumer Society,* 263–334, 327–28; Raven, *Judging New Wealth,* 219–33; David Trotter, *Circulation: Defoe, Dickens, and the Economies of the Novel* (Houndmills, UK: Macmillan, 1988), 18–45.

26. Habermas, *Structural Transformation,* 85, 51, 56.

27. Habermas attributes consciousness of the "disorganization of civil society" to the nineteenth century (*Structural Transformation,* 119). But many eighteenth-century object narratives indicate that such awareness existed when the public sphere ostensibly emerged. Bourdieu's elaborate analysis of the cultural field, in which different public activities (from the literary and artistic to the economic and political) occupy different fields of production, offers perhaps a more flexible model, one that can accommodate public dissension. However, Bourdieu's focus on the nineteenth century limits each field to "a separate social universe having its own laws of functioning independent of those of politics and the economy" (162), a model that is less applicable for eighteenth-century British culture. See Pierre Bourdieu, *The Field of Cultural Production: Essays on Art and Literature* (New York: Columbia University Press, 1993). Object narratives, which integrate various professional discourses, from law and politics to medicine and aesthetics, ignore disciplinary boundaries. Thus, while Habermas may generalize the eighteenth-century public sphere in overly unified terms, Bourdieu's analysis would, for the eighteenth-century field of cultural production, be too restrictive.

28. "Adventures of a Quire of Paper," 449. Subsequent quotations from this work are cited parenthetically in the text.

29. Stories that appeared in magazine form include "The Adventures of a Bad Shilling," "The Adventures of a Half Guinea," "The Adventures of a Half Penny," "The Adventures of a Shilling," and "The Adventures of a Three-Shilling Bank Token" (Mayo, *The English Novel in the Magazines,* 442–43). Book versions include *The Adventures of a Silver Penny* (London, 1786); *The Adventures of a Silver Three-Pence* (London, [1800?]); *Argentum: or, Adventures of a Shilling* (London, 1794); *Aureus; or, The Life and Opinions of a Sovereign* (London, 1824); *The Birmingham Counterfeit; or, Invisible Spectator: A Sentimental Romance* (London, 1772); Thomas Bridges, *The Adventures of a Bank-Note,* 2 vols. (London, 1770–71); Charles Johnstone, *Chrysal; or, The Adventures of a Guinea,* 2 vols. (1761), 4 vols., expanded ed. (London, 1765); and Helenus Scott, *The Adventures of a Rupee* (London, 1782).

30. Bridges, *Adventures of a Bank-Note,* 1:3.

31. Marc Shell, *The Economy of Literature* (Baltimore: Johns Hopkins University Press, 1978), 86, 63.

32. On how coffeehouses, playhouses, pleasure grounds, and musical venues contributed to the establishment of the eighteenth-century public sphere, see Habermas, *Structural Transformation,* 32–43.

33. See Mayo, *English Novel in the Magazines,* 508.

34. Scott, *Adventures of a Rupee,* 91.

35. The insistence in these stories on the value of speech may stem from the privilege orality was granted. On oral authority in the seventeenth century, see Martin Elsky, *Authorizing Words: Speech, Writing, and Print in the English Renaissance* (Ithaca, NY: Cornell University Press, 1989), 209–223. On oral authority in the eighteenth-century, see Alvin Kernan, *Printing Technology, Letters and Samuel Johnson* (Princeton, NJ: Princeton University Press, 1987) 12–16, 71–102. In both "'Oral Tradition': The Evolution of an Eighteenth-Century Concept," *Tradition in Transition: Women Writers, Marginal Texts, and the Eighteenth-Century Canon,* ed. S. J. Alvaro Ribiero and James G. Basker (Oxford: Clarendon Press, 1996), 161–76, and *Writing and European Thought 1600–1830* (Cambridge: Cambridge University Press, 1994), 92–118, Nicholas Hudson discusses the interchange between spoken and written language in eighteenth-century literature. On the interplay between handwriting and print in the seventeenth century, see Jonathan Goldberg, *Writing Matters* (Stanford, CA: Stanford University Press, 1989), 136–37. See also Harold Love, *Scribal Publication in Seventeenth-Century England* (Oxford: Oxford University Press, 1993), 288–310, on the continuing value print culture placed on scribal production in the eighteenth century.

36. See Benedict Anderson, *Imagined Communities: Reflections on the Origin and Spread of Nationalism* (London: Verso, 1983), 56–83; Pierre Bourdieu, *The Field of Cultural Production: Essays on Art and Literature* (New York: Columbia University Press, 1993), 112–41; Habermas, *Structural Transformation,* 12–54.

37. Tony Bennett, "Putting Policy into Cultural Studies," in *Cultural Studies,* ed. Lawrence Grossberg, Cary Nelson, and Paula Treichler (New York: Routledge, 1992), 27, 28.

38. Quoted in Devendra P. Varma, *The Evergreen Tree of Diabolical Knowledge* (Washington, DC: Consortium, 1972), 36, 41.

39. *Birmingham Counterfeit,* 46, 1.

Hackwork: It-Narratives and Iteration

Mark Blackwell

> It seems to me that this Genus of composition has never been properly distinguished or ascertained; that it wants to be methodized, to be separated, classed, and regulated.
>
> —Euphrasia, in Clara Reeve, *The Progress of Romance*[1]

> Novels being the chosen recreation of an uncritical multitude, there was a market for anything readable; hence competition among booksellers for copy . . . Thus the manufacture of novels speedily became a flourishing trade, and a supply was forthcoming from a crowd of hacks, in the regular pay or at the service of the booksellers.
>
> —Ernest A. Baker, *The History of the English Novel*[2]

> They were at the leading edge of an age which was moving toward an age like our own, at home with the machine and with utter ambivalence.
>
> —Hugh Kenner, *The Counterfeiters: An Historical Comedy*[3]

IT-NARRATIVES POSE A NUMBER OF PROBLEMS FOR SCHOLARS OF eighteenth-century prose fiction. They enjoyed their greatest popularity after the mid-century high point of Fielding's and Richardson's achievements and before what Homer Obed Brown calls the "institution" of the novel via the great anthologizing projects of the early nineteenth century.[4] Indeed, their waxing production in the 1770s, '80s, and '90s links them irrevocably to decades long viewed as the nadir in the glorious ascendancy of the novel as a form, a period rife with shameless imitation, failed experimentation, and quickly expiring topicality. In *The Development of the English Novel* (1899), reprinted more than twenty times between 1899 and 1924, Wilbur L. Cross expressed the longstanding scholarly consensus: "Excepting Jane Austen's, the novels published between 'Humphry Clinker' (1771) and 'Waverley' (1814) were written mostly for the amusement or the instruction of the day, and, having served their purpose, they deservedly lie gathering dust in our large libraries."[5] Ian Watt's seminal *Rise of the Novel* (1957) did little to change this view; the 1770s, '80s, and '90s are the years accounted for least satisfactorily by Watt's still influential "rise-of-the-novel" thesis.[6] Moreover, though the history of prose fiction between Sterne and Austen has received increasing critical attention and has been elucidated by (largely feminist) projects of recovery that have revived interest in long-overlooked novels, the formulaic sameness of most it-narratives chills the enthusiasm of all but the most intrepid advocates for forgotten texts. Morris Dickstein has usefully distinguished those who treat literary history "as a branch of history" (the "cultural" approach) from those who consider it "a branch of criticism," tracing the triumph of the latter, "critical" approach—and a concomitant thinning of the literary canon—to the mid-twentieth-century hegemony of New Criticism.[7] Yet even exemplars of the "old" cultural approach and its encyclopedic impulse such as Ernest Baker had little sympathy for the likes of Charles Johnstone's *Chrysal* (1760–65), which went through twenty editions between 1760 and the close of the century and was later collected in Sir Walter Scott's *Ballantyne's Novelists' Library* (1822), together with a biographical sketch of Johnstone. Despite *Chrysal*'s inclusion in Scott's influential canon-making anthology, Baker dismissed the work and its literary kin as "a misuse and often prostitution of the craft of the novelist, an easy means of emptying a store of anecdote, miscellaneous observations, surreptitious libels, and what-not. Their literary interest," he pronounced, "is insignificant."[8]

Champions of the it-narrative may be inclined to interpret Baker's characterization as an anachronistic misreading distorted by Jamesian ideas about the craft of the novelist. Yet Baker's judgment does little more than paraphrase an early review of Helenus Scott's *Adventures of a Rupee* (1782):

> This mode of making up a book, and styling it the Adventures of a Cat, a Dog, a Monkey, a Hackney-coach, a Louse, a Shilling, a Rupee, or—any thing else, is grown so fashionable, that few months pass which do not bring one of them under our inspection. *It is indeed a convenient method to writers of the inferior class, of emptying their common-place books, and throwing together all the farrago of public transactions, private characters, old and new stories, every thing, in short, which they can pick up, to afford a little temporary amusement to an idle reader.* This is the utmost degree of merit which the best of them aspire to; and, small as it is, more than most of them ever arrive at. The slight performance before us is perhaps one of the best of its little species, and may give half an hour's entertainment to a coffee-house critic, or a lounging traveller, as the style is tolerably easy and correct, and some of the materials are not unentertaining.[9]

The anonymous reviewer distinguishes "writers of the inferior class," here depicted as undiscriminating purveyors of odds and ends, from a nameless but superior literary set. The reviewer assumes a like distinction between a "little species" of writing, quickly sketched as "the Adventures of a Cat, a Dog, a Monkey, a Hackney-coach, a Louse, a Shilling, a Rupee, or—any thing else," and another, greater species that transcends the world of "fashionable" ephemera, presumably by offering more than "a little temporary amusement" or "half an hour's entertainment." This reviewer may be writing decades before the "institution" of the novel, yet already the sort of criticism that makes a canon of "great" novels possible—the sort that "can mediate between the growing number of artists and the expanding middle-class audience, uncertain of its bearings in the brave new world of culture," as Dickstein puts it—has begun its work.[10]

Eighteenth-century it-narratives are significant exactly because they register the moment in the commodification of prose fiction when "the novel" begins to emerge as a respectable literary form through its differentiation from "little species," subspecies, subgenres—in short, hackwork.[11] Alvin Kernan has written that "a print-made anxiety about writing" resulted in "eighteenth-century writers' efforts to make themselves something other than laborers in the book factory":

> Print may have determined that henceforth all writers would be some kind of, to put it most crudely, Grub Street hack, but this life of *labor* rather than *work* was obviously unacceptable to the most intense writers of the day; and though they had to accept print realities to some degree, they also expended large amounts of energy and undertook great risks . . . to carve for themselves an acceptable poetic mask.[12]

Yet it-narratives confront us with writers resigned to their role as laborers turning out print-based consumables in response to the demand—the fashions—of a specific time and place.[13] Indeed, the vogue for it-narratives marks the appearance of what we now call genre fiction and of niche markets for formulaic literary commodities.[14] Period reviews of these works evince this important, emergent distinction. But so do the works themselves. Their writers' cognizance of, and anxiety about, the niche they occupy is revealed by their shameless co-optation of voguish narrative idioms, by their insistent allusions to hack culture, and by the framing devices that signify their self-conscious participation in a generic tradition.

Hack Writers and Hackneyed Stories

Eighteenth-century reviewers of it-narratives never tire of noting that their conventions are hackneyed. By the early 1770s, the reviewer of *The Birmingham Counterfeit* (1772) could complain, "a Birmingham shilling recites its travels and adventures, on the hacknied and worn-out plan on which the *Adventures of a Guinea*, with a multitude of other Invisible Spies, have been written," thereby noting the work's participation in a distinctive if undistinguished tradition.[15] The reviewer of *The Adventures of a Watch* (1788) was equally unkind to "Adventures of this kind," describing them as

> so hackneyed, that genius itself could scarcely lend them grace, or learning convey to them importance. Neither have any share in this work. All has been told before, in a better manner; and the reflections are trite, and tediously expanded: in short, all the bookmaker's art is exhausted; all the typographer's ingenuity employed, to spin out the meagre materials into a trifling and insipid volume. The author of the Hackney Coach has wound up this paultry machine: it will go for a few hours, and then be silent, we hope, for ever.[16]

The genre is not the distilled essence of authorial "genius" or "learning," but a commodity, a material product of the bookmaker and typographer's labor, a soulless "machine" whose ephemerality is its only recommendation. This reviewer renders it-narratives the equivalent of eighteenth-century automata, such as Jacques Vaucanson's duck or his flute player, "paultry" counterfeits fit only for a few hours entertainment, belated exemplars of a fad whose time has passed.[17] The reviewer's distinction between typographical ingenuity and authorial genius, between fiction that resembles a clockwork thing and fiction that seems alive, recalls an analogous distinction implicit in the previously cited review of Scott's *Adventures of a Rupee.* By describing it-narratives as a "little species" fit to divert one during an idle hour, that reviewer figured such fictions as pets and slyly insinuated their inferiority to proper novels, a greater species that proffers the literary equivalent of lasting human companionship. In both cases, the difference between original fiction and hackneyed counterfeit, between lasting literary achievement and diverting ephemera, is conveyed through categorical distinctions—inanimate mechanism versus animate organism, animal pet versus human companion—that it-narratives play at challenging.

The reviewer's charge that *The Adventures of a Watch* has been spun out, its "meagre" substance "tediously expanded," echoes a like accusation in an earlier review of *The Adventures of a Hackney Coach* (1781): "a book, unfortunately for authors, must consist of so many pages, and be spun out some way or other; what has a poor writer to do, therefore, but to fill it up as well as he can with something which he has ready cut and dried for the occasion?"[18] Both reviewers' use of the word "spin" harks back to Swift's *Battle of the Books* (1704), in which a spider serves as an apt emblem of a modernity in which authors display an inexhaustible capacity to spin line after silken line from nothing at all. Critics of the earliest it-narratives occasionally invoke a Scriblerian world overrun with hacks, as in the *Monthly Review*'s account of *The Adventures of a Black Coat* (1760), which laments the writer's decision to add "to the herd of Authors; which, indeed, is numerous enough."[19] Indeed, the critics know whereof they speak, as they themselves rely on conventions of disparagement (terms such as "spin" and "hackneyed") to fill up their reviews and consort with the very pack of authors whose growing numbers concern them.[20]

The great champion of that herd in the second half of the century was Samuel Johnson, perhaps because he was its most successful member. As Lawrence Lipking notes, "No previous author, or at any rate no celebrated author, can be so firmly associated with hackwork."[21] In a well-known essay in *The Adventurer,* Johnson dubbed his own era "The Age of Authors," hypothesizing that "there never was a time, in which men of all degrees of ability, of every kind of education, of every profession and employment, were posting with ardour so general to the press." Johnson recognized that, "of the innumerable books and pamphlets that have overflowed the nation, scarce one has made any addition to real knowledge, or contained more than a transposition of common sentiments and a repetition of common phrases."[22] Yet Johnson rendered that commonness and that repetition a worthwhile achievement in an earlier and equally famous number of *The Rambler.* Johnson maintained that there is an obscure, indigent "race of beings" who "live unrewarded and die unpitied" because "their usefulness is less obvious to vulgar apprehensions" than that of "the husbandman, the labourer, the miner, or the smith." He admitted that "only a very few [of these "authors of *London*"] can be said to produce, or endeavour to produce new ideas," calling the dull majority "the drudges of the pen, the manufacturers of literature," and likening them to "other artificers" intent only on delivering "their tale of wares at the stated time": "they perceive no particular summons to composition, except the sound of the clock; they have no other rule than the law or the fashion for admitting their thoughts or rejecting them; and . . . their productions are seldom intended to remain in the world longer than a week." Well before Walter Benjamin, Johnson is addressing the work of writing in an age of mechanical reproduction, considering the ways in which a highly differentiated marketplace of readers demands varied sorts of textual manufactures, and claiming a place for "the *Ephemerae* of learning," which "have uses more adequate to the purposes of common life than more pompous and durable volumes. Every size of readers requires a genius of correspondent capacity . . . As every writer has his use, every writer ought to have his patrons."[23] The reviewer of *The Adventures of a Bank-Note,* for one, seems to have taken such lessons to heart. In the spirit of Johnson, this reviewer professes that one's critical endeavors must be scaled to the scope of the writer's talents: "Not to allow some compassion to laborious dullness, would be cruel and inhuman." Nonetheless, even writers with relatively modest ambitions—"the entertainment of the public"—must be "severely reprehended" when they do not "exert" themselves to serve their distinctive audience.[24]

It is perhaps anachronistic to see Johnson as describing a publishing world much like our own, in which niche marketing encourages a particular sort of literary commodity to be manufactured for a narrowly construed target audience—in which different "sizes" of contemporary readers consume fantasy fiction, or mysteries, or some more specialized subcategory, buying feminist science fiction, say, or following the work of a particular writer of police procedurals. Yet James Raven cites "customer identification" as an important factor in the late-eighteenth-century print trade and underscores the industry's development of fresh "methods of attracting and retaining new readerships."[25] Clara Reeve, for one, depicted the literary world of 1766 in terms of the calculus of supply and demand, noting that "the manufacturers of Novels" worked "constantly" to provide "an Annual Supply for the Circulating Library."[26] Johnson sketches a literary marketplace shaped by consumer demand as well, one in which any writer meeting that demand serves as useful a social purpose as the miner or the smith. To be sure, Johnson does not mean to abandon qualitative evaluations of literary merit, as his emphasis on different sizes of readers and writers and his implicit distinction between rule-bound, clock-watching textual mechanics and other sorts of authors intimates. Differences of social rank here stand in for distinctions of literary quality, and Johnson deploys the same language of mechanical manufacture oft used by critics to disparage hastily assembled, clunkily constructed it-narratives. Nonetheless, Johnson envisions—and defends—a highly differentiated literary field, one that suits a social world equally complex, stratified, and changeable.[27]

At least one critic may have had Johnson's *Rambler* essay in mind when reviewing the best-known and most successful it-narrative of the eighteenth century, Johnstone's *Chrysal.* Writing in the *Monthly Review,* this critic complained that the novel was perhaps "too much tinctured with misanthropy," remarking that such pessimism about human nature is not uncommon among "such as are *hackneyed in the ways of men.*"[28] Johnson had used the phrase in a different context, remarking that the ephemeral writers he was "endeavouring to recommend have been too long *hackneyed in the ways of men* to indulge the chimerical ambition of immortality."[29] *Chrysal*'s reviewer associates the phrase with writers who harbor no illusions about the world or their fellow humans, while Johnson links it to authors who understand all too well the limited scope of both their talents and their professional prospects. In his *Dictionary* (1755), Johnson employed the phrase, "He is long *hackney'd* in the ways of men," to illustrate the meaning of the verb "to hackney," defined as "to practise in one thing; to accustom to the road." Johnson attributed the phrase to Shakespeare; it seems to be a misquotation of King Henry's speech to his wayward son in *I Henry IV,* wherein the king complains that Harry has become "So common-hackneyed in the eyes of men, / So stale and cheap to vulgar company."[30] The application of the phrase to writers—especially fiction writers—is apt, as it distinguishes promiscuous circulation and an excess of publicity from something else, something more elevated. More importantly, it unavoidably evokes reviewers' frequent complaints that it-narratives are hackneyed (trite, commonplace, stale, unoriginal) and, through cognates such as hack and hackney, hints that such works are composed by garret-dwelling hirelings, plodding drudges, imitators—those who reduce themselves and their work to mere things through a form of literary prostitution, those who, like hackney horses and hackney coaches, make the same dull round again and again.[31]

It may have been with the figure of the hack in mind, and its association of writers for bread with coaches for hire, that Jonathan Swift used a vehicular metaphor to describe the literary habits of Grub Street's denizens in *A Tale of a Tub:*

> The Grubaean Sages have always chosen to convey their Precepts and their Arts, shut up within the Vehicles of Types and Fables, which having been perhaps more careful and curious in adorning, than was altogether necessary, it has fared with these Vehicles after the usual Fate of Coaches over-finely painted and gilt; that the transitory Gazers have so dazzled their Eyes, and fill'd their Imaginations with the outward Lustre, as neither to regard or consider, the Person or the Parts of the Owner within.[32]

Swift's narrator associates hack writing with manneristic excess, with a baroque adornment that obscures the matter at hand; thus the passage begins by criticizing the tendency of "Grubaean" writers to obfuscate meaning with stylistic "Lustre," to adorn their rhetorical carriages to the disadvantage of the vehicles' semantic occupants. As the coach metaphor implies, the embellishment is intended to signify the distinction of the owner's identity, the uniqueness of the occupant's ideas, yet it contributes nothing to the vehicle's capacity to convey its passenger to the intended destination. Quite the contrary—the coach's ornamentation becomes an end in itself, so dazzling viewers that its "outward Lustre" blinds them to what lies within. The passage of course serves as an example of what it describes. The *Tale*'s narrator soon finds himself "shut up" in the vehicle of his own coach metaphor, so that by the end of the excerpt above his purpose seems to be not to analyze literary style, but rather to make a point about vehicular aesthetics and self-adornment. Hence the narrator's later definition of "True Criticks" as "Discoverer[s] and Collector[s] of Writers Faults" who become "so entirely possess'd and replete with the defects of other Pens, that the very Quintessence of what is bad, does of necessity distill into their own: by which means the Whole appears to be nothing else but an *Abstract* of the *Criticisms* themselves have made."[33]

Like the critic who becomes "possess'd" by the very stylistic faults he enumerates, and like the carriage owners who become unnoticed embellishments to the equipages originally intended to display them to advantage, Swift's narrator loses himself in his analysis of the Grubaean literary aesthetic and metamorphoses into an example of what he decries. That the narrator considers this stylistic transmigration to have broader resonance is suggested both by his immediate invocation of Pythagoras and by his subsequent admission that his first critical annotations treat not a classical text, but *"Tom Thumb,* whose Author was a *Pythagorean* Philosopher" and which "contains the whole scheme of *Metempsychosis,* deducing the Progress of the Soul thro' all her Stages."[34] Indistinction, identity transfer, iterability—paradoxically, these are the accompaniments of an embellished individuality, be it textual or personal. For it is not just meaning but people who are obscured at passage's end, concealed by the very trappings intended to render them singular, distinct, individual. Swift's coach seems not an anonymous hackney but a unique carriage emblazoned with the decorative touches that declare the personal taste of the owner. Were the coach also to bear the owner's arms, it would render its occupant's identity the product of a dialectic of family heritage and aesthetic individuality. Yet the capacity of style to be copied, the ease with which it replaces (or effaces its difference from) that which it adorns, together with the fact that genealogy functions as a sort of lineal metempsychosis that renders the individual a mere vehicle for the family name—all of this begins to unravel the distinction between anonymous circulation in a hackney coach and anonymous circulation in a gilt carriage, and between the carriage and its owner.

The *"Novelty of my Vehicle"*: Imitating Sterne's Inimitable Style

The reviewer of *The Adventures of a Hackney Coach* grumbled most noisily about the work's heavy reliance on Shandean idiosyncrasies:

"Nor can we in any of the other characters discover the marks of taste and genius which so eminently distinguished the truly original writer whom our author seems ambitious of imitating. A servile copy of *Sterne*'s peculiarity of expression, his sudden transitions, exclamations, &c. without his force, spirit, and sensibility, will never recommend a writer to public attention."[35] Despite this critic's distinction between Sterne's peculiarities, which may be mimicked, and his inimitable force, spirit, and sensibility, several writers of it-narratives, and a number of their contemporaries, gambled on the iterability of Sterne's "marks of taste and genius."[36] Hence, as Wilbur Cross remarks, "the sentiment and gesture of Sterne were diffused everywhere," though J. M. S. Tompkins complains that this diffusion merely gave rise to "that insupportably tedious vulgarization of Sterne's technique by which his imitators hoped to capture something of his unique and inimitable spirit."[37] Period commentators were also aware of the trend; Clara Reeve, for instance, remarked that "*Sterne,* like all other Original writers has been followed by a swarm of imitators, not one of which deserve mention among works of eminence in this class of writing."[38]

Some it-narratives, such as *The Adventures of a Bank-Note* (1770), copied Sterne's comic, mechanico-physical descriptions of humans and their passions, as in the novel's description of the "hobby-horse" of a mercer whose dedication to the efficient endorsement of banknotes renders him "a piece of clockwork," or its depiction of Mrs. Ruby-nose's means of venting her spleen: "The method that Mrs. Ruby-nose used to dismiss her anger, was to clap herself into an arm-chair with such a whang, that it shook the hot vapours from her brain, and sent them in a hurry down into a capacious store-room called her victualling-office."[39] Among the most amusing invocations of Sterne in an it-narrative comes in *The Life and Adventures of a Fly* (1789?), which recycles the famous scene from *Tristram Shandy* in which Uncle Toby's release of a fly serves as the basis of Tristram's sentimental education. Four-year-old Tommy Pearson is visited by "cousin Larry"—the eight-year-old Master Laurence Sterne—who helps Tommy decide what to do with a fly he has caught: "Go to the window which you see is open, put him out, and say, 'Go thy ways, poor sluttering thing; it were very hard indeed, if in this wide world there were not room enough for *me* and *you* to live;' and then shut down the window, and let him fly a-way."[40]

The author of *The Adventures of a Hackney Coach* literalizes the metaphor of mechanical imitation through a dedicatory epistle that attributes the text's genesis to a pen inherited from Sterne:

> Chance put into my hand an old worn-out pen of Yorick's; . . . 'This Pen,' whispered my Genius, 'may do wonders yet;—whip out your knife,—put it in repair;—if this world presents a blank of ingenuity, take a trip to that of

5. Derivative of both William Hogarth's *Taste in High Life* and his *Marriage a la Mode* series, this homely 1769 engraving, entitled *High Life at Noon,* attempts to exploit Sterne's popularity as well, using a prominently displayed clock and an allusion to *Tristram Shandy*'s clock-winding scene to point its commentary on sexual impropriety. The leaf displayed in the monkey's paws reads, "A Dissertation / on Winding up / the Clock by / Tristram / Shandy." Courtesy of The Lewis Walpole Library, Yale University.

> invention! you are certain of the Prize of Fame, while you brandish this renowned Talisman!'—This sweet whispering found a pleasing passage to my heart.—I sat down by my fire-side; examined the treasure of my memory—found it contained a mine for my purpose, without spurring my Pegasus into imaginary regions:—Truth took her seat beside me; examined the contents;—and found they corresponded with her registry. I put them into form—and am happy in presenting them to the heart of sensibility.[41]

The talismanic pen is a marvelous figure for the Sterne fetish that swept England in the wake of *Tristram Shandy* (1759–67), and for an automaticity of writing that Sterne himself endorsed: "The truth is this—that my pen governs me—not me my pen."[42] The pen associates Sterne with the materiality of writing, with a technology of style that renders the author its instrument. This writing implement—and the style it bears—can circulate like the coins, snuffboxes, gloves, and coaches, and the stopwatches and tobacco pipes and hats in Sterne's works, objects that hover uneasily between merely mediating exchanges of language and feeling between human possessors and becoming so brimful of sentiment and subjectivity that they come to life as animate, independent interlocutors. Yet the pen also permits the writer access to an unplumbed interiority—"the treasure of my memory"—that seems to render both imagination and imitation unnecessary, thereby reconciling the viewless depths of the singular self with portable, mobile properties belonging to no one in particular. On the one hand, Sterne's mannerism and his heavy reliance on textual predecessors created an opening for literary franchisers eager to exploit a marketing opportunity by peddling Sterneana. On the other hand, Sterne's "novelty" distinguished his work from the "tame imitation" that "makes almost the whole merit of so many books."[43] Yet that novelty also inspired—or modeled—originality, much as scenes of sentimental pathos prompt real tears that nonetheless proceed from an identification with, and assumption of, another's feelings. As Vicesimus Knox pointed out in the course of lamenting the threat posed to the "dignity of the republic of letters" by "novels, pamphlets, and newspapers," "Nothing is so irregular and anomalous, but it may become fashionable; and when it is once fashionable, it will be made a model."[44] Sterne's fiction made inimitable novelty a genre whose formula could be distilled to serve readers hungry for more of the same.[45]

Like Sterne's *Sentimental Journey through France and Italy* (1768), for instance, *The Adventures of a Hackney Coach* opens by thrusting its readers into the middle of a conversation and provides little to orient them to their surroundings: "'This is the most fashionable Coach on the stand,' says a pretty young lady, stepping into me, with all the hilarity of soul that distinguish the cheerful children of prosperity."[46] But a more insistent imitation of Sterne's manner may be found in *The Adventures of a Watch* (1788):

> Methinks I hear a critic voice exclaim, How! A Watch pretend to prate! politically too—Hold, my good Sir; why not? I am thoroughly wound up, therefore cannot help going, beside, belonging to a statesman, surely I may claim some little right to enter into the state of the nation; which, were I to examine particularly, the account might possible [*sic*] run thus—Some thousands
>
> In a roguish state,
> Ditto in a distracted state,
> The poor in a starving state,
> Overseers in a gutling state,
> The late M— —y in a losing state,
> The present in a recovering state,
> Rakes in a shattered state,

> Bruisers in a battered state,
> Some few in a blessed state, and
> Numbers in a damned state.

> But that I may not reduce my readers to a yawning state, I shall begin my story, which shall commence from my perfect state; for to relate the various tortures I underwent before I was finished, would, I'm sure, be too affecting to a person of feeling. Feeling, *apropos*—a word on that business—To handle a feeling subject properly, requires some consideration, for though numbers may speak feelingly, yet to write so is rather novel, notwithstanding there are a number of novel writers. But waving this remark, and to proceed methodically, we will principally take a peep at

> Fine feeling,
> No feeling,
> Some feeling,
> Fellow feeling, and
> Feeling the pulse.[47]

The passage is little more than a catalogue of Sternean effects. There is the pretence of a sprightly narrator engaging with readers, critics, interlocutors; the narrative self-consciousness; the digressiveness with its concomitant sense of "unplanned-ness" and disorder; the quickness; the attention to feeling—including a distinct allusion to the pulse-feeling scene in *A Sentimental Journey;* the too emphatic echo of Sterne's famous lists (of Roman shoes, for instance, in *Tristram Shandy,* or of travelers near the opening of *A Sentimental Journey*); and, of course, the jokes about a voluble watch, doubtless intended to recall Yorick's anxious reflections on the materialist self and the clockwork universe. In its way, however, the excerpt is a remarkable tour de force, a knowing précis of the conventions of *Tristram Shandy* and *A Sentimental Journey,* a mannerist caricature of Sterne's most characteristic mannerisms. Like the automata popular in the eighteenth century—ducks, flautists, harpsichordists—the garrulous watch may not fool its readers into believing that timepieces can think, or into regarding its story as a long-lost work by Sterne, but it succeeds in raising questions about the distinctions between real and artificial life, between originals and copies, between literature and what J. C. T. Oates terms "the rubbish of literature."[48]

The complex relationship between so-called originals and copies can be traced in the career of George Kearsley, who published both *The Adventures of a Watch* and *The Adventures of a Hackney Coach.* In both cases, his commitment may have been less to the it-narrative as a genre than to the market for Sterne and Sterneana, the "vogue for things Shandean and sentimental"—that is, the Sterne brand.[49] In the fifteen-year period between 1775 and 1790, Kearsley was involved in the publication not only of these Sterne-influenced object tales, but also of *Letters from Yorick to Eliza* (1775), the ten-volume *Works of Laurence Sterne* (1780), *The Beauties of Sterne* (1782), and *The Letters of Maria, to which is added, an account of her death* (1790). It should be noted that Kearsley also published a number of the other *Beauties* anthologies mentioned in Leah Price's *The Anthology and the Rise of the Novel,* including *The Beauties of Fielding* (1782), *The Beauties of Goldsmith* (1782), *The Beauties of Johnson* (1782), *The Beauties of Swift* (1782), *The Beauties of the late Revd. Dr. Isaac Watts* (1782), *The Beauties of Milton, Thomson, and Young* (1783), *The Beauties of Pope* (1783), *The Beauties of Shakespeare* (1783), *The Beauties of the Spectators, Tatlers, and Guardians* (1787), and *The Beauties of the Rambler, Adventurer, Connoisseur, World, and Idler* (1787).[50]

The example of Kearsley forces one to think anew about the paradoxes of what Jacques Derrida terms "the law of genre."[51] One paradoxical aspect of the old saw about the pervasive influence of Sterne's originality on the "minor" fiction of the 1760s, '70s, and '80s—a story retailed by such twentieth-century critics as Cross and Tompkins, as well as by period reviewers—is the fact that Sterne's work incorporated that of his own literary forebears so freely and inventively. As Ian Campbell Ross puts it, "Sterne was a great admirer of encyclopaedias, compilations, and digests—works of popular entertainment characteristic of the age, from which he borrowed, stole, paraphrased, and misquoted at will."[52] Sterne's borrowings have been old news since the 1790s, when John Ferriar's *Illustrations of Sterne* (1798) began the process of identifying Sterne's sources, especially Burton and Rabelais.[53] Yet, as the recent work of Thomas Keymer suggests, Sterne was a "voracious reader of new fiction" equally indebted to the ephemeral titles of the 1750s.[54] Keymer makes clear that Sterne, like his imitators, manipulated the commodification and packaging of his novels for gain while inheriting from novelistic predecessors many of the typographical and material experiments with the "printedness" of his work that we now consider so original.[55] Indeed, Keymer demonstrates that Sterne's "exuberant manufacture of fashionable print" and his "recycl[ing]" of "the output of others" render him different in degree, not in kind, from his hack-writing contemporaries.[56]

In this context, it may make sense to regard *Tristram Shandy* and *A Sentimental Journey* not as literary models for a number of derivative it-narratives that take a Shandean stamp in order to exploit the vogue for Sterne—as with the watchcases, tea waiters, sugar bowls, butter dishes, shoe buckles, bud vases, and bracelets that were illustrated with a picture of Maria of Moulines—but as the best-remembered participants in a number of loose, amorphous generic experiments, two of which are now reified as the novel of sentiment and the it-narrative.[57] The "borrowing" likely worked in several directions at once, issuing in a complicated intertextual relationship between early it-narratives that influenced Sterne, Sterne's own fiction, compilations of Sterne's *Beauties*, and continuations and elaborations of his works (including later it-narratives that exploit Sterne's popularity, such as *The Adventures of a Watch* and *The Adventures of a Hackney Coach*). Sterne himself displays an acute awareness of the complexity of literary borrowing in *Tristram Shandy*, not only in the famous passage wherein Tristram criticizes plagiarism in language stolen from Burton, or in his unacknowledged application of Locke's theory of property to Walter Shandy's own tendency to appropriate others' ideas, but also through Tristram's reflections on the generosity that signifies his own "true genius": "never do I hit upon any invention or device which tendeth to the furtherance of good writing, but I instantly make it public; willing that all mankind should write as well as myself."[58] Whether Tristram is publicizing his own inventions or peddling devices he has "hit upon" in others' work remains unclear, perhaps by design.

Hence the difficulty of tracing Sterne's connections to the it-narrative, popular at the height of his fame.[59] Most critics who have attempted to take the measure of Sterne's debt to the form have identified the starling episode in *A Sentimental Journey* as a symptom of his interest in circulation tales.[60] In the revised version of "Personal Effects and Sentimental Fictions" that she has contributed to this volume, Deidre Lynch enumerates some other itinerant objects in *A Sentimental Journey*—La Fleur's *gage d'amour* and Tristram Shandy's monogrammed handkerchief, now in the possession of Maria of Moulines—that supply "miniaturized narrative[s] of circulation" and thus provide further evidence of Sterne's relationship to the ephemeral fiction of his day. The latter example is especially interesting, for by underscoring the parallel between intertextual allusion and the circulation of things from hand to hand (the handkerchief passes not only from Tristram to Maria, but also from *Tristram Shandy* to *A Sentimental Journey*), it complicates our ideas about ownership and borrowing—about what it means for something to belong to a discrete text or an individual person.

Yorick himself, I would suggest, functions as a sort of it-narrator. After all, *A Sentimental Journey* recounts Yorick's circulation on the continent, his glancing contact with others serving as the occasion for reflections and feelings that remind him that, the "most *physical précieuse* in France" and "all her materialism" to the contrary, he is not "a machine."[61] Yorick's need to reassure himself that he is not merely a thing, a mechanism or collection of parts, is apposite here, as is the slack, episodic narrative of his wanderings, reminiscent of the haphazard motion of various it-narrators who bounce from possessor to possessor, gathering their stories.[62] Like many it-narratives, *A Sentimental Journey* is marked by its circulating narrator's frequent if fleeting encounters with human beings who command his attention only temporarily, encounters usually occasioned by an exchange.

Yet it is not only in *A Sentimental Journey* that Sterne betrays his interest in it-narratives. The "ill-fated sermon" that serendipitously falls from Uncle Toby's copy of Stevinus—an absent-minded Yorick left it nestled in the book's pages—is the object of a crucial inset circulation tale in *Tristram Shandy:*

> Ill-fated sermon! Thou wast lost, after this recovery of thee, a second time, dropp'd thro' an unsuspected fissure in thy master's pocket, down into a treacherous and a tatter'd lining,—trod deep into the dirt by the left hind foot of his Rosinante, inhumanly stepping upon thee as thou falledst; —buried ten days in the mire,—raised up out of it by a beggar, sold for a halfpenny to a parish-clerk,—transferred to his parson,—lost for ever to thy own, the remainder of his days,—nor restored to his restless MANES till this very moment, that I tell the world the story.

Though the sermon does not recount its own wanderings, it does metamorphose into a person, an "it" endowed with human attributes. The transformation is accomplished through apostrophe ("Ill-fated sermon! Thou wast lost"); through the narrator's assertion that it was inhuman for Rosinante to tread on the sermon, a claim that imputes human feelings to Yorick's horse and his manuscript; and through the narrator's earlier depiction of Stevinus and the sermon as human companions: Yorick "sent *Stevinus* home, and his sermon to keep him company."[63] The sermon's contingent transit from hand to hand and its powerlessness to control its trajectory recall the fate of numerous circulation-novel protagonists, lost things all, while at the same time serving as a commentary on the aleatory dimensions of *Tristram Shandy* itself; after all, the story of the sermon succeeds the reading of the sermon, which issues from its unforeseen discovery in Stevinus, which was itself consulted because Stevinus was the inventor of a sailing chariot brought to Uncle Toby's mind by the unexpected arrival of Dr. Slop, whose entrance interrupts Toby and Walter's discussion of the nature of women, itself a diversion from what one might expect to be the main event: Elizabeth Shandy's effort to give birth to the eponymous Tristram. Moreover, the allusion in the passage above to the sermon's being "buried . . . in the mire" and then "raised up out of it by a beggar" evokes the metempsychosal meanderings of many it-narrators, some of whom are figuratively reborn into a new life with each new possessor, others of whom are mobile spirits who either find themselves inhabiting a particular animal or object (as in *The Sopha* [1742], the English translation of Crébillon fils's novel) or pass through a series of very different material embodiments (as in *The Adventurer* 5 [November 21, 1752]). Finally, the found manuscript story, so common in it-fictions as either a framing device or an interpolated narrative, also forms part of this overdetermined moment in Sterne's text.

Note too the odd way in which Yorick becomes identified with the sermon—their unhappy fates seem mutually determining—just as Stevinus the author is metonymically equated with his text, or as Tristram Shandy and *Tristram Shandy* become inextricable from one another. There is something unsettling about the thought of Yorick carelessly "popp[ing] his sermon . . . into the middle of *Stevinus*," just as there is something disconcerting about the narrator describing the prebendary of York's appropriation of the sermon as an intrusion upon Yorick's physical remains, a means of "plunder[ing] him after he was laid in his grave." Misusing another's text and violating a corpse become indistinguishable in this passage, as do the objects ennobled by it-narratives and the narratives themselves, all classed as circulating things. Sterne quickly moves readers from morbid to comic musings upon these confusions; no sooner does Tristram inform us that he hopes "to give rest to *Yorick*'s ghost;—which . . . *still walks*" than he reveals his ambition to put Yorick back in circulation. "In case the character of parson *Yorick,* and this sample of his sermons is liked," Tristram reports, "there are now in the possession of the *Shandy* Family, as many as will make a handsome volume," and they are for sale. Both Yorick's sermon and his "character" are resurrected, rescued from obscurity and reborn as circulating volumes. Yorick's sermons are an assembled text ("as many as will make a handsome volume") not unlike a crazy-quilt it-narrative whose episodes serve merely to pad it out, to "make" its volume. Both sorts of volume are like Stevinus's sailing chariot as well—textual contrivances that promise to transport their readers, print mechanisms that circulate promiscuously. Yet Yorick's sermon differs from most it-narratives in that it still bears some trace of its writer. Like the critics who distinguish Sterne's unique style from that of his slavish imitators, Walter Shandy is convinced by "the stile and manner" of the sermon that "it was Yorick's, and no one's else."[64]

The tale of the caged starling in *A Sentimental Journey* is Sterne's sliest and most explicit acknowledgment of his indebtedness to the it-narrative or novel of circulation. Yorick's sympathy for the bird is of course evoked because of his own anxieties about foreign imprisonment for traveling without a passport. The starling speaks, plaintively crying "I can't get out" again and again, and though Yorick recognizes that its notes are "mechanical"—as are, he fears, his own sentimental responses—he is moved nonetheless. However, the bird is no sooner purchased for Yorick than it is passed from hand to hand:

> In my return from Italy I brought him with me . . .—and telling his story to Lord A—Lord A begged the bird of me—in a week Lord A gave him to Lord B—Lord B made a present of him to Lord C—and Lord C's gentleman sold him to Lord D's for a shilling—Lord D gave him to Lord E—and so on—half round the alphabet—From that rank he passed into the lower house, and passed the hands of as many commoners . . .
>
> It is impossible but many of my readers must have heard of him; and if any by mere chance have ever seen him—I beg leave to inform them, that that bird was my bird, or some vile copy set up to represent him.[65]

Yorick goes on to inform his readers that he has added the poor starling as the crest to his coat of arms, making it the sign of his own identity. Yet Yorick's coat of arms, like Swift's gilt carriage, seems incapable of securing his inalienable identity. Indeed, his arms now serve as an emblem of his identity's capacity to circulate, to be traded from hand to hand or even copied, despite his emphatic assertion of ownership—"that bird was my bird." The scene may thus function as a winking allegory of the ways in which a voluble "stearn" had recently been put on the market, recalling both the circulation of Sterne's *Tristram Shandy* among a mixed readership and the triumphant tour of Sterne himself among his fashionable patrons, often impersonating the characters he had written—or, in Jonathan Lamb's words, "imitating his imitations."[66] One's writing, like one's celebrity, can take on a life of its own, and one's originality, one's very identity can come to consist in repeat performances of a character one has written—or even of lines written by another, as the Count de B****'s confusion of Yorick with Shakespeare's jester suggests, and as the poor starling's own iteration of a characteristic phrase it has learned by rote likewise demonstrates.[67] The serial encounters, the potential for different iterations of the starling, and its own mechanical repetition of the same phrase make this episode seem both an inset it-tale and an allegory of the illimitable spread of cookie-cutter it-fictions.

Yorick sympathizes with the starling's imprisonment, with its isolation in a foreign setting, with its powerlessness to control its future course ("I think there is a fatality in it—I seldom go to the place I set out for," he muses), and perhaps with its repeat performance of a copied identity, its endless parroting of another's language.[68] Yet after his efforts to free the bird fail, he seems content to leave it caged, even showing himself quick to assert his proprietary interests in it. Like the Tristram who simultaneously imputes spirit or subjectivity to Yorick's lost sermon, thinking its recovery will lay his ghost, and treats it as a possession that will soon circulate as a printed text, Yorick vacillates strangely between sympathetically identifying with and objectifying the bird, between considering it as another speaking subject that should enjoy certain rights and treating it as a commodity, a valuable and amusing curiosity.[69] The pathos of the bird's imprisonment is offset by Sterne's odd reduction of its serial possessors to alphabetical tokens of its trajectory, markers who cumulatively trace its story from A to Z. This ambivalent relationship recalls the dynamics of many it-narratives, in which a pin or a penny seems imprisoned by its dependency on its owners, yet also renders those owners instrumental to its own purposes by assembling their tales into the fabric of its distinctive, loquacious "thinghood"—by, in Yorick's phrase, "miss[ing] nothing [it] can fairly lay [its] hands on."[70] These ambivalences run parallel to the problem of sentimental commerce in *A Sentimental Journey,* in which tears are traded for currency—coins offered in charity, a pair of gloves purchased to extend an affectively charged moment, snuffboxes exchanged as tokens of sympathetic fellow-feeling—and sentimental encounters become collectibles, spots of time whose serial ordering become the story of one's life—a story little different from that of, say, a gold coin whose trajectory through the circuit of exchange constitutes its narrative identity. Like the anonymous hacks writing it-narratives, Sterne rides his hobbyhorse at the boundary between the world of objects and the world of human relationships, concerning himself, as John Pocock puts it, "with the administration of things and with human relations conducted through the mediation of things."[71]

It-Narratives and Generic Self-Consciousness

It is probably mere coincidence that Yorick's reflections on the mechanics of feeling in "Nampont: The Postillion" bear a vague resemblance to the experiences of the protagonist of *The Travels of Mons. Le Post-Chaise* (1753), whose emotional states are so tightly linked to the physics of its motion that an unpleasant stint in a livery stable "reduc'd my usual Sprightliness of running eight Miles an Hour, into a melancholy Crawl of not above three."[72] Yet it is a telling coincidence. One thing that distinguishes *A Sentimental Journey* and *Tristram Shandy* from scads of it-narratives is Sterne's reluctance to claim generic kin, to affiliate himself with a particular class or style of contemporary writing.[73] While discussing Sterne's self-consciousness about the originality of *Tristram Shandy* and his efforts to differentiate himself from fellow writers, Christopher Fanning remarks that "recognizability is at odds with difference, the distinguishing feature of originality."[74] Like the sentimental Yorick, Sterne's fictions try to pass as citizens of the world. As Yorick is ill at ease with religious, national, and linguistic allegiances that impede the flow of tears, commerce, and travelers, that confine and isolate ("Tut! said I, are we not all relations?"), so Sterne's novels resist easy generic classification and exceed conventional narrative structures, spilling past their putative beginnings and endings.[75] How curious, then, that Sterne so often serves as the exemplary English novelist between Fielding and Austen.[76]

By contrast, many it-narratives display a remarkable generic self-consciousness, adhering to generic formulae that establish their market position and hail readers eager for more of the same. Keymer, for one, considers novels of circulation to have become sufficiently "fashionable," and their generic identity sufficiently recognizable by the mid-1750s, to have inspired a writer like John Kidgell, in *The Card* (1755), to exploit readers' expectations about the form in order to serve his own ends.[77] Writers of it-narratives sometimes manifest their consciousness of genre through imitation, as in the example of Sterne cited above, or the less frequent but no less insistent invocation of Fielding. *The Life and Adventures of a Cat* (1760), for instance, falsely identifies "the late Mr. Fielding" as its author and includes mock-Homeric moments reminiscent of *Tom Jones:* "It was about the meridian hour, when the Sun is vertical over the heads of mortals, in plain English, it was about twelve o'clock high noon."[78]

More often, the generic identity of it-narratives proceeds from the works' recognition of their implication in hack culture. The frame narrator of *Memoirs and Interesting Adventures of an Embroidered Waistcoat* (1751), for example, is a struggling writer who, armed with "a little Money in my Pocket" after the "Success of a late Pamphlet of my writing," makes for the pawnbroker's shop to collect the sword and tye-wig he needs to cut a figure at the theater, little suspecting that he will encounter a talking waistcoat.[79] In the 1752 third edition of *The History of Pompey the Little; or, The Life and Adventures of a Lap-Dog,* Francis Coventry added a chapter "Describing the miseries of a garreteer poet" and another entitled "A poetical feast, and squabble of authors."[80] The former identifies the collapse of the patronage system as the condition of literary modernity, as Mr. Rhymer's request for "a small gratuity" fails to move Lord Marmazet: "I have no money to fling away on poets and hackney-writers; let the fellow eat his own works, if he is hungry."[81] Marmazet's reduction of Rhymer's writing to mere matter anticipates Coventry's description of a table in Rhymer's "aerial garret" that "served to hold the different treasures of the whole family," including "the first act of a comedy, a pair of yellow stays, two political pam-

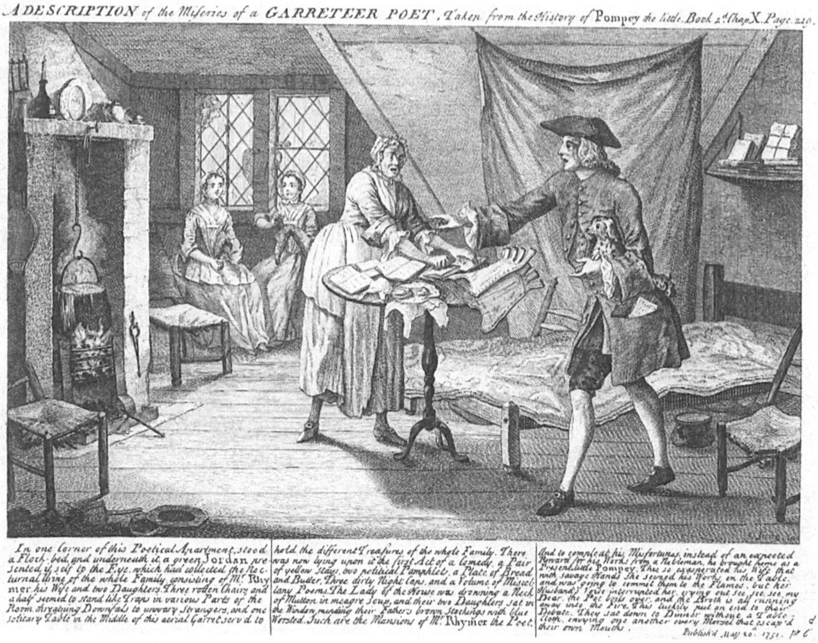

6. Unknown, *A Description of the Miseries of a Garreteer Poet,* 1751. Etching and engraving. Courtesy of The Lewis Walpole Library, Yale University.

phlets, a plate of bread-and-butter, three dirty night-caps, and a volume of miscellany poems." Though Rhymer asserts a distinction between "the mechanical trades" and the poet's calling, abusing his wife for "a vulgar notion of things" that leads her to prefer "frying grease in a tallow-chandler's shop" to "listening to the divine rhapsodies of the *Heliconian* maids," his own table betrays him, jumbling food and filthy clothes with writing and thus displaying objects associated with the needs of the body cheek by jowl with what we have learned to call intellectual property.[82] The erosion of various categorical distinctions is explored in these chapters about hack writers, from Marmazet's insistence on referring to Rhymer as "dog" and "hound," to his decision to offer Rhymer a Bologna lapdog in lieu of hard currency, to the writers' debate about whether "brutes think and have intellectual faculties" or "are mere machines."[83]

The epigraph to *The History and Adventures of a Lady's Slippers and Shoes* (1754) suggests that, in a jumbled literary marketplace wherein important distinctions between pleasure and pain, authors and hacks have become obscured, it is but a short step on the great chain of authorship from scribbling humans to prolific things:

So common now are Authors grown,
That ev'ry Scribler in the Town,
Thinks he can give delight.
If writers then are got so vain,
To think they pleasure when they pain,
No wonder Slippers write.[84]

In *The Adventures of a Black Coat* (1760), the tattered manuscript of a "long-visaged" scribbler has been "strangely smeared and stained" while in the care of a theater manager, for it has served "in taking the tea-kettle off the fire, and other such worthy employments"; indeed, the manager must remove the manuscript "from under a coffee-pot that stood in the window" in order to return it to its careworn, unfortunate author.[85] In these works, hack writers are things, mere instruments of a culture that commodifies texts, thereby "smear[ing] and stain[ing]" writing with the excess of materiality associated with teakettles, coffee-pots, and plates of bread and butter.

In *The Memoirs and Adventures of a Flea* (1785), the narrating flea serves as a perfect figure for the parasitic hack whose work depends on others. The flea unsentimentally embraces the impermanence of its literary production—"the indulgence of an hour or two . . . is all I ask"—by recognizing the likely correspondence between the longevity of its *Life* and its expected lifespan, admitting that its autobiography "will live as long as an insect like myself ought, or can be supposed to live; one way or other I shall be of public utility. I may some time or other have my papers useful in pastry-cooks shops, or in the yet more shining temple of that ever necessary goddess 'yclept Cloacina."[86] In the spirit of Johnson's *Rambler* essay championing "the *Ephemerae* of learning," the flea gamely—and slyly—pronounces itself willing to contribute its little all for the greater good, transforming the traditional satiric fate of Grub Street writing—absolute reduction to its material elements through adaptation as food wrapper or toilet paper—into a noble if humble contribution to the public welfare.

The Adventures of a Cork-Screw (1775) sentimentalizes the figure of the hack more emphatically than does *The Adventures of a Black Coat,* opening with a frame narrative in which a chance encounter with a beggar woman on the Pont Neuf in Paris leads to the discovery of the manuscript of the *Adventures of a Cork-Screw.* Intent on helping the poor woman bury her dearly departed husband, the frame narrator proceeds to the prison where the man died to collect his possessions and assess their worth. The narrator meets a prisoner who lists the deceased's worldly goods, which include "one old ragged coat, a pair of rusty breeches, part of a tyewig, some old books, and a large parcel of paper entirely spoiled, being scribbled all over; for the man was very fond of scribbling, though I never knew any good come of it."[87] Appreciation for the dead hack's literary leavings becomes a sign of refined sensibility that distinguishes the narrator from both the prisoner, who scorns scribbling, and the jailor, an "inhuman wretch" who mocks the narrator's interest in the papers: "a fine purchase you have got, for I am sure they would not fetch six-pence at a chandler's shop."[88] Corpse and corpus become inextricably linked ("Fetch me down those papers you speak of, let me have them, and I will pay the price of redemption for the dead body"), for regarding one as mere spent matter entails treating the other as lifeless, worthless stuff, while collecting and publishing the papers redeems both the body and the life of the scribbler who penned them.[89]

In *The Life and Adventures of a Fly,* hack writing as narrative redemption—or recycling, or iteration—also becomes a central thematic element of the frame narrative, one that rhymes with the convention that the "pre-owned" objects and animals depicted in it-narratives are renewed through their contact with new possessors. "It was in consequence of some circumstances of distress in which I was lately involved," the frame narrator informs us, "that the manuscript was discovered, from which the following history has been printed." The narrator goes on to relate that, inspired to turn writer-for-bread by his financial coming-down-in-the-world, he hired a garret,

> and it was in a corner of this poor apartment, that I found, neatly folded up, and carefully tied round with a piece of silk ribbon, a manuscript clearly written, and entitled, *"The Life and Adventures of a Fly"* . . . Having made proper enquiry to be satisfied that it was the property of no other person, I put it into my pocket, and offered it for publication to my worthy friend *the Bookseller at the Corner of St. Paul's.*

As in so many it-narratives, the found-manuscript device becomes a means of exploring writerly agency. Texts are but another sort of previously owned goods that speak through their owners rather than of them, bearing the marks of their own history. Viewed this way, the found text becomes a figure for a kind of genre fiction that treats the individual writer as a mere instrument, a material link between the protocols of the generic formula and the demands of the literary marketplace—"*the Bookseller at the Corner of St. Paul's.*"[90] Despite their modal and tonal distinctions, then, all of these works register their status as a species of hack writing, whether ironically or tearfully.

Nonetheless, what most insistently marks the generic identity of it-narratives, especially in the final decades of the eighteenth century, is their acknowledgment that they are participants in a novel movement. The anonymous author of *The Sedan* (1757) cites classical tradition—in particular, the history of the fable—to justify telling a story in which an inanimate object speaks:

> Aesop, Phaedrus, and others (among the antients) have given it under their hands, that brutes and fish have spoke, and so much to the purpose too, that nobody has yet over-ruled their arguments.—Gay, among the moderns, also has passed his word, that animals and birds, besides parrots, (two thousand years afterwards) occasionally did the same, and in his hearing too: but Ovid swears that inanimate things have had speaking faculties; trees, rocks, rivers, with all the train of seemingly dull and dumb-founded matter. How this may be philosophically proved, is not my business: there are idle philosophers enough in this great metropolis . . .[91]

However, later it-narratives tend to invoke a more recent, more proximate tradition. The preface to *The Birmingham Counterfeit* (1772), for instance, notes that "to give all the qualities of human nature to inanimate beings is no new thing, nor needs it, in cases like this, any particular apology":

> Modes and fashions are no less variable in the Republic of Letters than in the *Beau Monde.* The love of Novelty seems natural to almost every individual . . . An inundation of Romances have overflowed the literary markets. Of this species of *humble imitators,* it is more than probable, that the editor of *The Birmingham Counterfeit* will not be the last Adventurer, since every week produces something *new* of the kind.[92]

The context does not make clear whether the "species" invoked here is the novel in general or the novel subspecies of it-fiction, yet the uncertainty is telling. It-narratives function as the type of the novel as a genre by mingling the transience of fashion with the persistence of continuous and relentless production ("every week produces something *new* of the kind"), the "love of Novelty" with slavish copying ("*humble imitators*"), the singularity of the unique instance with the ubiquity of mass production ("an inundation of Romances have overflowed the literary markets").

The talking timepiece in *The Adventures of a Watch* not only identifies with other "scribblers," but also quickly establishes its place in a mushrooming literary genealogy:

> As Authors have made lap-dogs, fleas, lice, bank notes, guineas, nay even Birmingham halfpence, though of very roguish appearance, give the history of their lives, why not adopt the example? The language of a watch is surely

> as intelligent as any of the above; beside, 'tis of essential service to us all . . . With these qualifications, shall not a watch be allowed the privilege granted to a louse? 'Tis true the one appertains to the head, the other only to the pocket, which, when well lined, is generally the most respected. Besides, 'tis no vulgar watch, but a watch of fashion! A gold Repeater, elegantly chased! Listen to it attentively![93]

The watch limns a genre of talking things that includes both object tales and animal narratives. However difficult it may now be to enumerate compelling, categorical criteria that distinguish it-narratives from spy novels, sentimental fictions, romans à clef, memoirs, and picaresque tales of human circulation, there is no doubt that many writers of the lives of things thought of their work as belonging to a discrete and recognizable literary kind, as one more unit in an established series: "And why not a learned *fly,* as well as a learned *horse,* a learned *pig,* or a sagacious *goose?*"[94] *The Adventures of a Watch,* for one, is cognizant of its role as a "Repeater," both in the sense that it collects and retails the stories of the watch's owners and in the sense that it chimes with other it-narratives, "adopt[ing] the example" of a clockwork genre mechanically reproduced in response to the "fashion" for it-fictions in order to gain access to well-lined pockets. It-narratives often offer readers a social panorama populated by satiric types, an "extensive view" of the sort sketched by Johnson in "The Vanity of Human Wishes" (1749); recall that the watch waggishly surveys the various human states—roguish, distracted, starving, and so on—that compose the nation-state, as well as the myriad types of feeling—fine, no, some, fellow—that constitute a sentimental culture. Just as insistently, it-fictions apply type-thinking to the literary marketplace, betraying their writers' profound awareness of writing and reading habits and their concomitant understanding of the centrality of monotony, routine, iteration to both the consolidation of generic identity and the forging of readers' loyalty.[95]

By the 1790s, when parents emerge as the target market for it-narratives aimed at children, writers are beginning to claim that they have appropriated the popular gimmick of the it-narrative to communicate home truths more effectively. Consider, for example, the preface to *The Adventures of a Pin* (1790):

> Being in company, some months ago, with several of the learned authoresses of the adventures of inanimate beings, such as peg-tops, pin-cushions, kites, &c. and likewise the compilers of memoirs of rather more rational (although dumb) animals; and hearing the great praise bestowed on such productions; it naturally occurred to me, that, under the title of "The Adventures of a Pin," as much amusement and instruction might be con-

> veyed, (to those who desire it), as either of my predecessors can boast of having circulated.[96]

The author of *The Adventures of a Pin* proposes to make circulation, and the novel of circulation, serve the ends of moral instruction. *Memoirs of a Peg-Top* (ca. 1790) likewise purports to put the conventions of the it-narrative to work for didactic children's literature, as its verse epigraph suggests: "These *Trifles* that amuse in life, / Promote a higher end, / Since *Reason* in this lighter dress, / With pleasure we attend."[97] Yet *Memoirs of a Peg-Top* also represents an advance in the generic self-consciousness of the it-narrative. First, things themselves are aware of the vogue for it-narratives and are anxious to capitalize on it to secure their share of the market. Chance still plays a significant role in this frame story, not through the discovery of an overlooked manuscript, but rather through the serendipitous placement of the peg top on a writing desk. Indeed, this fable of literary production underscores the aleatory and material dimensions of writing, as a lucky conjunction of objects makes writing possible, and as things replace people both as the authors and as the subjects of narrative:

> As I have heard that a *Pincushion*, a *Dog*, a *Halfpenny*, and a *Bank Note*, have each written a history of their adventures, I thought to myself one morning, when I was left upon a writing-desk, That it would be a convenient opportunity for me to imitate such examples, and that the memoirs of a Peg-Top might prove equally entertaining with any of the before mentioned histories. So resolving to recollect the various scenes I had passed through, I determined to present *my adventures* likewise to the world, and share in the fame of those Authors, who had bestowed their labors to immortalize a particular animal or toy, while the rest of their species were consigned to neglect or oblivion.[98]

The allusion to precursor texts—"a *Pincushion*, a *Dog*, a *Halfpenny*, and a *Bank Note*"—persists, but one senses that this allusion, like the frame narrative recounting the origins of the it-tale, is offered ironically by a writer who understands that explaining where the story came from and acknowledging one's participation in a tradition of it-narration have themselves become conventional hallmarks of the genre. By the final decade of the eighteenth century, generic self-consciousness has become a doubly significant marker of generic belonging.

It-narratives are an interesting test case for questions about the generic identity and the theory of the novel in the second half of the eighteenth century. They mark the increasingly uneasy relationship between so-called genre fiction and literary fiction at a moment when genericity has grown increasingly problematic—when proper novels must at once register their participation in generic categories and appear sui generis, unique, novel; when a traditional hierarchy of genres is slowly being reshaped by market forces; and when the fashion for novel reading experiences is becoming difficult to tease out from the vogue for fresh versions of the same experience. The commodification of "the novel" and the iterative mechanics of literary aesthetics in this period may help explain why a definitive history of prose fiction between Sterne and Austen has proven so elusive.

Notes

1. Clara Reeve, *The Progress of Romance, through Times, Countries, and Manners,* 2 vols. (Colchester, 1785), 1:7–8.

2. Ernest A. Baker, *The Novel of Sentiment and the Gothic Romance,* vol. 5 of *The History of the English Novel,* 10 vols. (1929; New York: Barnes & Noble, 1957), 15.

3. Hugh Kenner, *The Counterfeiters: An Historical Comedy* (1968; rpt. Baltimore: Johns Hopkins University Press, 1985), 13.

4. See Brown's *Institutions of the English Novel: From Defoe to Scott* (Philadelphia: University of Pennsylvania Press, 1997), especially the "Introduction: Beginning with No Beginning" and chapter 6, "The Institution of the English Novel."

5. Wilbur L. Cross, *The Development of the English Novel* (1899; New York: Macmillan, 1924), 82. In like spirit, Leah Price refers to "the planned obsolescence of late-eighteenth-century fiction" (*The Anthology and the Rise of the Novel* [Cambridge: Cambridge University Press, 2000], 90).

6. See Clifford Siskin, *The Work of Writing: Literature and Social Change in Britain, 1700–1830* (Baltimore: Johns Hopkins University Press, 1998), 155: "the moment the novel actually did rise—rise literally in quantitative terms—is the moment we have paid it relatively little attention . . . The 1780s and 1790s . . . were precisely the decades when the novel took off." Thomas Keymer notes "the tendency of revisionist studies [of the rise of the novel] to cut out in mid-century" (*Sterne, the Moderns, and the Novel* [Oxford: Oxford University Press, 2002], 23).

7. Morris Dickstein, "Popular Fiction and Critical Values: The Novel as a Challenge to Literary History," *Reconstructing American Literary History,* Harvard English Studies 13, ed. Sacvan Bercovitch (Cambridge, MA: Harvard University Press, 1986), 30–31, 37.

8. Baker, *The Novel of Sentiment,* 52.

9. *The Critical Review* 52 (December 1781): 477–80 (emphasis mine).

10. Dickstein, "Popular Fiction," 34. In the words of Ian Campbell Ross, "as books of every description flooded from the nation's presses, no single individual could hope to read even a fraction of the works which the booksellers placed before them. How, then, to choose, or know, what was of real value?" (*Laurence Sterne: A Life* [Oxford: Oxford University Press, 2001], 218). See John Feather, *The Provincial Book Trade in Eighteenth-Century England* (Cambridge: Cambridge University Press, 1985), 50–51, on the function of the *Monthly Review* (begun in 1749) and the *Critical Review* (begun in 1756) as aids in book selection.

11. On the emergence of "'the' novel" and "the elevated novel" in the mid-eighteenth century, see William Warner, *Licensing Entertainment: The Elevation of Novel Reading in Britain, 1684–1750* (Berkeley and Los Angeles: University of California Press,

1998), 287–91. Also see Hilary Englert's essay in this volume, which addresses this developing hierarchy of literary value from the perspective of eighteenth-century debates about literary property.

12. Alvin Kernan, *Samuel Johnson & the Impact of Print* (1987; rpt. Princeton, NJ: Princeton University Press, 1989), 84, 86–87.

13. James Raven explains that "literature, like other fashion and leisure wares, was taken up by entrepreneurs with a sharp eye to the market" (*Judging New Wealth: Popular Publishing and Responses to Commerce in England, 1750–1800* [Oxford: Clarendon Press, 1992], 42–43). Shaun Regan notes that, beginning in the 1750s, "more conciliatory attitudes towards writing's relationship with commerce . . . began to emerge"; hence perhaps the more frequent and more sympathetic depictions of professional writers in the late eighteenth century ("Print Culture in Transition: *Tristram Shandy,* the Reviewers, and the Consumable Text," *Eighteenth-Century Fiction* 14.3–4 [2002]: 291).

14. "From the eighteenth century forward," Warner writes, "formula fiction of various sorts . . . haunts the legitimate novel as its double, challenging its claim to be the only fiction worth reading" (*Licensing Entertainment,* 292). Yet Warner neglects to pursue the implications of this claim in the crucial decades *after* Richardson and Fielding.

15. *Monthly Review* 46 (May 1772): 540.

16. *Critical Review* 65 (June 1788): 569.

17. On Vaucanson, see, for instance, Jessica Riskin, "The Defecating Duck, or the Ambiguous Origins of Artificial Life," in *Things,* ed. Bill Brown (Chicago: University of Chicago Press, 2004), 99–133. For a more broadly suggestive musing on "counterfeitable man" in the eighteenth century, see Kenner, *The Counterfeiters.*

18. *Critical Review* 51 (April 1781): 287.

19. *Monthly Review* 22 (June 1760): 548. Indeed, the reviewer's barb is derived from the novel itself, whose anonymous author begins by lamenting the current oversupply of writers: "In this age of *Magazines* and *Chronicles,* the *cacoethes scribendi* hath infected the town so much, that almost every *shop,* or *work-room,* harbours an author; and *gentlemen* of the *file* now leave their more useful labour at the *vice,* and toil to *polish periods.* When such *gentlemen* assume the pen, I hope it will not be deemed vanity, if I decline standing as candidate for literary fame, and declare myself not desirous of sharing with the *honours* that may be bestowed on their labours" (*The Adventures of a Black Coat* [Edinburgh, (1760?)], ix–x).

20. On this point, see Regan, "Print Culture," 296–97.

21. Lawrence Lipking, *Samuel Johnson: The Life of an Author* (Cambridge, MA: Harvard University Press, 1998), 9.

22. Samuel Johnson, No. 115 (Tuesday December 11, 1753), The Idler *and* The Adventurer, ed. W. J. Bate, John M. Bullitt, and L. F. Powell, vol. 2 of the *Yale Edition of the Works of Samuel Johnson* (New Haven, CT: Yale University Press, 1963), 457, 460.

23. Samuel Johnson, No. 145 (Tuesday August 6, 1751), *The Rambler,* 5th ed., 4 vols. (London, 1761), 3:214–15.

24. *Critical Review* 30 (November 1770): 395.

25. Raven, *Judging,* 43.

26. Reeve, *Progress,* 1:36.

27. Compare Vicesimus Knox, who notes that "readers [are] more numerous at present than in any preceding age" and asks, "Is the pleasure and improvement of the classes, both numerous and respectable, to be neglected?" Knox enumerates "the liberal merchant, the inquisitive manufacturer, the country gentleman, the various persons who fill the most useful departments in life, without pretending to literature," as distinct members of a broad, mixed reading public that supports "novelty of publication" (*Winter Evenings, or, Lucubrations on Life and Letters,* 2nd ed., 2 vols. [London, 1790], 1:7, 9).

28. *Monthly Review* 23 (August 1760): 157–58.

29. *Rambler,* 3:215.

30. *The Norton Shakespeare,* ed. Stephen Greenblatt (New York: Norton, 1997), 1196 (3.2.40–41). The phrase also appears in Thomas Edwards's sonnet "*To the Author of* Clarissa," which asserts that Richardson has won "The grateful tribute of each honest heart / Sincere, nor hackney'd in the ways of men" (*The Sonnets of Thomas Edwards* [1765; Los Angeles: Augustan Reprint Society, 1974], 328).

31. It is worth noting that most of the *OED*'s earliest citations for "hack"—at least those most closely related to the semantic range discussed here—date to the early eighteenth century; most of those for "hackneyed" date to the middle of the eighteenth century, among which is a reference to Johnstone's *Chrysal.*

32. Jonathan Swift, *A Tale of a Tub with Other Early Works 1696–1707,* ed. Herbert Davis, vol. 1 of *The Prose Works of Jonathan Swift* (Oxford: Blackwell, 1965), 40.

33. Ibid., 58.

34. Ibid., 40–41.

35. *Critical Review* 51 (April 1781): 285–86.

36. On this phenomenon, see Baker, *Novel of Sentiment,* 98–99; Anne Bandry, "Imitations of *Tristram Shandy,*" in *Critical Essays on Laurence Sterne,* ed. Melvyn New (New York: G. K. Hall, 1998), 39–52; and Ian Campbell Ross, *Laurence Sterne: A Life* (Oxford: Oxford University Press, 2001), 16–18.

37. Wilbur L. Cross, *The Development of the English Novel* (New York: Macmillan, 1924), 83; and J. M. S. Tompkins, *The Popular Novel in England, 1770–1800* (1932; rpt. Lincoln: University of Nebraska Press, 1961), 50. On Sterne's imitators in late-eighteenth-century miscellanies, "one of the dreariest chapters in magazine history" (336), see Robert D. Mayo, *The English Novel in the Magazines, 1740–1815* (Evanston, IL: Northwestern University Press, 1962), 336–46.

38. Reeve, *Progress,* 1:31. Vicesimus Knox, for one, seems to have thought the vogue had passed by the late 1780s: "if the rage had continued for that kind of writing that is denominated the SHANDEAN, many men of parts and abilities would have endeavoured to imitate it, though it is confessedly irregular and indefensible by the best laws both of right reason and sound criticism" (*Winter Evenings,* 2:461–62).

39. *The Adventures of a Bank-Note* (London, 1770), 62, 87.

40. [Stephen Jones], *The Life and Adventures of a Fly* (London, [1789?]), 64–66.

41. [Dorothy Kilner], *The Adventures of a Hackney Coach,* 3rd ed., corrected (London, 1781), 5–6.

42. From a letter to Sir William Stanhope quoted in Arthur Cash, *Laurence Sterne: The Later Years* (London: Methuen, 1986), 309. A like passage occurs in *Tristram Shandy:* "Ask my pen,—it governs me,—I govern not it" (Laurence Sterne, *The Life and Opinions of Tristram Shandy, Gentleman,* ed. Melvyn and Joan New, vols. 1–3 of *The Florida Edition of the Works of Laurence Sterne* [1759–67; Gainesville: University Presses of Florida, 1978–84], 2:500). George Saintsbury remarks on the artificial and mechanical aspects of Sterne's style: "And yet laboriously figured, tricked, machined as it is—easy as once more it may be to prove that it is artifice and not art—that fact remains that . . . it is triumphant: and that English literature would be seriously impoverished without it" (*The English Novel* [1913; rpt. Folcroft, PA: Folcroft, 1969], 131–32).

43. *Annual Register* 3 (1760): 247; attributed to Edmund Burke and quoted in *Tristram Shandy,* ed. Howard Anderson (New York: Norton, 1980), 481.

44. Knox, *Winter Evenings,* 2:462.

45. As Frank Donoghue puts it, "'Laurence Sterne' had been turned into an institution" (*The Fame Machine: Book Reviewing and Eighteenth-Century Literary Careers* [Stanford, CA: Stanford University Press, 1996], 75). On "the lunatic fringe of Sterneana," see

J. C. T. Oates, *Shandyism and Sentiment, 1760–1800* (York, UK: Cambridge Bibliographical Society, 1968), 23ff.

46. [Kilner], *Adventures of a Hackney Coach,* 1.

47. *The Adventures of a Watch!* (London, 1788), 6–9.

48. Oates, *Shandyism,* 4.

49. Ibid., 4.

50. Price notes that "nearly every fictional subgenre to emerge at this moment [the late eighteenth century] borrowed the discontinuous structure of the anthology" (*Anthology,* 91). Clearly, there is a relationship between the *Beauties of Sterne,* some of whose selections are narrative set-pieces detached from the broader narratives from which they hail, and the loose, episodic form of most it-narratives, especially those published by Kearsley during the same decade in which he was churning out volumes of *Beauties.* Still, it is worth noting that such structural discontinuity did not begin with the vogue for anthologies; short stories included in periodicals, interpolated tales in novels, and disjointed episodic narratives, such as early novels of circulation (or it-fictions or spy novels), prepared the ground as well.

51. "The Law of Genre," trans. Avital Ronell, *Glyph* 7 (1980): 202–32.

52. Ross, *Sterne,* 218.

53. On changing attitudes toward Sterne's borrowings, see Melvyn New, "Introduction: Four Faces of Laurence Sterne," in New, *Critical Essays,* 4–5.

54. Keymer, *Sterne,* 59. On this point, see also Christina Lupton's unpublished essay, "Speaking Things, Sterne, Stage-Coaches, and the Self-Conscious Narrator: 1751–1768."

55. Keymer, *Sterne,* 63–72.

56. Ibid., 153. Keymer asserts that "Sterne's originality was clearly not in foregrounding and interrogating conventions on which everyone, post-Fielding, was playing," but maintains nonetheless that Sterne could "simultaneously plunder and ingeniously outdo" his "immediate competition" even when relying on the same "hackneyed raw material" (59).

57. W. B. Gerard, "Sterne in Wedgwood: 'Poor Maria' and the 'Bourbonnais Shepherd'," *The Shandean* 12 (2001): 78–88. John Brewer discusses the wide circulation of the Maria print in *The Pleasures of the Imagination: English Culture in the Eighteenth Century* (New York: Farrar, Straus and Giroux, 1997), 462–63. Peter de Voogd describes a fan dating from 1796 which depicts three scenes from *A Sentimental Journey* in "Sterne All the Fashion: A Sentimental Fan," *The Shandean* 8 (1996): 133–36. Oates cites *Ways to Kill Care* (1761), which registers how quickly Tristram Shandy became a modish name for horses and lapdogs (*Shandyism,* 9–10). Frank Donoghue credits the reviewers of *Tristram Shandy* for "inventing . . . the English sentimental novel" by shaping Sterne's composition of the later volumes of *Tristram Shandy* and *A Sentimental Journey* through their exhortations that affect be privileged over learned satire (*Fame Machine,* 81).

58. New, *Tristram Shandy,* 1:408; 1:262–63; 2:762.

59. Two tantalizing but inconclusive facts: First, Sterne's alternative title for *A Political Romance* was *The History of a Good, Warm Watch-Coat.* Both its title and its satirical allegory link it most obviously to Swift's *Tale of a Tub,* but the style of that title also, if unwittingly, invites confusion with it-fictions. Second, perhaps the earliest painting of Sterne was executed by Thomas Bridges, a Yorkshire friend who left Hull for London in 1759, became a hack writer, and published *The Adventures of a Bank-Note* in 1770–71. See Ross, *Laurence Sterne,* 191, and Arthur H. Cash, *Laurence Sterne: The Early & Middle Years* (London: Methuen, 1975), 210–211, 299–300. For jogging my memory about Sterne's friendship with Bridges, I am indebted to Tim Parnell's "'Writing a Romance': *Tristram Shandy* and its Traditions Reconsidered," read at the 37th Annual Meeting of the American Society for Eighteenth-Century Studies in Montreal, March 30, 2006.

60. See Markman Ellis, *The Politics of Sensibility: Race, Gender, and Commerce in the Sentimental Novel* (Cambridge: Cambridge University Press, 1996); Liz Bellamy, *Commerce, Morality, and the Eighteenth-Century Novel* (Cambridge: Cambridge University Press, 1998); and Deidre Lynch, "Personal Effects and Sentimental Fictions," *Eighteenth-Century Fiction* 12.2–3 (2000): 345–68, a version of which appears in this volume. Ellis was the first critic to remark on the connection between the starling scene and the novel of circulation or it-narrative (76–77).

61. Laurence Sterne, *A Sentimental Journey through France and Italy,* ed. Graham Petrie (New York: Penguin, 1986), 28.

62. See Lynch, "Personal Effects," 361.

63. New, *Tristram Shandy,* 1:166.

64. Ibid., 1:166–67.

65. Sterne, *A Sentimental Journey,* 96, 99.

66. The fact that "stearn" and "starn" are Yorkshire terms for "starling" reinforces the notion that the bird's circulation emblematizes Yorick's—or Sterne's—own tale of itinerancy (Ellis, *Politics of Sensibility,* 74; see also Lynch's essay in this volume). Lamb's words are drawn from "Sterne's System of Imitation," *Modern Language Review* 76 (1981): 794–810; rpt. in New, *Critical Essays,* 33–34.

67. Sterne, *A Sentimental Journey,* 110. John Allen Stevenson terms this phenomenon "the commodification of personality" and alludes briefly to "the resulting loss of distinction between a person and a product," though he does not reflect on the iterability of Sterne's "distinctive voice of personality" ("Sterne: Comedian and Experimental Novelist," *The Columbia History of the British Novel,* ed. John Richetti [New York: Columbia University Press, 1994], 161).

68. Sterne, *A Sentimental Journey,* 102.

69. For a differently inflected reading of this scene, see Jonathan Lamb's "Modern Metamorphoses and Disgraceful Tales," in Brown, *Things,* 221–23.

70. Sterne, *A Sentimental Journey,* 51.

71. J. G. A. Pocock, "Virtues, Rights, and Manners," in *Virtue, Commerce, and History* (Cambridge: Cambridge University Press, 1985), 44.

72. Sterne, *A Sentimental Journey,* 64–65; *The Travels of Mons. Le Post-Chaise* (London, 1753), 6. Lupton argues for a more decisive connection between these texts in "Speaking Things."

73. Hence Keymer's distinction between Sterne's "concrete and localized allusions" to the learned-wit tradition and the "ghostly palimpsestuous structures" that intimate his elusive intertextual relationships with contemporary sources; Keymer emphasizes Sterne's tendency to allow connections with contemporary texts "to remain implicit" (*Sterne,* 11, 157, 160). In Donoghue's terms, one might also frame Sterne's reticence to embrace his affinity with contemporaries serving "an emergent mass audience," despite his "surrender to a consumer public," as the residue of his never relinquished "belief that being an author entailed a special affinity with the aristocracy," a sign of his "incomplete" transition to "the realities of the open market" (*Fame Machine,* 71, 66, 59).

74. "'The Things Themselves': Origins and Originality in Sterne's Sermons," *The Eighteenth Century: Theory and Interpretation* 40.1 (1999): 31–32.

75. Sterne, *A Sentimental Journey,* 92.

76. Keymer describes *Tristram Shandy* as "the most typical work of 1760s literature" (*Sterne,* 164). My point—and Fanning's, I take it—is that Sterne's typicality and his originality are inextricably related to one another. Contemporary marketing lingo—with its talk of "branding," "brand identity," and "brand loyalty"—provides a useful lexicon for the transformation of the unique into a type that may be peddled en masse, for the ways in which the prevailing instance comes to be considered the exemplary

original. We may speak without irony or anachronism, I think, of the "branding" of Sterne and of the pirating of that brand in the final decades of the eighteenth century.

Derek Attridge's discussion of singularity is apposite here. Attridge describes singularity as "generated . . . by a configuration of general properties that . . . go beyond the possibilities pre-programmed by a culture's norms, the norms with which its members are familiar and through which most cultural products are understood. Singularity . . . is constitutively impure, always open to contamination, grafting, accidents, reinterpretation, and recontextualization. Nor is it inimitable: on the contrary, it is eminently imitable, and may give rise to a host of imitations" (*The Singularity of Literature* [London: Routledge, 2004], 63). Such a description may make Sterne's oeuvre seem the quintessential event of singularity, in Attridge's terms. Yet Attridge's firm distinction between singularity and "its opposite, for which there are many names (triteness, imitativeness, banality, *hackwork*, cliché, stereotype)" (my emphasis), like his description of singularity as functioning "like a signature" (64) (recall Sterne's signing of the later volumes of *Tristram Shandy*), seems to me to simplify the relationship between the singular and the generic by sanitizing the constitutive impurity of literary singularity.

77. Keymer, *Sterne*, 71.

78. *The Life and Adventures of a Cat* (London, 1760), 26–27.

79. *Memoirs and Interesting Adventures of an Embroidered Waistcoat* (London, 1751), 1–2.

80. Francis Coventry, *The History of Pompey the Little; or, The Life and Adventures of a Lap-Dog*, ed. Robert Day Adams (London: Oxford University Press, 1974), 163, 168.

81. Ibid., 163, 164.

82. Ibid., 163, 164, 167.

83. Ibid., 163, 164, 171.

84. *The History and Adventures of a Lady's Slippers and Shoes* (London, 1754).

85. *The Adventures of a Black Coat* (London, 1760), 35–39.

86. *The Memoirs and Adventures of a Flea* (London, 1785), 6–7.

87. *The Adventures of a Cork-Screw* (London, 1775), x.

88. Ibid., vii, xi.

89. Ibid., x.

90. [Jones], *Fly*, x–xvii. Regan notes that one period defender of professional writers, James Ralph, described them as situated between the "punishing regime" of the booksellers and "the debased tastes of the book-buying public" ("Print Culture," 291).

91. *The Sedan*, 2 vols. (London, 1757), 1:1–2. On other period attempts to establish a philosophical basis for speaking objects and animals, see Mark Blackwell, "The People Things Make: Locke's *Essay concerning Human Understanding* and the Properties of the Self," *Studies in Eighteenth-Century Culture* 35 (2006): 77–94.

92. Preface, *The Birmingham Counterfeit; or, Invisible Spectator*, 2 vols. (London, 1772), 1:n.p.

93. *Adventures of a Watch!*, 1–4.

94. [Jones], *Fly*, 21.

95. On the importance of "formulaic sameness" in a roughly contemporary genre—Gothic fiction—see Mark Blackwell, "The Gothic: Moving in the World of Novels," in *A Concise Companion to the Restoration and Eighteenth Century*, ed. Cynthia Wall (Oxford: Blackwell, 2004), 146–48.

96. *The Adventures of a Pin* (London, 1790), i.

97. [Mary Ann Kilner?], *Memoirs of a Peg-Top* (London, [1790?]).

98. Ibid., 7.

Occupying Works: Animated Objects and Literary Property

Hilary Jane Englert

> The *Property here claimed* are all *ideal;* a Set of Ideas which have *no Bounds or Marks* whatever, Nothing that is capable of a *visible* Possession, Nothing that *can sustain any One* of the Qualities or Incidents of Property. Their *whole Existence* is in the *Mind* alone; *incapable* of any *other* Modes of Acquisition or Enjoyment, than by *mental* Possession or Apprehension; safe and invulnerable, from their own *Immateriality:* No *Trespass* can *reach* Them; no *Tort affect* them; no *Fraud or Violence diminish or damage* them. Yet these are the *Phantoms* which the Author would *grasp* and *confine to Himself:* And these are what the Defendant is charged with having *robbed* the Plaintiff of.
>
> —Justice Yates, *Millar v. Taylor* (1769)

> O incredulous wretch, (exclaimed the voice) I will now convince thee that this is no phantasma or hideous dream . . . thou will then be firmly persuaded that I am an actual, independent existence; and that this address is not the vague delirium of a disordered brain.
>
> —Tobias Smollett, *The History and Adventures of an Atom* (1769)

FAMOUSLY INTERVENING IN THE BRITISH COPYRIGHT DEBATES OF THE eighteenth century, Justice Joseph Yates declared the entire category of literary property "extraordinary," the very assertion of its existence "strange and singular."[1] We might imagine the Smollett narrator also given voice above as Yates's interlocutor in the dispute over the immaterial substance of literary property, just coming into conceptual and legal being at the point of his novel's publication.[2]

The most immediately apparent peculiarity of *The History and Adventures of an Atom* is the narrative device announced by its title; indeed, its protagonist-narrator is not entirely human. As a physical atom—a particle of the very human body it takes as its audience—the narrator of this work exemplifies an eighteenth-century narrative contrivance, increasingly popular in imaginative prose of the 1760s, '70s, and '80s. While these were just the decades in which public interest in the question of literary property reached its highest pitch, and indeed, in which the definitive legal battles over early statutory copyright were waged, the connection is more than mere historical coincidence. As has been amply demonstrated by recent historians, it was through conflict over copyright that an author's property in his own literary compositions crystallized, a property whose legal, economic, and cultural existence was finally deemed as "actual and independent," if also as "strange and singular," as that of Smollett's adventuring atom-narrator.[3] As I will argue, this curious sort of narrator and the particular narrative paradigm it authorizes were mobilized to negotiate the intricate relations among the conceptual categories, practices of literary labor, and institutional arrangements at the heart of the eighteenth-century controversy about whether, to what extent, and how the law should regulate the unauthorized appropriation and reproduction of written works.

The History and Adventures of an Atom is prefaced by an "advertisement" from the fictional publisher, S. Etherington, to the reader, detailing the manuscript's origins and the commercial transaction by which he has acquired its copyright. This explanation is ostensibly designed to foreclose the possibility of litigation brought by either a disgruntled bookseller contending copyright infringement or a public figure alleging character defamation. "In these ticklish times," Etherington's preface submits, "it may be necessary to give such an account of the following sheets, as will exempt me from the plague of prosecution" (3). The sanitizing history of the work's passage from manuscript to book is offered in the context of the law, underscoring the close proximity in the public imaginary between institutions and practices of publishing and legal controversy during the period. What this framing device "advertises" is its novel's place within a subgenre of popular fiction whose nonhuman narrators are consistently mobilized to figure the period's shifting and increasingly public relationships among professional writers, the book trade, readers, and their competing property claims.

At least sixty different works of eighteenth-century fiction "written from a non-human point of view" have been catalogued, dating from Alain René Lesage's 1707 *Le Diable boiteux* (translated as *The Devil upon Two Sticks* in 1708), the work modern critics commonly cite as the paradigm for many of the supernatural narrators throughout the century.[4] A year after the English translation of this demon-narrated work appeared, Charles Gildon's *The Golden Spy* extended the trope's logic of exaggerated mobility, inaugurating what would become the widely imitated inanimate object-narrator, and more specifically, the money-narrator.[5] Meanwhile, early-century periodicals introduced a set of satirical modes and narrative conventions designed to expose vice and folly from an array of unusual perspectives. Among these were the mock-heroic and mock-sentimental adventure stories told from the point of view of a widely circulating everyday object. First elaborated in the 1710 *Tatler* 249, "Adventures of a Shilling," the satirical adventure story continued to be rehearsed in essay-serials and miscellanies throughout the first half of the century, often in combination with other modes of magazine fiction, specifically the dream narrative or dream vision, the oriental tale, the secret history, and the letter-series.[6] Mid-century writers of long prose fiction published in volume form appropriated these commonplaces of periodical fiction, constructing narratives on a logic of seriation, episodic accumulation, and piecemeal assembly. It was not until the third quarter of the eighteenth century, however, that nonhuman narration gained coherence as the defining characteristic of a fully codified, indeed thriving, category of the novel. Aileen Douglas traces the "vogue" for what she calls "it-narrators" to the publication and enthusiastic reception of Charles Johnstone's 1760 novel, *Chrysal; or, The Adventures of a Guinea,* the popularity of which—three editions in three years—authorized Johnstone to prepare an expanded, four-volume edition, which was published in 1765, prefaced by a grateful account of the "uncommon favour" with which the public had met the original novel.[7] This four-volume version was graced with equal success and ran through over twenty editions by 1800, only falling out of favor and print, as its modern editor, E. A. Baker, speculates, once the targets of its topical satirical portraits were no longer recognizably contemporary.[8] Indeed, Roger D. Lund cites George Sherburn's confidence that as "the most notable, or even notorious of the novels featuring nonhuman narrators . . . *Chrysal* spawned a host of imitations," and James Raven describes the Johnstone novel as the "most reprinted and imitated spy novel" of the era.[9]

Novelists of the second half of the eighteenth century seized on the narrative device introduced by Lesage and popularized by Johnstone, organizing their works around narrators with heightened awareness, an itinerant nature, and special capacities for surveillance, as though competing for the ultimate in penetrating, incisive perspectives. Indeed, from the middle of the 1750s through the 1780s, satirical writers looking for fresh viewpoints from which to expose sites of hypocrisy, scandal, and folly compiled the observations and insights, the experiences and adventures of a striking array of animals, demons, wandering human souls, and spirits imprisoned in inanimate objects and currencies. Before the end of the century, readers had been entertained by the first-person experiential accounts of a lapdog, a flea, a louse, an atom, a number of devils, a row of chimneys, and several transmigrating souls and spirits temporarily inhabiting articles of clothing, pieces of furniture, moving vehicles, and household utensils—among them a black coat, a lady's slippers and shoes, a waistcoat, a petticoat, a fan, some jewels, a pin and pincushion, a mirror, a corkscrew, a bedstead, a sofa, a cane, a ring, a goose quill, a hackney coach, a sedan chair, a stage coach, and a watch. In addition, various forms of currency assumed narrative power and agency—including a banknote, a guinea, a shilling, a counterfeit shilling, a halfpenny, a rupee, and a silver piece.[10]

While critical attention has recently been turned to this literary historical curiosity variously designated the "object-narrator," "eccentric-narrator," "it-narrator," and "circulating protagonist," its chief feature—the feature designed to explain the narrator's animation, its special powers of observation, and its capacities as a storyteller—has been largely neglected by modern scholars. The ordinarily inanimate and insensible "objects" who relate these tales invariably frame them with elaborate, self-referential accounts of the order of the universe—a universe populated by innumerable incorporeal agents, inhabiting its material substances and giving voice to their perspectives. The furniture, articles of clothing, household instruments, and forms of currency that narrate their adventures in these novels are capable of doing so—are capable in fact of *experiencing* their passages through the world *as* adventures—because they are neither essentially inanimate nor material. The "object-narrator" is, in fact, conventionally a supernatural agent—a spirit or demon—or a human soul, condemned to occupy its object or objects as a form of karmic or divine punishment. Fundamentally protean, invisible, and untethered to any one material embodiment or perspective, these fictional observers enjoy both a radical mobility and a capacity to access the deepest recesses of the social world, resulting in a theoretically limitless series of encounters, transactions, and exchanges.

The narrator of the 1772 novel, *The Birmingham Counterfeit; or, Invisible Spectator,* for instance, explains its double identity as both "Counterfeit," the spirit of deceit, and its current physical embodiment as a counterfeit shilling: "having, ever since the creation, been the author of so much mischief as an animate being, I soon found myself degraded to my present station, a Birmingham shilling; but, as a spirit, still retain the same faculties of hearing, seeing, and thinking."[11] Likewise, the narrator of Crébillon fils's *Sopha,* published thirty years earlier, blames "Brahma" for imprisoning his soul within the upholstery and mercilessly leaving his sensibilities and consciousness intact.[12] The anonymous writer of the 1775 *Adventures of a Cork-Screw* confines his narrator's spirit within a household utensil "as a punishment for the unbounded scenes of debauchery and wickedness [he] committed while on earth."[13] Like Gildon's golden spy, who recounts the proliferation of its "Transmigrations . . . multitudes of Masters, and shapes full as various," nonhuman narrators frequently invoke an Eastern philosophical doctrine to make sense of their animated materiality.[14] Crébillon fils's narrator, for example, prefaces his account by identifying himself as an "adherent of the Brahmin sect [who] believe in metempsychosis" (23). "Incorporeal," but not invisible, momentarily shapeless, but not imperceptible, Johnstone's Chrysal, who repeatedly "condense[s] into an incorporeal substance in the form of a spirit," supplies an involved account of the supernatural system of which it is a part: "In the oeconomy of nature, to ease the trouble, and keep up the state of its great author, a subordination of ministerial spirits executes the system of his government in all its degrees; one of whom, for the greater order and expedition, is made to actuate every divided particle of matter in this immense universe" (4). Nine years after the publication of the first edition of *The Adventures of a Guinea* (just four years after that of the four-volume version), Tobias Smollett's "indestructible" particle of matter explains both his double status as spirit and substance and his unlikely narrative powers by invoking "the transmigration of souls, a doctrine avowed by one Pythagoras, a philosopher of Crotona" (10). Unmistakably, if allusively, positioning the work within what by 1769 was already recognizable as a narrative tradition, the atom's interlocutor instantly recognizes the spiritual possession before him, terrified by "the conceit of being in presence of an atomy informed with spirit, that is, animated by a ghost or goblin" (5).

Indeed, Smollett's Nathanial Peacock, the dutiful scribe who records the storytelling atom's tale, serves to remind us of another conventional feature, as vital to this subgenre as it is obscured by the designation "object-narrative," namely, the ambiguous multiplicity of the narrative's origins. Not only is the nonhuman narrator both spirit and object, the "nonhuman narrative" is invariably the product of collaboration. In other words, the fictive author of the narrative rarely is simply or identically the object-inhabiting spirit whose narration is featured in that work. Instead, these novels typically divide the labor of narration and literary production between at least two agents, one of whom is possessed of an extraordinary, often supernatural narrative perspective, another of whom serves as surrogate to the reader, documenting the tale and assimilating its substance to a first-person narrative account of the interaction. A relationship between two separate figures—the narrator of adventures and the human figure who documents them—is apparently cultivated to reconcile the narrative's extraordinary conditions of production to the basic organizing principles of novelistic realism. Still, this complex discursive dynamic is elaborated far in excess of the demands of probability, indicating the form's powerful stake in representing the fundamentally relational character of the compositional process. Framed as dynamics of disclosure and receptive engagement, the novels of this subgenre contain elaborate, self-conscious, and often highly theorized dramatizations of their own construction, raising questions about the nature of authorship, originality, imitation, influence, literary property, and literary theft.

What the spirits and souls of these novels desire most is to be freed, not only from their physical confines, but from their invisibility and imposed silence. In most cases, the spirit's release, if temporary, conditions the possibility for its tale to be told; another figure is required to release the spirit, to incite it to discourse, to receive and internalize its experiential narrative, and to formalize that narrative as a written composition. Once Lesage's devil persuades a local student to liberate him from the glass phial in which he has been confined, for instance, he assumes human shape and bestows his narrative as reward. Johnstone's Chrysal promises its confessor to reveal "the mysteries of nature" by providing the narrative of its traffic through the world as an animated piece of gold, "to trace the operations of nature through her most secret recesses . . . by a detail of the various incidents of [her] being, in [her] present state" (2–3). The spirit sprung from his steel captivity in *Adventures of a Cork-Screw* rewards his liberator with tales of "the variety of persons, their characters and their histories, in whose hands [he has] been" (5).

According to convention then, once the spirit is released, it presents its narrative of private experience, scandalous observation, and revealed secrets as a gift to a figure whose exclusive privilege it is to appropriate that narrative and redeploy it as his own work. It is only once the adventurer is no longer hidden by its material embodiment, once it is rendered perceptible as spiritual substance, that the narrative constituting the basis of the novel may materialize and, moreover, that an author may take credit for it. In this way, the narrative of nonhuman adventures dramatizes the liberation of the spirit of the literary work from its physical confinement as printed material.

Indeed, like the unsuspecting confidants and confessors who, to their shock and discomfort, discover in their sofas, corkscrews, and coins storytelling spirits that would ordinarily go unnoticed by the human world, the eighteenth century strained to recognize the literary work as the rightful object of property lurking within the books and periodicals they increasingly purchased and read. The reader's access to the spirit-inhabited object-narrator as both spiritual *and* material recalls the strenuous cultural effort to conceptualize and legitimate literary property as, precisely, "immaterial substance." Indeed, as we will see, the transmigrating narrator works to represent and expose that effort as a fundamental mystification of the literary labor, responsibility, and property rights of writers whose work bore little resemblance to the emerging legal paradigm of literary production as the sovereign enterprise of a single, inspired, original author.

Throughout the copyright debates of the third quarter of the eighteenth century—during the period, that is, of the transmigrating narrator's greatest popularity—arguments on behalf of an author's rights in his works were rehearsed and elaborated. Those arguments directly engaged with the incorporeality and alleged elusiveness of the literary object. Perhaps the most pressing theoretical question at the heart of this great legal battle was whether the immateriality of the literary object foreclosed its status as property, whether immaterial property could be said to exist at all. If copyright was to be a perpetual protection, then it had to be legally recognized as a form of property and not merely a right. Standing in the way of this recognition was the insistence by both Scottish and English justices and attorneys that the abstract literary work was no property at all: the Roman basis of Scots law maintaining that to constitute a tenable legal entity, a property had to have a "real," that is physical, existence. Thus, as John Feather has succinctly put it, "although a book or a manuscript was certainly a piece of property, Scots lawyers were generally very doubtful whether the same could be said of the text."[15] If their doubts were to be allayed, a clear and legally ascertainable difference had to be established between the perpetual property in the "work" retained by its author (or the author's assigns once the manuscript was published, sold, and publicly circulated) and the property in the book transferred to the buyer upon purchase. That is, the abstract literary work had to be both distinguishable from its material manifestations and susceptible to its owner's unambiguous possession.

In other words, the claim on behalf of copyright as a distinct form of property rested on a conception of the literary object as *both* material commodity and textual abstraction. Indeed, transmigration might have furnished a helpful metaphor in the articulation of this conception. As early as 1747 William Warburton, in *A Letter from an Author to a Member of Parliament Concerning Literary Property,* defends the perpetuity of an author's claim to his works with a taxonomy designed to distinguish literary property from other more familiar forms. According to Warburton's schema, each category of property demands a different scope of ownership, property in an object produced by mental labor, "as in a *Book* composed," encompassing the work's abstract essence—the "doctrine contained" in the work—as well as the paper imprinted with that doctrine.[16] It is this "doctrine" that Warburton insists remains the rightful property of its author, even should he possess no printed copies of that work. Twenty years later, William Blackstone follows Warburton in characterizing the identity of a printed text as dual, consisting of a material and an immaterial component.[17] Dividing the immaterial component into content and form, he suggests that it is this latter *formal* element that serves as the basis for the author's property claims. While Warburton had described the essence of a work as its "doctrine" or content, Blackstone locates the author's property in the work's "sentiment and language," detached (that is to say, detachable) from its material habitation in any one copy or edition. For him, "the same conceptions, clothed in the same words, must necessarily be the same composition; and whatever method be taken of exhibiting that composition to the ear or the eye of another, by recital, by writing, or by printing, in any number of copies or at any period of time, it is always the identical work of the author which is so conveyed" (2:406). On his model, the book buyer's claim to ownership of the material object, of the physical as well as substantive aspects of the book, could be upheld, as could the reader's property even in the *content* of its ideas. The *form* of these ideas, on the other hand, the manner or method in which these ideas were presented, would remain the property of the author.

In light of the transmigrating-narrator fiction, the literary composition as delineated by Warburton and Blackstone looks very much like the material object animated by a spiritual agent, the manuscript, book, or magazine piece (copy or edition) animated by the work. In 1774 William Enfield plaintively reiterated Blackstone's argument:

> AFTER a literary work is produced or composed, it may subsist in various forms: it may remain lodged in the author's memory; it may be recited *viva voce;* it may be written, or it may be printed: but in all these forms it is still the same work; and these are only incidental circumstances which do not at all change its nature, or affect its identity . . . This is indeed a kind of property invisible and untangible; but it is not on that account the less real.[18]

Supernatural and otherworldly, the transmigrating narrator indeed parallels the concept of literary property in its precarious realness and in the challenge it presents to perceptibility. As though to testify to just this analogy, Henry Fielding in his 1743 spirit-narrated *A Journey from this World to the Next* traffics in playful descriptions of "immaterial substance." The transmigrating soul narrating the work struggles against the limitations of human language to represent the fabric of the next world, unknown to this one, and yet eminently real, invisible yet perceptible, spirit yet substance:

> Perhaps, Reader, thou may'st be pleased with an Account of this whole Equipage, as peradvanture thou wilt not, while alive, see any such. The Coach

> was made by an eminent Toyman, who is well known to deal in immaterial Substance, that being the Matter of which it was compounded. The Work was so extremely fine, that it was entirely invisible to the human Eye. The Horses which drew this extraordinary Vehicle were all Spiritual, as the Passengers . . . and as for the Coachman, [he] was a very thin Piece of immaterial Substance.[19]

As Fielding teasingly notes here, the very cognitive exercise of grasping immateriality could be broadly characterized as a new cultural imperative for the increasingly commercialized eighteenth century. In Mark Rose's view, it was according to the logic of the advanced marketplace that "the solidity of apparently concrete referents was dissolving, replaced in many different but interconnected spheres by the circulation of signs."[20] Indeed, both Rose and Catherine Ingrassia have suggested that arguments on behalf of literary property paralleled arguments advanced to legitimate another eighteenth-century innovation: paper money. "Thus money also became fantasmic, a matter of the circulation of signs abstracted from their material basis. Furthermore, just as literary property was underwritten by the personality of the author, so the acceptability of commercial paper depended on the credibility of the note issuers and of the endorsers through whose hands they had passed."[21]

Rose garners support for this discursive parallel by observing that Lord Mansfield, in addition to arguing strenuously on behalf of the perpetuity of the author's natural property in his works, was "an instrumental figure in establishing banknotes as a legitimate form of money." In the 1758 case, *Millar v. Race,* in which "a defendant sought to avoid payment of a banknote by claiming it was not property but merely evidence of a debt," Mansfield accused the defense of relying on a "false comparison." In Mansfield's terms, banknotes were "treated as Money, as Cash, in the ordinary course and transaction of Business, by the general Consent of Mankind." As Rose points out, the same conceptual work required to legitimate banknotes was made necessary by the "abstractness of literary property." This was work that Lord Mansfield both modeled and encouraged in both cases, arguing as he did in *Millar v. Taylor* (1769) that the author's property in his works was "detached from the manuscript, or any other physical existence whatsoever."[22] In the same case, on the other side, Justice Yates drew an explicit connection between stock investment and the purchase of copyright by booksellers, that is, the commercial risk taken in printing a text that might or might not sell. Reinforcing the parallel between literary property and financial speculation, Yates refused to extend either category a stable place within the modern legal-economic system:

> Immense *Ideas* of Property were raised in the South Sea Stock, in the Year 1720. In that year, innumerable Rights of this Kind were bought and sold; and these Transactions passed between Parties whose Ideas were as sanguine as any Authors could be, 'that the Ideas They sold were real Property:' and yet the Subjects that were sold were, in Truth and Fact, *no* real Property.[23]

An unyielding opponent of literary property, Justice Yates nonetheless joined advocates of perpetual copyright in the view that it offered writers their only possibility of retaining ownership over some aspect of a literary composition even after that composition had been published and publicly circulated. Echoing Blackstone's terminology, with perhaps a hint of mockery, Yates contended that the defendant in *Millar v. Taylor* had "not meddled with any *Property* of the *Author's;* unless the very *Style and Sentiments* in the Work were *His*" (65). Of course, it was precisely this suggestion of the prosecution that Yates most vehemently rejected. However much the ideas, sentiment, language, and style of a literary work served as evidence of its author's "invention and labour," as they could never be demarcated by proper, discernible "Limit, Extent, and Bounds," because ideas could not be stamped with "*Indicia* or *distinguishing* marks," Yates insisted that they could not constitute property (65–66, 76). Because "Nothing *can* be an *Object* of Property, which has not a CORPOREAL Substance," Yates argued, any scheme to fix property in ideas was "quite wild" (71, 66). If the author were to be recognized as the undisputed proprietor of his works, he had to be able to demonstrate sole possession or "occupancy" of that precise, circumscribed property. On Yates's account, "Property is founded upon *Occupancy*"—occupancy of a new property, known as invention, and/or the occupancy of a vacant property and the "bestowing cultivation upon it," known as labor (66). Neither ideas, sentiments, nor literary style can constitute an object of property because they cannot be occupied, "for otherwise, How should *other* Persons be apprized They are not to use it?" (66). Since the very value of a published work depends precisely upon others using or occupying it, by the act of commercial publication, authors invite others both to purchase their work and to take up their thoughts. In this way, publication of a work dissolves, rather than establishing, both its author's occupancy and his property claim. In Yates's scoffing pronouncement, "the Occupancy of a *Thought* would be a new Kind of Occupancy indeed" (66).

And yet, it was precisely a "new kind of occupancy" that Blackstone sought to establish in insisting that every author has property "in his own original literary compositions" (405). As long as the work in question can be determined to have originated with its author—to be discernibly "original"—it is necessarily in his first possession. In *An Argument in Defence of Literary Property* (1774), Francis Hargrave reiterates and explicates Blackstone's analysis, delineating a work's originality as a function of its author's individual personality. Reasoning that every author has a "mode of combining and expressing . . . ideas" entirely peculiar to himself, that "a literary work *really* original, like the human face, will always have some singularities, some lines, some features, to characterize it, and to fix and establish its identity," Hargrave casts a work's "originality" as the source of its identifying marks and its author's occupancy.[24]

Indeed, Yates's fellow Justices in the Court of King's Bench found this logic persuasive. In their separate opinions, Justices Willes, Mansfield, and Aston each posit the author's distinctive personality as the basis and guarantee of his works' "distinguishing marks." In so doing, the majority opinion reinforces the emerging construction of the author as the single, ultimate authority over his own work, and of the work as the reflection of the author's singular agency. According to Aston, the work carries on it the impression of the particular mind that produced it, whether that impression is formalized on the title page or not. Indeed, it is this impression that renders the literary work the author's exclusive and manifest property: "It is *a personal, incorporeal* Property, *saleable* and *profitable;* It has *Indicia certa* . . . I confess, I do *not know,* nor can I comprehend *any Property more emphatically a Man's Own, nay, more incapable of being mistaken, than his literary Works.*"[25]

Aston's assurance that every text necessarily exhibits its author's "earmarks" and his explication of an author's property in his works on the model of property in one's life and person represent a significant historical shift in assumptions about the nature of both the author and the work. Whereas early modern conceptions of literary production had cast the writer as a vehicle or conduit, mediating creative forces larger than both himself and his readers, eighteenth-century arguments on behalf of literary property relocate the origin of and responsibility for the work in its author. Seeking new grounds for literary proprietorship, proponents of perpetual copyright retained the early modern notion of the inspired author, but dramatically shifted the source and implications of the inspiration. While previous centuries had attributed a work's greatness to some intervention by a deity or muse, mid-eighteenth-century literary property discourse internalizes inspiration, reformulating it as experiential and affective. As Martha Woodmansee puts it, "'inspiration' came to be explicated in terms of *original genius*" and the author was cast accordingly as the origin of the singular forces that animated his works.[26]

Proponents of perpetual copyright skirted the ambiguity at the heart of this shifting notion of artistic inspiration by positing legal occupancy of a work on the basis of the author's original workmanship, his uncontested and sovereign invention. Because the work originally takes up residence in the mind of its creator, inspiring or possessing its author, that individual may claim legal occupancy and possession of it as literary property. For Blackstone, the conception of literary form emanating organically from the peculiar perspective, experience, or genius of the writer secured that writer's claim to both legal ownership of his text and to its authorship in the modern sense. Whereas previously, respectable authorship was conditioned by the essentially social requirements of financial independence or landed status, taste, or commercial disinterestedness, arguments on behalf of perpetual copyright and proprietary authorship during the second half of the eighteenth century substituted for these standards individuating notions of personality, novelty, and most importantly, originality. On this new model, it was possible to ratify an alliance between aesthetic and commercial conceptions of literary value, even as its implication that all writers might lay claim to original work threatened to undermine distinctions of literary merit. Originality in a new sense emerged here as a measure by which to differentiate respectable authorship from the hackwork of the writer-for-hire. As Mark Rose points out, it was thus that "Johnson distinguished between the large number of 'drudges of the pen, the manufacturers of literature, who have set up for authors' and the few actual authors, who 'can be said to produce, or endeavour to produce new ideas.'"[27] Though the emphasis on originality in literary production was not new, the connection between a privileged creative genius and originality had, in John Brewer's words, "never before been made so forcefully."[28]

Indeed, it was through legal and public discussion that originality came to serve as the basis of a writer's claim to both property in his literary labor and status as a reputable author. By the same logic, it was out of the discourse of originality that standards for the measure of literary value and authorial legitimacy were distilled. Suggestively conflating legal and literary critical commitments, Lord Hailes, in the 1771 case *Hinton v. Donaldson,* contests the possibility of property inhering in a work without literary merit, his criterion for which is quite clearly invention in the sense of uniqueness and novelty—what he calls "originality." Because Stackhouse's bible—the book whose copyright was allegedly violated—consisted of a collection of excerpts from other works, it could lay claim to neither newness nor originality, neither literary merit nor property status.

> The London booksellers *enlarge* the common-law right by conferring the name of *original author* on every *tasteless compiler* . . . [Stackhouse] was as very a compiler as ever descended from a bookseller's garret. The incorporeal substance of Stackhouse's ideas is a non-entity. And yet, in the opinion of *The Sages in St. Paul's Church Yard,* Stackhouse is no less an original author than Hooker or Warburton.[29]

The exception taken by Hailes to the "tastelessness" of mere compiling as distinct from "original" authorship, coupled with the disdain he evinces for the trappings of Grub Street, for its base "dependents" merely executing plans designed by profit-hungry booksellers, reinforces the concept of originality as conferring both aesthetic and social respectability. Indeed, "compilation" here might well stand in for the range of collaborative and imitative compositional practices associated with literary hackwork. What is new and striking is the equation Hailes draws between this conception of authorial originality and literary property—an equation effected by his use of the term "incorporeal substance" to refer to both the (allegedly nonexistent) originality of Stackhouse's work and the literary property he would claim. For Hailes, only original authors—authors conveying new ideas or sentiments in new styles—could be regarded as the creative originators of their works or credited with the occupancy of literary property. If the design of the work or the ideas contained within it are borrowed from another source (or many sources), then so too must the property claim be located elsewhere. In insisting that the "incorporeal substance of Stackhouse's ideas is a non-entity," Hailes does not disavow the concept of incorporeal property—it is not literary property per se that he dismisses as "ideal"—but the claim to authorship made by every tasteless compiler, every collaborative or imitative writer-for-hire, every unoriginal literary producer.

And yet, in a field of literary production in which piracy, plagiarism, and a range of forms of collaborative authorship were common practice, questions about how the originality of a literary composition was to be reliably determined were not so simply resolved. Increasingly over the course of the century, the debate over copyright gave way to the elaboration of an idealized model of authorship as the creative enterprise of one self-identical, inspired, and sovereign individual—a model conspicuously remote from the scenarios and circumstances of the actual literary labor for which commercial writers were beginning to expect increased compensation. If everyday objects, possessed and animated by storytelling spirits with distinct perspectives, initially appear to figure the double character of literary property as both material commodity and textual abstraction in a way that would support the arguments of Warburton, Blackstone, and Hargrave, the scenes of authorship dramatized in these novels persistently complicate distinctions between originals and copies, the new and the borrowed, proprietary authors and tasteless hacks.

To be sure, the discourse of proprietary authorship suppressed much of the reality of the eighteenth-century book trade—in particular, the longstanding, if informal, arrangements that guaranteed stationers' legal ownership of copyrights and unyielding editorial control over the works they printed, the commonly collaborative, shamelessly imitative compositional strategies mobilized by writers to meet the demands and deadlines imposed by copy-holding stationers, and the profoundly formulaic and fragmented character of much popular imaginative prose. Indeed, despite the statutory vesting of copyright in "the author" at the beginning of the century, writers rarely retained either property in or control over their literary labor. Rather, more often than not, an author received a meager lump sum for the outright sale of his or her copy, a payment that could easily be spent before the work was even published.

Accordingly, many relatively successful professional writers supplemented the income they earned from the sale of "original" works with various kinds of hackwork, or what Ian Watt has called "casual labor—proposals, dedications, introductions, epilogues, compilations, translations, and so forth."[30] Not merely an imitator, the writer-for-hire was expected to comfortably, masterfully navigate a range of formal, discursive, and stylistic territories. Smollett, for one, a figure who early in his career might have boasted something like hack expertise, has been described as belonging to "the glorious company of English hack writers who have turned their hands to anything. Verse, drama, travel, political writing, a treatise on midwifery, translation—he translated Cervantes, Lesage, and Voltaire—and a history of England in many volumes poured from his pen."[31] The kind of work performed by the literary laborer was defined primarily by its lack of unified purpose, or fixed character, the hack himself routinely disdained and caricatured as disordered, scattered, and inconstant. Indeed, for proponents of "original" authorship, the catholic sensibility and versatile literary capabilities of the writer-for-hire bespoke a suspicious lack of integrity. In other words, his greatest offense, greater even than his alleged talentlessness, appears to have been his shape-changing and dexterous ventriloquism: the consummate hack could write in any and all styles and genres assuming any set of political or ideological commitments. This mercurial figure slipped in and out of literary and discursive modes and attitudes as so many costumes, frequently enough over the course of one, albeit fundamentally miscellaneous, work. Indeed, the hack himself might more accurately be characterized as a dramatic role available to all commercial writers during the period, rather than a practical designation marking the border between legitimate and disreputable writers. In light of common practices and arrangements governing popular literary production during the period, the prescriptive, regulatory nature of this phantom border comes into focus.

David Saunders adds another dimension to our understanding of hackwork as a common compositional mode, explaining the consistently broken, rambling narrative structure of the eighteenth-century popular novel as an effect of the principles of "extension" and "augmentation," which he claims organized much literary production and book manufacture during the period.[32] Novelists looking to churn out volumes quickly sought to liberate themselves from the constraints of narrative continuity and the unity of formal design by adopting makeshift unifying mechanisms that could accommodate diverse modes and materials. This left them free to insert interpolated tales, digressions, and tenuously relevant or downright extraneous passages, perhaps written earlier for another project but never used, written after the fact and carelessly injected into a text of insufficient length, or pinched from another writer altogether. Even in the construction of his novels, Smollett has been described as having "padded mercilessly and shamelessly" for the sake of length and, of course, the increased pay that length brought with it.[33] Indeed, Henry Fielding has been accused of "filling spaces with anything that came to hand until the last moments" during the rush to complete his *Miscellanies*, the collection containing *A Journey from this World to the Next*.[34]

Both eighteenth-century and modern critics understand the transmigrating narrator as just this sort of device invented to facilitate and excuse the "assemblage" logic governing its novel's construction. Derived at once from picaresque satire, secret histories, romans à clef, fabulous journeys, and spy narratives of late seventeenth and early eighteenth centuries, as well as from the conventional dream narratives, oriental tales, and satirical and sentimental adventure stories of early eighteenth-century periodical fiction, these narratives reimagine the picaro satirist as, in Ronald Paulson's description, "a convenient persona for reporting current events" with a critical edge and "sharp style."[35] Modern scholars follow eighteenth-century critics in viewing the transmigrating narrator and the narrative-of-adventures paradigm that it authorizes as principally designed to create the impression of coherence and continuity among disparate discursive and generic modes, narrative features, character sketches, incidents, interpolated tales, and digressions. Ernest A. Baker, for one, characterizes the device as merely "an easy means of emptying a store of anecdote, miscellaneous observations, surreptitious libels, and what-not," adding that its "literary interest is insignificant."[36] Roger Lund reinforces this view, referring to *Chrysal* as a "rambling collection of journalistic essays, character portraits, historical set pieces, and moral reflections."[37] Walter Allen describes the same novel's use of the transmigrating narrator as "not original" and the structural design it engenders as "a dead end in fiction."[38]

Clearly, the liberal borrowing from already published works to form "new" compositions, the slavish adherence of "new" works to popular generic paradigms, and the slapping together of assorted materials penned by various figures and published as "new" titles troubled the emerging conception of authorship underwriting literary property. As such, these practices, and the popular fictional works whose narrative construction appeared to broadcast them, were offered in accounts like that of Justice Hailes above as the abject sacrifice to the legitimation of that conception. The popular, ephemeral novels told from nonhuman perspectives were just the sort to be dismissed in these accounts. And yet, no less than the legal thinkers and polemical writers on the great question concerning literary property, novels narrated by transmigrating spirits inhabiting inanimate objects raise questions about the nature, boundaries, and location of literary value and literary property, as though in defiance of the discursive and institutional structures that increasingly insisted on their low status. Both material possession and supernatural agent, both matter and spirit, the transmigrating narrator appears to embody and celebrate precisely the doubleness or mixed nature of literary property as defined by Warburton and recapitulated by Blackstone. And yet, as the final section of this essay will explore, the adepts and interlocutors who in turn take responsibility and credit for the "authorship" and publication of these works serve to complicate claims about the occupancy of literary property, the privileging of literary originality, and the sovereignty of literary composition.

Henry Fielding's *A Journey from this World to the Next* (1743) features narration by a disembodied soul referred to as "the author." In the middle of chapter 10, the role of narrator is seized by another transmigrating soul, that of Julian the Apostate, whose lengthy interpolated tale charts his various incarnations, and then again by Anne Boleyn's spirit, a fragment of whose autobiographical account appears. Although both sections unfold in an uninterrupted first-person voiçe and together constitute the greater part of the work, they are entirely bracketed by quotation marks to sustain the premise of the original narrator and demarcate his authorial status. Authorship is further complicated by the work's status as a found manuscript whose origins are unclear, and by the assumption of responsibility for the work by the worldly "editor," who rearranges and actively annotates it in preparation for publication and who writes its preface. The commanding tone and scholarly character of the editor's footnotes, as well as his use of the first-person plural, reveal him to have taken property in the work and to have assumed a certain accountability for both its form and substance. Indeed, he assumes an officious propriety over the work, even as he is routinely met with the indeterminacy of its author's intended meaning. Glossing the author's description of his liberation from his body through his own nostrils, after which he "cast [his] eyes backwards upon it," the editor points to a petty logical inconsistency, and then justifies its appearance in the text uncorrected: "Eyes are not perhaps so properly adapted to a spiritual Substance: but we are here, as in many other places, obliged to use corporeal Terms to make our selves the better understood" (7). Conflating the author's intentions in devising the formulation and his own in standing behind it, the editor encourages the reader to identify with both figures as though at the scene of the narrative's construction. While the "we" who are "obliged" to use figurative language to make "ourselves" clear explicitly refers to both the author and the editor, the reader, too, is implicated in the dilemma, as it is both a pressing and a universal one—that of the inadequacy of our language and experience to apprehend incorporeal substance. The cultural and epistemological struggle to conceptualize literary property is here subtly invoked as the proper frame in which to contemplate the diffuse nature of authorial responsibility and autonomy.

The scene of narrative construction represented in *A Journey* disperses the authority of literary production that proponents of proprietary authorship insisted ought to remain within the author's province. We may recall, for example, Lord Mansfield's complaint that under limited terms of copyright protection the author becomes

> no more Master of the Use of his own *Name*. He has no Control over the *Correctness* of his own Work. He can not *prevent Additions*. He can not *retract Errors*. He can not *amend;* or *cancel* a faulty Edition. Any One may print, pirate, and perpetuate the *Imperfections,* to the Disgrace and against the Will of the Author; may propagate Sentiments under his Name, which he *disapproves, repents* and is *ashamed of.*[39]

In discussing the perils of piracy, the havoc that unauthorized editions and reproductions allegedly make of original works, Mansfield posits a single, autonomous, and self-identical author, one whose control over the constitution of his work and whose power to govern its reception demand legal protection on the same grounds that the law protects individuals from character defamation. Yet the particular anxieties articulated depict the material and institutional conditions of eighteenth-century literary production in a way that exposes Mansfield's scenario of authorship as a fiction, a fantasy.

As Fielding's miscellaneous text dramatizes, stables of writers, editors, and stationers actively, if not always cooperatively, participated in constructing both the content and the form of published works during the period. Authorship itself was dispersed through a number of forces, institutional spaces, and stages of production, even as copyright law was being constructed to mythologize writers as the originators, rightful owners, and sovereign rulers of what they wrote. The subgenre inaugurated here by Fielding and codified over the next several decades cannily inscribes that mythology, indicating its inadequacy to describe or organize commercial literary culture.

We may take Charles Johnstone's *Chrysal; or, The Adventures of a Guinea* as an elaborate instance of this representational enterprise. The enabling fiction of this narrative is a storytelling scenario in which a spirit inhabiting a coin visits an adept who will later chronicle the coin's adventures. Peculiarly, the spirit demands complete silence of the amanuensis. While the spirit repeatedly expresses the utmost commitment to allaying her listener's doubts and confusion and the greatest interest in communicating her adventures clearly and coherently, her guiding assumption is that the most reliable transmission of knowledge may take place without interruption by the recipient.[40] Of course, this assumption can only be reinforced supernaturally: with recourse to the spirit's uncanny insight, her ability to "enter into the hearts" and minds of her possessors and "read" their sentiments and thoughts without the mediation of their self-disclosure. Chrysal warns the student: "I can see your thoughts; and will answer every doubt which may arise in your mind at the wonders of my relation, without the interruption of your enquiries, as *awful silence is the essence of my converse,* the least breach of which puts an end to it for ever! Listen then in mute attention, nor let a breath disturb the mystic tale!" (3). Though the spirit's objective is to convey her tale seamlessly to the amanuensis, the latter is forbidden to participate actively in the formation of the narrative, even in the form of audible response.

The conditions the spirit places on its narration enact a fantasy of singular, consolidated, sovereign authorship, ultimately undermined by the necessity of the amanuensis. In completing the fantasy of total authorial control, these conditions figure the impossible denial at the heart of the discourse of proprietary authorship, a denial of the multiple hands involved in the actual processes of literary production, of readers' unruly interpretive agency, and of the ungovernable influence of external forms and ambient ideas on even the most solitary compositional process. The belabored articulation of a desire for a narrative method that might enable an unmediated transfer of knowledge only serves to cast that method as an illusion and to underscore the contingency and elusiveness of both reading and writing. To eliminate this contingency—to avoid Mansfield's (mis)interpretation, amendments, and errors—the unruly element in the dynamic must be contained, the reader rendered a passive receptacle for the narrative, and the author monumentalized as singular, sovereign, and absolute. The "least breach" of the contract between narrator and reader destroys the fantasy. The objective here is not merely the accumulation and exercise of power. Rather, Chrysal's central concerns are epistemological. Both narrator and narrative persistently return to questions about how knowledge, affect, and discourse may be reliably transferred from one being to another. In answering these questions they make conspicuous recourse to the preposterous supernatural machinery that conditions Chrysal's singular intuition.

Oddly enough, this intuition is explicitly characterized as a version of reading. Chrysal's access to her master's interiority furnishes contact with the other spirits who permanently inhabit the spaces of his or her heart and mind, which internal recesses are organized as a constellation of fully adorned living rooms, each corresponding to one of its master's principal internal states and containing the inscriptions of his or her character. Chrysal describes an adventure while in the possession of the particularly anguished Traffic: "Curiosity prompted me to learn the cause of his distress: I therefore immediately entered into his heart, to read the events of his life, which I doubted not but I should find deeply imprinted there" (7). Within the physical confines of Traffic's human consciousness, the spirits perform an unmediated and silent but singularly reliable communicative exchange. "I *looked at her,* my desire to know the meaning of what she was doing, and to signify the cause of my visit, to which she returned me this answer in *a glance,* that interrupted not her work" (8). In less than a moment, Chrysal receives the explanation of the spirit she has incited to discourse, "looked" as it is, rather than spoken. The reader of the novel, on the other hand, must trudge through several rather tedious pages of quasi-scientific psychological discourse ostensibly offered as the naïve experiential narrative of the spirit of memory, however much it seems to corroborate contemporary philosophical systems. Explicitly, if loosely, authorized by Lockean sensation psychology, identity-formation is framed here as textual inscription and access to it understood on a paradigm of reading. The internal processes are described as mechanical operations, governed by a host of inhabiting spirits, and resulting in traces eminently legible to them.

The narrative's interest in sensation psychology and its implications for human identity bear directly on its conception of authorship, which, as we have seen, combines an emphatic but unconvincing sovereignty with a heavy reliance on appropriative acts of reading. Chrysal's insistence on absolute authorial control is complicated, if not thoroughly undermined, by her perpetual engagement with other texts and her wholesale assimilation of those texts to her narrative. Notwithstanding the involvement of a number of mediating forces in the construction of the narrative—the explicitly writerly roles played by the other spirits with whom she communicates, the characters whose experiences make up the substance of the narrative, and, most importantly perhaps, the scribe responsible for transforming the narration into a written account—Chrysal expects the supernatural mechanisms by which she communicates to preserve her narrative authority. Moreover, her seamless communicative mode and the condition of silence she places on the exchange would appear to ensure that the adept will both receive and transmit her narrative unadulterated, further reinforcing an authorial claim designed to mystify the mixed origins of the work itself.

Chrysal's narrative, hardly the epitome of original genius, self-consciously figures the work of nonauthorial writing, the collection of tales and experiences, episodes and anecdotes, characters, observations, and texts imported from elsewhere into a work of questionable unity and dispersed authorship. This particular configuration of ambiguous and varied contribution and the assertion of authorial command figures a collision between the essentially collaborative nature of eighteenth-century literary production and the conception of singular, organic, proprietary authorship being articulated in the courts. Indeed, as we have seen, the next two decades saw the emergence of a minor literature greatly indebted to Johnstone's narrative of adventures, one that persistently dramatizes the tension, even incommensurability, between this emerging conception of literary property founded upon authorial originality and the notoriously unoriginal character of so much eighteenth-century popular novelistic production and book-manufacture—just the character, that is, that it plainly exemplifies.

Even as animated object-narrators register the copyright debates by guiding readers through the conceptual work required to recognize incorporeal property, the very same features of these novels dramatize a paradigm of literary production that severely undercuts the argument on behalf of proprietary authorship taking shape in the courts. Tales recounting the adventures of transmigrating narrators not only instantiate a kind of literary production without integrity, they thematize and normalize it for a readership eager to rally around this newly codified subgenre and imbue it with fashionable status. Moreover, in depicting the scene of writing as essentially collaborative (however unwitting its contributors may be) and rendering incoherent the division of labor in the production of the narrative, the transmigrating narrator erodes precisely the assumptions about authorial control and responsibility, original genius, and creative inspiration reinforcing arguments on behalf of perpetual copyright during the period. This copiously imitative subgenre complicates the very nature of authorship, over and above pointing to common cases in which isolating individual, autonomous, inspired authors was impracticable. These works suggest that all authorship is some version of collaboration, if only in the loose sense implied by the notion that "inspiration," ideas, and creative forces come from everywhere, even when they are channeled through a single, relatively autonomous agent. By making this case during the period in which the definition, boundaries, and implications of literary property were being fiercely debated, these novels expose the construction of the sovereign author as a mystification without undermining the legitimacy of their own proprietary claims. In other words, they suggest that even the most derivative and conventional narratives deserve recognition as literary labor and legal protection as literary property, on the grounds that literary value and vitality are generated through dialogue, collaboration, circulation, and recontextualization.

As fictional representations of the book trade during the period make clear, popular commercial writers were highly conscious that the fiercest advocates of literary property were wealthy stationers looking to secure their copyrights against infringement by other printers and publishers, and eventually by writers themselves. Indeed, the legal thinkers representing these business interests elaborated their arguments on a logic that both discredited and disenfranchised the great number of writers who constituted the field of commercial literature. Privileging a notion of originality as the figure for an author's character and the distinguishing—indeed, authenticating—mark of his works, these arguments were designed to naturalize a set of assumptions about the nature of literary production that not only failed to accommodate the interests of writers-for-hire, but sold them out to the interests of the very businessmen claiming to speak for them. Sufficiently canny to recognize that their professional futures hung in the balance of the great cultural battle over literary property, writers of fashionable but critically disreputable—minor, miscellaneous, ephemeral—literary forms sought to imagine a property claim on grounds entirely different from those they saw articulated in the courts. The transmigrating narrator was one device used by popular novelists to stake their claim to proprietary authorship, even as they challenged literary property arguments that offered their own anonymous, collaborative, unapologetically commercial enterprise as the sacrifice to the property rights of the authors of "original" works of literary excellence.

NOTES

1. James Burrow, *The Question Concerning Literary Property, Determined by the Court of King's Bench on 20th April, 1769, in the Cause Between Andrew Millar and Robert Taylor: with the Separate Opinions of the four Judges; and the Reasons given by Each, in Support of his Opinion* (1773), in *The Literary Property Debate: Seven Tracts, 1747–1773,* ed. Stephen Parks (New York: Garland, 1974), 100.

2. Tobias Smollett, *The History and Adventures of an Atom,* ed. O M Brack (1769; Athens: University of Georgia Press, 1989), 6. All further references to this work will be cited parenthetically.

3. See John Feather, *A History of British Publishing* (London: Routledge, 1988); Toni Benjamin Kaplan, *An Unhurried View of Copyright* (New York: Columbia University Press, 1967); Lyman Ray Patterson, *Copyright in Historical Perspective* (Nashville, TN: Vanderbilt University Press, 1968); Mark Rose, *Authors and Owners: The Invention of Copyright* (Cambridge, MA: Harvard University Press, 1993); Trevor Ross, "Copyright and the Invention of Tradition," *Eighteenth-Century Studies* 26.1 (1992): 1–27; David Saunders, "Copyright, Obscenity and Literary History," *ELH* 57.2 (1990): 431–44 and *Authorship and Copyright* (London: Routledge, 1992); David Saunders and Ian Hunter, "Lessons from the 'Literatory': How to Historicise Authorship," *Critical Inquiry* 17.3 (1991): 479–509; Martha Woodmansee, *The Author, Art, and the Market: Rereading the History of Aesthetics* (New York: Columbia University Press, 1994); Martha Woodmansee and Peter Jaszi, eds., *The Construction of Authorship: Textual Appropriation in Law and Literature* (Durham, NC: Duke University Press, 1993).

4. Richard K. Meeker, "Bank Note, Corkscrew, Flea and Sedan: A Checklist of Eighteenth-Century Fiction," *Library Chronicle* 35 (1969): 66. While eighteenth-century writers cited *Le Diable boiteux* as their direct influence, Lesage's work was itself an adaptation of Guevara's 1641 *El Diablo Cojuelo,* which features a devil who removes all of the rooftops of Madrid, exposing the entire city's private operations for the amusement and instruction of a favored companion. The conceit adopted by Lesage inspired a number of explicit imitations, including several editions of the 1756 anonymous "translation," *The Devil upon Crutches in England; or Night-Scenes in London. A Satirical Work. Written upon the Plan of the celebrated* Diable Boiteux *of Monsieur LeSage;* Samuel Foote's farce, *The Devil upon Two Sticks,* produced in 1768; and *The Devil upon Two Sticks in England,* a continuation by William Combe, published in 1790. See Ronald Paulson, *Satire and the Novel in Eighteenth-Century England* (New Haven, CT: Yale University Press, 1967), 221.

5. Charles Gildon, *The Golden Spy,* ed. Malcolm J. Bosse (1709; New York: Garland, 1972), 6. All further references to this work will be cited parenthetically.

6. Robert Mayo, *The English Novel in the Magazines 1740–1815* (Evanston, IL: Northwestern University Press, 1962), 38.

7. Aileen Douglas, "Britannia's Rule and the It-Narrator," *Eighteenth-Century Fiction* 6.1 (1993): 65–82; Charles Johnstone, *Chrysal; or, The Adventures of a Guinea* (1760; New York: Arno, 1976). A version of Aileen Douglas's essay appears in this volume.

8. Baker, quoted in Roger D. Lund, *British Novelists, 1660–1800,* vol. 39, part 1 of *Dictionary of Literary Biography* (Detroit, MI: Gale Research, 1985), 293.

9. Sherburn, quoted in Lund, *British Novelists*, 294; James Raven, *Judging New Wealth: Popular Publishing and Responses to Commerce in England, 1750–1800* (Oxford: Clarendon Press, 1992), 45–46.

10. See Meeker, "Bank Note," and Toby A. Olshin, "Form and Theme in Novels about Non-Human Characters, a Neglected Sub-Genre," *Genre* 2.1 (1969): 43–56.

11. *Birmingham Counterfeit; or, Invisible Spectator. A Sentimental Romance* (1772; New York: Garland, 1975), 44. All further references to this work will be cited parenthetically.

12. Claude-Prosper Jolyot de Crébillon, *Le Sopha* ([Paris], 1742), 28–29. All further references to this work will be cited parenthetically.

13. *Adventures of a Cork-Screw* (1775; New York: Garland, 1975), 4. All further references to this work will be cited parenthetically.

14. Gildon, *Golden Spy*, 9.

15. John Feather, *A History of British Publishing* (London: Routledge, 1988), 81.

16. William Warburton, *A Letter from an Author, to a Member of Parliament Concerning Literary Property* (London, 1747), rpt. in *Horace Walpole's Political Tracts (1747 and 1762), with Two by William Warburton on Literary Property (1747 and 1762)*, ed. Stephen Parks (New York: Garland, 1974), 8.

17. William Blackstone, *Commentaries on the Laws of England*, 4 vols. (1765–69; Chicago: University of Chicago Press, 1979), 2:405–6. All further references to this work will be cited parenthetically.

18. William Enfield, *Observations on Literary Property* (London, 1774), rpt. in *The Literary Property Debate: Eight Tracts, 1774–1775*, ed. Stephen Parks (New York: Garland, 1974), 11.

19. Henry Fielding, *A Journey from this World to the Next*, ed. Ian A. Bell and Andrew Varney (1743; Oxford: Oxford University Press, 1997), 9. All further references to this work will be cited parenthetically.

20. Rose, *Authors and Owners*, 129.

21. Ibid. While a full discussion of the money-narrated novel is beyond my scope here, Thomas Bridges's 1770 *Adventures of a Bank-Note* provides perhaps the powerful instantiation of this parallel between new, abstract money forms and incorporeal property. See Catherine Ingrassia, *Authorship, Commerce and Gender in Early Eighteenth-Century England: A Culture of Paper Credit* (Cambridge: Cambridge University Press, 1998), and James Thompson, *Models of Value: Eighteenth-Century Political Economy and the Novel* (Durham, NC: Duke University Press, 1996), esp. chapter 2, "Money as Sign."

22. Rose, *Authors and Owners*, 129.

23. Burrow, *Question*, 80.

24. Francis Hargrave, *An Argument in Defence of Literary Property* (1774), rpt. in *Francis Hargrave; Four Tracts on Freedom of the Press, 1790–1821*, ed. Stephen Parks (New York: Garland, 1974), 6–7.

25. Burrow, *Question*, 47, 52.

26. Woodmansee, *Author*, 36–37.

27. Samuel Johnson, *Rambler* 145 (August 6, 1751), quoted in Rose, *Authors and Owners*, 119.

28. John Brewer, *The Pleasures of the Imagination: English Culture in the Eighteenth Century* (New York: Farrar, Straus and Giroux, 1997), 150.

29. James Boswell, *The Decision of the Court of Session upon the Question of Literary Property in the Cause of Hinton against Donaldson* (Edinburgh, 1774), rpt. in *The Literary Property Debate: Six Tracts, 1764–1774*, ed. Stephen Parks (New York: Garland, 1975), 6.

30. Ian Watt, *The Rise of the Novel: Studies in Defoe, Richardson and Fielding* (Berkeley and Los Angeles: University of California Press, 1957), 25.

31. Walter Allen, *The English Novel: A Short Critical History* (New York: E. P. Dutton, 1954), 68.

32. J. H. Howard, "Literature and Regulation: A Study of the Development of Literature and Literary Practice in Relation to the Laws Regulating Publication in the First Half of the Eighteenth Century" (PhD diss., University of Leeds, 1965), 135, quoted in Saunders, *Authorship and Copyright,* 70.

33. Walter Allen cites the case of *Peregrine Pickle,* in which Smollett inserted the "quite irrelevant" 150-page interpolated tale "The Memoirs of a Lady of Quality," which he claims "he certainly did not write himself" and "was probably paid to put in" (*The English Novel,* 68).

34. Simon Varey, *Henry Fielding* (Cambridge: Cambridge University Press, 1986), 29.

35. In his discussion of "secret histories," "spy-narrators," and *chroniques scandaleuses,* Paulson cites Ned Ward's *The London Spy* (1698), Tom Brown's *Amusements Serious and Comical* (1700), and Mary de la Riviere Manley's *The Island Adjacent to Utopia* (1725), as well as Charles Gildon's adaptation of Apuleius's *Metamorphoses* (1709), in which the golden ass is replaced with the more domesticated lapdog, a conceit that would be borrowed by Francis Coventry in 1751 (Paulson, *Satire and the Novel,* 119–21). See also Ioan Williams, ed., *Novel and Romance 1700–1800: A Documentary Record* (New York: Barnes and Noble, 1970), 1–26, and Mayo, *The English Novel.*

36. Ernest A. Baker, *The Novel of Sentiment and the Gothic Romance,* vol. 5 of *The History of the English Novel,* 10 vols. (1929; New York: Barnes and Noble, 1957), 52.

37. Lund, *British Novelists,* 293.

38. Allen, *The English Novel,* 81.

39. Burrow, *Question,* 116.

40. Chrysal later clarifies her gendering of pronouns, only to underscore the ambiguous implications of her first person singular: "(I see you wonder, that I speak of this spirit, though the SELF of a man, as if it was a female; but in this there is a mystery; every spirite is of both sexes, but as the female is the worthier with us, we take our denomination from that.)" (8).

Circulating Anti-Semitism: Charles Johnstone's *Chrysal*

Ann Louise Kibbie

IN MAY OF 1753, THE HOUSE OF COMMONS PASSED A BILL (ALREADY passed by the House of Lords) making a very limited change in the process for the naturalization of aliens. Since 1609, British law had required that all aliens applying for naturalization undergo the Sacramental Test: that is, those seeking citizenship had to receive the sacrament of communion in the Anglican Church before Parliament would consider their petitions for naturalization. The Jewish Naturalization Act (popularly referred to as the "Jew Bill") sought to allow Jews who had resided in Great Britain or Ireland for at least three years to initiate their petitions for naturalization without submitting to this precondition. By any objective assessment, the aims of the bill were modest. Resident Jews seeking naturalization would still have had to go through the expensive and slow process of privately petitioning Parliament, only now they would not have to commit an act of apostasy first. The passage of the bill was not, however, the end of the story. Although it received royal assent in June, by December of the same year a virulent campaign in the press and in pamphlets forced the repeal of the Jewish Naturalization Act before it had been applied in a single case.[1]

In an essay on representations of "outlandish" Englishmen in Georgian drama, Michael Ragussis urges scholars to turn their attention to "the centrality of the Jews" in the popular culture of the mid-eighteenth century, calling for a study of the "wide circulation of (and debate over) the figure of the Jew, particularly after the Jew Bill debacle."[2] In the following essay, I hope to contribute to such a study by focusing on a work that, although it was enormously popular in the later eighteenth century and remained well known into the nineteenth, has received little extended critical attention: Charles Johnstone's novel *Chrysal; or, The Adventures of a Guinea*. First published in 1760, then considerably expanded in 1761 and again in 1765, *Chrysal* participates somewhat belatedly but nonetheless maliciously in the backlash precipitated by the abortive passage of the Jewish Naturalization Act. Johnstone explicitly reminds his readers of the controversial bill through the character of Aminadab, a stereotypically treacherous Jew who hints that he used bribery to try to ensure its success. Such a glancing reference to contemporary history is not unusual in Johnstone's novel, which incorporates many recent events into its narrative, and this alone might make *Chrysal* no more than a footnote in the study of reaction to the Naturalization Act. But as part of the larger issue of, as Ragussis puts it, the "circulation" of the imaginary figure of the Jew, Johnstone's novel represents an especially interesting and important case.

Aminadab's story is only the first of a number of episodes in *Chrysal* in which Johnstone depicts Jewish treachery. The series of crimes that Johnstone associates with the figure of the Jew leads from the attempt to invade and undermine English national identity through the Naturalization Act, to the plan of a Jewish community in Germany to celebrate Passover with the slaughter of a group of Christian children, to the successful debasing of British currency by Jewish "clippers" abroad. The second of these instances, invoking the most monstrous anti-Semitic myth of the blood libel, would seem to render the other two examples trivial. Indeed, it is only the blood libel episode that attracts Frank Felsenstein's attention to *Chrysal,* in his groundbreaking study of the cultural history of anti-Semitism in England, *Anti-Semitic Stereotypes: A Paradigm of Otherness in English Popular Culture, 1660–1830.* In Felsenstein's analysis, Johnstone's reference to Jewish ritual murder stands as an isolated and grotesque manifestation, in an increasingly skeptical age, of a deracinated medieval myth. It seems to me, however, that Johnstone's themes of national identity, currency debasement, and blood libel are irreducibly connected. In my discussion of *Chrysal,* I hope to complicate Felsenstein's reading in two ways. First, by placing Johnstone's novel alongside other examples of eighteenth-century narratives of currency, I will focus on the ways in which *Chrysal*'s own participation in the backlash against the Jewish Naturalization Act intensifies that genre's intrinsic interest in anxieties surrounding national identity and citizenship. Second, I will discuss how Johnstone's symbolic association of the blood libel episode with the later mutilation of English currency endows the *economic* crime with the Gothic horror of the earlier episode: a horror that *Chrysal* itself circulates and recirculates as its legacy.

As Christopher Flint has observed, while the speaking objects of the eighteenth-century it-narrative tend to "seek a unified national identity," they are also at the same time "subject to a variety of dislocations that . . . complicate the meaning of citizenship."[3] Nowhere is this more apparent than in the narratives of coins that make up a significant number of these fictions: the guineas, shillings, rupees, and pennies that render up accounts of themselves over the course of the century.[4] While the involuntary peregrinations of other speaking objects may or may not detach them from a sense of an immutable national identity, for the speaking coins such dislocation is embedded in the very essence of their beings. The "character" that allows money to pass as currency is, first and foremost, the stamp of a national identity; it is not surprising that these coins exhibit a militant, if ineffectual, patriotism.[5] In the first of the eighteenth-century narratives of currency—for example, Charles Gildon's *The Golden Spy* (1709)—a handful of coins from different countries cannot inhabit the same breeches pocket without quarreling, and their owner is "oblig'd to interpose [his] Authority for the preservation of the Peace."[6] This attempt at pacification does not prevent the proud guinea of the bunch from delivering the following panegyric to England's greatness:

> what Nation can compare with the English, who are not content to be rich and free themselves when almost all the World is in slavery, but extend their power to the Relief of all the distressed on the Continent; shewing themselves as dreadful to the Enemy by Land, as on the Seas, which is their proper Dominion; and tho' it be a little World of itself, yet is able to strike a Terror by the force of its Arms and the Valour of its Natives, into the greater.[7]

Given the coins' fervent identification with the country whose stamp they bear, and given the analogy between currency and blood that pervades the seventeenth- and eighteenth-century discourse on money and trade, readers might expect these narratives of currency to tell a straightforward story of nationalistic pride, in which true English "blood" circulates healthily, conveying English values at home and abroad. The stories that these coins actually tell, however, indicate that the questions of currency and nationality are far more vexed than we might at first imagine, making these narratives a rich site for exploring eighteenth-century anxieties concerning citizenship and naturalization.

While the gold in Gildon's tale is of divine origin (it is part of the Jovian shower that descended into the lap of Danae), the subsequent narratives of currency, beginning with Joseph Addison's story of a talkative shilling, published in the *Tatler* 249 (November 11, 1710), shift their focus from the mythological to the material, stressing the coins' genesis in the bowels of the earth, far from English soil. Addison's shilling begins the story of its life with the information that it was "born . . . on the Side of a Mountain, near a little Village of Peru," reminding us that, if we traced their lineage thoroughly enough, most British coins made of precious metals would prove to be of foreign extraction.[8]

An emphasis on money's foreignness is, of course, not entirely new to the eighteenth century. For example, in Ben Jonson's *The Staple of News* (1625), the personification of money, Pecunia, is referred to as the "Infanta of the Mines," and her glittering genealogy is traced to "the "Spanish Mines in the West-Indies."[9] As Anthony Parr notes, in identifying Pecunia with Spain, Jonson "capitalizes on contemporary hostility to Spanish wealth."[10] This is a hostility contemporary to eighteenth-century readers as well, for whom Spain represents a nightmare version of colonialism against which England's own imperial and colonial ambitions appear entirely benevolent and humane. *The Adventures of a Silver Penny* (1787), one of a number of narratives of currency produced as part of the evolving genre of children's literature later in the eighteenth century, makes this especially explicit. Before commencing the tale proper, the author informs his young readers that "every thing that is far fetched and dear bought, must be, according to the general opinion, very valuable." Therefore, despite its seeming insignificance, "the little hero of this piece . . . must be very valuable indeed": "dear bought it must be, since the Spaniards, to whom this gold and silver country [Peru] now belongs, in order to get possession of it murdered innumerable thousands of innocent Indians, and made slaves of those they did not murder."[11]

Against this vision of Spanish exploitation, the narratives of currency offer an optimistic vision of a kind of metallic assimilation, not unlike the utopian ending of Alexander Pope's *Windsor-Forest,* in which English commerce itself offers a corrective to the crimes perpetrated by the rival nation, as the "new World," "launch[ing] forth to seek the Old," finds in England a bright future of trade without "Conquest" or "Slav'ry."[12] Transported to England in the primitive form of an ingot, which it refers to as its "Indian Habit," Addison's shilling is then, in its own words, "refined, *naturalized,* and put into the British Mode, with the Face of Queen Elizabeth on one Side, and the Arms of the Country on the other" (*Tatler* 249, 3:270, emphasis mine). By the end of its story, it has reached a kind of apotheosis: as part of the great recoinage of 1696, our shilling undergoes a further refinement by fire and emerges "with greater Beauty and Lustre than [it] could ever boast of before," now bearing the image of King William.[13] Originally an alien, the naturalized coin even becomes a muse of English letters, boasting that, in its renewed form, it has inspired "the finest Burlesque Poem in the *British* Language," John Philips's *The Splendid Shilling* (*Tatler* 249, 3:272, emphasis in original).

The "naturalization" of this foreign metal, its inscription as English, simply mirrors, in a less bitterly satirical way, the artificial creation of a national "character" that Daniel Defoe mocked in *The True-Born Englishman.* Describing "That Het'rogeneous *Thing, An Englishman,*" Defoe claims "A *True-Born Englishman*'s a Contradiction, / In Speech an Irony, in Fact a Fiction," and that the term itself is "A Metaphor invented to express / A Man *a-kin* to all the Universe."[14] The English are, in Defoe's words, a "compounded Breed," "Making a Race uncertain and unev'n, / Derived from all the Nations under Heav'n."[15] In the narratives of currency, the ironic inverse of acknowledging that England's true (legitimate) coins are originally foreign issue is the realization that only counterfeit coins can claim to be of strictly English composition, an irony that Richard Bathurst exploits in the story of a counterfeit halfpence that he published in *The Adventurer* in April 1753. This story would merely be a slavish imitation of Addison's tale of a shilling, were it not for the original twist of recounting the adventures of a member of the criminal class of coins. Just as Addison's Isaac Bickerstaff has fallen into a reverie while contemplating a shilling lying before him on a table, so Bathurst's narrator falls into a "half-slumber" after musing on a counterfeit halfpence lying among his change, a sight that leads him to lament "the adulteration of the copper-coin."[16] Bathurst is not simply giving voice to the conventional conservative lament for the loss of a Golden Age; his sense of the debasement of the English coin accurately registers a crisis in English currency that affected all types of specie. By the early decades of the eighteenth century, the current coins of all types had become "worn and underweight," and, insufficient for the day-to-day demands of trade, these coins were "supplemented" through a thriving (if dangerous) business in counterfeit coins.[17]

Disconcertingly, Bathurst's counterfeit presents the appearance—albeit faded—of royalty. Like Addison's shilling, it bears the image of King William, although this impression is "now scarcely visible, as it was very much battered"; and the words it speaks issue "from the royal lips stamped on its surface." The image itself is a false one, however; what the coin asserts through these putatively royal lips is its own baseness. "Sir!" it confesses, "I shall not pretend to conceal from you the illegitimacy of my birth, or the baseness of my extraction . . . I received my being at Birmingham not six months ago" (*Adventurer* 43:255).[18] This paradoxical association between the illegitimate coin and the trueborn Englishman is a trope that persists into the nineteenth century with Sidney Laman Blanchard's "Biography of a Bad Shilling," published in Dickens's journal *Household Words* in 1851. The anti-hero of Blanchard's tale is decidedly homegrown, the offspring of "the zinc door-plate of a solicitor" and "a pewter flagon residing at a very excellent hotel, and moving in distinguished society."[19] When an initiate to the counterfeiting profession refers to this shilling and its brethren as "bad money," a veteran sharply reprimands him, "Hush, hush . . . no offence to the home coinage" (62).

Bathurst and Blanchard both associate this counterfeit "home coinage" with the figure of the Jew. It is a "Jew-pedlar" who originally puts Bathurst's false coin into circulation. "I was transported, with many of my brethren of different dates, characters, and configurations, to a Jew-pedlar in Dukes Place, who paid for us in specie scarce a fifth part of our nominal and extrinsic value," it recounts; these coins are then dispersed to "coffee-houses, chop-houses, chandler-shops and gin-shops" (*Adventurer* 43:255).[20] Blanchard's "Bad Shilling" is conceived when its parents meet in the "melting-pot" of a "Hebrew gentleman" (60–61). The image of the Jew's melting-pot verges on the oxymoronic, as it is the figure of the Jew himself that stands for the alien that cannot be subsumed into Englishness. During the controversy over the Jewish Naturalization Act, the *London-Evening Post* would pronounce that Jews "are, in the eye of the Law, Aliens in the highest degree: *perpetui inimici,* perpetual enemies."[21] For an especially powerful and compact expression of the belief in this perpetual alienation, we can turn to Sir Edmund Isham's speech to the House of Commons on the same subject:

> Let us consider, Sir, that the Jews are not like French refugees, or German Protestants: these in a generation or two become so incorporated with us, that there is no distinguishing them from the rest of the people: their children, or grandchildren, are no longer French or German, or of the French or German nation, but become truly English, and deem themselves to be of the English nation. But the unconverted Jews can never be incorporated with us: they must for ever remain Jews, and will always deem themselves to be of the Hebrew not the English nation.[22]

In both Bathurst's and Blanchard's narratives, this figure that cannot be assimilated into Englishness proliferates a false value that can be taken, at least temporarily, for coin of the realm, transforming the legitimate mobility of "circulation" into the fraudulent fluidity of "passing." Filled with shame at its own imposture, Blanchard's "shilling" confesses, "Like the counterfeits of humanity, whose lead may be seen emulating silver at every turn, my only desire is—not to be worthy of passing, but simply—to pass" (61).[23]

It is an historical coincidence that Bathurst should have published the tale of his counterfeit halfpence, with its casual allusion to Jews' participation in the undermining of the British currency, in April of 1753, the same month that saw the introduction of the Jewish Naturalization Act in the House of Lords. In the anti-Semitic rhetoric that will flood the press in the months to follow, this association of the Jews with the debasement of the currency takes on a greater urgency and violence. In this discourse, counterfeiting is overshadowed by the crime of actually mutilating the nation's currency: the crime, that is, of "clipping." And, in his own contribution to the anti-Semitic discourse inspired by the Jewish Naturalizaton Act, Johnstone will connect this assault on the nation's currency with the most murderous fantasy of Jewish crime: the blood libel.

While Addison's foreign-born shilling arrived in England in its unminted, "savage" (and therefore nationless) state, Johnstone's guinea, likewise born in Peru, already bears the marks of a rival nation when it immigrates to England: it is a Spanish doubloon. Once on English soil, however, Chrysal immediately and seemingly painlessly "change[s] [his] Spanish appearance for the fashion of the country," reveling in "the beauty and convenience of [his] new figure."[24] Both Addison's shilling and Johnstone's guinea describe their inscription or reinscription with a national character as a superficial transformation, simply involving a change of "Mode" or "fashion." This initially casual or fluid attitude toward citizenship will disappear after Chrysal's own naturalization, however. Appearing as it does in the wake of the controversy over the Jewish Naturalization Act, Johnstone's novel itself offers evidence of the intensification of British anxieties about citizenship, anxieties that are displaced onto the loathed figure of the nationless Jew.

Despite the attempts of the foremost historian of the Jewish Naturalization Act, Thomas W. Perry, to minimize the importance of anti-Semitism in motivating the backlash against the bill by attributing the bitter controversy to especially venomous party politics, it is indisputable that the campaign against the Act was waged in great part by recirculating the hoariest anti-Semitic stereotypes. There is no overestimating the hysterical rhetoric of the opponents of the Act. "If [England] is worth our keeping, why are we going to give it away to the worst and most despicable People this Day in the Sight of God and Man?" asked one anonymous pamphlet.[25] The *Westminster Journal* of June 9, 1753, warned that the bill would introduce "even the worst species of foreigners among us, to share all the glorious advantages of Englishmen by a NATURALIZATION."[26] Writers in the public and the private press indulged in what James Shapiro has rightly called "the crudest sort of racial prejudice."[27] *A Modest Apology for the Citizens and Merchants of London, Who Petitioned the House of Commons Against Naturalizing the Jews* argued that

> It is a Matter of Fact, that the Jews do live in continual Uneasiness, tormented and haunted, like Murderers, with a Legion of Horrors: Their

> Crimes deserve these severe Lashes of Conscience, and how severe they are you may read in their very Faces. You know a Jew at first Sight. And what then are his distinguishing Features? Examine what it is peculiar that strikes you. It is not his dirty Skin, for there are other People as nasty; neither is it the Make of his Body, for the Dutch are every whit as odd, aukward Figures as the Jews. But look at his Eyes. Don[']t you see a malignant Blackness underneath them, which gives them such a Cast, as bespeaks Guilt and Murder? You can never mistake a Jew by this Mark, it throws such a dead, livid Aspect over all his Features, that he carries Evidence enough in his Face to convict him of being a Crucifier.[28]

Another pamphlet describes the Jews as

> a most rebellious, disobedient, gainsaying, stiff-necked, impenitent, incorrigible, adulterous, whorish, impudent, froward, shameless, perverse, treacherous, revolting, backsliding, idolatrous, wicked, sinful, stubborn, untoward, hard-hearted, hypocritical, foolish, sottish, brutish, stupid, ungrateful, Covenant-breaking Nation or People; a Seed of Evil Doers, a Generation of Vipers.[29]

"And shall it be recorded," the passage concludes, "that *Britannia,* the first among the Christian States, ever admitted such a Nation or People as this to become one People, and to enjoy the Privileges of a true born Englishman?" (13). Although one proponent of the Jewish Naturalization Act attempted to counter this xenophobia by reminding his readers that "England is a Composition of Foreigners, whose Forefathers were as much Strangers as the Jews can possibly be," for the opposition there was no longer any Defoean irony in the phrase "true born Englishman."[30]

Johnstone's Aminadab is the offspring of the anti-Semitic rhetoric of the opponents of the Jewish Naturalization Act. He enters Chrysal's narrative as a representative of the eighteenth-century version of the figure of the Jewish usurer that haunted the sixteenth- and seventeenth-century literary and economic imaginations. Discussing this earlier bogeyman, the usurer, Shapiro writes,

> Undoubtedly, English depictions of Jews as usurers during [a] period when the concept of lending money at interest was undergoing such rapid and startling revision strongly suggest that such representations were in part projections: Jews enabled the English to imagine a villainous moneylender whose fictional excesses overshadowed their own very real acts of exploitation.[31]

The image that Shapiro presents here of the years from 1571 to 1624—the image of an era of "startling revision" in attitudes toward what we would now call capital, a revision that is experienced as profoundly dislocating, even frightening—would just as accurately describe the late seventeenth as well as the eighteenth century, with its economic innovations (such as the creation of the Bank of England and of the National Debt, the evolution of paper currency and new instruments of credit), and economic traumas (such as the explosion of the South Sea Bubble). Shapiro's point about the projection of English economic anxieties onto the figure of the villainous Jew is relevant to this later period of financial revolution as well, although the usurer is replaced in the eighteenth century by a more up-to-date figure, the stockjobber. This transformation is encapsulated in its pithiest form in the Prologue to George Granville's 1701 adaptation of *The Merchant of Venice,* in which the ghost of Shakespeare addresses the audience to inform it of the new play's revision of the villain: "Today we punish a stockjobbing Jew."[32] It is as just such a "stock-jobbing Jew" that the character of Aminadab enters Johnstone's novel as well. While the words of Shakespeare's ghost are meant to testify to the mildness of the play to follow, which promises to exhibit "Less Heinous Faults" than those exposed in its source, *Chrysal*'s own exploitation of this revised figure of the Jew gives the lie to the claim that the more "modern" manifestation of the stereotype of the Jew is any less a subject of loathing.[33]

When we first meet the stockjobber in *Chrysal,* he is visiting a woman referred to only as Her Grace or the Countess, and their conversation turns to the disappointment of the defeat of the Act, a disappointment that is mutual because the Countess, who had been bribed to support its passage, had hoped for even further profit from its success. "Fear not," she comforts Aminadab, "though I could not procure an establishment for your whole nation, as I would have done, I certainly will for your family . . . Your son shall be made a BARONET at least; you have riches enough to support the title" (2:41). Aminadab has no intention of awaiting the outcome of yet another promise, however, and he flees to Holland with a small fortune of the Countess's money, which she has asked him to invest. At this point, the character of Aminadab intersects with the figure from England's literary heritage that the opponents of the Jewish Naturalization Act repeatedly invoked as an example of the ceaseless perfidy of the Jews: Shylock himself.[34] Like his predecessor, Aminadab sees himself as taking a just revenge on Christians. "What do we mix with them; what do we serve them; what do we bear their abominations, their insults for, but to make our own advantage of them?" he asks. "Fools! vain presumptuous fools! to imagine that any benefits, any gratitude can bind us to them; or change the innate hatred of our souls, to a sect, that has been the cause of our dispersion and ruin" (2:114). To this general antipathy, Aminadab adds the motive of the repeal of the Jewish Naturalization Act:

> Have I not laboured hourly for this Gentile woman without payment! Did she not join to defraud our people of a greater sum than this, to which my mite was added too, under the pretence of procuring us a settlement! and did she not refuse to return it, when the attempt failed of success. What then is this, but a just retaliation? a fulfilling of our law, that says, *An eye for an eye, and a tooth for a tooth?* (2:114–15).

And if Granville's revision of *The Merchant of Venice* assured its audience that it would witness "less Heinous Faults" than those represented in the original, in *Chrysal* Shylock's ghost returns with a vengeance, paving the way for the even more murderous representations of the figure of the Jew to come.

Although the alliance of convenience between Aminadab and "this Gentile woman" has now broken down, it plays an important role not just in introducing the topic of the Jewish Naturalization Act into the novel, but in furthering Johnstone's larger commitment to linking his fictional world and the world of real personages and events. The unnamed Countess, who would have been immediately recognizable to contemporary readers as the royal mistress, the Countess of Yarmouth, loathed for her rapaciousness, is just one of the many famous and infamous men and women of the day to make an appearance in *Chrysal*'s pages. That this "real-life" content was considered a major selling point for the novel is evident from a 1760 prepublication advertisement, which announces that "there will be speedily published, under the emblematical title of the 'Adventures of a Guinea,' a dispassionate, distinct account of the most remarkable transactions of the present times all over Europe, with curious and interesting anecdotes of the public and private characters of the parties principally concerned in these scenes."[35]

Especially in light of this advertisement, *Chrysal*'s interest in real people and real events would simply seem to be an example (in fact, with its constant parade of celebrities, the most perfect example) of what Aileen Douglas has referred to as "the commodification of the rich and famous," a commodification that she identifies as a main source of the object narrative's popularity with readers.[36] With their promise to provide "access to the casual, intimate, and mundane acts of public figures," Douglas writes, these narratives "[expose] the purely personal to marketable effect, blurr[ing] the distinction between private and public." In this precursor of the modern celebrity industry, "the historical individual" is separated "from the commercial use of his or her name and actions."[37] Douglas's emphasis on the alienation and marketing of celebrity identity is consistent with an emphasis in studies of the eighteenth-century novel on the vulnerability of the real to a kind of incursion by fiction. *Chrysal,* however, exemplifies a kind of reverse incursion in which the real-life characters and events endow the fiction with their own truth value. In borrowing the strategies of the roman à clef and the *chronique scandaleuse,* Johnstone's novel participates in what Catherine Gallagher, in a discussion of the proliferation of keys to novels in the eighteenth century, has referred to as a "rage for reference," "the period's desire to open every book to some extra-textual reality."[38] (In fact, a key to *Chrysal* supposedly provided by Johnstone himself was eventually published in 1814.)[39] In the case of *Chrysal,* this rage for reference has an especially pernicious effect, as the recognizably "real" content of the novel, the guinea's circulation among thinly disguised celebrities and its alleged eyewitness accounts of real events, helps to underwrite a myth that was reinvigorated by the controversy over the Naturalization Act: the myth that Jews engage in the ritual murder of Christian children at Passover.

Johnstone sets his account of Jewish murderousness on foreign soil. Circulating from owner to owner, Chrysal eventually finds itself in Germany, where it falls into the hands of a Jewish butcher, who is also a money-clipper. Chrysal's own beauty and wholeness distinguish him from his companions: "The beauty of my appearance, for I had hitherto escaped mutilation, made my master, who was an adept in that art, think it improper to throw me among his diminished heap, as I should but make their loss the more remarkable" (2:155). His master, therefore, places him in his purse. That very evening his new master leaves work early "to purify and prepare himself for the celebration of the most secret and mysterious ceremony of [his] religion . . . the sacrifice of *Passover,* which," Chrysal explains, "by a secret tradition, never committed to writing . . . was changed from the typical offering of a lamb, to the real immolation of human blood, for which purpose the most beautiful children were purchased at any expence, and under any pretext . . . and brought from all parts of Europe, to these ceremonies" (2:155). Because, Chrysal adds, "some traces of natural affection might remain, even in hearts divested of the feelings of common humanity," and in order to "stimulate superstition by hatred and revenge," the Jews sacrifice only Christian children (2:156). Chrysal then moves quickly to the scene of the sacrifice: "All things being prepared, the victims were brought to the altar naked and bound, the instruments for slaying, and the fires for roasting them (for horrour to human thought! they were to have feasted on their flesh) in readiness" (2:160). Just as the butchers (including Chrysal's master) are about to begin the sacrifice, a band of soldiers bursts in, and a different slaughter ensues: "The house was in a moment a scene of horrour beyond description. Most of [the Jews] fell instant sacrifices to this resistless rage. Happier far in having so speedy an end put to their sufferings than the few survivors, who saved their lives for that moment, by throwing themselves among the dead" (2:161).[40] We are told that the next day, after a speedy trial, the surviving Jews were "all publickly burned alive on the very spot, where they were to have perpetrated their guilt" and all of their property "confiscated to the use of the state" (2:164).

Although some contemporary critics did express general disapproval of the vehemence of Johnstone's tone in *Chrysal,* nowhere is this episode singled out for special discussion.[41] Modern critics as well have attempted to accommodate the horrors of this passage by including it in a larger context of a general satire. Malcolm Bosse, in his introduction to the facsimile edition of *Chrysal* published by Garland Press in 1979, insists that the blood libel scene should be read in the context of what he calls a "constellation" of episodes that satirize false religion.[42] Thus, for example, the Jesuits Chrysal meets reveal themselves to be hypocrites who use their position to prey on naïve believers, committing or countenancing the most shocking crimes to increase their own wealth and power. Aileen Douglas also classes this episode with a number of scenes exposing "the vices of various international groups."[43] But, unlike the scenes of vice and corruption with which Bosse and Douglas would group it, the episode of the blood libel in *Chrysal* has no moral or satiric purpose. Money itself (in the form of Chrysal) is not, as in the other episodes, itself a motive. It is not a price, a bribe, or even an object of desire: it simply presents itself as an eyewitness to what a modern tabloid would call a "shocking true story."

Other critics have tended to hurry over Johnstone's exploitation of the blood libel as an embarrassment. Baker, after acknowledging that Johnstone's guinea "is also an anti-Semite, at a time when hatred of the Jews was inveterate all Europe over," simply dispenses with the scene of narrowly averted ritual murder by pronouncing that "this sort of thing is merely ridiculous," compared with what he sees as the more egregious personal attacks on real individuals that Johnstone engages in over the course of his narrative.[44] Later critical discussions of *Chrysal*'s invocation of the blood libel engage in the same displacement that Hillel Kieval so acutely describes as a tendency in responses to ritual murder trials in nineteenth-century Europe. These trials tend to be understood, Kieval observes, as " 'unnatural' intrusions of medieval persecutions and their attendant mental structures on to the domain of the modern and the rational."[45] Even the critic who devotes the most time to serious discussion of this episode in *Chrysal,* Frank Felsenstein, seems torn between the acknowledgment that, in *Chrysal,* we are confronted with the persistence of anti-Semitic stereotypes, and a wish to view Johnstone's invocation of the blood libel as an idiosyncratic anachronism. On the one hand, commenting generally on anti-Semitism in the eighteenth century, he observes that

> in the so-called age of Enlightenment, the nation that half a millennium before had been the first in medieval Europe to expel its Jews, a nation that (as far as records reveal) was also the first to promote the myth of the Wandering Jew and the obscenity of the blood libel, showed a purblind refusal to let go of its primitive superstitions with anything like the genial acquiescence that many later scholars would have us suppose.[46]

Felsenstein's point here is an important corrective to a tendency, on the part of earlier scholars, to ignore aspects of the eighteenth-century world that did not fit into a story of the steady march of enlightened progress. When he turns his attention specifically to *Chrysal,* however, Felsenstein dismisses Johnstone's "cast[ing] contemporary Jews as child-eating savages" as "merely straining to the last ounce the sensationalist element in the blood libel myth and enfeebling its already tenuous bond with its roots in a bygone medieval theology."[47] In this passage, with its emphasis on strain, enfeeblement, and attenuation, Felsenstein implies that Johnstone's use of the blood libel represents the last gasp of an exhausted myth. In his reading, the severance of the blood libel's roots in medieval theology would seem to hasten its demise. On the contrary, I would argue that Johnstone's modernization and secularization of the blood libel provides the eighteenth century with a reinvigorated version of the myth, one that fits, by association, with current anxieties regarding nationalism and the health of the nation's currency. By putting this story in the "mouth" of a coin, Johnstone helps to keep this libel in circulation in a new world of global commerce.

In the introduction to his excellent (and, unfortunately, as yet unpublished) abridged edition of *Chrysal,* Michael Abraham Mandelkern remarks, on the influence of the Jewish Naturalization Act on *Chrysal,* that Johnstone's personal anti-Semitism was "so strong, it seems clear that it did not require a bill in order to activate it."[48] While this may or may not be true, the insistence on detaching Johnstone's case from a more wide-ranging anti-Semitism has the effect of reducing it to an individual pathology, rather than acknowledging it as part of a larger cultural moment. In fact, Johnstone's use of the blood libel is part of a reinvigoration of the myth that begins with the anti–Naturalization Act writings, writings that not only retail old charges of ritual murder but insist on the ongoing nature of the crime. *An Appeal to the Throne Against the Naturalization of the Jewish Nation, &c.*, for example, describes

> the high Contempt and Despite [which the Jews] have frequently discovered against the Person and Passion of Christ, *which they have maliciously acted over and over again,* in representation, not only by piercing his Image with Swords and Spears; by abusing the Sacramental Bread; and by crucifying a Ram at Easter; but by crucifying several Christian children on Good-Friday; as could be instanced by seven or eight facts in England alone. (16–17, emphasis added)

A bit later the same pamphlet refers to charges

> that the Jews in Paris did every Year steal some Christian Child or other brought up in the King's Court, and carrying him to a secret House or Vault, did on Good Friday or Easter Day, in Contempt and Derision of Christ, and the Christian Religion, crucify him on a Cross: And that such is their Malice to Christ, that *neither Fines, nor Imprisonments, nor Death itself are able to deter them from acting the like Tragedies over again, as often as Opportunity serves.* (18, emphasis added)

According to the pseudonymous Archaicus, in *Admonitions from Scriptures and History, from Religion and Common Prudence, Relating to the Jews,* "The Writers of all Ages . . . have born Witness of the cruel and implacable Malice the Jews have ever born against Christians . . . by stealing, and torturing, and oftentimes crucifying Christian Children," and "always," he adds, "doing them all the Mischief in their Power, and murdering them by all the Tortures they could devise, by Thousands."[49] The insistence on the frequency of these crimes ("oftentimes") is repeated a bit later: "Out of their said Law, they infer the Legality of torturing Christian Children, throwing them into Wells and Pits, and even Crucifying them; as they have oftentimes done in several Places, and more than once or twice even in our *England.*"[50] Such charges became part of the very fabric of eighteenth-century anti-Semitism after the abortive passage of the Jewish Naturalization Act, and it is against this distinctly eighteenth-century context that we must view the blood libel scene in Johnstone's novel.

In the final anti-Semitic episode of *Chrysal,* the guinea will itself be transformed from mere eyewitness to victim. On falling into the hands of the Jewish butcher, the coin has remarked on its own unmutilated state. The importance of this seemingly trivial detail becomes clearer later on, when Chrysal's subsequent mutilation at the hands of Jewish clippers makes explicit the links among the scattered anti-Semitic episodes of the novel. The story of Chrysal's mutilation, which takes place in Portugal, reintroduces us to Aminadab's son. Now orphaned, the young Aminadab has come to Portugal to seek his uncle, who rejoices to see him, especially as the youth has been initiated into the "mysterious art of lessening the weight, without effacing the image" of gold coins, particularly British coins (2:273). (Note the echo of the "mysterious ceremony" of Passover.) Here, Johnstone alludes to a charge made repeatedly in the anti–Naturalization Act literature: that Jews are constantly engaged in an assault on England's currency, an assault that is most emphatically physical in nature. Uncle and nephew rejoice in a shipment of British coins, "all new from the mint" (2:274). This lot includes Chrysal, who now becomes the victim of a disfiguring assault. "I fell one of the first sacrifices to [this] art, which deprived me of a fourth part of my weight, and of all my beauty," it laments (2:274).

Chrysal is not the first of these speaking coins to suffer such violence. In a comically horrific representation of assault and battery—even, with its sexual puns and double entendres, of rape—Addison's Elizabethan shilling recounts falling into the hands of an "Artist" who "with an unmerciful Pair of Shears cut off my Titles, clipped my Brims, retrenched my Shape, rubbed me to my inmost Ring, and, in short, so spoiled and pillaged me, that he did not leave me worth a Groat" (*Tatler* 249, 3:272).[51] Unlike young Aminadab and his uncle, the criminal "Artist" here is not identified as Jewish. In fact, the very absence in Addison's tale of what would become, later in the century, an automatic association between the clipper and the Jew helps to reveal an essential shift in the representation of money itself. This shift involves an issue that, while it may seem somewhat minor compared to the horror and violence of the blood libel episode, plays an essential role in linking Johnstone's representation of the threat of ritual murder with his representation of assaults on the currency itself: the issue of money's gender. After the trauma that Addison's Elizabethan shilling undergoes at the hands of the unspecified "Artist," it experiences what it refers to as a "Change of Sex" (*Tatler* 249, 3:272). As part of the recoinage of King William's solo reign, it is recast, emerging from the furnace like a phoenix from the ashes, bearing a new, masculine stamp. This change of sex is, of course, accidental—as the gender of the monarch has changed, so too does the gender of the coin. But this transformation enacts in miniature a larger transformation in the imaginative representation of currency. In the Elizabethan and Jacobean precursors to the eighteenth-century narratives of currency, the many plays, poems, and prose pieces in which money is personified, such personifications are almost invariably female.[52] In the eighteenth-century narratives of currency money is regendered, and this change of sex, so lightly touched on in Addison's tale, becomes crucial in the wake of the Jewish Naturalization Act controversy, allowing Johnstone to represent the vulnerability of this masculinized body to a specifically Jewish predation. If in Addison's tale "clipping" described a kind of sexual assault on a feminized currency, in Johnstone's tale, as in the anti-Semitic rhetoric of the backlash against the Naturalization Act, clipping merges with what is seen as the Jewish threat to the masculine body, circumcision, which is described as a kind of castration.[53]

In a final turn of the screw, both uncle and nephew are undone. As a way of stealing all of his uncle's earthly goods, the ungrateful nephew betrays him to the Inquisition. Immediately after the uncle's execution, the nephew himself is discovered in the very act of debasing his coins, "a crime," Chrysal notes smugly, "never forgiven in any state" (2:276), and the nephew too is put to death. "Of all the human sufferings I had yet seen," Chrysal remarks of the nephew's punishment, "except in the case of the sacrificers," that is, the case of the Jews in the blood libel episode, "this gave me the greatest pleasure" (2:276). Chrysal's insistence on an equation between the would-be ritual murder and the crime against the body of the nation through the mutilation of its currency is part of a long-lived association. In *Anglo-Judaeus, or the History of the Jews Whilst Here in England* (1656), William Hughes argued that the oppression of the Jews is attributable to three causes: they "make it their annual practice to crucifie children, conspire against City and people, [and] still clip and spoil the coyn."[54] William Prynne, in *A Short Demurrer to the Jews* (1656), writes that "Jews had been formerly great clippers and forgers of money, and had crucified three or four children in England at least, which were the principal causes of their banishment."[55] We find the same conflation in the anti–Naturalization Act writings. "How faithful they have been to this English Nation, let any impartial Reader judge," writes the anonymous author of *An Appeal to the Throne Against the Naturalization of the Jewish Nation*: "*They who shall out of Scorn and Hatred of our Profession, crucify Children, lay violent Hands on tender Infants (and that by common Practice) they who shall clip, counterfeit, and mangle our Coin*" (33, emphasis in original).

Chrysal's "mangling" marks the beginning of the end of his circulation as currency. He returns to London, where he must become "an idle spectator of [economic] transactions, for young Aminadab had made such depredations on me, that no one in London would accept me at my original value" (2:291). Finally, despite "the diminution of [his] size," he is given, like Bathurst's counterfeit halfpence, to "a Jew pedlar" who, in turn, "passed me off . . . to a pawn-broker, at a division of the loss" (2:297). (Like clipping itself, pawnbroking is a "mysterious trade" [2:298].) In the final transaction of the novel, the pawnbroker passes Chrysal off to a poor man who happens to be an "adept," an alchemist in search of the secret of transmuting baser substances into gold. Chrysal is about to reveal this secret when his new owner, afflicted with hunger, farts, and the offended guinea simply disappears, leaving behind no trace except his narrative itself, the account of his life that he delivered to the adept. When Johnstone himself expanded the novel from two to four volumes, he did so not by *continuing* the story, but by expanding the body of the narrative that he had already published, elaborating further on episodes already present in the original narrative, or writing new episodes to be inserted into the existing body of the text. This can be seen as an imitation of the narrative innovations of Lawrence Sterne (and, indeed, the publication of *Tristram Shandy* had an enormous impact on the later narratives of currency), but it is also, in fact, necessitated by the ending that Johnstone has put in place. We could say that Chrysal's mutilation, by forestalling the possibility of further exchange, both makes possible the story itself and also represents a point beyond which that story cannot proceed. In this way its mutilation, which creates a fatal break in its circulation, is both the precondition for and the terminus of its narrative.[56]

But *Chrysal* has a sequel, of sorts. In 1824 the pseudonymous Peregrine Oakley published *Aureus; or, The Life and Opinions of a Sovereign,* in which the coin-narrator pays explicit homage to Johnstone's guinea. In his prefatory remarks, the sovereign describes the encounter that has inspired him to deliver his own "golden publication."[57] He and his current companions are happily resting in a purse when their attention is drawn to a coin that maintains a haughty distance from the others, seeming "to think himself superior to all the rest of us . . . and to hold us in that sort of contempt which is displayed by a patrician of high blood when he contemplates a peer of recent creation" (10–11). The analogy is an apt one, as this coin is indeed a member of the monetary aristocracy, as proud of the "pure and unadulterated metal in his composition" as any human blue blood could be of his ancestry. In fact, the coin can do the human snob one better. Where a person can only speak somewhat abstractly of the family blood that courses through his veins, the coin claims that "he was formed of a portion of the identical substance from which was moulded his renowned ancestor of the name CHRYSAL" (11).

Having awed his listeners with his lineage, the guinea (for we now know it *is* a guinea) exhorts them to follow Chrysal's example: "if you would but rouse yourselves to exertion, and cherish a proper sense of your own condition, you would blush at your want of ambition, and strive to acquire . . . celebrity in the future annals of fame" (13). What Chrysal has passed along to his unnamed descendant is not just a respect for literary fame, however. In a passage that recalls Chrysal's mutilation at the hands of Aminadab's son, but that intensifies its attention to the details of physical violence, Chrysal's descendant describes the torments of falling into the hands of Jewish clippers: "Whenever . . .

any of our royal race were seen abroad, we were seized upon with savage ferocity, by those infidel dealers in barbarity, the Jews; who, without any remorse of conscience, inflicted upon us the most unfeeling acts of cruelty and torture, by clipping pieces out of our bodies—our very noses off our faces—and burning us in furnaces or crucibles, till we lost every trace of our original formation" (12). Thus, what continues to circulate in this later narrative of currency, in its indebtedness to *Chrysal,* is not only Johnstone's famous guinea, but the figure of the Jew as the sadistic mutilator of the body of the nation. In her acute discussion of narratives of currency, Deidre Shauna Lynch writes that money, "a marker of social agreement," "memorializes the convention that draws persons into a community of mutual dependence—into a social space."[58] In the use that these works make of the figure of the Jew, however, we can see that such community is affirmed only through the violent exclusion of what is seen as a threat to circulation, of what is identified as "unpassable."

Notes

Research for this essay was supported by an NEH Summer Stipend and a Bowdoin College Kenan Fellowship.

1. Although his thesis that the backlash against the Jewish Naturalization Act was less about anti-Semitism than it was about bitter party politics has been challenged by more recent scholars, Thomas W. Perry's *Public Opinion, Propaganda, and Politics in Eighteenth-Century England: A Study of the Jew Bill of 1753* (Cambridge, MA: Harvard University Press, 1962) remains the most thorough overview of the bill and its aftermath. For other insightful discussions of the bill that take issue with Perry, see Frank Felsenstein, *Anti-Semitic Stereotypes: A Paradigm of Otherness in English Popular Culture, 1660–1830* (Baltimore: Johns Hopkins University Press, 1995), 187–214; and James Shapiro, *Shakespeare and the Jews* (New York: Columbia University Press, 1996), 195–224.

2. Michael Ragussis, "Jews and Other 'Outlandish Englishmen': Ethnic Performance and the Invention of British Identity under the Georges," *Critical Inquiry* 26.4 (2000): 797.

3. Christopher Flint, "Speaking Objects: The Circulation of Stories in Eighteenth-Century Prose Fiction," *PMLA* 113.2 (1998): 212. A version of Flint's essay appears in this volume.

4. In addition to *Chrysal,* the eighteenth-century works that I include in this category, in order of publication, are: Charles Gildon, *The Golden Spy* (London, 1709); Joseph Addison, "Adventures of a Shilling," *Tatler* 249 (November 11, 1710); Richard Bathurst, [The Tale of a Counterfeit Half-Pence], *The Adventurer* 43 (April 3, 1753); Thomas Bridges, *Adventures of a Bank-Note* (London, 1770–71); *The Birmingham Counterfeit; or, Invisible Spectator* (London, 1772); Mr. Truelove [pseudo.], *The Adventures of a Silver Penny* (London, 1780); Helenus Scott, *The Adventures of a Rupee* (London, 1782); "R.J.," *The Adventures of a Silver Penny* (London, 1787); and *Argentum; or, Adventures of a Shilling* (London, 1794).

5. Thomas Bridges's banknote represents an anomalous case. Rather than being

stamped with a national character, the banknote is inscribed with a private identity. As the banknote explains, "The person that deposits cash for a bank-note may properly be called its father," and these fathers are "noblemen's stewards, placeman's gentlemen, city usurers, knowing stock-jobbers, bankers' clerks, and bishops' toll-gatherers" (1:5). The model of paternity operating here is also a model of authorship, and, indeed, the father of this particular banknote is a hack writer. For a discussion of the object narrative's relation to evolving anxieties about modern authorship, see Christopher Flint's essay in this volume.

6. Gildon, *Golden Spy,* 39.

7. Ibid., 40.

8. *The Tatler* 249 (November 11, 1710), ed. Donald F. Bond, 3 vols. (Oxford: Clarendon Press, 1987), 3:269–70. All subsequent quotations from this work are cited parenthetically.

9. Ben Jonson, *The Staple of News,* ed. Anthony Parr (Manchester, UK: Manchester University Press, 1988), 1.6.42, 2.2.12.

10. Anthony Parr, Introduction to Jonson, *The Staple of News,* 117 n. 11.

11. *The Adventures of a Silver Penny* (London, 1780), 9–10.

12. Alexander Pope, *Windsor-Forest,* in *Poetry and Prose of Alexander Pope,* ed. Aubrey Williams (Boston: Houghton Mifflin, 1969), lines 402, 408.

13. As the profile of King William reminds us, many of these British coins (legitimate and illegitimate) bear the images of foreign-born monarchs. In her discussion of the evolution of British nationalism, Linda Colley refers to the successions of William of Orange and George I as "successive acts of iconoclasm." For a sense of how such a break with the rules of dynastic succession could be reconciled with a sense of English nationalism, Colley turns to Henry St. John, Viscount Bolingbroke, who "argued that a [foreign] British monarch could still make himself the vital center of politics, the father of his people." In the words of Bolingbroke, "the spring from which this legal reverence . . . arises is national, not personal" (*Forging the Nation 1707–1837* [New Haven, CT: Yale University Press, 1992], 47). To take Colley's argument a bit further, we might say that it is not simply that an emerging English nationalism is *capable* of incorporating the foreign monarch into itself, but that it is partly the very foreignness of these monarchs that *necessitates* the construction of British nationalism.

14. Daniel Defoe, *The True-Born Englishman,* in *British Literature 1640–1789,* ed. Robert Demaria, Jr. (Oxford: Blackwell, 1996), 1.280, 1.317–18, 1.321–22.

15. Ibid., 1.116, 1.118–19.

16. Richard Bathurst, [The Tale of a Counterfeit Half-Pence], *The Adventurer* 43 (April 3, 1753): 255, 253. All subsequent quotations from this work are cited parenthetically.

17. John Styles, "'Our Traitorous Money Makers': The Yorkshire Coiners and the Law, 1760–83," in *An Ungovernable People: The English and their Law in the Seventeenth and Eighteenth Centuries,* ed. John Brewer and John Styles (London: Hutchinson, 1980), 173–74. Styles notes that visitors to England "found the plethora of false coin of all kinds worthy of special remark" (177). Further complicating any sense of a purely English currency, the insufficiency of gold coin was partially remedied by the circulation of Portuguese moidores as legal tender in England; by 1742 these foreign coins "were described as 'in great measure the current coin of the Kingdom'" (176).

18. Bathurst's false coin takes its place in a distinctly English tradition of defiant illegitimacy, which includes *King Lear* and Richard Savage's *The Bastard,* both of which make pointed use of the familiar metaphor between coining and biological reproduction. With only slight adjustment, Edmund's speech in Act I of King Lear could be applied to the counterfeit coin itself: "Wherefore base? / When my dimensions are as

well compact, / . . . and my shape as true, / As honest . . . issue? Why brand us / With base? with baseness?" (*King Lear,* 1.2.6–10).

19. Sidney Laman Blanchard, "Biography of a Bad Shilling," in Mary Poovey, *The Financial System in Nineteenth-Century Britain* (New York: Oxford University Press, 2003), 60. Subsequent quotations from this work are cited parenthetically in the text.

20. As Todd M. Endelman points out in his discussion of the association of Jews with distributing counterfeit coins, "the clustering of lower-class Jews in street trades, which required them to be constantly making change, was responsible for their notoriety in passing bad coins." He adds that this notoriety, at least until the final decades of the eighteenth century, seems to have been unfounded: "There were no convictions of Jews at the Old Bailey for any offences involving counterfeit coins, including their manufacture and distribution, before 1782." Beginning in the 1790s, however, Jewish fruit vendors "began to appear fairly regularly at the Old Bailey for passing bad coins" (*The Jews of Georgian England, 1714–1830: Tradition and Change in a Liberal Society* [Philadelphia: Jewish Publication Society of America, 1979], 207–8.)

21. In *A Collection of the Best Pieces in Prose and Verse Against the Naturalization of the Jews* (London, 1753), 46.

22. Quoted in Felsenstein, *Anti-Semitic Stereotypes,* 192.

23. Although the connotation of racial or ethnic impersonation may seem anachronistic, that "passing" could be employed in this sense as early as the beginning of the eighteenth century is clear from Joseph Addison's own use of it in the first number of *The Spectator* (March 1, 1711), when Mr. Spectator tells the reader that he "sometimes pass[es] for a *Jew* in the Assembly of Stock-Jobbers" (in Donald F. Bond, ed., *The Spectator,* 5 vols. [Oxford: Clarendon Press, 1965], 1:4 [emphasis in original]). For a discussion of the surprising frequency with which Gentile characters engage in the impersonation of Jews in the Georgian drama, see Ragussis, "Jews and Other 'Outlandish Englishmen,'" 792–93.

24. Charles Johnstone, *Chrysal; or, The Adventures of a Guinea,* 4 vols. (1760–65; New York: Garland, 1979), 1:69. Subsequent quotations from this work are cited parenthetically in the text.

25. J.E., *Some Considerations on the Naturalization of the Jews* (London, 1753), 6.

26. In *A Collection of the Best Pieces,* 43.

27. Shapiro, *Shakespeare and the Jews,* 197.

28. *A Modest Apology for the Citizens and Merchants of London, Who Petitioned the House of Commons Against Naturalizing the Jews* (London, 1753), 9.

29. *An Appeal to the Throne Against the Naturalization of the Jewish Nation, &c.* (London, 1753), 12–13. Subsequent quotations from this work are cited parenthetically in the text.

30. *The Case of the Jews Considered, With Regard to Trade, Commerce, Manufactures and Religion, &c.* (London, 1753), 10.

31. Shapiro, *Shakespeare and the Jews,* 99.

32. George Granville, *The Jew of Venice,* in *Six Restoration Adaptations of Shakespeare,* ed. Christopher Spencer (Urbana: University of Illinois Press, 1965), 29.

33. Ibid., 28.

34. In his invaluable discussion of the role Shylock played in opposition to the Jewish Naturalization Act literature, James Shapiro writes that just as "some of the darker currents of early modern English attitudes toward the Jews informed Shakespeare's *The Merchant of Venice,*" so, in the controversy over the Jewish Naturalization Act, when "these same cultural stereotypes were dusted off and tried out again on an English public," the authority of Shakespeare provided them with a "culturally sanctioned form." He continues: "Shakespeare, the national poet, and *The Merchant of Venice,* the best-

known English work about the Jews, provided confirmation of the insidious threat Jews posed to the economic, sexual, and religious life of the nation" (*Shakespeare and the Jews*, 199–200).

35. Quoted in the sketch of the author's life that prefaces the 1821 edition of *Chrysal* (London: Hector M'Lean). Modern critics have seen in this reference to real life the secret of *Chrysal*'s staggering popularity. As Ernest A. Baker writes, "A work professing to reveal political secrets and to give the seamy side of the life of the best abused men of the time was bound to be a popular success" (Introduction to *Chrysal; or, The Adventures of a Guinea,* by Charles Johnstone [n.p.: Library of Early Novelists, 1907], vi). Similarly, Michael Abraham Mandelkern remarks, "It is easy to discern exactly what the audience saw in the novel: it was widely read as a supposedly truthful account of the personal lives of some of the most famous people of the era." "The brilliant success of *Chrysal*," he adds, "was due to the lifelikeness of the portraiture and the sprinkling in of well-known incidents" (Introduction to *An Abridgement of Charles Johnstone's "Chrysal, or the Adventures of a Guinea" with Introduction and Annotation* [Ph.D. diss., City University of New York, 1996], viii).

36. Aileen Douglas, "Britannia's Rule and the It-Narrator," *Eighteenth-Century Fiction* 6.1 (1993): 68. (A version of Douglas's essay appears in this volume.) Not all of Johnstone's contemporary readers approved of this aspect of his novel. In August 1760, a critic for the *Monthly Review* expressed some reservations about Johnstone's representation of public figures: "we cannot but think the description he gives us, of some of the most distinguished characters of the age, too unfavourable for the truth." The objection was more pointed in the *Critical Review*'s assessment (in August 1765) of the expanded edition of the work:

> We can however by no means approve of this manner of writing, which was first introduced into the English language by the authoress of the Atalantis, to stigmatize the whig administration under Queen Anne. The true secret of its success lies in taking off some strong, noted, feature, which marks the person so as not to be mistaken; and then the author is at liberty to tack to it every circumstance of infamy and falshood, that can either gratify his own malice, or promote the sale of his work.

37. Douglas, "Britannia's Rule," 69.

38. Catherine Gallagher, *Nobody's Story: The Vanishing Acts of Women Writers in the Marketplace, 1670–1820* (Berkeley and Los Angeles, University of California Press, 1994), 125, 124.

39. This key is found in *An Olio of Bibliographical and Literary Anecdotes and Memoranda Original and Selected* (London, 1814), 13–21.

40. The officer who has staged this rescue explains that he was "informed, when he served in Poland, in his youth, that the Jews had a custom of stealing and sacrificing, or murdering infants, on the night when they celebrated their Passover" (2:163).

41. While *The Monthly Review* placed the blame for the work's pessimism with Johnstone's fellow man—"it is a reflection, melancholy as true, that those who by experience know the most of mankind, have the worst opinion of them"—a writer for the *Critical Review* insisted that Johnstone's monstrous depictions of human vice were a failure of the satirist's skill. When such representations "[exceed] what the utmost villainy can effect," the critic writes, "the satyrist loses his aim" (*Monthly Review* [August 1760]; *Critical Review* [May 1760]).

42. Malcolm Bosse, Introduction to *Chrysal* (New York: Garland, 1979), xxv.

43. Douglas, "Britannia's Rule," 78.

44. Baker, Introduction to *Chrysal,* xiv. According to Baker, the "one offence of Johnstone's that cannot be forgiven" is "his ribald attack upon [George] Whitefield": his

"lying but circumstantial account" of the great evangelist's history and character, he adds, "must have convinced ignorant readers that the saint was a hypocritical rogue." "A man with the journalistic art of relating as fact the things he wants believed, with very little conscience," Baker continues, "Johnstone produced, in spite of his excesses, or by reason of them, one of the most damaging indictments of the public men he hated that was ever used in political warfare" (xiv). This personal libel exercises Baker in a way that the group libel does not.

45. Hillel J. Kieval, "Representation and Knowledge in Medieval and Modern Accounts of Jewish Ritual Murder," *Jewish Social Studies* 1.1 (1994): 54. Endelman's remarks on the blood libel follow this pattern of reading its appearance as the echo of an essentially medieval pathology: "To discover the survival of medieval beliefs about the Jews well into the eighteenth century comes at first as something of a shock. The Georgian period, with its calm veneer of political stability and its apparent high regard for rationality, would seem to be an incongruous setting for the blood libel . . . and other medieval superstitions . . . Yet, more than a few otherwise sensible men, most of whom were adherents of the High Church party, continued to hold beliefs about the Jews that were in no significant way different from those held several centuries before" (*Jews of Georgian England,* 87).

46. Felsenstein, *Anti-Semitic Stereotypes,* 2.

47. Ibid., 154.

48. Mandelkern, *Abridgement,* 17.

49. Archaicus [pseudo.], *Admonitions from Scriptures and History, from Religion and Common Prudence, Relating to the Jews* (London, 1753), 18.

50. Ibid., 24.

51. "Clipping" itself is just such a pun, also meaning "to embrace." Elizabethan and Jacobean writers made much of this double meaning. For example, the poet John Taylor writes, in the voice of a shilling, "In this I onely differ from a Whore, / We both have wicked followers great store: / The Whore they may kisse, clip and coll, and strip, / Me they may safely kisse, but never clip" (*A Shilling or, The Travailes of Twelve-Pence* [London, 1621], lines 559–62).

52. Among the many works that include female personifications of money are Robert Wilson's two plays, *The Three Ladies of London* and *The Three Lords and Three Ladies of London;* Richard Barnfield's long poem *The Encomion of Lady Pecunia;* the anonymous poem *The Massacre of Money;* Thomas Dekker's prose piece, *Worke for Armorours;* and Jonson's *Staple of News.* In the economic satires of the eighteenth century, it is not money but the figure of Credit that is represented as feminine.

53. As Shapiro remarks briefly in a note, "Not until the eighteenth century is a connection drawn between clipping coins and clipping foreskins" (*Shakespeare and the Jews,* 256 n. 40). The ubiquitous references to circumcision in the anti–Naturalization Act literature range from the constant use of the epithet "circumcisors" to castration fantasies. *The Craftsman* of July 7 wrote mockingly that "As it is apparent . . . that the christian religion has no longer a footing in this country, it may not be improper to repeal the sacramental test, and to substitute in its room the act of circumcision" (*A Collection of the Best Pieces,* 55). A series of satirical news items appeared in the *London Evening-Post* of August 9: "Mr. W—— the famous Jewish solicitor, being of a gross habit, and not a very sound constitution, (having been prevailed on by his Hebrew clients to undergo the ceremony of circumcision) . . . lies dangerously ill" (*A Collection of the Best Pieces,* 82). Another item indulges in a pun at the expense of a member of Parliament, who plans "to undergo the operation in time, that thus any wound or scar he should receive by the cicatrizing instrument, might have time to heal against the next general election, and himself be in a condition of standing again as one of the city members" (*A Collection of the Best Pieces,* 83).

54. Quoted in Felsenstein, *Anti-Semitic Stereotypes*, 40.

55. Quoted in Shapiro, *Shakespeare and the Jews*, 52.

56. As Jonathan Lamb observes of object narratives in general, it is frequently "the irregularities and suspensions of exchange," the "break[s] in the circuit of exchange," that enable the narrative itself, although "this break often annoys the things themselves, who seem unaware that it is the *sine qua non* of their speech" ("Modern Metamorphoses and Disgraceful Tales," *Critical Inquiry* 28.1 [2001]: 155).

57. Peregrine Oakley [pseudo.], *Aureus; or, The Life and Opinions of a Sovereign* (London, 1824), 14. Subsequent quotations from this work are cited parenthetically in the text.

58. Deidre Shauna Lynch, *The Economy of Character: Novels, Market Culture, and the Business of Inner Meaning* (Chicago: University of Chicago Press, 1998), 96.

Corkscrews and Courtesans: Sex and Death in Circulation Novels

Bonnie Blackwell

CRITICS IAN WATT, MARGARET ANNE DOODY, NANCY ARMSTRONG, Ruth Yeazell, and Josephine Donovan all account for the "rise of the novel" differently. Yet each confirms by his or her selection of paradigmatic novels that "the contemplation of character is the predominant pleasure in modern arts narrative."[1] Doody finds "literary self-consciousness" in Alexandrine narrative, and so disputes Watt's dating of the novel's rise but not the fundamental task of novels themselves, which is to convey the nuances of human psychology from author to reader.[2] The distinction Watt and Armstrong give to Richardson's *Pamela* (1740) in their studies is founded upon the pleasures afforded by examining Pamela's richly contradictory motives; when Armstrong contends that the modern subject is female, she does so because of women's passion for recording the "written representations of the self [that] allowed the modern individual to become an economic and psychological reality."[3] Donovan's interest in female reeducation in Mary Davys's *Reformed Coquet* (1724) and Charlotte Lennox's *The Female Quixote* (1752), and Yeazell's in the "modest woman's affinity for a private letter" in *Evelina* (1778), betray the same pleasure taken in the "sweeter banquet of the mind."[4] Indeed, when a novel such as *Roxana* (1724) or *Memoirs of a Woman of Pleasure* (1748–49) has a female first-person narrator, but does not provide rich opportunities for the examination of her motives or character, we decry the author's failure to capture female subjectivity authentically.[5] To authorize the intimate contract between narrator and reader, readers schooled in the Western apotheosis of the individual selected, out of a diverse tradition, novels like *Clarissa* (1748–49), which gratify our notions of the uniqueness of the individual. Such novels are particularly verbose on the subject of the interrelatedness of a woman's sexuality and her mortality: Clarissa is never more charmingly herself, Belmont claims, than in the death she engineers to atone for Lovelace's rape.[6]

The intimacy and immediacy of such writing is a recommendation for the reader, who finds companionship in the first-person narrator during the most solitary of activities, reading. Yet in savoring the novel of interiority, we overlook the pleasures of a prominent subgenre of novel written expressly to thwart eighteenth-century fiction's newly achieved illusion of psychological depth: novels with an object-narrator, which proliferated in France and England between 1730 and 1795. Rather than asserting the uniqueness of each character in his or her death, these novels focus on an inanimate object precisely because it outlives many owners. The object-narrator, often a mass-produced item such as a banknote, seems a paradigmatic example of asexual reproduction; yet, with remarkable consistency, the object-narrator serves as a surprising pretext for the exploration of female sexuality. In these novels, object-narrators consistently juxtapose their own circulation with that of a woman, who, by dispersing her favors among many men—usually the owners of the object-narrator—shortens her life and wastes her fragile beauty. The resiliency of the object-narrator is captured in its ability to recover from reversals; often it holds hostage the reincarnated spirit of a human (usually male) who will endure many more miniature deaths. Its endurance throws into high relief the transitory nature of female value as both object and woman pass through the hands of many users. Ultimately, the object-narrator is both witness to and metonym for the waning market value of a woman once initiated into sexuality. The moral of these novels is that the "planned obsolescence" of commodities under capitalism is nowhere more poignant than in the ephemeral value of the female courtesan or streetwalker.

In a single generation, more than a dozen novels were written by as many different English authors to showcase inanimate, mechanical, or nonhuman principals; others treated an intangible concept, such as commonsense, as the hero; one even takes for a protagonist a piece of legislation, Hardwicke's 1753 Marriage Act, tracing the effects of that agent upon several human beings exactly as another object-narrator novel follows a pet or a snuffbox. Titles from this sequence include the anonymous *The Secret History of an Old Shoe* (1734) and *The Adventures of a Black Coat* (1750), Francis Coventry's *The History of Pompey the Little* (1751), John Shebbeare's *The Marriage Act. A Novel* (1754), Charles Johnstone's *Chrysal; or, The Adventures of a Guinea* (1760), Montagu Lawrence's *The Life and Adventures of Common Sense: An Historical Allegory* (1769), Tobias Smollett's *The History and Adventures of an Atom* (1769), Thomas Bridges's *The Adventures of a Bank-Note* (1770–71), the anonymous *The Adventures of a Cork-Screw* (1775), M. Truelove's *Adventures of a Silver Penny* (1780), Mary Ann Kilner's *The Adventures of a Pincushion* (1780?) and *Memoirs of a Peg-Top* (1785), and the anonymous *Argal; or the Silver Devil, being the Adventures of an Evil Spirit* (1794). John Kidgell's

The Card (1755) masquerades as a novel with an inanimate protagonist, but the allegorical comparison of commodity and subjectivity is limited to a close reading of the frontispiece—a playing card. Despite its deviation from the form, *The Card*'s ruse is an indicator of the marketability of the object-narrated novel at mid-century.

England's publication boom in object-novels was matched by an attendant fad in France, where the literary caprice of the object-narrator also thumbed its nose at detailed portraits of subjectivity in, for example, Rousseau's *La Nouvelle Héloïse* (1761). In one French permutation of the craze, a lady's fan relates the adventures of her owner in *Mercure de France* (1755); in another, a pair of stoves discourse knowledgeably on human behavior in *Entretiens des cheminées de Paris, ouvrage rempli de caracteres vrais et fidellement copiez d'après les originaux* (1736).[7] Like its predecessor, Cervantes' *El Coloquio de dos Perros* (c. 1604), in which two dogs discuss such human traits as philosophizing, gossiping, and hypocrisy, *Entretiens* had recourse to intimate domestic observers to explain human frailty. Unlike the stoves, Cervantes' dogs use the doctrine of reincarnation to explain the presence of human subjectivity, and the related propensities of speech and storytelling, in the nonhuman protagonist who tells the tale. Reincarnation enables the satire of Tobias Smollett's *The History and Adventures of an Atom* (1769), an elaborate allegory for George III's court narrated by an atom who undergoes "a great number of vicissitudes" to be incarnated as a grain of rice, a bit of duck, and the cell contributed by Ephraim Peacock to make his son Nathaniel, who records the story. Mainly, though, the atom resides in the perineum of "Fika-Kaka," a Japanese minister meant to represent Thomas Pelham-Holles, first lord of the Treasury from 1754–56 and 1757–62. From this privileged position, the atom is able to see all the rites of "osculation *a posteriori*" by which corrupt government operates.[8]

No one devoted more care to reincarnation as a narrative pretext for the object-narrator than Claude Prosper Crébillon fils in his novel *Le Sopha* (1740). *Le Sopha* was the French nouvelle with an object-narrator that English contemporaries could readily obtain; Horace Walpole awaited *Le Sopha* anxiously and received it joyfully in February 1742, when Lord Chesterfield imported three hundred copies into England and Walpole was at last able to read this tale, which he declared "admirable."[9] *Le Sopha* updates *A Thousand and One Arabian Nights* with "such a story as Scheherazade would tell" if she were still alive, and if she were more interested in interior décor than interiority.[10] *Le Sopha* is a satire on the war between the sexes, narrated by Amanzei, a man who spent many years living as a series of serviceable divans (his spirit occasionally moved from house to house) upon which Ottoman concubines practiced their trade. As Mimi Hellman notes, eyewitness accounts are a normal thing upon which to base one's authority as a narrator, but being present as a sofa is not.[11] The virtue of being a sofa is that the inanimate position allows the reader a complete physical intimacy akin to that of a servant: "as few men are heroes to their valets, so may I safely affirm that few women are saints to their sofas" (26).

Pamela's letters bewitched Mr. B with emotional and intellectual intimacy without physical possession, in a striking reversal of the Squire's previous sexual relationships with women.[12] *Le Sopha* allows the reader physical closeness with the women of the tale, but not an entrée into female mental solitude wherein we could empathize with their secret hopes and fears. Proximity without intimacy will, *Le Sopha* proclaims, render a woman as charmless as Pamela's letters made her desirable. *Le Sopha* corroborates what Jonathan Swift never tired of asserting about women: that confidential access to their persons and dressing rooms will render a man impotent with rage and disgust.[13] Amanzei claims that his imprisonment in a sofa is a punishment for his lack of self-discipline during his human life, but the excuse is a flimsy one: we see through a series of anecdotes of women being caught and beaten for infidelity that the true purpose of the story is to assert the uniformly unchaste and perfidious nature of women.

In her essay on *Le Sopha,* Mimi Hellman writes that in this French it-novel, the "relationship between furniture and people is one of both enticement and uneasiness. The sofa is sumptuous and convenient, perpetually able to receive the body and to display it to advantage. At the same time, however, it is an agent of surveillance, as ready to discern the flaws of its users as it is able to enhance their charms."[14] While Hellman convincingly argues that objects of interior décor operated like "vigilant, other-oriented individuals" able to "anticipate and accommodate flexibly the terms of every situation" in eighteenth-century France, what interests me is that the language of objects (decoration, luxury, consumption) employed both by Hellman and by authors of English novels with object-narrators persistently points to the homology between the object-narrator and the sexually exploited female body.[15] The body of the female courtesan or streetwalker is also "sumptuous and convenient"; as Bernard Mandeville writes in *A Modest Defense of the Publick Stews* (1724), some women "have shook off all Pretence to Modesty" and "more or less, profess themselves always in a Readiness to be enjoy'd"—that is, are no more judicious or discriminating than a sofa.[16] Mandeville's text, like the it-novels, explores the possibility for exploiting the willing self-effacement of females in the marketplace. The most "vigilant, other-oriented individuals," then, are successfully socialized women. The central contradiction of female lives explored by the it-narrative is how women may remain uniformly yielding and compliant so that they might be patient, submissive mothers and wives, yet be prevented from surrendering their power to the wrong owners. So while Hellman shows that "objects were exemplary social actors" in eighteenth-century décor, my reading of the it-novel explains how women were exemplary social objects, and how transforming objects into actors and narrators throws that fact into high relief.[17]

Despite their currency in the period, such works have received scant critical attention because we have not been able to satiate our modern tastes for character development in their breakneck accounts of anecdotal meetings and dizzying exchanges: some of the agents pass through dozens of owners' hands in their romps, which may take as many as four volumes to accomplish. Yet, as I propose to demonstrate, the implicit goal of novels narrated by objects is shaping "an ideal woman out of the stuff of novels."[18] Though it does not explore the psychology of the narrator itself, the circulation novel presents a powerful cautionary tale about the dangers of female sexual autonomy. Object-narrators urge the female reader not to avoid her objectification by men, which appears as an inexorable fact of life, but to take care to be possessed by only one male so as to assure her longevity and safekeeping.

I
Why Male Object-Narrators Should Be Read as Female

Nancy Armstrong writes, "[Robinson] Crusoe was more female . . . than either Roxana or Moll" (16); I contend that Pompey the Little, a male Bologna Spaniel, is more female than all three. In his early life, Pompey, who is a gift to an Englishman from his favorite Italian courtesan, enjoys the biological prerogatives of a male with no responsibility for his abundant sexual appetites: his youth in the house of Lady Tempest in London is marked by "gallantries" in which he fathers some "very pretty puppies"; the affair is even immortalized in an epistolary correspondence (written by his owner), so that it leaves a literary record, like a proper eighteenth-century romance.[19] Strikingly, however, once his owner Lady Tempest is taken with a sexual distemper and visited by all the commiserating ladies of London who had themselves "contracted a stain," Pompey's sexual exploits as a male are palpably at an end; thereafter, he functions in the text as a female picaroon along the lines of Moll or Roxana (54). Transformed by female sexual misconduct into a hapless victim of men's desires, Pompey is taken to Cambridge by young Master Qualmsick, a carefree student (whose name is a memento of his mother's hypochondria). While in Cambridge, Pompey befriends all the prostitutes Mr. Qualmsick frequents, such as "the three Miss Higginses, whose Mother kept the Sun Tavern; Miss Polly Jackson, a Baker's Daughter; the celebrated Fanny Hill, sole Heiress of a Taylor, and Miss Jenny of the Coffee-house" (235). He also is pressed into service to impersonate the natural child of Betty Trollop, and in that guise is laid at the doorstep of the College's Master of Arts, Mr. Williams (236–39). In addition to being coddled and fussed over by the Cambridge harlots, Pompey embodies their fleshy crimes in a prank that intimates how pervasive whoring is among even the most sober of the college.

Though petted and spoiled like a kept woman, Pompey has a tendency to swap owners while wandering in the streets or the pleasure gardens at Vauxhall, a quality that evokes a common streetwalker more than a high-class courtesan. When former owner Lady Tempest finds Pompey in St. James's Mall at precisely the spot where she lost him eight years before, she and the dog's present owner have a brief tussle, which more than hints that the actual topic is female sexual virtue, to which neither interlocutor has a very strong claim. First, Lady Tempest asserts that she remembers losing this dog eight years before, and her rival asserts that " 'tis impossible to remember a Dog after eight Years absence." Lady Tempest counters,

> "I protest, my Dear, I know not what Sort of a Memory you may be blest with, but really, I can remember Things of a much longer Date; and as a fresh Instance of my Memory, I think, my Dear, I remember you representing the Character of a young Lady for near these twenty Years about Town." "Madam," returned the Lady of inferior Rank, now inflamed with the highest Indignation; "you may remember yourself, Madam, representing a much worse Character, Madam, for a greater Number of Years. It would be well, Madam, if your Memory was not altogether so good, Madam, unless your Actions were better." (257)

Pompey is not merely a beloved object for women to fight over: he is an emblem for the tractability of females everywhere, and represents their tendency to be lead into precisely the kind of scandalous life that Lady Tempest embodies as an antiquated courtesan of London. When the two women go to court to determine rightful ownership of the dog, the judge rules that there is nothing "peculiar" in the loyalty of dogs that would warrant such legal action. A dog is certainly property, the judge says, based upon the amount of care and love invested in the creature by the human owner. Women, too, had the legal status of property in the courts. Yet, since the affection men extend to their pets and their whores is not strictly reciprocated, in the judge's reckoning, there is no guarantee that a domesticated dog or a kept woman feels obligated to one master. Indeed, he says, "their prodigious Attachment to Man inclines them to follow any body that calls them, and that makes it difficult to fix a theft . . . a Dog be of a *following Nature,* as I observed, and may be sometimes tempted, and seduced, and inveigled away in such a Manner, as makes it difficult . . . to fix a Theft on the person seducing" (263, emphasis original). There can scarcely be any doubt that the real subtext here is female sexual inconstancy, which Pompey externalizes for his rival owners, in effect manifesting their own sexual histories in miniature. Occasionally, *Pompey the Little*'s narrator, who is not the dog himself but an omniscient male voice, will warn female readers against giving their favors and indulgence to "ungrateful wretches" who will "shew no Mercy to your slightest Failings, but expose and ridicule your Weakness in Ale-houses, Nine-pin-alleys, Gin-shops, Cellars, and every other Place of Rendezvous" (51). The analogy between object and woman persistently illustrates that object-status and submission to ownership is the lot of women, but that possession by "insolent, brutal, ungenerous Rascals" degrades a woman forever.

The Adventures of a Black Coat (1750) replicates the same moral exhortation for women—possessed you must be, but take care to have a genteel buyer—but changes the vehicle from a pet to a shopworn garment. This novel depicts the short, desolate life of a harlot, represented metonymically by a formal frock coat that has been worn by so many strange men that now no one wants to be seen in it. The tale opens with a speaking coat unhappily lodged in a wardrobe within the shop of a tallyman, a merchant who buys, sells, and rents used clothing. The setting amidst rented clothing evokes prostitution immediately, since eighteenth-century traffics in used clothing and used bodies were inextricable. Via the tallymen, prostitutes could cheaply obtain fashions to help them ply their trade; via light-fingered jilts who picked men's pockets during intercourse, tallymen had access to a steady supply of gentlemen's watches, handkerchiefs, and linens. (In *The Beggar's Opera* [1723] Miss Diana Trapes, the tally-woman whose name indicates her origins as a streetwalker or "traipse," keeps good shoes and fine damask dresses to "trick out young ladies, upon their going into keeping."[20]) Given the well-known interdependency of tallymen and harlots in the eighteenth century, the clothes shop becomes an acceptable way to speak figuratively about brothels and whores, all without an improper or explicit word ever appearing on the page.

"Sable," our narrator, is a worn-out black coat of passé design who addresses the entire narrative to a fresh white coat of a more modish cut. The latter's appearance in the clothespress rings the death-knell for the aged Sable: "Thy presence, Spark, warns me of my approaching dissolution; but when I cast a retrospect over my former life, and behold thy native purity and unblemished form, I cannot but pity the many and various misfortunes thou art, in all probability, heir to."[21] Though Sable addresses White as "Spark," a name for a male lover, the novel repeatedly underscores the feminized predicament of garments rented by men. Their ability to circulate is based upon their attractiveness, their apparent newness, however feigned with dyes and fierce brushing, and their serviceability. Sable's lesson for White is that even the most crisp and attractive will be discarded without a thought after a few uses. This life of contingency, circulation, and neglect is a female one.

In the pornographic subtext of *The Adventures of a Black Coat,* Sable is a sober version of the hackneyed prostitute Phoebe in *Memoirs of a Woman of Pleasure,* whose role is to instruct a novice Fanny Hill in the skin trade; however, Sable's lecture reveals the regrettable consequences rather than the potential pleasure of sex work. In this novelistic convention, the novice is nothing less than the reader within the text, whose objections are smoothed over by the narrator's skillful handling of the embedded reader. The white coat achieves absorption of the moral instantly, even before hearing the narration of Sable's life history. Indeed, Sable's appearance is more instructive for the reader-within-the-text than her story: "when I behold thy queer shape and rustic aspect, I cannot but return thy pity, and offer up my prayers against longevity" (5). Given James Boswell's estimation that the life span of a London streetwalker was approximately two years from her first going on the town until disease, violence, or execution ended her life, the white coat's plea for a brief life seems both realistic and prescient.[22]

The Adventures of a Black Coat allegorizes not just any woman long on the town, but obliquely records an often forgotten segment of the British population: African, Afro-British, and Afro-Caribbean prostitutes in eighteenth-century London. One of the two strongest cues to this tale's racial nuances is, of course, the name Sable, which anticipates Olaudah Equiano's phrase, "the sable females," whose sexual interest he is keen to attract, and the "sable race" whose wrongs his autobiography seeks to redress.[23] The other is Sable's London origins: it was made a mourning coat for a "commoner of distinguished abilities" to wear to Parliament and St. James's after the death of a Princess (7). St. James's court, Pall Mall, and Jermyn Street housed London's most select brothels, including highly specialized ones for exotic beauties. Sable's name and "birthplace" direct the reader's attention to London's entirely black bordellos, Black Harriot's and Ebony Bet's, located in Pall Mall's environs and known to cater to the nobility and especially to the House of Lords, at least twenty of whom were regular visitors who found "sable females" desirable and elusive.[24] In hinting delicately at a racial subtext for its object-narrator, *The Adventures of a Black Coat* anticipates the escaped slave narrative of *Pompey the Little;* since Pompey was the second most popular name given to male slaves by English owners of the eighteenth century, Pompey's wanderings and captures evoke an escaped slave narrative.[25] Indeed, like prostitutes, London's largely unacknowledged population of slaves and free blacks provides ample opportunities to explore the questions of ownership, circulation, and freedom into which the object-narrated novel delves.

From its origins in the glossier side of London prostitution, the coat passes to a domestic servant, who sells it to a merchant in Monmouth Street. Initially, Sable takes to this life of casual hire agreeably because it welcomes the fresh adventures temporary rentals by strangers afford: "Here properly I may say I began to exist; my heart dilated with joy at the prospect of seeing life, and associating with the various characters that visit this place" (8). Yet the rigors of enveloping so many new and unaccustomed male bodies quickly begin to wear Sable thin: "I was soon introduced to the class of *occasional gentlemen* each of whom I had the mortification to see frequently depart from our prison of dust and moths" (8). These gentlemen echo poignantly in the mind of the reader who is cognizant of a population of men who sampled a woman for a time, then dropped her, leaving her behind in a filthy "prison." On a more literal level, Sable appears to use "occasional gentlemen" to refer to the fine men's coats rented for special occasions from its own clothes-press, in keeping with the thinly held pretext that the men's clothes are themselves male. Sable worries that these other coats are being taken out more frequently; indeed Sable soon spends more time in the wardrobe than on the arm of some gallant, "many objecting to me on account of my size, which was then far above the common, tho' now, as you may see, below it, having lately been curtailed by the degrading scissors of a botcher and refused by more from my colour" (8). Sable has apparently been altered by a poor tailor, but the language of butchery and subsequent physical deterioration conjures prostitutes' injuries at the hands of doctors who performed dangerous abortions and venereal cures. These common wages of a strolling woman's trade are rendered visible and corporeal by the coat's ragged tail, where the remnants of many surgeries are visible to the world.

Sable is kept for a while by Teague, an Irish actor with broad shoulders and a bold, impertinent manner who stretched out other coats trying to find one that would be equal to his "Herculean breadth." On his back, Sable predicts whippings and soakings in ponds, anxieties that gloss a common eighteenth-century prejudice that Irishmen were extremely violent toward prostitutes and mistresses.[26] The "Hibernian Roscius" sells Sable back to the tallyman after his ambitions to go on the stage are thwarted by a stage manager at the Drury Lane Theater (10). When a fine gentleman comes to try Sable on, Sable has been stretched out of shape by Teague's manly form. It wishes to conceal this distortion so that it might go back into keeping and escape a life of casual renting: "I was fearful of being somewhat too large, but the desire I had to accompany this agreeable youth, made me contract every thread to clasp him; and I so far succeeded that he seemed equally pleased with me as I with him" (11). The language of constriction and pleasure echoes the conventions of mid-century pornographic novels, and would be recognized by worldly readers as consonant with prejudices that experienced women's vaginas were stretched out by intercourse; plucky Sable heroically strives to meet these desires by mimicking constriction during intercourse to please her renter. The convention of contraction and constriction during intercourse is quite rife in *Memoirs of a Woman of Pleasure,* and in the genre of whore's biography more generally. In Charles Walker's biography of Sally Salisbury, one whore is ambivalently celebrated for retaining her narrow passage after many years in the profession, to the point where she actually imperils the men who value her taut interior muscles: "She was most remarkable for the Elasticity of her Parts, and a Certain Spring in her Motion, which endangered the Rider."[27]

In a final gesture towards *The Adventures of a Black Coat*'s true subtext as a demimondaine tale, Sable ends life as a doctor's coat in the salivation wards at St. Thomas's hospital in Southwark (89). Southwark, an area near London Bridge notorious for cheap, seedy brothels, was also home to a charity hospital for poor women. A salivation ward takes its name from the dangerous and debilitating mercury treatments for venereal disease, which produced massive amounts of saliva; indeed, the spitting of liters of fluid from the mouth, though really just a symptom of mercury poisoning, was taken to be a sign of progress against the disease.[28] Upon the back of the Doctor, Sable sees in the salivation wards a young woman named Susan Sirloin, whom the coat encountered in a previous incarnation as a butcher's daughter who was prone to romantic fancies (89). If Sable is a worn-out garment, Susan Sirloin is a piece of meat too long on the market that now turns people's stomachs; her father's profession as a butcher both gives professional credence to the name and refers back to the trauma of Sable's own botched surgery which, in turn, predicts the fate of young Susan here in the venereal ward. Sable is prevented from concluding its tale with a moral since White (the auditor coat) is abruptly rented by another man, a circumstance which "leaves Sable's last sentence broken [off]" (90). The reader is left to stitch together the moral from Sable's patchwork of suggestive homologies between the sexual woman and the frayed garment.

Exchange woman for coat, and the meaning is clear: A young woman begins life on the town as a courtesan operating in the toniest region of St. James's court, passes through the hands of abusive renters, and ends her days in a venereal hospital south of London Bridge, where she takes a last look at the other tragic women who have followed her path.

As the interlocutor coat in *The Adventures of a Black Coat* indicates, the reader-within-the-text is a convention that comes early to the novel of circulation; already an experimental form, the it-novel integrated other provisional techniques into its web of artifice. *The Secret History of an Old Shoe* (1734) is the object-narrator novel in its embryonic stages, a hybrid of verse and prose. In this case, the object's biography is told in verse, interspersed with the prosing interruptions of the embedded reader, whose banal expectations from narrative are matched by his unremarkable diction. This reader-within-the-text claims not to understand the new convention of an inanimate protagonist, and querulously asks for the heroic men of romance and epic whose qualities were circumscribed but inspiring. The narrator, who is the implied author rather than the object, defends the choice of the Old Shoe as central protagonist, "Despising all the idle Cant / Of Criticks learn'd or ignorant." Conceding that his it-novel's "Theme [is] a Scandal to the Muses," the author proclaims that the merit of the tale is that it as odd as it is true, "the story of a good old Shoe."[29]

The shoe is defended from critics who would call it an insipid or ill-conceived protagonist. The implied author insists that utter triviality, not pedigree, makes this consumer object worth celebrating. Indeed, this insistence upon the ubiquitous, unremarkable nature of the protagonist is one of the key features within the circulation novel symbolizing its true subject, the sex worker. The novel of interiority insists upon the uniqueness of Pamela, Clarissa, and Evelina, but the it-novel explores the lives of women who are as available and cheap as rented clothes:

'Tis not a Shoe was ever wore
By Saint or Pilgrim heretofore;
Nor Relick fetch'd from Holy Place,
Imparting mere mysterious Grace,
Nor Kin at all that we can guess
To Slipper of his Holiness.
It is not, as I said before,
A shoe that Martyr ever wore;
Nor Wooden Shoe, that Type exotick
Of Tyranny and Pow'r Despotick;
Nor do Historians mention whether
It is of red, or sable Leather;

A dancing, or a pushing Shoe,
At Paris made, or by Carpue;
Or fashioned to relieve the Gout,
Or wore by Lord, or Lady; or;
Or grac'd the foot of neat Jane Shore,
Or some more clumsy modern whore.

(7)

Despite the implied author's claim not to know the provenance of the shoe, it does not take long for the object to become aligned with women of imperiled virtue, from the she-tragedy heroine Jane Shore to the common-as-muck strolling woman of the night. Soon the story comes to focus upon a woman named Sweetissa, who has just "Learnt, like her Mother, th'ancient Knack, / Of gently falling on her Back" (9). The implied author does not blame Sweetissa for giving up her virtue, but rather wonders that she kept it as long as she did, considering where she lived: "She breathes that fatal Clime to Maids, / To widows, wives, and Husband's heads, / Where Virtue takes too slender Root / To yield a very lasting Fruit, / And is more difficult to Rear / [Than] Melons near the frozen Bear" (9–10). At this point, the obstreperous embedded reader clamors to know the name of this region so inimical to female virtue, and is rewarded with the key to the riddle: the court of St. James and the nearby Pall Mall, which "has so peculiar a Houtgout in it . . . that the Flavour of Venery is to be smelt in every Street by the most Indifferent Odorist" (10). Pall Mall is, of course, the very place where Sable the Black Coat began her career. In this neighborhood,

This Bauble, or this common Bubble
That gives Mankind such Plague and Trouble
This fleeting Thing, call'd Maiden-Head,
That in one short-lived Minute's fled
Like other Merchandise was sold
And barter'd for as Statesmen's gold,
For not the anxious Care of State,
Sworn enemy to amorous Heat,
Had Power to quell, so fierce a Flame,
What some th'unruly Member name.

(10)

The passage on female virtue conjures two other crucial cultural icons of the previous decade, the 1720s: one is the South-Sea Bubble, and the other is *The Beggar's Opera,* where a duet between Lucy Lockit and Polly Peachum—"I'm bubbled, I'm troubled, bamboozled and bit!"—provides the rhymes and alliterations of this riddle on Maidenhead.

Both *The Beggar's Opera* and *The Secret History of an Old Shoe* satirize the transitory nature of value, comparing female virtue to junk bonds or the promises of highwaymen: none of the three is backed by anything permanent or reliable.

Eventually, Sweetissa is admitted to be the daughter of a man named Skirrus, a fake Latinate tag that strongly hints that Sweetissa may represent Maria Skerrit, an actress and the acknowledged mistress of Robert Walpole for many years at the time of the *Old Shoe*'s publication. When Sire Skirrus dies, his "concerning Daughter [. . .] Took his fate, / As greedy Fishes do to a Bait, / She view'd the Moment he departed / With less concern than if he'd farted. / No vulgar filial Tears she paid / The ghostly, graceless Parent-shade" (12). Indeed, his passing conveniently allows Sweetissa to "Wh— —e without control / And make this prove Occasion lucky / To draw more largely on her Ducky" (13). Sweetissa goes into the keeping of an "am'rous Knight" and simultaneously draws "Sappho, chief of Female Friends" into her "snare of Lewdness." Indeed, the author speculates that Sweetissa may truly be a sapphist herself, since she experiences shame in front of women when having bodily functions which she does not scruple to conceal from her male lovers (14). Alternating between Sappho and the Knight, dismissing one to make "the beast with two backs" with the other, Sweetissa bears the Knight's child and receives a settlement paid "upon the convex of her bum" (19). The caviling embedded reader becomes restive with all this loose talk, though the author points out that he is merely quoting the great Shakespeare. The reader, who never endorsed the use of a shoe as the protagonist, now claims to be tired of waiting for the return of the shoe to the narrative. Finally, the tale returns to where it began, as we are told that the shoe's role in the story was to hide his fortune from Sweetissa and other women making claims on his fortune: the Knight "pack'd [his] Jewels and the Cash, / Together, like so much Trash, / Then pent them up in Hugger-mugger, / In private Hole to lye the Snugger" (22). The next day the servants are called and "the Cavity is over-haul'd, / When lo! The Treasure shews to View, / Entrenched within the good old Shoe" (22). Though the Knight chooses the hiding place of the shoe to protect his wealth from paternity claims such as Sweetissa's, the shabby and discarded whore is continually equated with the depreciated old shoe, so that the kept woman of greedy appetites comes to emblematize the "private hole" where a man's wealth lies snugly. The final irony, then, of *The Secret History of an Old Shoe* is that a man's efforts to protect his fortune from his whores ends in the concentration of all his wealth in their hands and bodies, in retribution for *his* body leaving its imprint upon the object he repeatedly occupied for his own pleasure.

In *The Adventures of a Cork-Screw,* our corkscrew-cum-narrator gives away the telltale analogy between kept woman and coveted commodity when he writes of Mrs. Lucy Lightairs, in whose possession he found himself prior to being stolen by her chambermaid:

> The death of her keeper a short time afterwards left her at liberty again, and every idea of virtue now obliterated, she pursued the path she had entered into without regret, and was at different times the property of the peer, the squire, the tradesman and others. We shall not follow her thro' the different scenes she passed through while with them, only observe, that when she caught the eye of a collegian she was in the possession of a noted jockey, who had left her at the races, to find her way up to town by herself.[30]

Mrs. Lucy, like the corkscrew, cannot travel unless someone deigns to pick her up and use her for the very thing she was made for: a courtesan, like a corkscrew, is for screwing. The very next chapter begins with the corkscrew detailing "the many different hands I passed through" (77); an earlier one ends, "it was about this time when I came into his possession, when this respectable nobleman was using his utmost influence to have a seat in the senate, appointed to be the guardian over a nation, when he had not sufficient prudence nor resolution to govern himself. Let us now quit this titled villain, and jog on with my new master to college" (34). The same language is used for corkscrew and courtesan (possession, passed through, property). There is occasion to examine the motives and feelings of neither corkscrew nor courtesan, but the reader is invited to contemplate the characters of the men who wish to own and use the corkscrew.

In *The Adventures of a Bank-Note,* our narrator is "born" to a bachelor poet, but is soon paid as reparation to the family of a greensick girl by the doctor who impregnated her to cure her lovesick distemper. The banknote then resides "in the torrid zone" of the widowed mother's thighs by day and in a "box" under her bed with tallow candles and snuff by night. Soon enough the daughter recovers from her confinement and marries, whereupon he is tucked between her breasts as a wedding present:

> What a change was here! O reader, think (if thou hast any sensation) of my happy situation! Dissolv'd in pleasure, I lay gasping and panting like a great carp in a fishmonger's basket, placed in a vale between two snowy mountains. I kept alternately surveying the sides, quite up to the summit; and then casting my eyes down to the valley that leads to ———. But I think some poet has described it better than I can: I will give you the words as nigh as I can recollect:

> Betwixt those hills a milky way there leads,
> Not to the heav'ns nor yet th' Elysian meads;
> But here's a path to greater pleasures shewn,
> For which the Gods have oft forsook their own.

> Whilst I was enjoying a situation great Jove himself would envy (was he alive now) would you think it possible that I could fish up something to be discontented as. Now whether you think it possible or not, I must tell you that I was very much discontented, because Nature had not formed my optics in such a manner as to look nine ways at thrice; and then whilst I was enjoying one part, I need not lose sight of the other; for want of which qualification I pined in the midst of plenty.[31]

This note is evidently printed with eyes, and, more amazingly, endowed with rich tactile sensations, so much so that he can accuse the reader of being insensate in comparison. He is also provided with a rich capacity for irony, since he manages both to describe the young woman as a pure and unspoiled natural wonder (snowy, Elysian) and to hint elliptically at baser terms of comparison (carp, fish) for her nether regions, where he longs to travel. The desire to consume luxury goods may be ingrained in human nature, but *The Adventures of a Bank-Note* suggests that the desire for lush consumer bodies may also be natural to banknotes and the commodities they may purchase. According to circulation novels, commodities want expensive, unattainable consumers, just as consumers want luxury goods. The anxiety *The Adventures of a Bank-Note* and other object-narrated texts manifest is a distinctly male one, that whores and courtesans may be critical of men's flaws and may prefer younger, wealthier, or more attractive purchasers. As these object-narrators cast a discerning eye over prospective owners to see if they are worth going home with, the one-sided nature of commodity fetishism and the sexual double standard are both interrogated, to the discomfort of male purchasers.

In the preface to *The Birth of a Consumer Society,* Neil McKendrick writes of the "consumer revolution" in eighteenth-century England, wherein men and women of all classes came to enjoy acquiring material possessions of a type and scale only afforded to the rich in earlier generations.[32] In circulation novels, commodities return the compliment and set out to acquire owners at a rapid rate. Like the people who purchase them, these object-narrators have short attention spans and a boundless appetite for variety. These objects flit from one owner to the other with no regard for the contract of purchase; they wander away in public parks, are left behind in brothels and inns, and secrete themselves in babies' bassinets, in the folds on carriage seats, in the cleavage of heaving bosoms, or between sweaty thighs. The locations continually underscore their relationship to female sexual commodification. The proliferation of object-novels in which the object is equated with the body of a prostitute betrays reservoirs of male anxiety about women's ability, as objectified possessions, to retain preferences and prejudices that ultimately render them knowing consumers of men. The accretive narration that builds up around a much exchanged object further bespeaks male uneasiness about the storage of sexual narratives and even male fluids in the body of a promiscuous woman. This anxiety must be considered in the context of metaphoric representations of vaginas as "city sewers" in Swift and other misogynists of the 1720s and '30s, as well as the medical authority of the day which asserted that women retained fluids and "impressions" of all the men they had known carnally, so that they could years later give birth to a child that resembled their first seducer. Novels narrated by objects exorcise male anxieties about their own pleasures in objectifying women, reenacting possession and circulation in a cathartic narrative sequence.

II
THE REINCARNATION OF OBJECT-NOVELS AS JUVENILIA

Given the consistently sexual and illicit nature of many it-novels, it may surprise some readers to learn that abruptly at the end of the eighteenth century, the subgenre was miraculously repackaged as children's literature, a guise it would maintain throughout the nineteenth and early twentieth centuries. This generic reworking was largely owing to the efforts of one woman, Mary Ann Kilner, who, with her sister-in-law Dorothy Kilner, built a considerable empire in adolescent fiction in the last decades of the eighteenth century. After Mrs. Kilner's *The Adventures of a Pincushion* and *The Memoirs of a Peg-Top* (both 1780s), it-novels become uniformly slim duodecimo volumes imbued with simple language and a grave concern for avoiding the imputation of unrealistic narrative structures. Gone are the three-volume romps through bordellos and taverns; gone is the jolly disregard for verisimilitude, evident in an inanimate object's ability to speak directly to humans or keep a minute-by-minute diary. Kilner's pincushion, by contrast, lies beside a pen for several weeks, unable to avail herself of the implement or ask a human to write her story, since "my language can only be understood by things as inanimate as myself." The pen is the implicit agent of the tale's transmission, since it "engaged to present these memoirs to the world, if it ever should be employed by the hand of kindness to rescue my name from oblivion."[33]

Mary Ann Kilner sets an important precedent of asserting the "make-believe" of the object-narrator's loquacity and literacy, one followed scrupulously by later it-novels. Kilner is, moreover, explicit about her wish to distance her project from the social satire of the earlier object-narrator novels:

> The pointed satire of ridicule, which could perhaps have given a zest to those scenes in which the subject of these papers was engaged, was not, in the opinion of the writer, at all proper for these readers for whom it was solely designed . . . Assuming, therefore, the title of an Historian, or Biographer, I shall take the liberty to speak for myself, and tell you what I saw and heard in the character of a Pincushion. Perhaps you never thought that such things as are inanimate could be sensible of anything which happens, as they can neither hear, see, nor understand; and, as I would not willingly mislead your judgment, I would, previous to your reading this work, inform you, that it is to be understood as an imaginary tale; . . . To use your own style, and adopt your own manner of speaking, therefore, you must imagine that a Pincushion is now *making believe* to address you, and to recite a number of little events, some of which really happened, and others might happen with great probability. (9–10)

This is sober stuff, intended to mark off the terrain of it-novels as the imaginary world of the playroom, to be kept within strict boundaries so that the novel's more pervasive illusions of probability and realism will win the day.

The element of the it-novel that clearly was "proper for the persons for whom it was designed," in Mrs. Kilner's estimation, was the transformation of sexual narratives into stories of commodity fetishism. For example, her pincushion, dropped inadvertently and pushed by a playful kitten under a bookcase, laments its lack of social life under the furniture in a way that alludes to young women's dangerous desires to bask in male attention in public places like balls and promenades: "Long have I remained in this dull state of obscurity and confinement [longing] to rescue my name from oblivion . . . Thought I, it is very hard that a pincushion so new, so clean, and so beautiful, that might have a thousand opportunities of seeing the different manners of mankind, should be thus secluded from company" (39–40). Beautiful young women are plainly meant to identify with the trapped pincushion and to see their social isolation as a beneficial imposition to keep them safe. Cheerful resignation to such retirement is recommended: "Though I fretted and fumed every day at my unfortunate condition, I never found it was at all improved by it, or that my ill humour in the least degree made me happier, or assisted my escape" (41). The pincushion is eventually rescued by movers and given to a housekeeper's daughter, who washes it in soapy water and renews it. Because it was sullied by neglect, not circulation, the pincushion stands for a lonely spinster who is redeemable, rather than a prostitute whose life cannot be salvaged. The preventive nature of the it-novel is now effectively transferred from reader (once spared a life of degradation by reading the cautionary tale) to object-narrator (now saved from abuse itself and left to contemplate alternate narratives rather than to enact them for our edification).

In *Memoirs of a Peg-Top,* the eponymous object is not only an inanimate narrator, but a keen reader of other such tales. It decides one morning when left upon a writing desk that if "a Pincushion, a Dog, a Half-Penny, and a Bank-note have each a history of their adventures" then it might as well recollect the pleasing scenes of its life.[34] This top, purchased by a widow for her ten-year-old son Henry as a consolation for sending him to boarding school, departs from the pattern of representing female sexual fragility. Instead, the top, a boy's toy, is quickly established as a penis substitute, so that playing with it becomes a figure for masturbation. The top considers Henry's habit of taking it out in church to admire it "highly blamable," but also understands why the boy would want to stroke it when he's feeling anxious and lonely: "Henry, who had been holding me in his hand without any design of playing from the time his mother began her discourse [telling him he has to go away to boarding school], had merely been rubbing me about with his fingers" (14). When the mother finishes her speech, Henry throws himself in her arms in a paroxysm of relief and anguish, in a catharsis highly suggestive of a masturbation scene, complete with remorse.

There are numerous scenes at the boys' school involving more symbolic sessions with the peg top. But the focus on male autoeroticism does not permanently crowd out the it-novel's endemic fascination with the fleeting nature of female sexual value. The female question recurs when a little girl named Sophy Jackson finds the peg top on the road and takes it home. Her two brothers humiliate her because she cannot make the top spin. One writes her a poem on the subject of her ineptitude:

> Why, Sophy! You had better the trial give o'er,
> Some other amusement attempt to pursue,
> For a top, my dear girl, is ill chosen for you.
> Go take up your doll, to your baby-house go.
> And there your attention much better bestow!
> Leave the Peg-Top behind, and behave like a miss,
> And I'll give you this picture, these nuts and a kiss,
> Like the dog in the manger, our sport you destroy,
> Nor receive for yourself either pleasure or joy;

From a motive so cross, if you offer to stay,
I declare I will toss all your geegaws away
Should I set on a stool with a needle and thread,
And dress up Miss Dolly, or put her to bed?
Or do you not think 'twould be pleasant to see
Master Neddie turned fribble, and pouring out tea?
And a boy just as well, sure, might trundle a mop,
As for you to attempt to be spinning a top;
I ne'er yet saw a lady at cricket engage.
Although you just now flounced away in a rage;
When you took up my bat with so awkward an air,
And I told you such toys weren't made for the fair:
Then let me persuade you the Top to resign,
Since 'twill spin in my fingers much better than thine.

(91)

In case the reader misses all the allusions to male sexual organs, to effeminacy caused by gender confusion, and to warnings against girl-children fondling such objects, there is another male masturbation scene nearby to underscore the message. Sophy's brother takes the top, and the object sighs gratefully: "Edward the eldest kept me up for near a minute, and I spun so well, as to sleep more soundly than I had ever done before" (89). The top, basking in the pleasure of sweet release, remarks that it is a shame that girls would ever be suffered to touch him, when Edward and his brother "afforded me as much satisfaction: for a Peg-Top of any emulation is as happy as its owner, when it is spun by a skillful hand, and when it is so fortunate as to excel, *will share with its Lord the pleasure and pride*" (89, emphasis original). Little girls are to play with dolls and wait for the day when some gentleman honorably makes them mothers through some mysterious process entirely divorced from the pleasures of stroking things found in boys' pockets.

Following Mrs. Kilner's example, the second generation of it-novels retains the conventional theme of the frailty of female sexual value, but the analogies are more oblique. The overt textual moral is how to avoid the imputation of being a spoiled, ungrateful, or untruthful girl; the idea that such a child will grow into a sexually promiscuous adult woman is only present as a distant innuendo. Notably, the work of piecing together that chain of causality is much more laborious after *Adventures of a Pincushion* than finding the link between object and sexual woman in the earlier novels of circulation. For example, in Mlle. Louise d'Aulnay's *Mémoires d'une poupée* (1840), the doll of the title approvingly witnesses a scene in which a badly behaved little girl is prevented from eating the wedding cake sent to her as a present by the bride, a girl just a few years older; the Freudian implication is that the naughty girl will not reap the fruition of properly structured sexual narratives (first marriage, then pleasurable reward) if she does not redeem herself soon. Attentiveness to the doll is the mark of little girls' suitability for motherhood, and the doll herself—a fastidious French fashion doll named Vermeille—is the antithesis of the scarlet woman to whom her name alludes. Indeed, she embodies a finicky sexual selectiveness that she passes along to her human companions, and by implication, to the implied little-girl reader. When the girls stage a wedding for Vermeille, based upon a desire for the trousseau rather than the consummation, the doll "foresaw nothing satisfactory or agreeable in this marriage. Some insipid punchinello or cherry-checked shepherd, forsooth! Who, without the smallest pretensions of his own, was to share my success in society, and more than probably supplant me in the affections of those I loved!" [35] Five potential grooms are offered and four are rejected: a shepherd for his "rusticity," a dandy because "he had the air of a puppy," a sailor, due to the separation and dangers of his profession, and a field marshall with many medals because of his age. Finally Prince Fortunio, a colonel of the Hussars, is accepted. A brilliant wedding and trousseau are planned and executed by the little girls. Regrettably, the doll-prince is killed on the way to the honeymoon when he puts his head out of the train window to get some fresh air and it is "dashed to atoms on a passing wall and his body rolled to their feet" (34). The doll (and the girls) avoid induction into sexuality by the speedy, and excessively brutal, removal of a male, who is himself a consumer object chosen to gratify female desires. Like *Memoirs of a Peg-Top,* the doll's story utterly mystifies the connection between sexual contact with males and the fulfillment of femininity in motherhood: the latter may be experienced or practiced for without the former via the use of appropriate commodities—being a mother is just dressing living dolls.

The Victorian flourishing of it-novels, this time expressly packaged as adolescent literature, includes Miss Black's *The Adventures of Little Downy, or the Story of a Field Mouse* (1832), Henry Harcourt's *The Adventures of a Cotton-Tree* (1836), and *The Adventures of a Fly* (1847). Each is an earnest education for children in the avoidance of cruelty and selfishness, and *The Adventures of a Cotton-Tree* throws in lessons in global trade for good measure. Finally, in 1889, an obscene it-novel, *The Autobiography of a Flea,* appeared with the falsely predated imprint of "Cyntheria, 1789" in an attempt to acquire amnesty under the umbrella of the previous century's tolerance of libertine writing. Indeed, the poetic preface predicts that this narrator will affect the presumably grown-up reader in more or less the way the peg top affects young Henry, although this narrative is more direct in stating what that means: "Aghast the modest reader stands / His ———— firm gripped in both his hands: / The red blood o'er his visage steals; / His eyes display the lust he feels; / His parted lips, his veins on fire, / Show how a Flea can raise desire, / With snorting Nostrils all aflame, / He flies to find some willing dame; / Enters her house,—pays down the "blunt"; / And blind with lust, calls out for ———."[36] Yet, for all its disregard for the hard-won propriety of the it-novel, *The Autobiography of a Flea* recognizes and respects Mrs. Kilner's wariness of the pretext that an inanimate object can talk:

> if the intelligent reader of these pages wonders how it came to pass that one in my walk,—or perhaps, I should have said, jump,—in life became possessed of the learning, observation and power of committing to memory the whole of the wonderful facts and disclosures I am about to relate, I can only remind him that there are intelligences little suspected by the vulgar, and laws in nature the very existence of which have not yet been detected by the advanced among the scientific world. (7)

The flea attaches himself to the thigh of a fourteen-year-old girl named Bella while she is in church, looking up her leg to the "thin and peach-like slit which just showed its rounded lips between them [the thighs] in the shade" (10). The flea then accompanies Bella on a late-night assignation with a young man named Charlie. The two have alfresco sex but are caught by their parish priest. Father Ambrose "absolves" Bella the next day with an act of oral sex; two other priests join in, and the romp is on. Bella repeatedly services her local clergy and even her uncle (with the assistance of her cousin, his daughter) to the point that "a flea of average intelligence only would have had enough of such disgusting exhibitions as I have thought it my duty to disclose" (59). The flea, who stays with her far beyond its allotted lifespan, says, "Bella continued to afford me the most delicious of pastures. Her young limbs never missed the crimson draughts which I imbibed, or felt, to any grave inconvenience, the tiny punctures which I was forced to make to obtain my living" (101). Clearly out of sync with the children's it-novels of the nineteenth century, *The Autobiography of a Flea* is also quite different from the eighteenth-century ancestors to which it misleadingly claims propinquity with its false imprint. The flea and the girl remain together; the plot is not driven by a need to narrativize the new capitalist process of circulation; and Bella is allowed to retain her youth and attractiveness, and does not swiftly decline and die like the women of other it-novels. The market urgencies that brought the object-narrated novel into being had faded, and all that remained was gross sensuality.

A Theoretical Conclusion

Long after the waning of the object-narrator in novels, objects continued to have something akin to character status in narrative cinema. Alfred Hitchcock had a name for the devices he masterfully deployed in his films: he called them MacGuffins, which makes them sound like a knowing Irish detective who shows up and unravels the twisted plot at key moments. In fact, MacGuffins are "something that the characters in the film care a lot about," such as Anna Thorwald's wedding ring in *Rear Window,* or Guy's monogrammed lighter in *Strangers on a Train,* both of which are treated by other characters as irrefutable proofs of guilt or innocence in the murder cases in question.[37] A lowly object becomes a MacGuffin in precisely the way that a Velveteen Rabbit becomes real: you have to love it enough, and magically, a transformation occurs. In the eighteenth-century context, Belinda's hair in *The Rape of the Lock* perfectly embodies (and parodies) the apotheosis of a MacGuffin, since it ascends to heaven and becomes a star after being appropriately mourned.

MacGuffins, like object-narrators, enact the truth of exchange value: they matter only insofar as a character invests them with meaning or a consumer covets them. In his treatment of Hitchcock's "formalist disdain" for the MacGuffin, Seymour Chatman writes that no matter how much the characters want an object, "its importance hardly qualifies the MacGuffin for characterhood." Yet he also notes that there are human MacGuffins, which are discussed and named as characters but remain potential, "a character *manqué*": Godot, for example, is "as human as a Beckett character can be," which is to say, not very much, and other characters invest him with a lot of meaning and care about him.[38] In Jane Austen's *Emma,* Frank Churchill's hypochondriacal aunt is another such character manqué, repeatedly invoked for her awesome power to command others and used as a pretext when Frank wants to come to Highbury to see his secret fiancée or storm out of town to punish her for coldness.[39]

The circulation novels of the mid-eighteenth century reverse the Godot problem: they offer MacGuffins made into heroes, MacGuffins whose lack of subjectivity infects the real humans in the book, turning them into enactments of typology, like the generic humans from the commedia dell'arte. These novels are a reductio ad absurdum of the picaresque, an episodic narrative loosely organized around a picaro, a rogue or scoundrel who recounts his or her escapades in the first person. In the true Spanish picaresque, the narrator is often a servant who recounts his adventures working for several employers, each meant to represent some archetype.[40] The picaresque thrived in sixteenth- and seventeenth-century Spain and France, and was imitated in the early eighteenth century by such English prototypes as *Moll Flanders* (1722). Picaresque protagonists are often male, and if female, are required to be prostitutes or loose women in order to account for the many sexual adventures requisite to the form. The formal exigencies of the genre, then, dictate a loose sexual character, for a virtuous woman with no sexual history has few adventures to recount. The inanimate picaresque avails the eighteenth-century English author of an important innovation, however. The prostitute or servant is replaced by a sofa, corkscrew, banknote, rupee, lapdog, or atom, who circulates as widely as any courtesan and experiences the same precipitous decline in status with age: as *The Adventures of a Bank-Note* says, the life-span of an object that passes through so many men's hands can be but three years at the utmost. Such a novel can achieve allegorically what *Moll Flanders* or *Roxana* achieves literally: a representation of the rapid diminution of a woman's value as she is fondled and possessed by many consumers. The occasion to examine the motives and feelings of the corkscrew is not provided, but in its absence, the reader is invited to contemplate the characters of the men who wish to own and make use of the corkscrew.

In analyzing the object-narrated novel, it may be useful to recall the distinction Aristotle makes in his *Poetics* between agent (*pratton*) and character (*ethos*): namely, that agents are necessary to the action, but character is a supplement that marks the beginning of that genuine intellectual pleasure, psychologizing the heroine. On the one hand, the novel of the inanimate protagonist allows the representation of female sexual value in base economic terms, and coincides with a novel like *Pamela* in defining sexual innocence as the sole determinant of a woman's market value. On the other hand, the object-narrator forces a reexamination of the rules of characterization which have pertained since Aristotle defined the ethos of character: *chreston,* the determination of base or noble qualities; the *harmotton,* or aptness of the qualities for the part required; the *homoios,* or idiosyncrasies that soften the character and add a touch of realism; and the *homalon,* or consistency, which makes the character uniform and believable.[41] For example, a war epic requires a soldier as its hero. His harmotton should be his bravery, which allows him to face guns and tanks with valor, but he may have as his homoios a fear of something absurdly harmless relative to the enemy he boldly confronts every day, such as mice, dogs, or women. The homoios opens up a narrative space for *analepsis,* or backstory, where we learn about a childhood event that planted the seeds of his endearing neurosis. An inanimate or insensate protagonist may fulfill only some of the four-part postulate of character. A corkscrew may have consistency, remaining twisted, metal, and altogether corkscrewy from preface to coda, but it can hardly aspire to homoios, or that personal mannerism that lends the illusion of depth to character. The narrator of *The Adventures of a Cork-Screw* attempts to speak for his own uniqueness when he says that he was displayed in glass by "one of the most eminent steel-workers in Woodstock" and is beautiful, "highly polished," and "curiously contrived" (7–8). These traits make him more recognizable and desirable than your average corkscrew, but they hardly amount to an eccentricity, much less an Achilles' heel or a true homoios.

The insensate protagonist, therefore, deprives the reader of what Roland Barthes called the "metonymic skid": the groping towards descriptives that would finally pin down the hero or heroine's character.[42] Clarissa is virtuous, sensitive, persecuted, paranoid, intelligent, beautiful, Sapphic, vain, self-satisfied, deluded, anorexic, frigid, and so on; in the attempt to find appropriate signifiers, the reader finds out what she thinks about love, rape, disordered eating, female friendship, and male homosocial bonds. The "exact combination of names" that would finally sum up a character yields a complexity of congruent and contradictory figures that make up the character's "'personality,' which is just as much a combination as the odor of a dish or the bouquet of a wine."[43] Indeed, when modern novelists have revived the trope of the object-narrator, they may choose, as Janet Harris does in *Blackberry Wine* (1999), a bottle of homemade wine for a narrator, whose bouquet of character is a given. In a related example, Tibor Fischer's *The Collector Collector* (1997) is narrated by a six-thousand-year-old bowl who accumulates and rates owners: it will say, for example, when a new character peers into its vessel, that, "still hoping for one hundred and sixty-seven, I find that Nikki's nose fits into the one hundred sixty-six classes I have already identified. It's number eighty-eight, or the begonia."[44] The key to the bowl as object-narrator is to understand that all the humans it encounters are strikingly less individual than itself; it is the only bowl of its kind still in existence, but we are all unremarkable facsimiles of features and personalities that it has met before. The it-novel has come full circle from representing tragically common desperate female lives to showing us the changelessness of human character.

But, unlike Fischer's fabulous one-of-a-kind bowl, in the eighteenth-century it-novel a banknote is just a banknote. At its moment of creation, it boasts nothing to distinguish it from other banknotes. As Thomas Bridges writes of his hero the banknote, he has "a pedigree not quite so long as Cadwallader's" (1:1), though he may acquire one through circulation, exchange, and aging. Someone may tear a corner or scribble a note, or the banknote may become frayed and faded. Yet the banknote, I argue, affords an opportunity for a "metonymic skid" of another kind: the representation of the entire system of capitalism via one of its symbols, the banknote; and, more aptly for my present reading, it allows the representation of women who are not as special as wealthy, sensitive, and individualistic Clarissa, but who are as numerous, interchangeable, and fungible as banknotes: courtesans and prostitutes. It is the determined credo of the it-novel to represent such women via metonymy. This substitution of prostitute for commodity produces insistent lines in *The Secret History of an Old Shoe* asserting the lack of individuality, provenance, or merit in the shoe-protagonist. Like banknotes, the courtesan has "a quick succession of adventures and acquaintance" (2:25), and like banknotes, the courtesan's life is "so short, few survive the year, but not one in fifty lives to be two years old." But the banknote answers that two years in high circulation is worth two hundred in the life of "a custard-eating parson," for "time is measured only by the slower or quicker succession of ideas" (2:26).

To return to the question with which I opened, let us revisit the issue of psychological depth in *Memoirs of a Woman of Pleasure.* Feminists have long complained that Cleland's Fanny Hill lacks interiority, depth, and nuance, and that her glossy two-dimensional character serves merely to illuminate the vices of the men who long for her. Yet, if we classify *Memoirs of a Woman of Pleasure* among the ranks of the object-narrated novel, then we acknowledge that the chief aim of the it-protagonist is to introduce the reader to a variety of psychological types in the packaging of picaresque. Fanny Hill, like the banknote, the corkscrew, and the atom, is a device for gaining admittance into the private motives and deeds of a number of human types, such as the "hackney'd thoroughbred Phoebe" who instructs her in "pollution"; Mrs. Brown the madam with the gaping beggar's wallet of a vagina; Mr. Crofts, who purchases Fanny's virginity; Charles, her first love; her fellow prostitutes Martha, Emily, Louisa, and Polly; Mr. H———, who keeps her; Will, the servant she uses to cuckold him; Mr. Norbert, the premature ejaculator; an unnamed, hearty sailor who attempts to soften his efforts to sodomize her with the genial motto, "any port in a storm"; and Mr. Barvile, the flagellant, who was one of those "unaccountably condemn'd to have his pleasure lash'd into him, as boys have their learning."[45] As Ruth Yeazell quips, "a nicer collection of sensualists and perverts one would be hard put to find."[46] Rather than a failed effort to capture female interiority, *Memoirs of a Woman of Pleasure* is yet another it-novel, this time narrated by an enthusiastic vagina; this body part joins a tradition, the object-narrated picaresque, that values the swift succession of character types more than prolix effusions upon the psychology of the heroine/narrator. My survey of the object-narrator tradition demonstrates that there is a viable feminist project in reading circulation novels, if we acknowledge them as one of the most estimable tools authors had at their disposal for exploring the exigencies of women's lives and their tendency to become trapped in entropic sexual narratives.

NOTES

1. Seymour Chatman, *Story and Discourse: Narrative Structure in Fiction and Film* (Ithaca, NY: Cornell University Press, 1978), 113.
2. Margaret Anne Doody, *The True Story of the Novel* (New York: Fontana, 1998), 152.
3. Nancy Armstrong, *Desire and Domestic Fiction: A Political History of the Novel* (Oxford: Oxford University Press, 1987), 8.
4. *The Odyssey of Homer,* trans. Alexander Pope (Rockville, MD: Wildside, 2003), 14.433; Josephine Donovan, *Women and the Rise of the Novel, 1405–1726* (New York: St. Martin's Press, 1999), 122; Ruth Bernard Yeazell, *Fictions of Modesty: Women and Courtship in the English Novel* (Chicago: University of Chicago Press, 1991), 123.
5. See, for example, Nancy K. Miller, "'I's in Drag: The Sex of Recollection," in *French Dressing: Women, Men, and Ancien Régime Fiction* (New York: Routledge, 1995), 99–102.
6. Samuel Richardson, *Clarissa, or The History of a Young Lady,* ed. Angus Ross (London: Penguin, 1985).
7. Mimi Hellman, "Furniture, Sociability, and the Work of Leisure in Eighteenth-Century France," *Eighteenth-Century Studies* 32.4 (1999): 438 n.
8. Tobias Smollett, *The History and Adventures of an Atom,* ed. O M Brack, Jr. (Athens: University of Georgia Press, 1989), 17.
9. *The Letters of Horace Walpole, Fourth Earl of Orford,* vol. 1, ed. Mrs. Paget Toynbee (Oxford: Clarendon Press, 1903), 178.
10. Claude Prosper Crébillon fils, *Le Sopha (The Sofa, A Moral Tale),* trans. Bonamy Dobrée (London: Folio Society, 1951). All further references to this work will be cited parenthetically.
11. Hellman, "Furniture," 415.
12. Samuel Richardson, *Pamela, or Virtue Rewarded,* ed. T. C. Duncan Eaves and Ben D. Kimpel (Boston: Houghton Mifflin, 1971).
13. See Jonathan Swift's "The Lady's Dressing Room," "A Beautiful Young Nymph Going to Bed," and "Strephon and Chloe," in *The Complete Poems,* ed. Pat Rogers (London: Penguin, 1983).
14. Hellman, "Furniture," 416.
15. Ibid., 435.
16. Bernard Mandeville, *A Modest Defence of the Publick Stews: Or, an Essay upon Whoring, as it is now Practis'd in these Kingdoms* (London: A. Moore, 1724), 8.
17. Hellman, "Furniture," 435.
18. Armstrong, *Desire,* 96. All further references to this work will be cited parenthetically.
19. Francis Coventry, *The History of Pompey the Little; or, The Life and Adventures of a Lap-Dog* (London: M. Cooper, 1751), 54. All further references to this work will be cited parenthetically.
20. John Gay, *The Beggar's Opera,* ed. Bryan Loughrey and T. O. Treadwell (London: Penguin, 1986), 103.

21. *The Adventures of a Black Coat* (Edinburgh: Alexander McCaslan, 1750), 5. All further references to this work will be cited parenthetically.

22. Julie Peakman, "London Prostitution and the Bills of Mortality," Invited Talk, Wellcome Institute of Medicine, London, July 20, 2004.

23. *The Interesting Narrative of the Life of Olaudah Equiano, or Gustavus Vassa, the African, Written by Himself*, ed. Angelo Costanzo (Toronto: Broadview Press, 2001).

24. Gretchen Holbrook Gerzina, *Black London: Life before Emancipation* (New Brunswick, NJ: Rutgers University Press, 1995), 73.

25. Trevor Burnard, "Slave Naming Patterns: Onomastics and the Taxonomy of Race in Eighteenth-Century Jamaica," *Journal of Interdisciplinary History* 31.3 (2001): 335. Laura Brown also reads *Pompey* as an allegorical slave narrative; see *Fables of Modernity: Literature and Culture in the English Eighteenth Century* (Ithaca, NY: Cornell University Press, 2003), chapter 6.

26. Bonnie Blackwell, "Alarmed at his Irish Proposal," in *Immodest Proposals: The Crisis of Sex, Dating, and Marriage in Eighteenth-Century Britain and Ireland*, unpublished book manuscript.

27. Charles Walker, "Epistle Dedicatory," in *The Adventures of Sally Salisbury* (London, 1723), B2.

28. Mary Spongberg, *Feminizing Venereal Disease: The Body of the Prostitute in Nineteenth-Century Medical Discourse* (New York: New York University Press, 1997), 70.

29. *Secret History of an Old Shoe* (Dublin: J. Dickerson, 1734), 6. All further references will be cited parenthetically.

30. *Adventures of a Cork-Screw* (London: T. Bell, 1775), 76. All further references will be cited parenthetically.

31. Thomas Bridges, *The Adventures of a Bank-Note*, 2 vols. (London: T. Davies, 1770–71), 1:51–53. All further references will be cited parenthetically.

32. Neil McKendrick, John Brewer, and J. H. Plumb, *The Birth of a Consumer Society: The Commercialization of Eighteenth-Century England* (Bloomington: Indiana University Press, 1982), 1.

33. Mary Ann Kilner, *The Adventures of a Pincushion* (London: John Harris, 1828), 27. All further references will be cited parenthetically.

34. Mary Ann Kilner, *Memoirs of a Peg-Top* (London, 1785), 1. All further references will be cited parenthetically.

35. Louise d'Aulnay, *Mémoires d'une poupée: Autobiographical memoirs of the life and adventures of a Doll*, trans. James Lindsay-Crawford, 24th Earl of Crawford (London: Thomas Hurst, 1840), 28. All further references will be cited parenthetically.

36. *The Autobiography of a Flea, Told in a Hop, Skip and a Jump, and Recounting all his Experiences of the Human, and Superhuman kind, both Male and Female; with his Curious Connections, Backbitings, and Tickling Touches; the whole scratched together and arranged for the Delectation of the Delicate, and for the Information of the Inquisitive* [London, 1887], 1. All further references will be cited parenthetically.

37. Chatman, *Story and Discourse*, 140.

38. Ibid.

39. Jane Austen, *Emma*, ed. Fiona Stafford (London: Penguin, 1996).

40. Chris Baldick, *The Concise Oxford Dictionary of Literary Terms* (New York: Oxford University Press, 1990), 168–69.

41. Chatman, *Story and Discourse*, 110.

42. Quoted in ibid., 134.

43. Quoted in ibid., 116.

44. Tibor Fischer, *The Collector Collector* (New York: Henry Holt, 1997), 13.

45. John Cleland, *Memoirs of a Woman of Pleasure*, ed. Peter Sabor (Oxford: Oxford University Press, 1986), 12, 24, 141, and 145.

46. Yeazell, *Fictions*, 113.

It-Narratives: Fictional Point of View and Constructing the Middle Class

Nicholas Hudson

CONTRARY TO THE IMPRESSION LEFT BY MANY STUDIES OF EIGHTEENTH-century fiction, most notably Ian Watt's still influential *Rise of the Novel* (1957), we cannot meaningfully speak of a "middle class" until this century's last two decades. Only then do authors such as Thomas Gisborne, Thomas Malthus, and Vicesimus Knox begin to use the expression "the middle class" or (more frequently) "the middle-classes."[1] And only then, as Dror Warhman has put it, was the middle class "imagined," albeit in different and competing ways.[2] Among conservative authors reacting to threats posed by the French Revolution, the "middle class" designated a loose grouping of the untitled gentry, the professions, and the upper merchant class, a coalition distinct from, though generally loyal to, the nobility, and allied in the desire to protect their privileges from the group eventually dubbed "the lower middle class": small shop owners, artisans, journeymen, petty officials. These lesser ranks, for decades the seedbed of radical politics, spent the period following the French Revolution pushing for de facto admission into the middle classes symbolized finally by the 1832 Reform Act—an event that, while superficially a victory for liberalism, in fact marked another step in the attempt to set a bottom limit to what Marxist historians have deceptively called "the bourgeoisie."[3]

Hence, what Marxists treat as a neatly defined material category actually represents a highly amorphous and uncertain site of ideological conflict.[4] The "middle class" was *constructed* in the realm of ideas, not facts. This does not mean, of course, that ways of constructing the middle class lacked material repercussions. The term "middle classes" was invented to protect the political advantages of certain groups roughly allied in their effort to resist pressure from "below"; the vocabulary of "class," in turn, ramified hugely during the nineteenth and twentieth centuries into a range of dialects deployed to organize material and political affairs, and even to create whole new systems. Nonetheless, recognizing the "imaginative" nature of the whole concept of class springs new questions about the role of literary writing, understood now not merely as the ideological superstructure of a material base, but as ways of imagining (and creating) a still gestating and uncertain economic and political order.

Here we come to our subject of "it-narratives." During a period of particularly intense social reorganization between 1750 and 1780, novels narrated from the point of view of nonhuman and inanimate objects pullulated through the bookstalls. What is the relation between this literary fashion and the idea of the middle class that reached something close to full articulation during the 1780s and '90s?

My attempt to shed light on this question will lean on the observation that the final creation of a "middle class" (particularly as imagined by conservatives) required not conflict but *reconciliation* between the old aristocratic elite and the newly, financially empowered merchant class. To a far greater degree than we usually recognize, the world of the City, home of Britain's business elite, was regarded with deep suspicion not just by the old elite but also by writers and professionals. Samuel Johnson, whose famous circle included no one from the merchant classes, reflected a very common unease when he wrote that "there will always be a part, and always be a very large part of every community that have no care but for themselves, and whose care for themselves reaches little farther than impatience of immediate pain, and eagerness for the nearest good . . . A merchant's desire, is not of glory, but of gain; not of publick wealth, but of private emolument."[5] Such hostility was particularly sharpened by the sight of vulgar "cits" elbowing their way into the privileges and entertainments usually reserved for the elite.[6] This erosion of traditional rank boundaries raised anxiety about the supposed moral and political disruption fomented by such "upward mobility"—a worry clearly registered in many it-narratives. At the same time, the key role that merchants and bankers played in Britain's increasing prosperity could hardly be denied, especially as the nation engaged in imperial wars expensively financed by the City and intended to secure mercantile interests. Like it or not, the coarse-spoken and avaricious cit—at least of the more prosperous sort—had to be trained to sit with reasonable decorum at the table of Britain's rulers. As for the old elite, in turn, it had to be educated to provide the model for moral and political leadership that its rakish heirs and vacuous beauties had notoriously failed to provide. Here were the exigencies that increasingly preoccupied the sermonizers, conduct writers, and the novelists of the century, especially during its second half.

How could novels narrated from the point of view of nonhuman objects serve this cause? Traditional fictional narratives, as I will explain, lacked the formal capacity to view English society from a perspective not strictly oriented by the rank and gender of the narrator. Without the resources of what Gérard Genette famously called "non-focalized" narration, every account had to be colored by the sociopolitical biases of the putative "author."[7] In Marxian terms, the novel was formally inclined to create "class conflict" rather than reconciliation. What English fiction increasingly required, on the contrary, was the ability to cast judgments and to create values that derived in no obvious way from one rank or another. The creation of apparently nongendered perspectives served this end because young women so obviously advanced or undermined, in their sexual and marital choices, the interests of their family groups and social milieux. The nobility had to be taught to live up to their traditional role as the nation's moral and political leaders. The merchants and bankers, in turn, had to be taught to influence power in ways reflective of national as opposed to narrowly selfish and venal motivations. The point of view of either of these groups could not be trusted. And so one turned to lapdogs, guineas, overcoats, corkscrews, hackney coaches, banknotes. Naturally, one does not need to read Wayne C. Booth's *The Rhetoric of Fiction* (as too few now do) to realize that these objects, like more recent forms of "impersonal" narration, did *not* in fact provide objective perspectives at all.[8] Just the opposite is true. These ancestors of modern non-focalized narration had their origin in the need to construct the illusion of a socially and politically noncommitted perspective—a goal that was meant both to include otherwise conflicting groups within a larger middle-class project and to exclude those that the emergent and unstable middle class wanted to exclude.

Let us begin with a text familiar to all recent students of the early novel, Aphra Behn's *Oroonoko; or, The Royal Slave* (1688). Implicit throughout this tale are the narrator's anxieties about her ability to achieve any kind of objective, and therefore authoritative, account of the hero she wants us to admire. The narrator claims to have been "myself an Eye-witness to a great part of what you will find here set down."[9] Yet this very admission of personal observation raises serious questions about what kinds of personal biases and weaknesses she brings to this task. She is only "a Female Pen," under which it was Oroonoko's "Misfortune," female-like, "to fall."[10] As this passage suggests, the narrator's relationship with the African prince in terms of class and power involves profound complications from which the eyewitness narration cannot escape. If, on the one hand, the royalist narrator views Prince Oroonoko from below as the tragic palimpsest of Charles I or sacrificial precursor of James II, she shies from condemning the same prince's enslavement by the Whiggish Captain, and seems happy enough to retreat into the gallery to watch, with sighs, the slaughtering of "Caesar," killer of tigers and sentimental victim of her own colonial caste.[11] In other words, the vaunted hero finally seems both heroic victim and helpless fool, both the proud remnant of a noble past and a literally castrated relic in the new age of capitalism and imperial expansion which buoyed Behn's own fortunes as an author.

To a postmodernist sensibility, such ambiguities may well generate a frisson of pleasurable indeterminacy. But such frissons result, at least in part, from the paucity of narrative resources at Behn's disposal. In subsequent decades, novelists remained similarly hampered by their inability to locate an "outside" point of view uninfected by the social, moral, and political perspectives of the putative narrator. For example, Defoe's first-person narrators represent precisely the kind of aggressive, amoral, and upwardly mobile figures so distrusted by the official morality of his time. And indeed Defoe tried to conform to this morality by filling his novels with righteous lamentations about the behavior of his protagonists—a moralism that still sounds weak and ambivalent because it is delivered by the same narrator recreating the excitement of his or her own push from obscurity to social prominence. Similarly, the primary charge leveled by critics of Richardson's *Pamela* (1740)—as prominently by Fielding in *Shamela* (1741) and Haywood in *Anti-Pamela* (1742)—concerned this novel's apparent encouragement of maidservants to manipulate the lustful yearnings of their superiors for their own social advancement. As Terry Castle has noted, Richardson apparently did not intend to send that message at all, for he strenuously distanced his heroine from approval for any such ambitions in his continuation of *Pamela*.[12] Yet the ambiguity in the first version cannot be dislodged even from the mind of a modern reader, for the heroine must dramatize the terror and excitement of her sexual encounters with her "master" while protesting in preening terms about her own grateful servitude and virginal innocence. The same problem continued to haunt Richardson in *Clarissa,* which he subjected to endless fiddling in the (unsuccessful) attempt to erase any suggestion that the aristocratic Lovelace embodies irresistible attractions for his middle-rank and pristine heroine. Even the proudly genteel Henry Fielding, who so roundly condemned the eroding social order of his time in his legal pamphlets, found himself unable to overcome the problems generated by focalized narration.[13] Offended by the apparent implication of Richardson's first novel that servant girls should navigate their masters' sexual desires towards personal advancement, Fielding moved after *Joseph Andrews* (1742) to a presiding third-person narrator capable of moral pronouncements. But his narrators, for all their brilliantly dexterous irony, cannot avoid creating the uncomfortable impression that they are muscling the reader towards preconceived and conservative judgments.

What all these authors share, in brief, is both an ideological program and a stylistic problem. The official program concerns the literary supervision of the upward mobility made possible by Britain's enriched economy, the agreement that these possibilities for social advancement potentially empowered the morally dissolute to seize the levers of the nation's political destiny. My use of the expression "*official* program" is pointed because, whatever the personal proclivities of socially ambitious people like Behn, Defoe, and Richardson, they recognized the exigency to conform to the early English novel's inherent hostility to abandoned individualism and amoral social aggression. The eighteenth-century novel is an essentially *conservative* genre—an admittedly unconventional argument that I have made at much greater length elsewhere.[14] Nevertheless, in the face of England's undeniably mercantile future, this conservatism could not imply the mere squashing of all forms of mercantile ambition. Here authors confronted what I have just called the "stylistic problem" shared by Behn, Defoe, Richardson, and Fielding. The devices available to these novelists would not permit the narrative to rise above the fray between old and new power, between the old elite and the encroaching influence of the City that, despite its proverbial vulgarity, was powering the enrichment of the nation and the literary marketplace itself.

Hence, the still unknown desideratum of these authors was the "objective," "impersonal,"or non-focalized narration developed in the nineteenth century. The full realization of this aim lay in the future. Yet between the first-person narratives of Behn or Defoe and the "omniscient" narrators of Austen, Dickens, or Eliot lay a transitional compromise: the it-narrative.

The fountainhead of this fascinating evolution in the conjoined modes of ideology and narrative form is a novel by a young Anglican priest and admirer of Fielding, Francis Coventry—*The History of Pompey the Little* (1751). The little hero of this funny little novel, a Bologna lapdog, performs an affectionate parody of Fielding's vagrant "young dog," Tom Jones, who seems equally at home with the local gamekeeper (and his randy daughter) and the high-society Lady Bellaston. Canine picaro, Pompey moves from owner to owner, alternating like a social yo-yo between a Bolognese whore and the lonely and dog-loving Lady Tempest, between the corrupt cabinet minister Lord Danglecourt and an oyster wench who trades Pompey for beer. The difference between Tom and Pompey is that Pompey, being a real dog, is incapable of moral judgment. The events recorded through Pompey's uncomprehending eyes belong on one level to the realm of objective "fact," though this objectivity does not stop Coventry from building up quite a clear argument for his own social vision—one that contributes to the creation of a conservative middle class equally critical of both aristocratic decadence and abject avarice in the City.

The social satire, that is, wags left and right. The satire of the old elite begins when the hilariously facile English gentleman Hilarius presents his souvenir of a Bolognese courtesan to his elderly friend Lady Tempest. Pompey, kidnapped in St. James's Park by the spoiled and sadistic child of an upstart merchant, will later witness the drunken arrogance of young noblemen who stagger after a night of dissolution from the Roundhouse to Parliament, and he plays "fetch and carry" with a citizens' petition tossed by the lolling and contemptuous cabinet minister, Lord Danglecourt. On the other hand, circulating through the mercantile ranks, Pompey joins a menagerie of crows and cats tortured by the children of some ridiculously vulgar parvenus, meets the base-born snob Count Tag who "always proportioned his Respect to the Rank and Fortunes of his Company," and overhears without understanding the domestic abuse and radical rantings of Councilor Tanturnian, whose "Passions were all centered on Money."[15] Pompey, whose own slobbery proclivities center on food and sex, has no judgment to make on any of this human nonsense. But we do. While never quite making this attitude explicit, Coventry impugns the extremes of both aristocratic irresponsibility and mercantile greed and stupidity. Heroism in this novel finds its measure in the ability to treat the hapless Pompey with a modicum of kindness and generosity. The winners of this prize are two of Pompey's friends who, while by no means exculpating the nobility from their egregious neglect of England's moral and political welfare, suggest that a conservative though progressive gentry loves dogs more than the rest. Lady Tempest comes nowhere close to embodying the negative connotations of her name: while her love of dogs is mocked in coarsely purulent terms by her servants, whom Coventry portrays as justly removed from any social and political influence, Pompey's panting return to the arms of his favorite mistress provides the novel's self-conscious and humorously wistful finale. The Milliner briefly adopts the unfortunate hero with a generosity clearly associated with the detail that she found "no charms in the Company of Tradesmen and stinking Shop-keepers," and that she is a similarly unfortunate gentleman's daughter who has sought the profession most associated with "People of Quality."[16]

In short, *The History of Pompey the Little* is a highly conservative book on the road towards a British "middle class," a category that, while internally embattled, would generally look up rather than down for its binding code of social manners. Although this novel glaringly exhibits the failures of the nobility, it also generally turns to the traditional aristocracy and gentry for models of virtue and generosity, reserving its most scathing attacks for those in the commercial community and serving class who treat Pompey merely as an object to be manipulated for sadistic amusement or to be traded like furry money. Pompey's "it-ness" serves a crucial role in advancing Coventry's ideological ends, for the use of his nonhuman perspective overcomes the narrative limitations that we have considered in previous novels. Unlike the first-person narratives of Behn, Defoe, Richardson, and Fielding, Pompey's inability to cast moral or political judgment on all that he witnesses creates the illusion of objectivity. This apparent objectivity is an illusion because Coventry's manipulation of the reader's moral responses has been merely shifted from explicit commentary to the way he dramatizes characters and events.

In important respects, therefore, this first it-narrative marks an important step towards the modern non-focalized narrative—a move closely associated with the drive to create a stable moral and political consensus in the upper-middle ranks and the old elite. Not only is a nonhuman narrator freed from the overt implication of moral or political bias, but a quotidian object like a lapdog, post chaise, corkscrew, or piece of money could circulate quickly and naturally through the whole gamut of social ranks in the way a human being simply could not. The guinea in Charles Johnstone's *Chrysal; or the Adventures of a Guinea* (1760) can "range through the whole territories of the society, to which I belong."[17] This virtually unlimited social range approximates, again, the kind of flexibility ultimately perfected by non-focalized narration. In one respect, however, it-narratives continued to suffer from an important limitation common to all first-person narratives: Pompey the lapdog—like the it-narrator in *The Travels of Mons. Le Post-Chaise* (1753) or Thomas Bridges's *The Adventures of a Bank-Note* (1770)—can only narrate events from the "outside" and is prohibited entrance into the minds and "hearts" of the characters. But certain it-narratives contrived, if somewhat awkwardly, to overcome even this limitation. The narrator of Johnstone's *Chrysal; or, The Adventures of a Guinea* is not the guinea itself, but rather a spirit trapped inside the guinea and released at the beginning of the novel by a latter-day alchemist. As an immaterial being, Chrysal can "*see* the depravity of human nature, when stripped of disguise and ornament," and moves not only through the whole social hierarchy but also in and out of the hearts of the characters.[18] Furnished with this extra device for moral judgment, Johnstone's vision of English society is explicitly much darker than Coventry's: we meet a general's "gentleman" with a taste for prepubescent girls; the corrupt whore of a lord who prowls the streets for custom on her time off; a merchant named "Traffic" whose "insatiable desire of riches" has rendered his heart hard and miserable; the daughter of a tradesman made wicked by her parents' foolish decision to raise her like a gentlewoman.[19] As this list indicates, Johnstone's satire, like Coventry's, takes aim at the corruptions of both the old elite and the newly wealthy. But his hostility to money and capitalism is, if anything, much deeper. He subjects the Dutch and Jews to vicious attacks for their supposedly inveterate lust for gold.[20] And Johnstone's curious choice of a (human) hero, the King of Bulgaria, addresses our perambulating guinea with the following philippic: "O thou source of every evil which distracts this wretched world . . . let me not be inflected by thy poison; let not my heart conceive a fondness for thee, farther than what thy native value of enabling it to do good justly entitles thee to."[21]

This technique of pairing an object with a supernatural being, a method later copied by the anonymous author of *The Adventures of a Cork-Screw* (1775), not only captured some of the advantages of the later "omniscient" narrator but also widened the author's rhetorical resources in commenting effectively on English society. Unlike a lapdog or a banknote, a spirit could pronounce moral judgments, making the author's views explicit. Yet because the spirit remained outside of human affairs, its judgments were not tainted by the class and gender bias inherent to a first-person narrative. And because the spirit remained attached to a peripatetic object, the author lost none of the social range facilitated by the it-narrative. In an important sense, in short, the kind of it-narrative invented by Charles Johnstone comes closest to being a full prototype of the non-focalized or omniscient narrator. As we will now go on to consider, this ultimate development in narrative technique is characterized by a similar pairing of rhetorical advantages: the omniscient narrator could go anywhere in English society or in the minds of the characters, but it remained "nonhuman" in the sense of having no evident gender or class, giving it the authority to pronounce with apparent "objectivity."

This evolution in the narrative form of the novel was being driven by the effort to establish an authoritative common ground between the aristocracy and the upper-middle ranks, and to regulate (not suppress) the disruptive energies of capitalism and the invasion of the lower-middle orders into the halls of privilege and power. Hence, such a deeply conservative novel as Frances Burney's *Evelina* (1778)—a work explicitly about the forging of a union between the middle-rank heroine and the aristocratic Lord Orville—borrows some of the characteristics of the it-narrative, though just as this form had began to wane. In many respects, the main narrator of this nominally epistolary novel, the eponymous heroine, behaves like an "it," as suggested even by her adopted name "Anville." Like an anvil, the heroine receives impressions of her experiences in London society without offering many moral judgments, especially early on. Unfixed as a lapdog or banknote by some preexistent social or moral commitment (she has been disowned by her genteel father, raised by a clergyman, and is carried about by her aunt, a former servant), inexplicably coveted like an itinerate guinea by everyone she meets, Evelina can circulate through a wide band of English society from the family of the hideous chandler Mr. Branghton at the bottom to her noble admirer Lord Orville at the top. Because Evelina is too demure to offer many moral judgments (except when her own sexual virtue is at stake), much of the ideological weight of the novel, as in an it-narrative, is shifted from direct authorial pronouncements to dramatization. And by virtue of Burney's considerable talent as a crafter of satirical drama, we are left in little doubt about her social likes and dislikes: she despises bumptious cits like the Branghtons or the Holborn beau Mr. Smith, recoils from crass parvenus like Madam Duval and the newly ermined Lord Merton, angers at the moral irresponsibility of corrupt noblemen like Sir Clement Willoughby, and is stirred to glowing admiration by the morally pristine aristocrat, Lord Orville. Yet these judgments appear, strangely, "objective" rather than imposed: if the genteel Henry Fielding has traditionally struck scholars as manipulative and elitist, the equally elitist Frances Burney has traditionally been praised by some of the same scholars as a Whiggish defender of "rights."

Evelina, that is, should be viewed as an "it-narrative" without an actual "it" doing the narrating. Technically, it offers little that is new. *Evelina* seems better than even the first and best of the it-narratives, Coventry's *Pompey the Little,* by sheer force of Burney's superior literary talent. But her fiction does point in prescient directions by indicating how a "non-object" narrator could facilitate much of the evident "objectivity" of the it-narrative. In this real way, she prepares the way for Jane Austen.

To say that Austen single-handedly created modern non-focalized narration, a form able to cast moral and political judgments without sacrificing the atmosphere of objectivity, would be inaccurate for at least two major reasons. First, previous authors such as Ann Radcliffe, whom Austen greatly admired, had created an omniscient narration virtually indistinguishable from that of Scott, Dickens, or Eliot. Unlike Austen's fiction, however, Radcliffe's continentally located novels seem largely bereft of any conscious social or political vision for England, whatever their conservative humor. Second, Austen's form of narration in fact continues to delight and fascinate us because its impertinent and confiding humor—and its creation of a distinctly saucy narrative personality—are so fetching and so reminiscent of the best eighteenth-century fiction. On a certain level, that is, Austen's novels are enjoyable because they are *not* "objective" at all. Nevertheless, Austen's defense of a modern form of middle-class hegemony has considerable authority because it speaks from a space that seems classless or even genderless in explicit ways—a space as "objective" and peripatetic as that of a wandering banknote or hackney coach, yet amenable to direct moral judgments such as those delivered by the spirit who inhabits Charles Johnstone's guinea. Austen's novels are ideologically powerful and creative of the British middle class, which was emerging as a self-conscious grouping during precisely the years of Austen's writing.

To trace the evolution of non-focalized narration from the it-narrative to Austen's fiction, let us begin with her earliest completed novel, a work that shows Austen moving away from previous narrative forms without having yet arrived at her mature style. To say that *Northanger Abbey* represents the *evolution,* rather than the achievement, of her mature style is not to deny the virtues of this witty and playful novel. But these virtues tend to be those of the best eighteenth-century fiction: it delights in its own ambiguity and self-conscious subjectivity, eschewing clarity and authority with regard to social and moral questions. While Austen's authorial persona exhibits some of the capacities of the omniscient narrator—she moves freely into the thoughts of the characters, for example—this persona clearly embodies a "first-person" perspective. Above all, this persona identifies herself as a woman with unapologetic class biases. "Let us not desert each other; we are an injured body," the narrator intones in a famous defense of other woman novelists; in a later scene, the narrator first telegraphs a compliment to a "sister novelist" (Burney) and then launches into a very un-Austen-like diatribe about men preferring ignorant to lively minded young women.[22] The persona's rootedness in the "respectable" gentry world of the Morelands and the Allens is made explicit from the very first lines of the novel, a bias revealed again by her strong ridicule of the pushy upstart Thorpes in Bath. It is significant that Austen generally avoids making the reader feel bullied or manipulated, for her tone remains consistently ironic and evasive, and her various judgments seem to flaunt their self-contradictions: for example, the narrator follows her defense of novelists with a scene that seems to imply just the opposite, heaping sarcasm on the "delicacy, discretion, originality of thought and literary taste" of Catherine and Isabella as they chat with girlish enthusiasm about recent fiction.[23] In short, the book is less than authoritative as a vehicle for Austen's form of social engineering. In its final pages, the narrator jokingly admits that the lesson of the book is unclear. And the novel's central issues and characters will no doubt invite unresolved debate among literary scholars for as long as *Northanger Abbey* is studied. Just what is Austen's attitude toward Gothic fiction, and modern fiction in general? Is Henry Tilney a worthy partner for Catherine, or something of a sexist cad? For that matter, is Catherine herself a slightly laughable simpleton or finally the "heroine" that she "trains" to be from the beginning of the novel?

We postmoderns may well relish these indeterminacies as arresting and elegant. But Austen herself was no postmodernist. She swept *Northanger Abbey* behind her and set about creating narratives with the sort of control over meaning that she clearly desired. In *Pride and Prejudice,* which still did not satisfy Austen's quest for diamond-like precision and authority, we witness a major step towards facilitating the kind of authority exerted by non-focalized narration. The "it" of *Northanger Abbey,* Catherine, moves up and down the ranks, from the Thorpes to the Tilneys, without a reliable compass to orient herself morally. At the same time, Austen's narrator in that novel lacks the ability of even Johnstone's genie, Chrysal, to make judgments that seem genuinely uncolored by personal prejudice. She is too "human." The very theme of *Pride and Prejudice,* by contrast, is the need to rise above personal prejudice to make "objective" judgments about the social order. As the history of criticism surrounding Austen suggests, a case can be built for various political orientations in her novels, from Marilyn Butler who has read Austen as a conservative Tory to Claudia L. Johnson who argued for her moderate liberalism.[24] My own view is that Austen should be read as a "conservative" but only in a sociological sense shared by both Tories and Whigs of her time: her novels make the case for a consolidated "middle class" flexible enough to embrace a fairly wide range of affiliations in contemporary party politics, and able to absorb acceptable members of previously distrusted social groups, particularly higher merchants and tradesmen, into a new ruling-order hegemony. This is an aim she validates through an apparently objective point of view fashioned through a set of strategies characteristic of modern "omniscient" narration.

Put plainly, and in keeping with the predominant mission of the eighteenth-century novel that I have traced, Austen builds a case for a "middle class" in which the old elite colludes with a rich though deferential merchant class in a common front against vulgar social climbers from below. "A daughter of a gentleman," Elizabeth Bennet, marries a "gentleman" of ancient family and noble connections, Mr. Darcy, a man who personifies the most sterling dictates of moral leadership expected from the old elite.[25] Especially given that she previously turned down Darcy's marriage proposal, Lizzy's enviable social rise seems invulnerable to the charge of upward-mobile ambition appropriately laid against her fluttering mother, the bilious bootlicker Mr. Collins, and the wrongly elevated libertine, Mr. Wickham. Mr. Darcy's exemplary moral authority, in turn, is clearly distinguished from the demands for implicit obedience exacted by his ridiculous aunt Lady Catherine De Bourgh. Though intolerant of immoral behavior and arrogant manners (the latter sin is one that he lays ruefully at his own door near the end of the novel), Darcy becomes a great social unifier of the new ruling class. This class embraces not only the genteel and worthily virtuous Lizzy (literally) but also the "well bred" and worthily virtuous merchant Mr. Gardiner (figuratively).[26] Darcy even invites Mr. Gardiner to come fishing on his estate, and the novel's very last paragraph reveals that he "loved" the merchant and his sober wife as much as Lizzy did.[27]

This is "constructing the middle class," English style, par excellence. But perhaps not a single reader is recorded to have recoiled from this novel as manipulative and obviously skewed. How do we account for the evident willingness of readers to admire this novel as a masterpiece of objective social realism? It is worth observing right away that the narrative structure of *Pride and Prejudice* exactly reverses that of *Northanger Abbey.* In *Northanger Abbey,* the main character is the "it," floating through the ranks like a startled lapdog, while the narrator, on the contrary, views events from a perspective explicitly colored by her class and gender. In *Pride and Prejudice* the narrator is the "it," recording the thoughts and feelings of her characters with apparent objectivity. It is Lizzy who must finally learn that her own proclivities for "pride" and "prejudice" have severely undermined her ability to judge objectively. The turning point comes when she reads and rereads Darcy's long letter explaining his past behavior, a document whose facts are confirmed by subsequent events in the novel, particularly Wickham's elopement with Lydia.

As Lizzy gradually comes to accept the accuracy of Darcy's values and actions, moreover, something crucial occurs in the narrative. Her judgments of people and events seem progressively more and more "objective." There can no longer be any reason to dispute her rising admiration for Darcy's moral authority, her unhappiness with Wickham's unworthy social elevation, her liking for the worthy merchant Mr. Gardiner, and so forth. These values no longer seem like the "prejudiced" or merely subjective perspectives of an individual of a certain class, gender, and situation; they seem like the apprehension of objective moral and social facts inherent in the world itself. Lizzy's physical point of view had always been quite close to that of the narrator, who seldom strays from the thoughts and feelings of the main character. As has been often pointed out, Austen's "free indirect discourse" converts a first-person form like a diary or series of personal letters into a third-person account. Previously, though, Lizzy had herself been vulnerable to the narrator's sly ironies. By the end of the novel, the narrator and Lizzy have become seamlessly unified in moral as well as physical terms. There seems to be nothing uncertain or provisional about the way Lizzy not only experiences but also *judges* the world.

If we cast our thoughts back one last time to previous novels, we will recognize that Austen has solved the paradox that had hindered the creation of authoritative social fiction. Richardson and Fielding basically shared the ideological aims of Jane Austen, though at an earlier stage: all were critical of aristocratic immorality and, just as strongly, socially ambitious "masquerading" in a culture where commercial enrichment had eroded the traditional hierarchy. But Fielding and Richardson, like all their contemporaries, lacked the resources of a narrative point of view without ambiguity or personal bias. The "it-narratives" of Francis Coventry and Charles Johnstone alleviate the limitations of first-person narrative by creating nonhuman narrators, throwing the weight of their conservative social critique onto the apparently "objective" dramatization of characters and events seen through the eyes of their objects. Johnstone, in particular, created a kind of awkward prototype of later non-focalized narration by joining an intelligent though nonhuman genie to his wandering guinea, making possible a direct, moral critique of English society. But the desideratum had not yet been achieved—this desideratum being a kind of narrative that could pronounce with apparently inarguable authority on the moral and social condition characteristic of the modern nation. To my knowledge, Jane Austen was the first to make the innovations that could completely realize that end. *Pride and Prejudice,* like her other fiction after *Northanger Abbey,* achieves the goal of making subjective, politically oriented judgments on society in a way that still seems objective and unbiased. Austen, so to speak, fully incorporated the genie in the guinea.

In the course of this endeavor, Austen helped to create a "middle class" that, though generally loyal to Church and monarch, would rule over Britain during its imperial heyday of the nineteenth century. The novels of this period no longer had to experiment in order to exercise the rhetorical advantages of non-focalized narration. Dickens, Gaskell, Eliot, Disraeli, and their contemporaries could use the novel as a vehicle for strong and unambiguous social critiques without sacrificing the effect of unprejudiced narration. This achievement in narrative form does not, of course, represent the be-all and end-all of modern fiction. Novelists like James, Woolf, and Joyce would turn back to sophisticated versions of first-person narrative, in part because they had lost any commitment to propping up the authority of the British bourgeoisie. Nonetheless, the it-narrative, along with its other sources of fascination explored in this volume, played the following pivotal role in the fanning possibilities of the modern novel: it experimented with narrative forms capable of making this genre a powerful instrument for defining the nature of the English middle class.

NOTES

1. See Thomas Gisborne, *An Enquiry into the Duties of Men in the Higher and Middle Classes in Great Britain,* 2nd ed., 2 vols. (1794; London, 1795), and Thomas Malthus, *An Essay on the Principle of Population, as it Affects the Future Improvement of Society* (London, 1798). On Knox's formations using the term "middle class" during the 1790s, see Dror Wahrman, *Imagining the Middle Class: The Political Representation of Class in Britain c. 1780–1840* (Cambridge: Cambridge University Press, 1995), 46–52.

2. See Wahrman, *Imagining the Middle Class.*

3. For more detailed discussion of the emergence of a self-defined "middle class" during the eighteenth century, see my *Samuel Johnson and the Making of Modern England* (Cambridge: Cambridge University Press, 2003), 11–32. Other discussions of "class" in the eighteenth-century include E. P. Thompson, *The Making of the English Working Class* (New York: Vintage, 1966), Harold J. Perkin, *The Origins of Modern English Society, 1780–1880* (London: Routledge and Kegan Paul; Toronto: University of Toronto Press, 1969), 176–217; W. A. Speck, *Stability and Strife: England 1714–1760* (London: Edward Arnold, 1977), 31–32; R. J. Morris, *Class and Class Consciousness in the Industrial Revolution, 1780–1850* (London: Macmillan, 1979), 12–20; J. C. D. Clark, *Revolution and Rebellion: State and Society in England in the Seventeenth and Eighteenth Centuries* (Cambridge: Cambridge University Press, 1986), 43; Penelope J. Corfield, "Class by Name and Number in Eighteenth-Century Britain," in Penelope J. Corfield, ed., *Language, History and Class* (Oxford: Blackwell, 1991), 101–30; John Richetti, "Class Struggle without Class: Novelists and Magistrates," *The Eighteenth Century: Theory and Interpretation* 32.3 (1991): 203–18; Jonathan Barry and Christopher Brooks, eds., *The Middling Sort of People: Culture, Society and Politics in England, 1550–1800* (Houndmills, UK: Macmillan, 1994); David Cannadine, *Class in Britain* (New Haven, CT: Yale University Press, 1998), 24–56.

4. For a defense of a traditionally Marxist division of "classes" in the eighteenth century, see R. S. Neale, *Class in English History* (Oxford: Blackwell, 1981), 68–99. Other Marxist scholars have, however, been more wary of applying nineteenth-century categories. See E. P. Thompson, "Eighteenth-Century English Society: Class Struggle without Class?" *Social History* 3 (1978): 133–65.

5. *Taxation no Tyranny* (1775), in *Political Writings,* ed. Donald J. Greene, vol. 10 of *The Yale Works of Samuel Johnson* (New Haven, CT: Yale University Press, 1977), 415.

6. On this complaint, see Terry Castle, *Masquerade and Civilization: The Carnivalesque in Eighteenth-Century Culture and Fiction* (Stanford, CA: Stanford University Press, 1988), 28, 63.

7. See Gérard Genette, *Narrative Discourse: An Essay in Method,* trans. Jane E. Lewin (Ithaca, NY: Cornell University Press, 1980), 189–94.

8. Wayne C. Booth, *The Rhetoric of Fiction* (Chicago: University of Chicago Press, 1961).

9. Aphra Behn, *Oroonoko; or, The Royal Slave,* ed. Lore Metzger (New York: Norton, 1973), 1.

10. Ibid., 40.

11. Ibid., 33.

12. Castle, *Masquerade and Civilization,* 140–41.

13. Henry Fielding, *Enquiry into the Causes of the Late Increase of Robbers*, ed. Malvin R. Zirker (Oxford: Clarendon Press, 1988), 67.

14. See my "Social Rank, 'The Rise of the Novel' and Whig Histories of Eighteenth-Century Fiction," *Eighteenth-Century Fiction* 17.4 (2005), 563–98.

15. Francis Coventry, *The History of Pompey the Little; or, The Life and Adventures of Lap-Dog*, ed. Robert Adams Day (New York: Oxford University Press, 1974), 149, 109.

16. Ibid., 168, 173.

17. Charles Johnstone, *Chrysal; or, The Adventures of a Guinea*, 2 vols. (London: 1760), 1:230.

18. Ibid., 1:145.

19. Ibid., 1:11.

20. See Ann Louise Kibbie's essay in this volume.

21. Johnstone, *Chrysal*, 2:167.

22. Jane Austen, *Northanger Abbey*, ed. Anne Henry Ehrenpreis (Harmondsworth, UK: Penguin, 1972), 58, 125.

23. Ibid., 60.

24. See Marilyn Butler, *Jane Austen and the War of Ideas* (Oxford: Clarendon Press, 1975); Claudia L. Johnson, *Jane Austen: Women, Politics and the Novel* (Chicago: University of Chicago Press, 1988).

25. Jane Austen, *Pride and Prejudice*, ed. Tony Tanner (Harmondsworth, UK: Penguin, 1972), 366.

26. Ibid., 177.

27. Ibid., 276.

III

It-Narratives in Transition

The Moral Ends of Eighteenth- and Nineteenth-Century Object Narratives

Lynn Festa

TALES TOLD BY THINGS ENJOYED THEIR HEYDAY IN THE EIGHTEENTH century, but they have an important afterlife in the late eighteenth and nineteenth century, when the world of satiric disenchantment described in earlier object narratives is transformed into the enchanted province of childhood. If the talking coaches, chatty pens, and long-winded waistcoats of the eighteenth century primarily solicit adult readers with their scandalous histories of human misconduct, nineteenth-century tales told by things turn from the quasi-public domain of the eighteenth-century novel of circulation to address themselves to the private world of children, creating a pedagogical wonderland in which animated objects and speaking animals delight and instruct humans. The peg top and pincushion, the German toy and the three-guinea watch of these later tales tender a kinder, gentler version of the world, one that fosters a child's communion with his or her beloved possessions. Sheltered from the realities of the external economy, the nursery furnishes a stronghold against the increasingly insistent clamor of Marx's commodity, a refuge where things remain things rather than values, and narratives can linger lovingly and longingly over the materials out of which the life histories of persons and things are wrought.

This essay compares the intertwining of moral and economic teleologies in eighteenth- and nineteenth-century versions of these tales. Whereas in the eighteenth century, the tales often anticipate the annihilation of the object—its destruction or disintegration into nothing as a reminder of the vanity of earthly things—the nineteenth-century tales bring objects to an Elysian Field of sentimental retirement. The talking doll and the pious grandfather clock featured in nineteenth-century narratives speak of a world in which property is restored to its "rightful" owner, in which objects instill moral lessons in their future masters while owners endeavor to become worthy of their possessions. The circulation of things in the children's tales is not governed by the abstract, impersonal forces of a market economy or even the social-climbing ambitions of their authors, but by affective relations between persons and their possessions. By juxtaposing the *vanitas* featured in eighteenth-century narratives—the satiric denunciation of the overvaluation of worldly things—with the sentimental reunion of beloved subject and object featured in the children's texts, this essay addresses the different ways eighteenth- and nineteenth-century examples of the genre endeavor to align the moral and economic ends to which things—and narratives—may be put.

The first section of this essay briefly traces the moral elements of eighteenth-century object narratives. The dispassionate, satiric gaze of the object strips away the material signs of social hierarchy to expose the real moral worth of persons; the omnipresent surveillance of persons by their possessions serves as a powerful reminder of the all-seeing eye to which all mortal creatures are accountable in the end. If the primary fault of the humans in eighteenth-century narratives is the overvaluation of worldly goods, the besetting sin in the later versions is the undervaluing of one's possessions: the failure to be a responsible caretaker. The nineteenth-century autobiographies of nonhuman characters, as I explore in the middle section of the essay, trace the education and upbringing of owner and object alike. In attributing sentience and emotions to things, the children's versions emphasize the parallels between the crafting of objects and the education of subjects; they invite younger readers to empathize with the feelings of their possessions in order to uphold a traditional hierarchy based on the reciprocal but unequal relations between owner and owned, master and servant. The pleasure taken by the pincushion and the peg top in being used by their owners is rivaled only by their delight in being crafted to such an end.

Whereas the eighteenth-century narratives revolve around the deceptiveness of things—above all, their capacity to remake people—and address the way market forces turn human beings into commodities, juvenile examples of the genre cope with the incursion of the commodity form into the sacrosanct world of personal possessions by constructing a domain insulated from the fungibility of the marketplace. The closing section of the essay explores the significance of the fact that objects are *not* interchangeable in the children's narratives: in their sentimental particularity, they are entitled to loving care and enduring patronage. The property relations created in children's tales are not personal but interpersonal; it is for this reason that Victorian objects achieve apotheosis through a sentimental reunion with their most virtuous owner. The tales things come to tell is not of their mastery over the devices and desires of men and women; instead, they explain how boys and girls become good masters and mistresses of that portion of the world over which they hold sway.

Satiric Instruction and Moral Didacticism

Recounted by waistcoats and watches, banknotes and counterfeit coins, eighteenth-century object narratives use public figures and current events as fodder for political and moral satire. Smollett's atom and Johnstone's guinea smuggle their readers behind the scenes to witness the complicity of merchants and thieves, statesmen and whores. Mute and unobserved, such objects easily eavesdrop on their owners. Their unobtrusive ubiquity allows them to weave in and out of public and private spaces unremarked, with the added advantage that a thing cannot be prosecuted for libel: "there was not a state secret but what I was let into," the ostrich feather tells us.[1] These tales recount the scandalous secret history behind the respectable surface, unveiling the pocked moral visage behind the unblemished public mask.

Although object narratives ostensibly offer the autobiography of things, the narrators are deeply preoccupied with humans: their desires, their needs, their aspirations, their flaws. They describe a world in which people do *not* exist in self-evident autonomy, aloof from objects, detached from and prior to the things that make and unmake their world. Instead they stress the ways people are made by their possessions. At a moment when the cheapness and availability of consumer goods allow individuals to purchase the trappings of a new social identity, the line between what one is socially and what one has or owns is mobile: "a man who possesses ten thousand pounds a year," the watch tells us, "cannot be a fool; for every one laughs at his jokes, feels his affronts, and sympathises with his—gold."[2] Individuals here engage in social relations using objects as their material proxies; they sympathize not with the man but with his gold. In the eighteenth-century narratives, the misguided worship of objects in a commercial society has allowed them to supplant the humans that own them.[3] Objects assume animistic powers in these tales, attaining such autonomy that they take on individual characters and recount their own tales. In a seemingly literal enactment of commodity fetishism, relations between persons have been overtaken by relations between things, as the lady's shoe talks to the slipper and the scissors pontificates to the needle.

The things have better morals than their owners; they despise their masters and seek to unmask them, stripping away the surface to reveal their true social origins and character. The black coat is so smart that he enables his owners to pass themselves off as gentlemen, while the addition of "Esquire" to the name inscribed on the banknote elevates the rank of its poet bearer: "your title to the title [of Esquire] will then be as indisputably a title, as your own title to your title page."[4] In making their owners appear more prosperous than in fact they are, the embroidered waistcoat and the petticoat facilitate all sorts of deception. But if objects give social status, they can also take it away: your possessions may snitch on you. When Jerrold's feather (one of the few instances of a satiric nineteenth-century it-narrative) warns that "there is peril in silk—there is danger in satin—yea, jeopardy in a bit of riband," it does not, as one might expect, go on to offer a jeremiad on the hazards of luxury or the perils of overvaluing worldly goods.[5] Instead, the feather warns of the tale-bearing propensity of material objects, the panoptic power of our possessions:

> Never, gentle reader, so long as you have a stitch about your anatomy, believe yourself alone. If thoughtless people could only know what their left-off clothes say about them, sure I am, they would resolve upon one of two things: either to reform their lives, or to go naked. Let no man harbour a black spot in his breast, and believe that his waistcoat is wholly ignorant of the stain . . . His very glove shall babble of the bribe that has burnt his hand . . . Ignorance of man! to believe that what is borne upon the body has no intelligence with the moral good or evil dwelling in the soul.[6]

Moving between literal and moral stains and blots, the feather transforms clothing into a material record of the sins of the wearer. The clothing that cloaks the body unveils the soul. Jerrold's Victorian account not only twitches off the moral fig leaf, it also institutes a system of surveillance. It is not a higher ethical principle but the fear of being blackmailed by one's coat that coerces the reader into self-policing virtue.

Seen through the impersonal eyes of their possessions, all humans are alike beneath the trappings of wealth and privilege. The object narrative does not affirm the particularity of the individual voice, the triumph of novelistic interiority; it celebrates the imperative to measure everyone by the same moral yardstick, irrespective of social rank and birth. "I have," the feather tells us, "found the coarse mind of the merest footman in the lackey peer; and in the Lady of the Bedchamber, the small envy, the petty heart-burning of Molly the chambermaid at the Star and Garter."[7] What matters, the objects ostensibly claim, are the moral attributes beneath the superficial mask—the virtues and vices that govern one's fate in the hereafter. Thus part of the purpose of these narratives is to remind readers that they will all come to the same end: "from dust we came, and to dust shall we return," the banknote gloomily pronounces.[8]

As a symbol of the vanity of worldly things, eighteenth-century object narratives in particular are meant to incite the reader to reflect on his or her own mortality, the transience of the material world to which person and thing alike belong. The nonhuman character, as Toby Olshin puts it, shows "how fallible a thing is a human being, how vulnerable, how ultimately powerless."[9] The waistcoat falls from the body of the lord to a dismal fate in a pawnshop; the gold ring is sold to "a refiner, who melted me down, and mixed my remains with other old gold, to experience a new resurrection; but never again in the particles of my *individual self,* to experience such a train of adventures as those with which the Reader had just now been presented."[10] Confronted by a spanking new "gay white coat," the black coat finds its high-minded resignation faltering before the prospect of his "approaching dissolution." It addresses its companion—and the reader—with dour admonitions about the future: "were it possible thou couldst foresee the train of misfortunes, which in the course of thy existence, and revolutions of thy fortune, thou wilt be subject to, that gay and happy mien would be changed to a gloomy and melancholy aspect."[11] Speaking objects like the coat invite readers to identify with the fate of the object, with its eventual deterioration or disintegration, in order to remind them that humans, like things, are subject to material erosion and death.

The satiric tales either conclude with a reminder of their status as print commodities—with the promise of further installments—or with the eclipse of the object itself. "Being now upon my last legs," the lady's slipper confesses, "I am only slipt on at night when she goes to bed . . . my lower parts fail, and time has made several chinks in me." The imminent death of the object shadows that of the subject. The things in which we invest our labors and which proclaim our wealth and stature do not outlast our mortal coil. "All I expect now," the slipper observes, "and I expect it with resignation, is to be thrown into the highway, or on the dunghill . . . to moulder away to the last shred."[12] People must attend to the spiritual lest they suffer the fate of their possessions. Like the still-life *vanitas,* the protracted attention to the object is meant to turn back on the subject, directing the reader's attention to the spirit over the body, the divine rather than the worldly. "May my movements never prove so unsteady," the watch piously concludes, "but when my springs grow weak through age, and my hands slow and tremulous from time, may I go to rest with A GOOD NAME!"[13]

The narratives remind us of the emptiness of material things, but they also—again like the *vanitas* still life—do the opposite of what they profess, by reveling in objects while purporting to reveal their insignificance. For all their ostensible interest in matters of the soul, object narratives are preoccupied with the well-being of the body. As invitations to look beyond themselves, the object narratives fail utterly. But as invitations to take seriously the moral issues at stake in the relation between subjects and objects, they are not quite failures. For they enable us to acknowledge the way the world of persons and the world of things are reciprocally made. In the juvenile stories to which we now turn, the fact that things speak becomes a matter of moral accountability within this world rather than the next. Whereas eighteenth-century texts invite their readers to identify with the object in order to recognize the fate to which all flesh is heir, the children's versions invite the reader to recognize the kinship between his or her education and that of the object or animal. The parallel between nonhuman narrator and all-too-human reader is not meant to produce meditation on death, but on the way one lives and learns. The London doll and the mouse are not memento mori, exposing the skull beneath the skin; instead, as we shall now see, they speak to remind young masters and mistresses of their obligations to the objects and animals under their stewardship.

Pedagogy and Children's Books

Unlike the objects featured in the satiric adult narratives, the doll, the thimble, the pin, and the whipping top seek to educate not to excoriate, to teach not to taunt. Whereas eighteenth-century object narratives endeavor to inculcate virtue through satiric discipline, the objects in children's tales disavow the desire to critique their owners; they aim to instruct rather than mock. "The pointed satire of ridicule," the pincushion observes,

> which would perhaps have given a zest to those scenes in which the subject of these pages was engaged, was not, in the opinion of the writer, at all proper for those readers for whom it was solely designed: to exhibit their superiors in a ridiculous view, is not the proper method to engage the youthful mind to respect: to represent their equals as the objects of contemptuous mirth, is by no means favourable to the interest of good nature: and to treat the characters of their inferiors with levity, the Author thought was inconsistent with the sacred rights of humanity.[14]

The children's versions replace ridicule and contempt with emotional blackmail: misbehavior is recounted in a sorrowful tone, reinforced by a threatened withdrawal of the objects' affections. In juvenile tales, the lash of satire is replaced by disquisitions on the proper behavior of boys and girls—with the added benefit that the moral lesson comes from a literally objective source. If you are a good boy or girl, your things will love you back. Thus the texts present models of good children—Miss Steady, Miss Allworth, George Reader—and bad—Tom Drift, Lady Dashley, Miss Shallow—to elevate particular ideals of conduct. The objects reward good behavior with affection for their virtuous owners, while frowning upon the misdemeanors of their corrupt possessors.

The shift from an adult to a juvenile audience may be partly attributed to market saturation: as the 1781 *Critical Review* wearily notes, "this mode of making up a book, and styling it the *Adventures* of a Cat, a Dog, a Monkey, a Hackney-coach, a Louse, a Shilling, a Rupee, or—anything else, is grown so fashionable, that few months pass which do not bring one of them under our inspection."[15] It may also be traced to the burgeoning mass market in children's literature fostered by publishers like Thomas Boreman, John Newbery, and John Marshall.[16] Although there were, of course, earlier texts explicitly designed for children, the 1744 publication of Newbery's *Little Pretty Pocket Book* is often seen to inaugurate the commercial boom in didactic and amusing works specifically targeting younger readers.[17] Capitalizing on Locke's recognition that children might be "cozen'd into a Knowledge of the Letters, be *taught to read,* without perceiving it to be any thing but a Sport, and play themselves into that which others are whipp'd for," Newbery's books were motley collections of tales, riddles, and songs.[18] "The avidity with which children peruse books of entertainment," the preface to Kilner's *Adventures of a Pincushion* (ca. 1780) contends, "is a proof how much publications proper for their attention are required."[19]

The emergence of this body of literature is often conjoined with the romantic celebration of the child, and yet the juvenile narratives told by objects are not easily absorbed into that model. Written largely by women educationalists—what Charles Lamb famously called "the cursed Barbauld Crew, those Blights and Blasts of all that is Human in man and child"—these narratives depict a child hemmed in by social and pedagogical constraints, dependent upon the labor of others.[20] Alan Richardson has noted that the romantic child's "distance from the social world, its seeming immateriality, in a word, its transcendence," seem crafted "to underwrite the wishful autonomy, the privileging of consciousness, and the devaluation of bodily experience for which feminist critics like Marlon Ross and Meena Alexander have disparaged male Romanticism."[21] Neither autonomous nor particularly self-conscious, the good or bad child in the object narrative is a far cry from the Wordsworthian boy. No intimations of individuated character trouble these semi-allegorical girls and boys. If anything, these texts endeavor to harness the imagination to prosaic ends, ensuring that even fanciful narratives be put to household use. Nevertheless, the writers of the tales and the romanticists draw on a shared literary tradition. Dorothy Kilner's *Life and Perambulation of a Mouse* (ca. 1783–84) and *Rational Brutes; or, Talking Animals* (1799), like Sarah Trimmer's *Fabulous Histories* (1786) and *Silver Thimble* (1799), evoke not only it-narratives like *The History of Pompey the Little; or, The Life and Adventures of a Lap-Dog* (1751), but also the speaking animals in the fables of Aesop and La Fontaine, the animated creatures in the fairy tales of Perrault (translated into English in 1729) and Madame d'Aulnoy (trans. 1707), and (later on) the haughty darning needle and steadfast tin soldier of Hans Christian Andersen.[22]

Whereas the eighteenth-century satires are composed of episodes often strung together without discernible plot or psychological motivation, the mobile narrators of the children's tales gather moral gloss, learning so that they may teach or preach to their young readers. This narrative conceit of a talking object or animal holds a child's interest, while the objects' itinerancy allows for variety of incident, tethered by the unifying thread of the objects' moralizing observations. Because the "dry detail of unconnected facts, however interesting in themselves," is not "well calculated to engage the attention of children," Lucy Peacock forms her 1800 natural history of the bee "into a regular succession of events set forth in such a manner as to interest their tender minds, that while they eagerly pursue the thread of the story, they may insensibly acquire a knowledge of facts, which cannot fail of exalting their ideas of the Supreme Being."[23] In short, these books delight and instruct by animating the objects of instruction.

Yet eighteenth-century critics disputed whether talking animals and objects are suitable vehicles of moral lessons for impressionable children. John Marchant, for example, condemned tales recounted by animals in his 1751 *Puerilia,* claiming that they lead the child to "believe that Brutes are endued with Reason and Understanding, which is to possess a young Mind with a false Notion, that Brutes are on a Level with the human Species."[24] The attribution of speech to animals erodes the differences between human and beast in the minds of children, disrupting the proper hierarchy of the natural world. Perhaps surprisingly, rationalist educators like Richard and Maria Edgeworth, Sarah Trimmer, John and Lucy Aikin, Anna Letitia Barbauld, and Mary Wollstonecraft admit the merits of moral tales told by animals and objects. Although these writers rejected fantastic or supernatural reading as detrimental to a child's education, railing against the bogeymen and fairy tales used by superstitious nurses to frighten small children into docility, they found tales recounted by animals or objects acceptable.[25] "Animals," Mary Wollstonecraft notes in her *Thoughts on the Education of Daughters* (1787), "are the first objects which catch their [children's] attention; and I think little stories about them would not only amuse but instruct at the same time, and have the best effect in forming the temper and cultivating the good dispositions of the heart."[26] The novelty of the narrator—whether an animal or an inanimate object—arrests the straying fancy of the youthful mind and gilds the didactic pill. "Reason," Wollstonecraft concludes, "strikes most forcibly when illustrated by the brilliancy of fancy."[27] Although the virtuous mother in Dorothy Kilner's *The Rational Brutes; or, Talking Animals* prefers instructive stories "which had really happened . . . to what is called *make-believe* stories," she makes an exception for a book that "supposed that birds and beasts, and fish, could talk and reason, which you know is quite impossible . . . called, the Gossipping [*sic*] Assembly of Dumb Animals."[28]

Nevertheless these texts bristle with reminders that the story is only make-believe in order to ensure that children not be deluded. The human author behind the text irrupts into the pincushion's account in order to address the credulous young reader:

> Perhaps you never thought that such things as are inanimate, could be sensible of any thing which happens, as they can neither hear, see, nor understand; and as I would not willingly mislead your judgment: I would previous to your reading this work, inform you, that it is to be understood as an imaginary tale; in the same manner as when you are at a play, you sometimes call yourselves gentlemen, and ladies, though you know you are only little boys or girls. So, when you read of birds and beasts speaking and thinking, you know it is not so in reality, any more than your amusements, which you frequently call *making believe.*[29]

By explicitly articulating the fictitious nature of the account, the author circumvents accusations of deliberately misleading her innocent reader. The pleasures of make-believe are all very well, provided the child understands the nature of the real world. This is a provisional fantasy, whose license is revoked with the closing lines of the text. In the end, boys and girls must return to the prosaic world of everyday life. (Notably even the children's play involves the bourgeois roles of the ladies and gentlemen they will eventually become.)

The attribution of sentience to the nonhuman narrator allows these tales to be read as lessons in childhood education. Like Condillac's statue, the things come into possession of their senses and consciousness in progressive stages. "Tick, tick, tick . . . It was the first time e'er / I had possessed the power to hear," the grandfather clock tells us. "And can it be this clatter is a part of me? / What am I? why awakened now, / Why am I called to life? and how?"[30] These objects are particular in their hand-hewn, nonindustrial being: they begin their lives as ore buried in the mountain or as feathers plucked from a bird: "I was a tree before I was a toy," the German toy confides. "I found myself growing, I did not know how, out of the ground, in the Black Forest."[31] The objects are all raised and educated on an individual basis; none of them are industrially manufactured. The manner of their crafting is lovingly described. If the toymaker's workshop initially sounds like a little shop of horrors—littered with "wooden legs and arms, and wooden heads without hair, and small bodies, and half legs and half arms, which had not yet been fitted together in the joints"—the making of the doll is a kind of gentle birth: "I passed into the hands of the most gentle of all the Sprat family, and felt something delightfully warm laid upon my cheeks and mouth. It was the little girl who was painting me a pair of rosy cheeks and lips."[32] The pincushion is made by the daughter of the house from scraps leftover from her mother's labors; the peg top is pronounced by his maker to be "the best top he had ever produced."[33] Even the pin—the epitome of the mass-produced commodity used by Adam Smith—is the singular product of labor.

The process by which objects gain value recalls that by which children become worthy. The heating and hammering of the needle parallel the physical discipline to which pupils are subjected: "how I thought the file hard, disagreeable, and rough," the needle tells us, "as many young folk have thought their teachers; how I was then heated in a fire till I grew as red as naughty boys who have been caned by their master, then left to cool in a basin of cold water, like the same boys shut up to think over the matter . . . education is a slow and troublesome matter, whether to children or needles!"[34] To assume its true shape, the needle must be beaten and bored (not unlike a student). Children and needles must be refashioned to produce their proper, useful role in the world. The style of education is differentiated by gender in these texts. Since, as Bonnie Blackwell argues elsewhere in this volume, the object narratives establish parallels between the exchange of objects and the traffic in women, the children's narratives must also deliver lessons about the proper circulation of bodies and the policing of sexuality. Whereas Kilner's pincushion, lost and neglected beneath a bookcase, instructs young girls to recognize that social isolation protects the virtuous girl from the hazards of the world, the peg top informs boys of the appropriate times and places to play with their peg tops.

The narratives both describe and perform the process by which childhood lessons are internalized, reproducing the mechanisms of examination and self-regulation that constitute education. Thus the watch describes its final polishing as a perversely Althusserian interpellation:

> I used to be handed over to a creature who took me up and examined me (as if he were a policeman and a magistrate combined), and according as I answered his questions he exclaimed, 'You're going too fast,' or 'You're going too slow,' and with that he set himself to 'regulate' me, as he called it. I was ordered to turn round, take off my coat, and submit my poor shoulders to his instrument of correction. But why need I describe this experience to boys? They know what 'regulating' means as well as I do![35]

Oscillating between literal and metaphorical domains, the anthropomorphized watch invites the reader to shift between abstract and physical correction. Neither watch nor boy should march to a different drummer. The watch is regulated so as to learn to regulate itself; it eventually becomes a self-monitoring mechanism in this clockwork universe.

Objects in the tales are represented as being in more or less voluntary servitude to their masters. "Whatever wooden office I was called to fill,—the handle of a pipe, or the case of a clock," the young sapling proclaims, "I must fill it to the best of my ability, and never torment myself at not being something else, or greater; then I should be both useful and happy."[36] Extolling the virtues of dutiful resignation and quashing aspirations beyond one's station, the sapling celebrates the status quo by advocating submission to one's rank and lot in life. "Why was I made, if not to be used?" the needle asks, while the pen "date[s] my adventures from the *day* in which I *first* became of service to mankind."[37] The superiority of human claims is not to be questioned. "Man has been gifted with a power called reason," the thimble explains to the needle; "by this he governs the world, by this he subdues creatures stronger than himself, and makes all things combine to serve him."[38] The children's narratives do not doubt the human right to dominion over creation, provided people behave correctly.

Yet there are people behind these objects and part of the purpose of the narratives is to articulate their place. In explaining how things are made, the Victorian versions of the narratives remind their juvenile readers of the myriad hands involved in the production of objects. The silver penny unfolds the labor hidden in its form, describing the depredations wrought upon the Indians by the Spaniards and the suffering of those enslaved in the Peruvian mines from which it came: "only think what a sad thing it must be, to be condemned for life to work under ground, without ever seeing the chearful light of the sun," the narrator admonishes the young reader. "That nice silver spoon, with which you eat your milk for breakfast, and the pretty silver cup, out of which you drink your beer at dinner time . . . were dug out of the bowels of the earth, at the expence of the death of thousands, and the slavery of many more."[39] The silver penny invites the reader to dilate upon the object in order to foster sympathetic identification with its makers. Although the penny does not particularize the plight of these distant sufferers by singling out one victim for attention, it homes in on specific objects owned and enjoyed by children in order to articulate individual complicity in the broader system. These texts remind children of exploitation elsewhere, exposing their dependence upon the labors of strangers. Yet they also obscure this labor by inviting the child to think about the feelings of the thing rather than those of the people behind the object.

I argued above that these narratives suggest a parallel between the education of a child and the making of an object. If one takes this parallel to its logical extreme, then it suggests the perturbing notion that children, like material goods, are instruments to be trained for use or exchange rather than ends in themselves. Composed at a moment when, as Viviana Zelizer notes, children's labor was becoming more rather than less valuable, the tales told by things move to shelter the child from such commoditization.[40] The education of the child, unlike that of the object, does not prepare him or her for the marketplace. These children are not destined to become servants or laborers, but ladies and gentlemen. Whereas the earlier satires acknowledge the commoditization of the human—the way persons as well as things are bought and sold on the market in the form of wage labor, political venality, marriage, and prostitution—the children's tales veer away from this recognition by confining the parallel between subject and object to their complementary functions as owner and owned.

The satiric bent of the earlier narratives cedes to a paternalistic model of reciprocal obligations, as the enmity that subsists between owner and possession in the eighteenth-century tales gives way to increasingly disempowered nonhuman narrators who must be educated and cared for. Whereas the eighteenth-century waistcoat, coin, and hackney coach threaten to unmask their owner's pretensions, the mouse, the pin, the doll, and the kitten represent the vulnerability of the child-reader before the depredations of a cruel adult world. Children, like animals and things, are often helpless bystanders or powerless victims. "How at that moment did I abhor my own existence," the mouse exclaims of the boys torturing his brother, "and wish that I could be endowed with size and strength sufficient, at once both to rescue him, and severely punish his tormenters."[41] Although the impotence of objects and animals echoes the powerlessness of children, the lesson to be gleaned is not, as in earlier narratives, Christian resignation but noblesse oblige. The child is invited to identify less with the suffering animal or misused thing than with the owner who treats his pets or possessions with care. By empowering the child through his or her greatness in relation to the Lilliputian world of the text, the narrative educates him or her in the rights, privileges, and obligations of ownership.

If the narratives by inanimate objects exalt the power of reason, celebrating human dominion over the raw materials of the natural world, those recounted by animals seek to instill a virtuous humility in their readers, reminding them of the obligations reason imposes upon humans. Children are enjoined to refrain from acts of wanton cruelty.

Newbery's 1789 *Life and Adventures of a Fly* features a cameo appearance by an eight-year-old Laurence Sterne, who advocates releasing a fly: "Go thy ways, poor fluttering thing; it were very hard indeed, if in this wide world there were not room enough for *me* and *you* to live."[42] Both the kitten of sentiment and the mouse rail against little boys who torture them, and the parents of the children make this message explicit. "What right," the father demands upon discovering his sons torturing a mouse, "have you to torment any living creature? . . . how . . . would [you] like, that either myself, or some great giant, as much larger than you as you are bigger than the mouse, should hurt and torment you?"[43] When the boys point out that adults kill vermin and insects, the father insists upon a distinction between necessary and gratuitous violence: "to take *pleasure* in hearing it squeak, and seeing it struggle for liberty, is such *unmanly,* such *detestable* cruelty, as calls for my utmost indignation, and abhorrence."[44] It is not the nature of the act (killing) but the motive and necessity underlying it. Purposeless violence is inhumane, even inhuman.

Cruelty by children to animals is attributed to a range of motives, from the failure to channel children's active impulses to natural depravity. Locke notes that children "often *torment* . . . Birds, Butterflies, and such other poor Animals which fall into their Hands, and that with a seeming kind of Pleasure. This I think should be watched in them . . . for the Custom of tormenting and killing of Beasts, will, by Degrees, harden their Minds even towards Men."[45] Unchecked, vicious impulses in children may lead to a lifetime of wickedness. "Some of the most execrable tyrants that ever disgraced human nature," *The Young Gentleman's and Lady's Magazine* contends, "began their career of cruelty with killing flies, and progressively went on to murder their fellow-men."[46] The child is the father of the man in this domino theory of moral corruption. The narratives by animals are intended to curtail the child's propensity to torture animals. By exciting "compassion and tenderness for those interesting and delightful creatures, on which such wanton cruelties are frequently exercised," tales recounted by animals, Sarah Trimmer contends, "convey moral instruction to the young reader."[47] The narratives invite the reader to put himself in the position of another: "How would *you,* dear reader, act, if *your* tail were wantonly pulled, or if *your* house were to be entered by an ugly stranger without invitation?"[48] Although adults have absorbed these enjoinders and become self-policing individuals, children must be instructed in the laborious production of sympathetic feeling.

Unlike the eighteenth-century satires, the children's tales do not ask us to think as if we were things or animals; they ask us to think as if things and animals were people. Because objects have feelings and memories, their treatment matters. The toyshop, the doll cradle tells us, "is haunted by all the dolls that Mr. Kramer sells that are treated badly. The thumps you hear are made by the head of a big wooden doll; for the girl who owned that doll, whenever she was angry with the doll, used to bang it on her nursery floor."[49] Things, we are told, have feelings and thus must be tenderly cared for and comforted. Even if mistreatment does not materially or visibly damage the toy, it has moral consequences. Neglect may hurt an object's feelings; it may injure or kill a pet. By articulating the consequences of children's heedless deeds from the point of view of the victim, the animated peg top and the speaking kitten create a heightened sense of accountability.

At the heart of these tales is the recognition of the difficulty of understanding another's pain, the incapacity of individuals to enter into the insular consciousness of others. "*You* would not attend to his cries," the father admonishes the boys torturing the mouse, "because you were *bigger,* and did not *feel* its torture. *I* now am bigger than *you,* and do not feel *your* pain."[50] The attribution of sensibility to nonhuman creatures creates the possibility of empathy by giving form to the damage inflicted upon otherwise voiceless entities. The expressive language uttered by the animal in pain or by the injured object begins, as Elaine Scarry puts it in *The Body in Pain,* "to externalize, objectify, and make sharable what is originally an interior and unsharable experience."[51] In the process, these tales invite readers to recognize not only the utility of objects, but the need to care for them. The capacity to feel for the sufferings of animals and objects instills in the child a sense of the obligations of possession. As I explore in the closing section of this essay, the interpersonal bonds fostered between nonhuman beings and their owners consolidate the child's future role as benevolent master or mistress.

Coming to a Good End

In ascribing feelings to animals and objects, children learn to love them and care for them, and the reward of good behavior is the love of one's possessions. Objects strive to escape from the clutches of wicked owners: "heartily sick of my captivity, for I cannot call it service," the silver thimble hopes "from day to day that I should fall into some more worthy hand," while the country doll prays "that I might be delivered from such a mother, and placed in the hands of a better one, who had more sense, and who was not so ill-humored and proud."[52] Relations of ownership prove to be interpersonal. Unlike eighteenth-century objects, however, children's things never revolt against their masters. Although they dislike falling into the hands of wicked girls and boys, they never mutiny.

Instead, the objects compete for the favor of their good masters, anticipating Disney's *Toy Story* by almost two centuries. The shoes in a lady's closet dispute "which was the mistress's favourite," while the saw, the awl, the axe, and the gimlet argue over who is most indispensable to the carpenter.[53] At times, the objects seem like courtesans jostling for royal favors; at others, they seem like lonely goods seeking only to be loved. The three-guinea watch turns "faint with jealousy" when supplanted by a gold watch and chain in its owner's affections and the London doll worries that "there were other dolls in the world who were far prettier and better made than myself."[54] "When he died," the grandfather clock tells us of his beloved owner, "I felt there was not one beside / To love me as in days of yore: / My happiness I thought was o'er."[55] The objects love their virtuous owners best, and the desire to be loved becomes the carrot to be earned by responsible behavior towards one's pets and possessions.

That the coat shrinks about the person, that the watch clutches at chains to try to stay attached to a desirable owner, legitimates the ownership of the many by the few.[56] The reason certain things belong to particular people is not class or economic privilege, nor the rapacity of an owner who would hoard what he or she already has; instead, you own objects because objects want to be owned by you. If all things return to the hands of the wealthy (or occasionally the virtuous poor), it is because all things belong in their hearts to particular people. These it-narrators tell a tale of moral entitlement; they want to be in the hands of the good and the good alone deserve them.

The entire plot of the 1883 *Adventures of a Three Guinea Watch* involves the watch's quest to be restored to his fair-haired, upright first owner, Charlie Newcome. It was hard, the watch declares, "after being the pride and favourite of a boy like Charlie Newcome, to find myself the property of Tom Drift" (80). "My first young master returned constantly to my thoughts" (153), it tells us, as it passes through the hands of a pickpocket, a receiver of stolen goods, a pawnbroker, a shopkeeper, a college student, a clergyman, and a sailor. When their paths cross midway through the book, the watch "looked at him [Charlie] and rejoiced, I felt I would give the world to be back in my old place in his pocket" (165). Objects objectively confirm the earthly rewards of virtue by desiring to belong to the good. This sprawling love affair ends happily. Through a set of truly remarkable coincidences, boy (now man) and watch are touchingly reunited in India during the 1857 Sepoy Revolt: "I may with truth say, I reached that night the happiest moment in my life. Indeed, as the young officer walked on, with me held tight in his hand, it would be hard to say which of us two was the happier" (212). In a true tale of heroism, the watch throws itself between Charlie and the bullet that would have killed him. After saving its master's life nearly at the price of its own, the watch retires to a place of honor in Charlie's curio cabinet. Liberated from all use value, the three-guinea watch becomes a memento, drawn out when the father tells the children how it saved his life.

Nor is this an unusual ending. If, as we saw above, the eighteenth-century tales end either with the annihilation of the object or the anticipation of its unremitting circulation in the market, the Victorian tales reunite objects with their most virtuous owner, or otherwise carry them into sentimental retirement. What once was lost will eventually be found. The restoration of property to its "rightful" owner constitutes a happy ending. The ability to keep something becomes a form of narrative stasis that forecloses the narrative. (Foreclosure of an economic sort is what propels things along.) Thus the ostrich feather is restored to the upstanding Captain Doriville who originally purchased it: "this," the feather exclaims, "is the happiest moment I have experienced since I left the extremity of my mother's wing!"[57] Unlike Marx's commodities, these objects do not forget their makers and caretakers. The doll is ecstatic to see the toymaker at the theater, while the clock is pleased to be conferred upon an old servant who "loved *me* with affection true, Ay, almost idolized whate'er / Belonged to any member dear / Of family so prized."[58] (Like the clock, the servant prizes objects not for their financial value but for their sentimental associations with the master's family.) The pin retires to a country estate, where it is ecstatic to find that "our nearest neighbours were my first and dearest friends, Mrs. Dormer and her lovely daughter."[59] The affective bond between things and their owners is so overpowering that the tales read more like a child's testimony in a custody battle than a narrative about an object: *Jarndyce vs. Jarndyce* rewritten into *Kramer vs. Kramer.*

The value these virtuous owners attribute to their possessions is affective rather than economic: object and owner love one another for their virtues rather than their monetary worth. Although "scarcely the shred of my former self . . . a poor discoloured, diminished thing," the feather finds happiness in the closing paragraphs of its story in its proximity to the virtuous Patty Butler, a "poor orphan feather-dresser" encountered earlier in the text.[60] The priceless silver penny falls into the hands of a poor but virtuous girl who tells the doctor who offers to buy the penny that "she would never sell me, and should be even very sorry to part with me, unless it was to somebody who would sometimes permit her to see me."[61] The silver thimble rejoices when the virtuous Miss Steady reclaims her from the clutches of the lying Miss Smallwit and explains that it remains a cherished treasure. Although "not worth a farthing" and unable to "be of the smallest service," the thimble is "still honoured with a place in a repository for keepsakes," guarded with "other baubles of little value but for the sake of their several donors . . . As a remembrancer it is just as valuable as any trifle in the box, and in itself has been very useful."[62] The value of the thimble stems from its absolute particularity; for Miss Steady, not just any thimble will do. Such sentimental value withdraws objects from infinite circulation, creating a refuge from the vast engines that run the economies of the world. Treasured things constitute a bid for humble objects to retain personal meaning in the face of broad systems of exchange.

The eighteenth-century object narratives with which we began satirize the overvaluation of worldly things by representing the moral and material end to which all persons and all things must come. By contrast, the conclusions of children's object narratives create a haven of sentimental retirement, exempt from the menacing fungibility of the world, in which objects and animals are loved for their own sake. The morality of benevolent responsibility and paternalistic mastery described in these texts draws younger readers into the roles of loving master and mistress, and creates powerful emotional bonds that lock persons and things together in relations that supersede the claims of mere property. In imposing narrative structure upon the vicissitudes of an arbitrary, impersonal, and contingent market, these tales gently guide objects into the hands of their proper owners while training those gentle hands to receive them. In these tales, the most absolute form of appropriation is sentimental possession.

NOTES

I would like to thank Marie-Christine Lemardeley, André Topia, and the members of the research group VORTEX at the Université de la Sorbonne Nouvelle (Paris 3) for sponsoring the conference "L'empreinte des choses," at which this paper was originally presented.

1. *The Adventures of an Ostrich Feather of Quality* (London: H. Bryer, 1812), 70.
2. *The Adventures of a Watch* (London: G. Kearsley, 1788), 185.
3. Aileen Douglas, "Britannia's Rule and the It-Narrator," *Eighteenth-Century Fiction* 6.1 (1993): 65–82; a version of Douglas's essay appears in this volume.
4. *Adventures of a Black Coat* (London: J. Williams, 1760), 4; Thomas Bridges, *The Adventures of a Bank-Note,* 4 vols. (London: T. Davies, 1770–71), 1:15. On object narratives and the emerging print market, see Christopher Flint, "Speaking Objects: The Circulation of Stories in Eighteenth-Century Prose Fiction," *PMLA* 113.2 (1998), 212–26, a version of which appears in this volume.
5. Douglas Jerrold, *The Story of a Feather* (London: Bradbury, Evans, 1867), 88.

6. Ibid., 86. For a similar passage, see *Aureus; or, The Life and Opinions of a Sovereign* (London: G. Wightman, 1824), 24.

7. Jerrold, *Feather*, 46.

8. Bridges, *Bank-Note*, 1:167.

9. Toby Olshin, "Form and Theme in Novels about Non-human Characters," *Genre* 2.1 (1969): 45.

10. "Adventures of a Gold Ring," *The Rambler's Magazine; or, the Annals of Gallantry, Glee, Pleasure, and the Bon Ton* 1 (July 1783): 256.

11. *Black Coat*, 1, 2, 2–3.

12. *The History and Adventures of a Lady's Slippers and Shoes* (London: M. Cooper, 1754), 27, 27–8.

13. *Watch*, 209–10.

14. Mary Ann Kilner [attrib.], *The Adventures of a Pincushion* (London: John Marshall, 1780), v–vi.

15. *Critical Review* (December 1781), quoted in J. M. S. Tompkins, *The Popular Novel in England, 1770–1800* (1932; Lincoln: University of Nebraska Press, 1961), 49.

16. Newbery published and sold histories, dictionaries, letter-writers, and juvenile magazines like the *Lilliputian Magazine* (1751–52), modeled on publisher Thomas Boreman's *Gigantick Histories* (1740–43). He also sold various patent medicines, including Dr. James's Powder, for want of which Goody Two-Shoes's father dies in Newbery's eponymous tale. See *Trade and Plumb-Cake For Ever, Huzza: The Life and Work of John Newbery, 1713–1767*, ed. John Rowe Townsend (Cambridge, UK: Colt, 1994).

17. On children's literature, see F. J. Harvey Darton's magisterial *Children's Books in England: Five Centuries of Social Life* (1932; Cambridge: Cambridge University Press, 1982). On the market for moral texts, see Mary V. Jackson, *Engines of Instruction, Mischief, and Magic: Children's Literature in England from its Beginnings to 1839* (Lincoln: University of Nebraska Press, 1989); Patricia Demers, *Heaven Upon Earth: The Form of Moral and Religious Children's Literature to 1850* (Knoxville: University of Tennessee Press, 1993); Samuel Pickering, *Moral Instruction and Fiction for Children, 1749–1820* (Athens: University of Georgia Press, 1993); and J. H. Plumb, "The New World of Children in Eighteenth-Century England," *Past and Present* 67 (1975), 64–95.

18. John Locke, *Some Thoughts Concerning Education*, 9th ed. (London: A Bettlesworth and C. Hitch, 1732), 230. On Locke and object narratives, see Samuel F. Pickering, Jr., *John Locke and Children's Books in Eighteenth-Century England* (Knoxville: University of Tennessee Press, 1981), 70–103.

19. *Pincushion*, vii.

20. Charles Lamb, *The Letters of Charles and Mary Ann Lamb*, ed. E. V. Lucas, 3 vols. (New York: AMS, 1968), 1.326.

21. Alan Richardson, "Romanticism and the End of Childhood," in *Literature and the Child: Romantic Continuations, Postmodern Contestations*, ed. James Holt McGavran (Iowa City: University of Iowa Press, 1999), 28. On romanticism and the child, see the other essays in this volume, as well as the essays in James McGavran, ed., *Romanticism and Children's Literature in Nineteenth-Century England* (Athens: University of Georgia Press, 1991).

22. On fables, see Kirsten Hoving Powell, "The Art of Making Animals Talk: Constructions of Nature and Culture in Illustrations of the Fables of La Fontaine," *Word and Image* 12.3 (1996): 251–73. See also Thomas Noel, *Theories of the Fable in the Eighteenth Century* (New York: Columbia University Press, 1975).

23. Lucy Peacock, *The Life of a Bee, Related by Herself* (London: John Marshall, 1800), vii, viii.

24. John Marchant, *Puerilia, or Amusements for the Young, consisting of a collection of*

songs, adapted to the fancies and capacities of those of tender years (London: P. Stevens, 1751), preface, iv.

25. The repudiation of fairy tales should not be understood as a simple sign of humorless moral rigidity, but must be contextualized in relation to the feminist claim to rational education. See Mitzi Myers, "Impeccable Governesses, Rational Dames, and Moral Mothers: Mary Wollstonecraft and the Female Tradition in Georgian Children's Books," *Children's Literature* 14 (1986): 31–59, and Mitzi Myers, "Romancing the Moral Tale: Maria Edgeworth and the Problematics of Pedagogy," in McGavran, *Romanticism and Children's Literature,* 96–128.

26. Mary Wollstonecraft, *Thoughts on the Education of Daughters* (London: J. Johnson, 1787), 16.

27. Ibid., 51.

28. Dorothy Kilner, *The Rational Brutes; or, Talking Animals* (London: Vernor and Hood, 1799), 2, 4.

29. *Pincushion,* 13. On the correlation of reason and adulthood, see Geoffrey Summerfield, *Fantasy and Reason: Children's Literature in the Eighteenth Century* (London: Methuen, 1984).

30. *Autobiography of a Clock* (Boston: William Crosby, 1852), 189.

31. *The Adventures of a German Toy* (Boston: W. V. Spencer, 1866), 7.

32. R. H. Horne, *Memoirs of a London Doll, written by herself,* ed. Mrs. Fairstar (London: Joseph Cundall, 1846), 2, 4.

33. *Pincushion,* 14–16; S.S., *Memoirs of a Peg-Top* (London: John Harris, 1828), 6.

34. *The Story of a Needle* (New York: Robert Carter, 1862), 12, 11.

35. Talbot Baines Reed, *The Adventures of a Three Guinea Watch* (London: The Religious Tract Society, 1883), 2. All further references will be cited parenthetically.

36. *German Toy,* 25.

37. *Needle,* 14; Dionysius, "Adventures of a Pen," *The European Magazine and London Review, containing Portraits, Views, Biography and Anecdotes* 50 (July 1806): 25.

38. *Needle,* 24–25.

39. *The Adventures of a Silver Penny, including many secret anecdotes of little misses and masters, both good and naughty* (London: E. Newbery, 1786), 10.

40. Viviana Zelizer, *Pricing the Priceless Child: The Changing Social Value of Children* (New York: Basic Books, 1985).

41. Dorothy Kilner, *Life and Perambulation of a Mouse,* 2 vols. (London: John Marshall, 1790), 1:37.

42. *Life and Adventures of a Fly, supposed to have been written by himself* (London: E. Newbery, 1789), 65. On the workings of sympathy in the object narrative, see Jonathan Lamb, "Modern Metamorphoses and Disgraceful Tales," *Critical Inquiry* 28.1 (2001): 133–66.

43. Kilner, *Mouse,* 1:45.

44. Ibid., 1:47. The mistress of the sentimental kitten distinguishes the cat's delight in a "nice sleek fat mouse" from her own humane trapping of vermin. See *Felissa, or the Life and Opinions of a Kitten of Sentiment* (London: J. Harris, 1811), 86; see also 112–14. See also James Steintrager, *Cruel Delight: Enlightenment Culture and the Inhuman* (Bloomington: Indiana University Press, 2004), esp. 37–59.

45. Locke, *Some Thoughts Concerning Education,* 178.

46. "Review of *The Sparrow,*" *The Young Gentleman's and Lady's Magazine,* ed. Dr. Mavor, 2 vols. (London: J. Walker, 1799–1800), 1:65.

47. Sarah Trimmer, *The Robins, or, Fabulous Histories, designed for the Instruction of Children, Respecting their Treatment of Animals* (1786; Boston: Munroe and Francis, 1822), vii.

48. Alfred Elwes, *The Adventures of a Cat and a Fine Cat Too!* (London: Routledge, 1857), 10.

49. *German Toy,* 90.

50. Kilner, *Mouse,* 1:48.

51. Elaine Scarry, *The Body in Pain: The Making and Unmaking of the World* (New York: Oxford University Press, 1985), 16.

52. Sarah Trimmer, *The Silver Thimble* (1799; Philadelphia: B. & J. Johnson, 1801), 96; Mary Curtis, *Memoirs of a Country Doll, written by herself* (Boston: James Munroe, 1853), 72.

53. *Lady's Slippers and Shoes,* 19; *German Toy,* 43–44.

54. Reed, *Three Guinea Watch,* 73; Horne, *London Doll,* 46.

55. *Clock,* 213.

56. See Reed, *Three Guinea Watch,* 192.

57. *Ostrich Feather of Quality,* 152.

58. Horne, *London Doll,* 106; *Clock,* 241.

59. Miss Smythies, *Adventures of a Pin, as related by itself* (Philadelphia: Samuel Longcope, 1802), 61.

60. Jerrold, *Feather,* 257.

61. *Silver Penny,* 124.

62. Trimmer, *Silver Thimble,* 112, 111, 112.

Discreet Jewels: Victorian Diamond Narratives and the Problem of Sentimental Value

John Plotz

> Of all the precious articles that constitute the representative signs of wealth, jewels are those which contain the greatest amount within the smallest compass. Hence the ease with which they may be concealed from the most searching eyes, and conveyed mysteriously and easily from place to place. Those advantages, peculiar to diamonds and precious stones, have rendered them objects of irresistible temptation to thieves in all ages and nations.
>
> —A. de Barrera, *Gems and Jewels*[1]

> She lay down among the broad leaves and cups, cradled by their interlaced stems, rocked by warm winds on the rocking water; she lay till the splash of fountains, and the chirp of nestlings, and the whisper of spiced breezes, and the chanted monotone of an innumerable choir, lulled to sleep her soul, lulled to rest her tumultuous heart, charmed her conscious spirit into a heavy blazing diamond,—a glory by day, a lamp by night, and a world's wonder at all times. Let us leave the fair body at rest, and crowned with lilies, to follow the restless spirit, shrined in a jewel, and cast ashore on Man-side.
>
> —Christina Rossetti, "Hero"[2]

It has recently been suggested that the historical span in which "things talk" ought to be extended considerably. Not only should we consider eighteenth-century speaking-object narratives, and familiar nineteenth-century debates on "dancing tables" and "commodity fetishes"; we ought also hear objects chatting all the way from the beginning of human history into the foreseeable future.[3] If we have been accustomed to terminate the account of "object narratives" with a few meek murmurings in the late nineteenth century, a quiet diminuendo of talking pocket-watches and clerical collars, we are now urged to advance our account of "things that talk" (to take the title of a recent Zone collection edited by Lorraine Daston) to include Hieronymous Bosch monsters and Rorschach blots.

This claim for object eloquence is not entirely new, of course. There is a familiar rationale for appraising the "social life of things" that anthropological discourse has systematically refined ever since Malinowski's accounts of "ka" exchange in the Pacific Islands. Its claims are securely bounded on the one hand by a Marxian sense (perhaps best articulated in Appadurai's 1986 collection, *The Social Life of Things*) that we can trace the ways economic value has been concretized in the objects that a society picks out as its inamorati; and, on the other hand, by the Maussian French (and latterly, American) attempts to discern the logic of the gift even in the capitalist age.[4]

Those boundaries, however, seem to have eroded slightly in the last decade, and we are beginning to see the emergence of various strongly worded exhortations to imagine that not simply human consciousness but something more elusive, and perhaps more transcendent, resides in the objects or things (an important distinction, as it turns out) that hover just at the edge of—or even just beyond—human cognition. The most striking phenomenological account of how things come to life is a sweeping and often ahistorical Heideggerian invocation of the phenomenology of the "Thing," which, unlike the merely usable, humanly cognizable object, lies beyond our cognition yet demarcates the parameters of human cognition.[5] But there have also arisen more historicized accounts of shifting conceptions of selfhood from the Enlightenment on.[6]

In fact, some recent work on the early twentieth century has advanced the idea that it might be possible to historicize the notion of the boundary between thing and person, so that determining what counts as an object, or a speaking object, and what counts as human attention to that object might be seen to reveal shifting ideas about the location of selfhood. Peter Galliston's recent "Images of Self," for example, gives an intellectual genealogy of the development and the mid-twentieth-century success of the Rorschach blot, talking thing extraordinaire.

By Galliston's account, Rorschach's insight, in his 1921 advocacy and distribution of a set of "Rorschach cards," was that a "degree zero" of thingdom in the form of ruthlessly engineered blots designed to evoke no "ordinary" human association would elicit from inside persons the true contents of their subjective selves.

> Not only did these cards talk; they did so in virtue of their form and color down to the smallest detail. If the blots suggested even a shard of human design, certain patients would seize on that fragment, losing their own ability to speak from within, For this reason, nothing was more important to Rorschach than creating and reproducing cards that would register as undesigned designs.[7]

The crucial contribution of this account is that it locates the problem of the "talking thing" not within the thing itself, but at the vexed boundary between self and world, where we are forced to articulate what kind of knowledge about the world exists only within persons, and what knowledge is actually latent in the world, waiting to be brought out. Galliston thus approaches afresh the same problem that Marx's account of dancing tables and the "commodity fetish" explores. Deciding what is "contained" in objects involves a series of prior, potentially ideological decisions about where you imagine human labor or human thought residing. Thus by Marx's account his contemporaries see as immanent within an object certain aspects of labor power that he thinks rightly belong not to the object but to the person whose work brought that object within the human economy.

By the 1920s, there was such a strong model of a coherent inner self, knowable only in its encounter with a "truly objective" outer world (that objectivity represented in Rorschach's case by pure meaninglessness), that a single test of seemingly loquacious objective reality was enough to elicit the whole of the person inside. The Rorschach blot, says Galliston, works only if the talkative object is so perfectly of the "objective" outer world that one can be sure that no other human agency was there before, so that what one says about the objects marks one's encounter with the pure outsideness of the world, in all its delightful and hence intensely meaning-laden rigidity: "The [Rorschach blot test] means that function of subjectivation (how subjects are formed) and objectivation (how objects are formed) enter at precisely the same moment. To describe the cards (on the outside) *is exactly* to say who you are (on the inside)."[8] Galliston's reading is important because it allows us to situate the Rorschach blot as a participant in a broader, early twentieth-century conversation about what it might mean for indisputably mute objects to "speak" the inner truth that they contain, to disgorge out of their abiding flatness some kind of depth that bespeaks the character of the persons with whom they abide.

Consider George Simmel's famous 1908 text on "Adornment," which takes up the question of what jewelry, and diamonds in particular, has to say about its wearers.[9] Diamonds strike Simmel as the best example for talking about the way in which objects external to us, but lain upon us like a set of clothes or a mask, work to produce both within the wearer and for observers a sense of an individual's "deep" or "genuine" character. The seemingly paradoxical way in which a diamond produces a sense of "deep" character coincides exactly with Rorschach's sense that only in the contemplation of those objects most pointedly stripped of any prior meaning of their own, save their meaning to us, can we find reassuring evidence of our own singular subjectivity.

For Simmel, jewelry is the exemplary instance of the way that the most personal of valuables is precisely the most impersonal, the most immersed in a shared knowable and priceable realm. What we most treasure inwardly is what's most valued in the outer world. To have a personal identity at all, he says, we are constantly participating in a public realm through which that personal identity is routed. On the one hand, through jewelry I establish a sense of personal worth and identity. On the other hand, jewelry's

> very elegance lies in its impersonality. That this nature of stone and metal—solidly closed within itself, in no way alluding to any individuality; hard, unmodifiable—is yet forced to serve the person, this is its subtlest fascination. What is really elegant avoids pointing to the specifically individual; it always lays a more generalized, stylized, almost abstract sphere around man—which of course, prevents no finesse from connecting the general with the personality. That new clothes are particularly elegant is due to their still being "stiff"; they have not yet adjusted to the modification of the individual body. [10]

Diamonds, that is, are the best of friends not despite their alienability, but because of it. Our commitment to a depth of character that points out a personality distinct from the reductive circulatory systems through which worldly value is established turns out in Simmel's account to be an illusion. The very alienability of a personal ornament (like those stiff, perfectly fitted but nonconforming clothes) lies close to its work of establishing my selfhood as something durable, deep, and valuable: "The essence of stylization is precisely this dilution of individual poignancy, this generalization beyond the uniqueness of the personality—which, nevertheless, in its capacity of base or circle of radiation, carries or absorbs the individuality as if in a broadly flowing river."

Simmel goes farther. Where one might expect to find only particular and distinct "genuine" individuals, Simmel argues we find jewelry, which precisely models (like a good, ultra-portable property) the very selfhood that's meant to be a thing apart from objects.

> The "genuine" individual, thus, is the person on whom one can rely even when he is out of one's sight. In the case of jewelry, this more-than-appearance is its *value,* which cannot be guessed by being looked at, but is something that, in contrast to skilled forgery, is *added* to the appearance. By virtue of the fact that this value can always be realized, that it is recognized by all, that it possesses a relative timelessness, jewelry becomes part of a super-contingent, super-personal value structure.[11]

Even selfhood's apparent depths, then, are modeled in the fully legible nature of the ornamental possession, because in jewelry the apparently inaccessible depth of character emerges to become part of a "superpersonal value structure" where such depth can exactly be realized.

Sentimental Objects: Pathetic Victorian Things

It may seem counterintuitive to begin an account of the loquacity of Victorian objects by looking at these early indices of twentieth-century psychological theories of impersonality. After all, when it comes to looking at Victorian fiction, doesn't Dorothy Van Ghent's compelling account of the importance of relentlessly particularized objects of sentiment still hold? Aren't the Victorians, as writers like Marshall and Jaffe have recently argued, beginning, in various ways inflected by liberalism, to move out from under the shadow of Adam Smith's rather economistic account of "moral sentiments" and calculable "sympathy" and into the realm of a fuzzy, warm, hard-to-quantify but easy-to-appreciate sympathy that hinges on admirable persons being what Charlotte Bronte called "singular"?[12] How much sense does it make to begin talking about the Victorian attachment to objects by pointing towards the steely impersonality of the Rorschach blot, if the one thing that we believe we know about Victorian objects—whether endowed with the power of speech or not—is how cozy, personable, and willfully individual they are?

Isn't this, after all, the era in which pub chairs invite you to curl up in them and Christmas puddings address their consumers by reciting their ingredients and their provenance, an era in which a sparkling grate and a glowing fire offer a level of intimate satisfaction that is not so evidently produced by the presence of human companions? If the Victorian age lends itself to talk about objects, then surely their psychological import, the way in which their singularity calls forth unsuspected reservoirs of emotion in the individuals attached to them, ought to be the object of our focus?

Galliston speaks of the process of "subjectivation" occurring with Rorschach blots in the face of the most extremely impersonal sort of "objectivation." Simmel speaks of diamonds that do not so much adorn their wearers as prick them out as "distinguished" or even as "deep," possessed of exactly the sort of psychological depth that Simmel's sociology makes into an illusion—the very same depth that Victorian texts seem dedicated on every level to discovering and glorifying. Doesn't the sort of sentimental outpouring that defines the Victorian return to a beloved hearth or a well-known print, a set of mourning rings and "hair jewelry," convince us that what Galliston calls "subjectivation" occurs, for the Victorian era, in the encounter not with "objectivation" in impersonal objects like diamonds or Rorschach blots, but with a latent "subjectivity" seen to reside within objects? If so, aren't we then charting out a Victorian era that is precisely as far apart from its Modernist successors as it is from its eighteenth-century forebears, those "object narratives" in which things speak on and on at great length so as to proclaim a fundamental identity between their consciousness and their exchange value?

The very starkness of that apparent opposition, however, points at a certain blindness in contemporary critical accounts of Victorian convictions about sentimentalized objects. It has been remarked that people find the need to assert something strongly only because they believe its opposite to be true. By that reckoning, what we encounter in Victorian texts that take on the life of objects directly is a series of arguments against the order of the age. In Victorian sentimental object narratives, we often find the passionate insistence that in such objects must lie depths of personality, coupled with the worry (or perhaps even the latent conviction) that just the opposite is the case: that such objects are no better than cold material, and that the human energies wasted upon them signify the real coldness that lies behind the seeming warmth of affective relations.

I believe that Modernist repudiations of Victorian accounts of depth in character and individuality in human nature can best be understood by charting the internal tensions already present within the Victorian notion of "sentimental objects." But such an account makes sense only once one understands the significance of the shifts required before the Victorian model of sentimental talkative objects could emerge. I hope a brief account of the distance between eighteenth-century object narratives and such diamond-centered narratives as Christina Rossetti's "Hero" will help explain why Victorian narratives that center upon the "secret life" of diamonds are a crucial lens through which to view the era's notion of the relationship between "sentimental" and "exchange" value—and hence the era's evolving ideas about the relationship of individuality to larger social structures.

The terms by which the eighteenth century understood the location of sentiment, and of value, within a speaking object differ radically from the way those terms are deployed in Victorian texts. Frame the comparison between early eighteenth-century object narratives and their Victorian successors around the question of what it means to possess empathy, and the contrast becomes immediately evident. The most famous instance of the genre, *Chrysal; or, The Adventures of a Guinea,* does not encourage readers to establish bonds with their money, since the "intuition" that allows the guinea to know characters' minds only works to the extent that those minds are obsessed with gold: simply to be a character in the novel is already to be defined by one's avarice.[13] It is typical of *Chrysal*-style object narratives that they erase the distinction between the circulation of sentiment—or desire, or any kind of amiable affection—and the circulation of cash.

As Adam Smith's *Theory of Moral Sentiments* (1759) understands it, sympathy between person and person arises from the effacement, not the perception, of individual particularity; in object tales as in other eighteenth-century novels, therefore, sentiment, like cash, comes across as pervasively liquid, producing for sympathetic identification indistinct and generic rather than singular and memorably distinctive characters.[14] Objects can play the role of hero perfectly because their whole personality seems engrossed in their role as fungible pieces of the realm of exchange (even the corkscrew in *Adventures of a Cork-Screw* is notable not for its bottle-opening but for its exchangeability).[15] Diderot's risqué *Les bijoux indiscrets* may be the perfect proof-text for what eighteenth-century logic requires when an author lights upon a kind of diamond tale. That the diamonds in question acquire their value only through the courtly game of selling sex (the diamonds are talking pudenda) epitomizes the inextricable and hence infinitely amusing intertwining of the talk of love and the cold hard reality of exchange value. Victoria would not have been amused.

One quick way to see the difference between an eighteenth-century account of objects that circulate in an undifferentiated sphere of cash and sentiment, and a Victorian account of objects as endowed with particular and irreproducible features (so that sympathy for any given object comes to depend upon its difference from all others), is to consider a transitional object narrative, the 1824 *Aureus; or, The Life and Opinions of a Sovereign.*[16] *Aureus* begins with the protagonist drawing itself up into a flaming pillar and telling the narrator, "I am Thy Sovereign"; the latent pun, however, hinges not on the authority that the King/coin has over the narrator, but on the fact that the coin is at once an exchangeable totem and a personable companion. Aureus turns out to be a sympathetic aid to two sisters trying to win the men of their dreams. Forsaking his fiscal duties—and that desertion is crucial—and even disparaging the very world of financial exchange, Aureus steps in to set them both on the path to loving matrimony by encouraging them to swap fiancés so that each may gain her heart's desire. When Aureus goes to a watery doom in a shipwreck, the readers are encouraged to feel as much for his loss as they would for any vanished mariner.

By the time of *Aureus*'s publication, then, what had seemed two compatible discourses in eighteenth-century object narratives (cash and feeling) are beginning to look like antithetical versions of circulation. It is not simply that one must trade love for money, as certainly happens in eighteenth-century narratives, but that the very move to treat things as exchangeable within a cash economy (rather than, as with the swapped fiancés, within a libidinal one) desecrates them. Love and money still circulate, but they must do so in incommensurate ways, and finding the circuits of love involves disavowing finance. Thus, successful movement in the circle of cash money proves an object's inability to be a bearer of sentiment—and vice versa.

This tendency comes to be so pronounced in the Victorian age that object narratives proper not only fade gradually away, but also become coated, in their rare remaining instances, by a kind of empathic adhesion that would have been unimaginable with Chrysal, or with one of Smollett's atoms. The era is not much for talking clocks or watches, but it is masterful at churning out talkative objects who, as it were, point to themselves and sweetly say what it is they contain and signify.[17] Unsurprisingly, this is a phenomenon largely confined to children's books—where, for example, soap bubbles loudly proclaim their ability to exemplify the rules of physics. In one of the widest circulating and best beloved of these books, Annie Carey's *Autobiographies of a Lump of Coal, a Grain of Salt; a Drop of Water; a Bit of Old Iron; a Piece of Flint* (1870), the reader is overwhelmed by a panoply of objects with distinct personalities, as loveable as Chrysal is fungible. In Carey's book, also published as *The Wonders of Common Things*, even coal gets personalized. "There are some members of our family of the name Lignite, who have preserved very distinct impressions of our former condition," a loquacious lump of coal proclaims, encouraging his young readers to construct a genealogy not just for coal in general (I used to be a Wood!) but for each lump in their own cellar.[18] It is striking to a later reader, as it would not have been to a Victorian one, that this volume works with such frenzy to establish a singular kind of attachment between the reader and any given object on display. It is almost as if the lesson constantly being adduced about the attachment of women to novels—that they could learn "facts" about the world only when these were swaddled in "a good story"—had been expanded into a general rule for any encounter with the universe: animate the physical world with personal sentiment, and children will swallow it whole. Chrysal's cold gold-soul seems a universe away.

Adamant Objects

In describing this genre of pedagogical science books, with its chatty soap bubbles and orotund raindrops, we may seem to have strayed from the commitment to diamonds as the adamantine arch-exemplar of the

Victorian commitment to sentiment at all costs, sentiment even where it might seem inevitable that cold hard calculation must intervene.[19] Surely the allure of the diamond narrative must proceed from something different?

Coal is not, by a thousandfold factor of compression, diamond; Conrad's *Victory* (1915) opens by bitterly remarking on that "deplorable want of concentration in coal . . . If only one could put a coal-mine in one's pocket—but one can't!"[20] Coal is trivial, only marginally valuable, so it would be juvenile to take its concretization of durable value seriously. Diamonds are different—they make an adult audience pay attention—as much attention, in fact, as children pay to coal. Not for nothing does Sherlock Holmes call them "the devil's petbaits," for their value elicits from within people whatever is ugliest in their own natures, driven by the knowledge that this one tiny bit of portable property contains a frozen lifetime of fiscal equivalence (the equivalence of years of harsh drudgery to a single easily lost set of stones being the horrible point of Guy de Maupassant's "The Necklace" [1884]).

Diamonds leave coal behind, however, not by repudiating the mixture of chatty attachment and durable value that coal displays in *The Wonders of Common Things,* but simply by intensifying that concatenation of sentiment and value for an adult audience. The exemplary Victorian texts turning on the "secret life" of diamonds all make this point about their location at the crux between two very different circulatory systems, one affective, the other fiscal. So it is that diamonds, rather than being creatures of pure sentiment, turn out to be very visibly *riven.* That is, these diamonds assume a significance that is at once determined by their exchange value and by a difficult-to-articulate rival, their sentimental value—a value that is certified by the fond associations, the auratic or cultural resonances that cluster round them. In sharp contradistinction both to eighteenth-century it-narratives and twentieth-century treatments of the life of objects, Victorian diamond texts are made up of a fascinating and shifting double vocabulary that, as in *Aureus,* attempts to put together (without ever actually coalescing) two divergent sorts of value.

It may help us to locate Victorian diamonds by turning not to Anthony Trollope's *The Eustace Diamonds* and Wilkie Collins's *The Moonstone,* but to a contemporaneous fairy tale in which the stone is still actually allowed to speak and to feel as a person would. Christina Rossetti's remarkable "Hero" (1870) is one example of how the twin discourses of absolute liquidity and absolute sentimental affect are combined discordantly for the purpose of producing a choice between the world of true value and the world of fluid exchange. The plot turns on a marriageable young woman named Hero, who lives close enough to what is called both Fairyland and Giftland (a telling dual nomination) to be granted a wish by the Fairy Queen. Her wish, "to become the supreme object of admiration," means that her spirit will become a kind of money, fungible enough to assume any shape so long as that object is the acme of admiration. The Queen "charm[s] her conscious spirit into a heavy blazing diamond,—a glory by day, a lamp by night, and a world's wonder at all times." Hero's spirit rushes off to be the hero of a story of dizzyingly swift transformations that would have made Marx proud (the fluidity of labor value incarnate). Her body meanwhile languishes back in Fairyland, the true blue object of her father's and sweetheart's affection, until the day when Hero's object-runnings miraculously come to an end and the body is returned to good Peter to marry—Hero's wishes in the world of exchange having presumably been removed by the process. It is as a diamond that Hero has her greatest glory and exacts the greatest price from the world—innocent sailors slay one another for her, caravans war over her, empires rise and fall in pursuit of her, and she glories in the pure naked need she can thus, adamantine, elicit.

The twin attributes of portable property in the Victorian age are here clearly in view: its tendency to slide through the coils of exchange, here known as "admiration" and performed by Hero's spirit, and its ability to stay at home producing companionate ties and long-lasting affection, here known as "love" and sanctified by Hero's pure white body. The question the story asks is whether those two attributes can be radically dissevered from one another. Hero on ice and Hero in the marketplace are manifestly one and the same thing, but the fairy-tale ability to split spirit and body solves an otherwise insoluble problem: that the object of my affection (sentimental, good) is also the object of my admiration (fungible, bad).

There is an obvious gender asymmetry at work here as in so much of Rossetti's work. A man can dream (as Hero's fiancé Peter does) of securing economic success by making and selling objects of value in the marketplace—making his labor alienable through a cash nexus, in Marxist terms. On the other hand, women have only their own body to exchange on the market. But the very fact that Hero is not only the story's named protagonist but also named as a story's protagonist—Hero is its *hero*—tips us off that Rossetti means us to read her as the very spirit of identification itself. Her desire to be the acme of admiration wherever she goes is incarnated even within the story, where, for as long as the tale lasts, she commands our undivided attention. The irony of her cynosure position, however, is that the admiration expressed for her can never profit her, since she is always sold but never selling: to be so admired is not to reap for oneself the rewards of what others are willing to pay, since to make the transaction one must be its object rather than the disburser of oneself.

Clearly, "Hero" marks an important departure from the basic lineaments of the eighteenth-century object narrative. Like *Aureus,* it departs from earlier texts in its commitment to rescuing an account of sentiment that enables articulate objects at once to proclaim their implication in a system of buying and selling and to point beyond that system into a somewhat similar realm where only affection and deep attachment ever circulate. What both texts leave unclear is how those two rival forms of circulation differ on the deepest level. The decision to address or obfuscate that distinction turns out to be one of the most crucial decisions that other such diamond-centered texts in the period have to face.

It is unsurprising that the Victorian era is the high-water mark for the production of jewelry made out of a beloved's or a dearly departed's hair. But Victorian interest in that sort of mawkishly sentimental and purely personal trinket by no means implies a disregard for the fiscal implications of jewelry as portable property. It is, after all, a mourning ring (these were ordered in job lots and came ready valued in five-shilling increments, both a token of respect and a usefully disbursable valuable) that Wemmick is referring to when he advises Pip to "get hold of portable Property."[21] For jewelry to be laden with affect is suitably Victorian; but for it to offer, as it does most notably in Thackeray's *Vanity Fair* (1848), a quick access to the world of fungibility, where esteem can be translated readily into property, is suitably Victorian as well.[22] The expressly made piece of jewelry, by virtue of its capacity to symbolize a kind thought from kin or companion—like the thirty-guinea ring acquired with an eye to its ready resale in *The Eustace Diamonds*—at once denotes the potential transmissibility of affect and the ready concretization of property into a handy take-away package.[23]

More or Less than an Heirloom: Trollope's *The Eustace Diamonds*

Trollope takes up the challenge implicit in Rossetti. For Rossetti, the allure of the fairy tale is that it allows one to split two streams of meaning and value that seem in ordinary life to run everywhere together, to make love and admiration keep their distance from one another. Without the luxury of the fantastical, Trollope inverts the problem and asks whether any set of circumstances might exist whereby there would be no way of making any such distinction—where fiscal and auratic value would interpenetrate one another so thoroughly that even distinguishing between heroine and villain would be difficult. Trollope certainly makes it clear in *The Eustace Diamonds* who is "meant" to be his heroine and who his villain, but in the very same breath he admits that his novel cannot sustain a heroine—and that if it did have one, it would have to be Lizzy, which is to say, its villainess. A strange confusion, indeed.

That confusion turns on no other question than the disposition of the diamonds that give the novel its name. They are objects whose perturbing effect on their owners is neither to make value available in fungible form, nor to stand in for a symbolic value higher than such fiscal worth. Instead, through these jewels a property-owning subject becomes trapped in a form of desire that produces not the realization of value by way of ornament, but the exact opposite: the construction of an ornament-dependent identity.

The Eustace Diamonds is best remembered as Trollope's Becky Sharp novel, in which Lizzie Eustace, queen of sharp dealing, vague deceit, and "perjury committed with regard to one's own property" (689), attempts to abscond with a 10,000-pound necklace stolen from her dead husband's estate. But the novel is just as much concerned with "the state of despondency into which she had fallen while the diamonds were in her own custody" (590). It is not just despondency, but diamond-induced irrationality that ends up being both "unnecessary" and "injurious" (686) to her own cause and those around her.

Vanity Fair is a primer in putting to nefarious use truly portable property—diamonds, banknotes, checks, and letters ripe for potential blackmail. But *The Eustace Diamonds* is a far more interesting account of the dangers entailed in an excessive attachment to any valuable property which seems alluring on account of its purported portability. When Lizzie complains of her necklace that "it has been like the white elephant which the Eastern king gives to his subject when he means to ruin him" (520), she tells an inadvertent truth about her (self-inflicted) plight. *The Eustace Diamonds* initially looks like the story of one person who is unable to give up the pursuit of money for the more satisfying pursuit of sympathy, professional success, or love. In fact, though, it is the story of a fetishized attachment to an object whose value, both financial and cultural, would lie only in its suitable exchange at an apt moment. Because Lizzie Eustace has forgotten the rules by which passion and interest dictate a change from time to time in object of adoration, she is ruined by it.

Lizzie's diamonds are potentially cash—in fact, her mission throughout the novel is to make them so—but they turn out never to be fully detachable from various ante-fiscal systems. Legally attached as "heirloom" (the claim is dismissed), practically attached as vulnerable personal property (they shuffle in and out of a protective iron box), sexually attached as the dower prize Lizzie uses to lure suitors (she aims for a Byronic hero and instead gets "Mealyus," the cozening, despicable Hungarian Jewish preacher), the diamonds are everything but a perfectly detachable commodity capable of realizing its value on the open market—or of representing to the public world the character of the individual whose name went with them.[24] Once Lizzie's relationship to them becomes one of insistent avarice—once they stop being an ornament whose value can be shared or realized in Simmel's sense—they supply her neither the benefit of a proper name nor the flexibility of a common asset. John Frow talks of the "lack of faith in the way we fail to attend to things, to their inherent speech, instead rendering them mere instruments of our will."[25] But the Eustace diamonds, for all that they are never fully depicted, turn out to possess a form of independent life.

In "Hero" objects speak to offer themselves for exchange with any other admirable object in the world: take me or trade me, they say, behaving just as Marx prescribed. In *The Eustace Diamonds,* however, the necklace is rightly classed by the sage lawyer Dove under the heading of "property so fictitious as diamonds" (695). They are not simply fictitious indirectly—because their worth is grounded in a shared disposition to grant arbitrary value—for their power lies in what they can make their possessors believe. The "risk of annihilation" Dove refers to is their vulnerability because they are portable rather than real property: who could reset or pilfer the acres of land to which the diamonds are compared? But any object whose worth for a single possessor begins to grow larger than can be justified or grounded in a common social fabric threatens to become a fetish, and not just its value but its very nature threatens to become illegible. Lizzie is of interest because she lowers herself not before a lover (Lucy Morris abjects herself before Frank and comes to no lasting harm) but before the fictitious subject of the necklace, a movement that if not sufficient to grant the necklace agency is at least enough to make her that object's abject subject in her turn.[26]

D. A. Miller has convincingly argued that Trollope novels generally depend upon a "merry war" that is depicted as merely a "belated copy . . . of a belligerent and heroic original," a "moderate schism" that allows plot to proceed by way of formal differences that cry out for a (readily achievable) resolution.[27] However, *The Eustace Diamonds* presents the story of a woman who moves outside those narrow disputational bounds. To other characters in the novel, the crucial questions of intersubjective and economic behavior involve taking up, and letting go of, objects of transitory but engrossing interest. Before she ties herself to her fiancé Frank and loses the power of ready attachment and detachment, Lucy Morris is acknowledged as the master of this activity:

to "take up your subject, whatever it was, and make it her own" (63). She knows better than anyone how to enter into and "be effective in the object then before her, be it what it might" (64).

Lucy is "a treasure" because she enters into these "objects" without personal interest, while others are less admirable because they pursue their own interests (Lord Fawn, thinking of promotion) or their own passions (Mrs. Hittaway his sister, liking to boss her family about). But all such characters are in any event united in their pursuit of readily assumable and detachable objects of interest: What will happen with the Sawab of Mygawb's pension? Does anyone truly favor Palliser's currency reform? What social scandal will occupy the Duke of Omnium's energy, so that he is not tempted to marry?

To all such adhesion, separation, and reattachment, however, there comes an end—first for Lizzie, in attaching herself helplessly to the diamonds, then for Lucy, in attaching herself to Frank. Though neither seems to realize it at first attachment, this means that both Lucy and Lizzie must prohibit themselves from adhering to any new object subsequently.[28] Having done so, they are committed to a particular object, and both Lizzie's self-serving detachments (fishing for several husbands at once) and Lucy's selfless ones (advocating for the Sawab of Mygawb) are brought to a close.

This is not to say Lizzie may not actually intend to continue her nefarious machinations. But with the diamonds as her newfound main object, such interested pursuits are doomed to fail. Her negotiations with Lord Fawn founder on the rocks, as she proves incapable of giving them up for the prudential considerations that she had thought motivated her. It might be argued that she discovers her avaricious commitment to the stones as an aspect of her own personality. However, the novel makes the attraction seem to stem from the stones, not from Lizzie herself. She finds herself stymied by her own desire to "stick with" the Eustace diamonds.

The problem of classifying attachment to portable properties persuades one Eustace lawyer to declare of gemstones that "the very existence of such property so to be disposed of, or so not to be disposed of, is in itself an evil" (753). Their looseness, or their ambiguous deviation from the norms of property disposition, are a kind of "devil's pet-bait" even for their apparent owner, who cannot help testing the limits of her power over them. That she does so with other sorts of property in the novel is hardly surprising; most notably, she is always exceeding her life-tenure perquisites by lopping down old trees on the Eustace family estate of Portray. But her battles with the imaginary entity of the necklace are something different: it's impossible to imagine a novel called "The Eustace Timber-Rights." Lizzie comes to be drawn to the necklace in itself, not because it enables her marital or fiscal circulation, nor even because it exempts her from such circulation. Rather, its iron box and patent key, the breathless trips up and down stairs it requires, and the almost sexual violations of her person it produces (in the way of searches, arrests, and robberies) intimate that she is succumbing to the power of the necklace itself.

Early in the novel conservatives are described as unhappy because they are "always in the right, and yet always on the losing side, always being ruined . . . and yet never to lose anything" (71). They can feel this sense of ongoing but nonexistent loss, in Trollope's account, because they do not depend, in reckoning up their happiness, on the possession of any one resource. And why should Lizzie feel any differently from such conservatives; she has 4,000 pounds a year, after all, so the diamonds (which will in any case be inherited by her own son) even at their highest value cannot possibly constitute more than a tenth of her wealth. Why not rest as easy as those happily unhappy conservatives? They are blessed with a series of detachable and reattachable grievances, while Lizzie has reduced her attention to a single object. Just as Lucy is required to find in Frank all that is good in the world, and renounce her friends and all mobile interests, Lizzie must quarrel with anyone who denies her free and clear title to her own pelf.

Lizzie becomes increasingly devoted to the actual physical process of tending to the diamonds: "And she would keep the key of that iron box with the diamonds and he would find out what sort of noise she would make, if he attempted to take it from her. She closed the morocco case, ascended with it to her bedroom, locked it up in the iron safe, deposited the little patent key in its usual place round her neck" (133). But this excessive incarnation of her possession dooms her. The diamonds themselves become more and more for Lizzie an obstacle to the very happiness that they are meant to underwrite; even her own traveling companion begins to think, "Who would willingly live with a woman who always traveled about with a diamond necklace worth ten thousand pounds, locked up in an iron safe?" (225). The diamonds that enchant Lizzie end up ruining her chances for real advancement, for the kind of exchangeable power that she might have if she boasted the savvy of the various female politicians interspersed throughout the Palliser books. She is not punished, as readers tend to assume, for being a bad girl. She is punished for being bad at being a bad girl.

Lizzie's trip to Scotland, accompanied by the diamonds, brings to the fore her incompetence in the most excruciating way possible, and finally makes explicit the analogy between the diamonds and female sexuality. Carrying the diamonds with her in a heavy iron box, Lizzie feels her zone of vulnerability growing, so that the whole container, her entire carriage, finally, seems as vulnerable as the thing contained.[29] Fending off the Eustace's lawyer, Lizzie feels herself stripped almost naked in her effort to protect the jewels: "There was now a little crowd of a dozen persons on the pavement, and there was nothing to cover her diamonds but the skirt of her traveling dress" (222). The diamonds' portability here is both sine qua non and curse, like that other necessary female property, her sex:

> During the whole morning she had been wishing that she had never seen the diamonds; but now it was almost impossible that she should part with them. And yet they were like a load upon her chest, a load as heavy as though she were compelled to sit with the iron box on her lap day and night. In her sobbing she felt the thing under her feet, and knew that she could not get rid of it. She hated the box, and yet she must cling to it now. She was thoroughly ashamed of the box and yet must seem to take pride in it. She was horribly afraid of the box, and yet she must keep it in her own very bedroom. (223)[30]

In the chronic repetition of the word "box," the diamonds are transformed into an enormously enlarged zone of sexual vulnerability; by boxing the diamonds Lizzie has not managed to take them out of circulation, as deposit in a real bank vault would imply. Instead, she has allied their movement with that of her own body, and made her own movement crushingly dependent upon the properties of her boxed jewels.

The phobic intensity of Lizzie's relationship to her diamonds in their box suggests that her attempt to navigate the shoals of fiscal and personal value is not a dead end, but a crux in Victorian notions about detachable personal property. And we can see how the diamonds dangle between sentimental fetish and cash instrument by contrasting them to Trollope's idea of a piece of property that profits by being both things at once. Trollope's own voyages, as detailed in *An Autobiography,* were accompanied by a striking tranquility about his most valuable property, his writing. Trollope boasts of having gone off to Australia with a light heart—just after finishing *The Eustace Diamonds*—because

> I also left behind, in a strong box, the manuscript of *Phineas Redux* . . . I also left behind me, in the same strong box, another novel called *An Eye for an Eye* . . . If therefore the "Great Britain" in which we sailed for Melbourne had gone to the bottom, I had so provided that there would be new novels ready to come out under my name for some years to come.[31]

A man who "never made any money selling anything but a manuscript" therefore shows himself adroit at the disposal of his one alienable property, so that his name can survive both "Great Britain" and his body. But, of course, the crucial difference here between Trollope and the lamentable Lizzie is simple: he can detach himself from this object of interest, profit from it, and move on. It is not that such vaults are inherently any safer than Lizzie's, but property stored within them is already half inserted into a system of alienable assets and affections. Like having a son halfway round the world, having novels available anywhere in the Empire gives Trollope not a specially precarious identity, but—to judge from his serene confidence—a specially aggrandized one.[32]

And objects such as his manuscripts are unapologetically endowed with sentimental and cash value simultaneously, in a way that profits from the dual systems rather than, as with Lizzie's necklace, falling between them with a thud. In Dickens, there is a profusion of objects, as Dorothy Van Ghent noted long ago, into which character's personalities or histories are poured. But Dickens generally goes out of his way to point out a disjunction between pricey and nostalgic objects: meltdownable teapots here, poignant treasures there.[33] Trollope to the contrary is famously willing to put on display his own triumph in entering precious personal treasures into the marketplace; indeed, his autobiography became notorious for his blunt boasts about having turned genius into "product" and inspiration into income. By contrast with Lizzie's impersonal but uncashable diamond, Trollope's own mobile writings look like a laudable contribution to an economy that pays him in cash and reputation both.

The Eustace Diamonds locates Lizzie's relationship to her diamonds at the far edge of plausible object-devotion, then, but it does not preclude comparisons altogether. The novel offers two telling parallels to Lizzie's attraction: Lucy's unswerving devotion to Frank, which fetishistically attributes to him good will and best intentions we know him not to possess; and Lucinda Roanoke's scrupulous, savage devotion to her aunt's desires, which she inscribes on her own mind and body by trying to marry solely to please her.[34] Lucy triumphs by renouncing, as Lizzie renounces, any interest in objects beyond the one she has chosen. Having chosen Frank, she can no longer enter into "objects" like the Sawab of Mygawb's pension: "I have nothing left to give . . . What I ever had is all given." As it happens, Lucy triumphs in marriage (it is not a thrilling plot: despite his protestations about Lucy's charms Trollope must have known by the name he gave the novel that Lizzie not Lucy would engross all attention).[35] However, at the crisis point, Lucinda does not find her own will amenable to her demands on it, and she goes mad.

The two endings suggest ways that Lizzie's fate—neither a disaster nor a triumph, compared to her alter egos'—might have differed had she not thrown herself abjectly before an object, but risked the complications of another person. Because "she still sticks to the diamonds" (333), however, they become a sticking point for all the various circulatory systems that have to run smoothly for a Trollope novel to reach closure: the circulation of cash, or family exchange, the traffic in women, and the traffic in emotions. The striking puzzle that the novel both poses and resolves is what it would mean for objects to become stuck not because they had dropped out of affective and economic circulation but because they were caught up in the coils of both. Simmel accounts for diamonds as (to borrow Galliston's description of the Rorschach blot) sites where "subjectivation" occurs precisely where "objectivation" does—if, that is, Simmel reads the allure of diamonds as their capacity to make us feel "deep" because we possess something so valuable. By contrast, Trollope is anatomizing the Victorian problem with valuables that seem at once fiscal and sentimental. Rather than the two systems cohering to float the valuable object forward, as in an eighteenth-century it-narrative or a Modernist account of animated things, objects' tension between being a marker of singular psychological depth and a token of objective, impersonal value causes immense narrative and conceptual problems.

Romancing the Moonstone

Once we understand that *The Eustace Diamonds* aims to render the necklace an object that necessarily circulates uneasily between cash and sentimental value—an object that bears with it potentially all the memories of an heirloom and all the convenient amnesia of a letter of credit—it becomes easier to see how certain other texts of the day also concern themselves with the question of how diamonds (or comparable commodities) might manage to intermit between expressions of personality (or circulating sentimental value) and of a surrounding fiscal system. Rossetti's "Hero" labored hard to produce a strong distinction between the desire for admiration that created the subject as a perpetually metamorphic self and a quasi-incestuous love that upheld perpetual sameness. But "Hero"'s almost absurd separation of the two kinds of circulatory value alerts us to a range of texts in the period that took the dual nature of the circulating valuable as an occasion to reflect, more ambivalently than Rossetti, perhaps, on the problem of cash value and its putative opposites. One text that undertakes the comparison between valuable and valued object is Wilkie Collins's *The Moonstone* (1868), a text that Trollope clearly had in mind when he came to write *The Eustace Diamonds*.[36]

Recent critical attention to *The Moonstone* has focused on the novel's relationship to the Imperial environs (India) from which its eponymous central player is drawn. The most convincing such account of the novel is Ian Duncan's description of the "Imperial panic" that structures it. By his reading, *The Moonstone* documents a "demonic counter-imperialism" in the form of the incursion of the diamond and its defenders (the priests of the shrine it was stolen from) into Britain itself. When that incursion is repelled, Duncan argues, what is left is "bright but fragile" restored "British order" so that the "diminished solution of domestic fiction" is counterpoised to a vast "world economy."[37]

What remains to be added to Duncan's cogent account, however, is an explanation for the conjunction of world economy and Asiatic culture that he rightly sees as the twin threatening forces at the edge of the book. For Duncan, "the mystery of the modern world coincides with its discursive status as a complex, dynamic, and global economy" (318). Here, however, Duncan collapses two forces that the novel seems to me to separate: the world economy on the one hand, and the mystery and threat of the East on the other. The sentimental attachments that Franklin Blake and Rachel Verinder form to the diamond (as family heirloom, as thing of beauty, as symbol of their love) are not exactly opposed to the mysterious forces that pull that diamond back to the East (the three priests who pursue it, the religious curse that hangs over it). Rather, they are a far weaker version of the same sort of mysterious desire. When Franklin Blake deposits the diamond in the bank, he can describe it "merely as a valuable of great price," but at no other time is its identity that simple.[38] The Moonstone is portable in England precisely because it is no mere commodity in motion; anything capable of bewitching a whole room of people to "shut out the light" and stare slack-jawed while "it shone awfully out of the depths of its own brightness, with a moony gleam, in the dark" (97) is clearly meant to have a residual value above or apart from its price.

Rachel's passionate attachment to the diamond, like Franklin's somnambulant one, is a pale domestic imitation of that much stronger force from abroad that Duncan labels "Asiatic romance," rightly arguing that it is imagined to pose a threat to British domestic tranquility. But the crucial force of the aesthetic attraction in *The Moonstone* resides, I think, in the affinity it creates between domestic and external desires. Both weak, domestic, aestheticized attraction to the gemstone and strong, long-distance, Hindu-priest devotion to its divine power are placed on one side of the equation.[39] On the other side is placed the real avatar of the world economy: European debt and European liquid markets.

Both Blake and Godfrey Abelwhite (thief and eventual victim of the moonstone) are in debt—one accrued his debts on the Continent, the other looks to go there to clear them—and those who are entangled in that world market have one idea only: to get to Rotterdam, liquidate valuables (such as the diamond, or their own good name, or their family ties; the male equivalent of prostitution, one might say, would be the sale of one's good name on these Continental markets), and thus reenter the free-moving stream of the marketplace. By the same token, the novel's opening threat, if Rachel refuses the poisoned gift from her uncle John Hearncastle, is that the stone will be cut up—its value increasing in dissolution because of a flaw at its heart—and sold to fund that ultimate form of pure fiscal mobility, "a professorship of experimental chemistry" (70).

The image of the flawed jewel only heightens an effect that Collins clearly strives for: the radical disjunction between diamond as money and diamond as site of sentiment. As long as the diamond remains uncut, the possibility of its double meaning is retained; in other words, the novel documents the period during which the stone, by being both potential cash and the instantiation of aesthetic value, also offers itself as a vulnerable marker of the fragility of both systems. Like the Eustace diamonds, it is burnable, cuttable, not only saleable but also damageable for as long as it stays intact. Translate it into some other form of value (let it cement a marriage, or fund a professorship) and it becomes merely a part of the smooth circulation of cash, or of emotional affect, which circulates like property in the right circumstances. So long as the moonstone remains intact and in the house, on Rachel's neck or Ablewhite's person, its insistent particular being troubles both systems—that which conveys cash value, and that which allows beauty, belief, or sentiment to circulate.

In highlighting as it does the perpetually doubled quality of the diamond, the way that it cannot help being torn between two competing sorts of value claims, *The Moonstone* explores the same set of questions that *The Eustace Diamonds* poses. Indeed, *The Moonstone*'s efforts to find a way to distinguish between the sentimental and the fiscal appeal of a precious stone, and its meditations on why that project will be doomed, resemble another telling moment from Trollope's Palliser novels, this one in *Can You Forgive Her?* (1864–65). When the cad George Vivasour flings a "love gift"—a ruby and diamond ring for his beloved (and despised) cousin Alice—onto the floor, one of the guard diamonds is dislodged.[40] Given that George has just taken from Alice as a "heart" token a "little ivory-foot-rule" because "nothing is too poor, if given in that way," it may seem that Alice, who does not love her cousin, will not be quick to recover the diamond—for all its cash value.[41] After all, if true sentiment is what matters most, what significance does such a pricey gem hold when even the heavily resonant gift of a folding ruler means nothing? In fact, though "it was not that she had any desire for the jewel, or any curiosity even to see it," Alice spends a long time looking in the grate for the lost stone before carefully hiding the ring away.

Marx argues in *Capital* that anything kept purely for personal use, or even preserved solely within the familial economy, need have no relationship to exchange value at all.[42] Marx divides objects between those valued in the personal or familial realm and those that fatally bear the marketplace's brand on them; as one gains exchange value, one loses the possibility of parsing things according to one of the systems of archaic value. But for Trollope, George's violence in separating diamond from ring, and his stupidity in thinking a thoroughly valueless folding ruler can be a suitable love token, both stem from the same basic mistake.

George has failed to grasp what the good Lucy Morris demonstrates with "a diamond of a tear . . . lurking" in her sympathetic and sympathizing eye: that diamonds are of value because they belong to a well-lubricated circulatory system in which emotions as well as valuables are well poised to make the rounds.[43] If the cash value of something as emotionally meaningful as a ring were to depart, so too would the sentimental value: Lucy's cheap gift to Frank is "not in the market," but it is also "purchased out of her own earnings" (320). Short of fantasized combustion, entombment, metamorphosis, or destruction, emotional and fiscal value ought not, perhaps even cannot, be dissevered from one another. The power of an heirloom may reside in nothing but iron—the "best pot or pan" may be an heirloom—but the sentimental value of a truly portable property has got to have an intimate, perhaps even a direct relationship to its cash value.[44] Lucinda may prefer a "gridiron" given with love to valuable silver, but in Trollope the separation of sentiment from value doesn't come so easily: only if the giver were poor enough that the purchase were a sacrifice would a gridiron manifest meaningful love (634). The peculiar and abiding interest of Trollope, then, is partially in his Simmel-like sense that the construction of a system of circulatable sentiment to run alongside the world of fiscal liquidity creates striking disjunctions that generally conceal the underlying homology between any object's cash value and its affective value. If those two values are not the same, they are still, in both Simmel's and Trollope's accounts, assembled out of the same logical elements and thus capable of standing in for, as well as contradicting, one another.

What for the Modernist sociologist Simmel is an inevitable feature of the world's circulating systems is, however, for the Victorian novelist the site of a peculiar tension, one that must be made palpable before any resolution can be attempted. *The Eustace Diamonds* introduces a disjunction within that exchange economy, a site where the abjection of subjects before objects becomes plausible in a fetish formation radically disjunct from the Marxian commodity fetish. By producing a particularity that sticks to the Eustace diamonds—whose attributes the reader never knows and whose appeal is not even alluded to—Trollope sets his sights, indirectly, on what can only be seen indirectly: those moments where adhesion interrupts flow. Lucy's shifting interest in the Sawab, like Lizzie's various marital prospects, is a predictable articulation of a well-ordered and well-lubricated system. Lizzie's adhesion to her diamonds, though—something like Lucy's attachment to the Frank Greystock whose goodness and inner essence she invents rather than perceives—is singular in a world of shifting occupations and possessions. The unexpected and almost unrepresentable vitality of the very portable property whose mobility ought to abet movement arrests the lives of subjects who fall prey to its control. But such portable property, precisely on account of its apparent banality, has the capacity to stand in for the very fact of particularity. Like persons, certain things come to be endowed with an abiding-because-indescribable strangeness within a world which threatens (by the time an older, more jaded Trollope produces *The Way We Live Now* [1874–75]) to be full of nothing but fungible things and persons. The portability of the hypostatized object—whether it be a compelling necklace or an unpredictable fiancé—thus offers hope that both objects and persons retain a depth precisely defined by being beyond the representative reach of the novel itself. It remains unclear, however, whether diamonds cast light on such depths—or reveal that they were nothing but shallows all along.

Notes

1. A. de Barrera, *Gems and Jewels: Their History, Geography, Chemistry and Ana.: From the Earliest Ages Down to the Present Time* (London: Richard Bentley, 1860), 367.

2. Christina Rossetti, "Hero," first published in *Commonplace and Other Short Stories* (1870), rpt. in *Victorian Love Stories*, ed. Kate Flint (Oxford: Oxford University Press, 1997), 143, (138–50). Further references appear parenthetically in the text.

3. Important recent contributions to this nascent field by such authors as Daniel Tiffany, Simon Schaeffer, Joseph Koerner, Charity Scribner, and Pater Galliston are collected in Bill Brown, *Things* (Chicago: University of Chicago Press, 2004), and in Lorraine Daston, *Things That Talk: Object Lessons from Art and Science* (New York: Zone Books; Cambridge, MA: MIT Press, 2004). See my review essay, "Can the Sofa Speak? A Look at Thing Theory," *Criticism* 47.1 (2005): 109–18.

4. Nicholas Thomas, *Entangled Objects: Exchange, Material Culture, and Colonialism in the Pacific* (Cambridge, MA: Harvard University Press, 1991); Marilyn Strathern, *The Gender of the Gift: Problems with Women and Problems with Society in Melanesia*, Studies in Melanesian Anthropology, vol. 6 (Berkeley and Los Angeles: University of California Press, 1988); Maurice Godelier, *The Enigma of the Gift* (Chicago: University of Chicago Press, 1999), as well as a raft of Godelier's students. It is this lineage Jacques Derrida

responds to in such recent work on the idea of the gift as Jacques Derrida, *The Gift of Death* (Chicago: University of Chicago Press, 1995).

5. See, for example, Bill Brown, "Thing Theory," 1–16, and John Frow, "A Pebble, a Camera, a Man Who Turns into a Telegraph Pole," 346–61, in Brown, *Things*.

6. Any explanation for the rise of Heideggerian and New Historicist interest in "the Thing" as an object of study would also need to account for the recent explosion of quasi-academic books with names like "history of a pencil" or "the chair" or "the story of a paperclip." Disavowing any theoretical presuppositions, these accounts are probably more like the New Historicist accounts of the thing/object interface, but they modestly position themselves as "just the facts, ma'am" narratives. That is a position that their authors clearly feel more comfortable embracing because their historical subject is, after all, only an inanimate object, whose very materiality seems part of the inarguability of the account itself: there's the thing, so what's to argue about?

7. Peter Galliston, "Images of Self," in Daston, *Things That Talk*, 271.

8. Ibid., 277.

9. Georg Simmel, "Adornment," in *The Sociology of George Simmel*, trans. Kurt Wolff (New York: Free Press, 1950), 338–44.

10. The passage continues: "Metal Jewelry . . . is always new; in untouchable coolness, it stands above the singularity and destiny of its wearer . . . Style is always something general. It brings the contents of personal life and activity into a form shared by many and accessible to many" (Simmel, "Adornment," 340–41).

11. Ibid., 343 (emphasis in original).

12. See, for example, David Marshall, *Surprising Effects of Sympathy* (Chicago: University of Chicago Press, 1988), Audrey Jaffe, *Scenes of Sympathy* (Ithaca, NY: Cornell University Press, 2000), and Catherine Gallagher, *Nobody's Story* (Berkeley and Los Angeles: University of California Press, 1995). For a contemporary influential account of the poignancy of the local that is evidence of the continuation of that Victorian logic of poignant particularity into present-day accounts of the eighteenth and nineteenth centuries, see Thomas Laqueur, "Bodies, Details, and the Humanitarian Narrative," in *The New Cultural History*, ed. Lynn Hunt (Berkeley and Los Angeles: University of California Press, 1989), 176–204. On Adam Smith and the novel, see Ian Duncan's instructive "Adam Smith, Samuel Johnson, and the Institutions of English," in *Scottish Invention of English Literature*, ed. Robert Crawford (Cambridge: Cambridge University Press, 1998), 37–54.

13. Charles Johnstone, *Chrysal; or, The Adventures of a Guinea* (1760–65; London: T. Cadell, 1794).

14. Adam Smith, *The Theory of Moral Sentiments*, ed. Knud Haakonssen, Cambridge Texts in the History of Philosophy (1759; Cambridge: Cambridge University Press, 2002).

15. I am heavily indebted here both to Deidre Lynch (*The Economy of Character: Novels, Market Culture, and the Business of Inner Meaning* [Chicago: University of Chicago Press, 1998]) and to Christopher Flint ("Speaking Objects: The Circulation of Stories in Eighteenth-Century Prose Fiction," *PMLA* 113.2 [1998]: 212–26) for their accounts of eighteenth-century object narratives. A version of Flint's essay appears in this collection.

16. Peregrine Oakley, pseud., *Aureus; or, The Life and Opinions of a Sovereign. Written by Himself* (London: G. Wightman, 1824).

17. The ultimate parody of this Victorian-object loquaciousness may be the talking cow in Douglas Adams, *The Restaurant at the End of the Universe*, 1st American ed. (New York: Harmony Books, 1981), which recommends that diners sample "my delicious fatty rump."

18. Annie Carey, *Autobiographies of a Lump of Coal; a Grain of Salt; a Drop of Water; a Bit of Old Iron; a Piece of Flint* (London: Cassell, Petter & Galpin, 1870).

19. Simon Schaeffer, "The Science Whose Business is Bursting," in Daston, *Things That Talk*.

20. Joseph Conrad, *Victory: An Island Tale* (London: J. M. Dent, 1923).

21. Marcia Pointon's account of the value inherent in memorial rings, which are both intensely personalized—bought by will for a friend's mourning—and fully commodified—incrementally valued for five through ten through twenty shillings—clarifies many of the meanings of diamond jewelry. See Marcia Pointon, "Intriguing Jewelry: Royal Bodies and Luxurious Consumption," *Textual Practice* 11.3 (1997): 493–516, and "Jewelry in Eighteenth Century England," in *Consumers and Luxury: Consumer Culture in Europe 1650–1850*, ed. Maxine Berg and Helen Clifford (Manchester, UK: Manchester University Press, 1999), 120–46.

22. It seems perfectly true to the logic of Victorian collecting, for example, that an October 2001 broadcast of the "Antiques Roadshow" had a woman delightedly discovering that her great-grandmother's intact collection of mourning hair-jewelry, apparently made of her great-grandfather's hair, would be worth about $3,000 should she decide to sell, which she gave every indication of wishing to do.

23. Anthony Trollope, *The Eustace Diamonds*, ed. Stephen Gill and John Sutherland (1873; Baltimore: Penguin, 1969), 633. Further references appear parenthetically in the text.

24. See Lee Holcombe, *Wives and Property: Reform of the Married Woman's Property Law in Nineteenth-Century England* (Toronto: University of Toronto Press, 1983), for an account of the four sorts of property that the law about Married Women's Property treated, ranging from real estate, to which women could have quite strong claims, to simple personal property, in which woman's possession was through the good grace of her husband; women's personal property (e.g., jewels) were thus disposable by will at his death, rather than remaining in her possession.

25. Frow, "A Pebble," 278; he is partially paraphrasing Hans Georg Gadamer, "The Nature of Things and the Language of Things," in *Philosophical Hermeneutics*, trans. and ed. David Linge (Berkeley and Los Angeles: University of California Press, 1976), 71.

26. As William Cohen has pointed out in *Sex Scandal: The Private Parts of Victorian Fiction* (Durham, NC: Duke University Press, 1996), Trollope's exploration of whether her necklace could have passed free and clear to Lizzie must have had something to do with the contemporary debates about the reform of Married Women's Property Law: in 1870 a law had passed that somewhat expanded the right of women to retain control of property after their husbands' deaths.

27. David Miller, *The Novel and the Police* (Berkeley and Los Angeles: University of California Press, 1988), 114.

28. When Lucy is married to Frank, and he is no longer a distant fetish but a present person, we can imagine her marriage allowing the diversion of her attention elsewhere—to other dramas in the Trollope universe. But as long as he remains apart, all her energy and her diamonds must go to keeping up belief in him.

29. This growth is a form of synecdoche, but it might also be thought of as a catachretic increase. Just as the word "limb" and "member" grew tainted by their association with improper body parts in the Victorian era, and just as piano legs were covered, because of their association with actual legs, so here the box grows as improper as the valuables it contains.

30. Marcia Pointon's account of the royal diamonds of Queen Charlotte stresses the double role that diamonds can play, in highlighting the beauty of a young female body (and marking a young woman's agency in refusing traffic in that body), or in contrasting, unfavorably, with her fading beauty as she ages ("Intriguing Jewelry," 510–12).

31. Anthony Trollope, *An Autobiography* (Berkeley and Los Angeles: University of California Press, 1947), 287.

32. This image of the manuscript as a sunk deposit back in a box somewhere contrasts interestingly with the peripatetic identity Trollope constructs for himself as hunter, mail collector, and writer on the fly. One anecdote in *An Autobiography,* for example, describes picking up mail in full hunting regalia, which matches well with his description of overcoming shame about writing on the train to work (discussed in Miller, *The Novel and the Police,* 175). But the box that holds onto these possessions behind the scenes complements that mobility: while Trollope himself may be broadly portable by train, or by horse, his manuscripts require a certain kind of professional authentication before they can be moved at all. Frank Churchill's unauthorized use of a horse belonging to the nouveau riche Mr. Nappie is a delightful jest in *The Eustace Diamonds* because any "gentleman" with good intent can bend the rules when it comes to expropriating a horse, but the same rules decidedly do not apply to professional questions like publication.

33. Van Ghent argues this point persuasively in *The English Novel: Form and Function* (New York: Harper and Row, 1953).

34. In "Heterosexual Exchange and Other Victorian Fictions: *The Eustace Diamonds* and Victorian Anthropology," *Novel* 33.1 (1999): 93–118, Kathy Psomiades details the relationship of all three women's marriage plots to contemporary debates, anthropological and otherwise, on "traffic in women" and marriage's relationship to fiscal exchange.

35. "The character of Lucy Morris is pretty; and her love is as genuine and as well told as that of Lucy Robarts or Lily Dale.

But *The Eustace Diamonds* achieved the success which it certainly did attain, not as a love-story, but as a record of a cunning little woman of pseudo-fashion, to whom, in her cunning, there came a series of adventures, unpleasant enough in themselves, but pleasant to the reader" (Trollope, *An Autobiography,* 285–86).

36. Trollope does not explicitly mention *The Moonstone* in discussing the writing of *The Eustace Diamonds* in *An Autobiography,* but his reference to how Collins would have handled the same situation makes it clear the novel was on his mind: "Wilkie Collins could have arranged these things (necklace thefts) with infinite labour, preparing things present so they should fit in with things to come" (286).

37. Ian Duncan, "The Moonstone, the Victorian Novel, and Imperialistic Panic," *Modern Language Quarterly* 55.3 (1994): 297–319. Further references appear parenthetically in the text.

38. William Wilkie Collins, *The Moonstone,* ed. J. I. M. Stewart, (1868; Harmondsworth, UK: Penguin, 1966), 80. Further references appear parenthetically in the text.

39. Jane Panton's fascinating 1886 novel, *Dear Life* (New York: D. Appleton, 1886), approaches the question of the gem's oriental valence slightly differently, disaggregating Oriental gems into those gained by theft and by miscegenation. That novel depicts two seemingly identical huge rubies, one marked as being "of the Lower Branch" (which enters England through a creole marriage) and one "of the Upper branch" (stolen, and hence forcibly removed by murder and re-theft). Panton's model makes it possible to imagine the portage of jewels by way of sentiment when they are forbidden to travel as material pelf.

40. I am very grateful to Nicholas Dames for mentioning this passage when I presented an earlier version of this article (Narrative Conference, March 2001, Houston, Texas).

41. Anthony Trollope, *Can You Forgive Her?* (1864–65; Oxford: Oxford University Press, 1973), 2:59–63.

42. Karl Marx, *Capital: An Abridged Edition,* ed. David McLellan (1867; Oxford: Oxford University Press, 1995), 1:13–22.

43. When Lucy is praised, it is because she is so attentive to all around her that their

particularity is asserted in the way that her gaze falls upon them: "the peculiar watery brightness of her eyes—in the corners of which it would always seem that a diamond of a tear was lurking . . . she would take up your subject, whatever it was, and make it her own" (Trollope, *Eustace Diamonds,* 63).

44. Trollope, *Eustace Diamonds,* 262.

Contributors

LIZ BELLAMY is a lecturer in English at The Open University and City College Norwich in the UK. Her publications include *Commerce, Morality and the Eighteenth-Century Novel* (1998), *Samuel Johnson* (2004), and an edition of Daniel Defoe's *Conjugal Lewdness* (2005) in the Pickering Masters series.

BARBARA M. BENEDICT is a professor of English at Trinity College in Connecticut. She is the author of *Framing Feeling: Sentiment and Style in English Prose Fiction, 1745–1800* (1994), *Making the Modern Reader: Cultural Mediation in Restoration and Eighteenth-Century Literary Anthologies* (1996), and *Curiosity: A Cultural History of Early Modern Inquiry* (2001), and the editor of *Wilkes and the Late Eighteenth Century* (2002) and Jane Austen's *Northanger Abbey* (2006). She has also published essays on eighteenth-century poetry, fiction, popular culture, and book history.

BONNIE BLACKWELL is an associate professor of English at Texas Christian University. Her research interests include film, feminism, the novel, and the eighteenth century, and her articles have appeared in such journals as *Genders, Camera Obscura*, and *ELH*. She is completing her book manuscript, *Immodest Proposals*, on marriage and satire in Britain and Ireland during the long eighteenth century.

MARK BLACKWELL is a professor of English and interim dean of the College of Arts and Sciences at the University of Hartford in Connecticut. He has recently published essays on Locke's theory of personal identity, on sublimity and the politics of taste in Burke's *Enquiry*, on narrative motion in Radcliffe's Gothic fiction, on allusion in Austen's *Sense and Sensibility*, and on social transplantation in *Emma*. His essay on live-tooth transplantation won the 2004–5 James L. Clifford Prize.

AILEEN DOUGLAS is a professor of English and director of postgraduate professional development at Trinity College Dublin in Ireland. She is the author of *Uneasy Sensations: Smollett and the Body* (1995) and the coeditor of *Locating Swift* (Four Courts Press, 1998). She is completing a manuscript, *Bodies of Writing: Script and the Individual, 1690–1840*, which explores changes in the conception and practice of writing in the period.

MARKMAN ELLIS is a professor of eighteenth-century studies in the School of English and Drama at Queen Mary, University of London. He is the author of *The Coffee-House: A Cultural History* (2004), *The History of Gothic Fiction* (2000), and *The Politics of Sensibility* (1996), and he coedited *Discourses of Slavery and Abolition* (2004). His current project—on what it means to be a critic in the early eighteenth century—is entitled *The Social Space of Criticism*.

HILARY ENGLERT was an associate professor of English at New Jersey City University, where she taught British literature and gender studies. The piece published here is part of a book she was completing entitled *Foraged Fiction: Locating Literary Value in the Eighteenth-Century Novel*.

LYNN FESTA is a professor of English at Rutgers University–New Brunswick in New Jersey and author of *Sentimental Figures of Empire in Eighteenth-Century Britain and France* (2006).

CHRISTOPHER FLINT is a professor of English at Case Western Reserve University in Ohio and author of *Family Fictions: Narrative and Domestic Relations in Britain, 1688–1789* (1998) and various essays on the eighteenth-century novel. He has recently published several articles on fiction and print culture and is currently working on a book project on the subject, entitled *The Fate of the Page: Fiction and Print in the Eighteenth Century*.

NICHOLAS HUDSON is a professor of English at the University of British Columbia in Canada and author of *Samuel Johnson and Eighteenth-Century Thought* (1988), *Writing and European Thought, 1600–1830* (1994), and *Samuel Johnson and the Making of Modern England* (2003), as well as numerous essays on the novel, the history of race science, the history of linguistics, and social class. He has just completed a new edition of Francis Coventry's *Pompey the Little*, and he is currently at work on a new monograph entitled *The Long Revolution: Literature and Social Class in Eighteenth-Century Britain*.

ANN LOUISE KIBBIE is an associate professor of English at Bowdoin College in Maine. Her publications include essays on John Cleland, Daniel Defoe, and Samuel Richardson.

JONATHAN LAMB is a distinguished research professor of literature at Vanderbilt University in Tennessee. He has published most recently on voyages to the South Seas during the eighteenth century. He is currently at work on two projects: *The Things Things Say*, tracing the emergence of the active and articulate thing in the eighteenth century, and *Scurvy, the Disease of Discovery*, devoted to the perceptual disorders of scurvy and their influence on the reportage of distant parts.

DEIDRE SHAUNA LYNCH is the Ernest Bernbaum Professor of Literature at Harvard University in Massachusetts. She is the author of *The Economy of Character: Novels, Market Culture, and the Business of Inner Meaning* (1998), and the winner in 1999 of the Modern Language Association Prize for a First Book. Her edited volumes include *Janeites: Austen's Disciples and Devotees* (2000) and, with Jack Stillinger, the new romantic-period volume of *The Norton Anthology of English Literature* (2006).

JOHN PLOTZ is the Barbara Mandel Professor of the Humanities at Brandeis University in Massachusetts and author of *The Crowd: British Literature and Public Politics* (2000). He is currently completing *Portable Properties: Problems of Cultural Transmission in Victorian Greater Britain*, from which his article is drawn; authors treated include George Eliot, R. D. Blackmore, Thomas Hardy, and William Morris. He has also begun work on a manuscript tentatively titled *Antisocialism, Mill to Arendt*.

Index

Note: **Bold** page numbers indicate illustrations, and *italicized* page numbers indicate tables. (When only one number of a page range is **bold** or *italicized*, illustrations or tables appear on one or more of the pages.)